# NO CRYING IN BASEBALL

## ALSO BY ERIN CARLSON

*Queen Meryl: The Iconic Roles, Heroic Deeds, and Legendary Life of Meryl Streep*

*I'll Have What She's Having: How Nora Ephron's Three Iconic Films Saved the Romantic Comedy*

# NO CRYING IN BASEBALL

*The Inside Story of*
**A LEAGUE OF THEIR OWN**
**BIG STARS, DUGOUT DRAMA,**
*and a* **HOME RUN** *for* **HOLLYWOOD**

## ERIN CARLSON

New York

Cover design by Amanda Kain
Cover illustration by Aaron Sacco


Hachette Books
Hachette Book Group
1290 Avenue of the Americas
New York, NY 10104
HachetteBooks.com
Twitter.com/HachetteBooks
Instagram.com/HachetteBooks

First Edition: September 2023

Published by Hachette Books, an imprint of Perseus Books, LLC, a subsidiary of Hachette Book Group, Inc. The Hachette Books name and logo is a trademark of the Hachette Book Group.

The Hachette Speakers Bureau provides a wide range of authors for speaking events. To find out more, go to hachettespeakersbureau.com or email HachetteSpeakers @hbgusa.com.

Books by Hachette Books may be purchased in bulk for business, educational, or promotional use. For information, please contact your local bookseller or Hachette Book Group Special Markets Department at special.markets@hbgusa.com.

The publisher is not responsible for websites (or their content) that are not owned by the publisher.

Print book interior design by Amy Quinn.

Library of Congress Cataloging-in-Publication Data

Names: Carlson, Erin, 1981– author.
Title: No crying in baseball : the inside story of A League of Their Own: big stars, dugout drama, and a home run for Hollywood / Erin Carlson.
Description: New York : Hachette Books, 2023. | Includes bibliographical references and index.
Identifiers: LCCN 2023017594 | ISBN 9780306830181 (hardcover) | ISBN 9780306830204 (ebook)
Subjects: LCSH: League of their own (Motion picture) | Baseball films—United States—History and criticism. | Motion pictures—Production and direction—United States—History—20th century.
Classification: LCC PN1997.L3826 C37 2023 | DDC 791.43/72—dc23/eng/20230503
LC record available at https://lccn.loc.gov/2023017594

ISBNs: 978-0-306-83018-1 (hardcover), 978-0-306-83020-4 (ebook)

Printed in the United States of America

LSC-C

Printing 1, 2023

*For Poppy—Go get 'em, tiger.*

"I have never wanted to grow up and stop playing."

—Penny Marshall

# CONTENTS


| | | |
|---|---|---|
| *Introduction:* | Dirt in the Skirt | 1 |
| *First Inning:* | An Underdog and Insider | 5 |
| *Second Inning:* | First Strike | 21 |
| *Third Inning:* | Another Swing at Bat | 31 |
| *Fourth Inning:* | The Hall of Famers | 49 |
| *Fifth Inning:* | The Tryouts | 75 |
| *Sixth Inning:* | Chicago | 107 |
| *Seventh Inning:* | Indiana | 137 |
| *The Bottom of the Seventh:* | Rockford Versus Racine | 167 |
| *Eighth Inning:* | Cooperstown | 191 |
| *Ninth Inning:* | Beyond the Outfield | 213 |
| | *Acknowledgments* | *237* |
| | *Source Notes* | *239* |
| | *Index* | *291* |

# NO CRYING IN BASEBALL

## *Introduction*

# DIRT IN THE SKIRT

GEENA DAVIS STEPPED UP TO HOME PLATE. SHE BENT HER KNEES, WRAPPED her hands around the bat, and tried to keep her eye on the ball as the camera rolled in silent judgment.

The camera. It saw everything and missed nothing. It exposed her as exactly what she was: an actress, the ultimate imposter, pretending to be a baseball player with superhuman ability and coming up awfully short. All the training in the world couldn't turn Geena into a professional athlete, nor could her rarified status as an Oscar winner hide the truth—that there, on a hot, dusty ballfield in the middle of nowhere, thousands of miles from the smog and mirrors and palm-tree shade of Los Angeles, she was merely a rookie. Every actress in Hollywood wanted her role. The audacity to believe they had what it took!

Geena had practiced hard for weeks. Elite coaches schooled her in the basics of America's storied pastime, instructing their eager student how to hit and catch and throw—the throwing, for her, was the trickiest—without doing damage to that face, those cheekbones, her moneymaker, her foot in the door.

On this day, her first at bat, she was supposed to smack a home run. Things were not going well. Pitch after pitch, take after take, Geena kept swinging with dismal results. The ball wouldn't go where it needed to go.

Penny Marshall, her director, paced back and forth behind the camera, a cigarette dangling from her mouth.

"Omigod, hit the ball, hit the ball, put me out of my misery!" she complained.

"Penny, that's not helping!" Geena said.

It was the summer of 1991, and Penny's trademark whine—to some, endearing; to others, exasperating—provided the soundtrack while she filmed *A League of Their Own* in the Midwest. Studio executives held their breath. Of course, Penny was talented. She had a special nose for what the masses wanted to see on the big screen. She hadn't gone to film school, nor could she explain the difference between this lens and that. She lacked the pretensions of aesthetes who won Oscars. Instead, she went for the emotional jugular without apology, intermingling happy and sad, good taste and schmaltz. That was the Marshall way.

While grappling with self-doubt, and a hostile crew, Penny had managed to make *Big* into a runaway success, and, in the process, she became the first woman director to gross more than $100 million at the box office. But among the corner-office set, she was often considered an expensive financial risk. She would go to grueling lengths to get the best shot, wasting countless reels of film. *Big*, an intimate set, had nothing on the scope and scale of *A League of Their Own*, which found Penny outnumbered by actresses who couldn't play ball, not to mention their ringers: the ballplayers who couldn't act. *How much money would she burn to capture convincing footage? Could Penny—hell,* anyone*—be trusted to deliver a decent movie about an obscure women's baseball league from the 1940s? And since men were assumed to enjoy sports movies more than their wives, girlfriends, and daughters, were Ordinary Joes actually going to buy tickets?* With Geena, and not Kevin Costner, behind the plate, the doubts amplified.

What transpired between Geena's at bat and Penny's final cut would silence the skeptics and defy conventional logic, especially when it was revealed that young girls adored the Rockford Peaches, memorizing the lyrics to the "Victory Song" that drove the crew nuts. An irresistible underdog tale featuring a rare female-led ensemble cast, *A League of Their Own* broke the mold to become the most record-breaking baseball movie of all time.

In hindsight, its appeal was obvious. But with anything new and untested, the unknowns piled up. Even Tom Hanks was a wild card. After a series of flops, he'd done what leading men like Costner and Cruise and Schwarzenegger almost never did back then: he demoted himself to character actor. He begged Penny to let him sulk in the dugout as the surly, drunken coach Jimmy Dugan, and she agreed despite studio reluctance.

Then there was Madonna. *How did the biggest pop star in the world not go stir-crazy during the eighty-eight-day shoot in Illinois and Indiana?* The Blond Ambition button-pusher, who ignited scandal amid the cornfields, yearned for New York City.

Nobody, not least of all Penny Marshall, could have ever envisioned that *A League of Their Own* would endure as a love letter to baseball and the real women who had played it professionally. Penny, a tormented soul with a relaxed exterior, initially dismissed much of her work as crap; she spotted weaknesses rather than triumphs. So how did she plunge onward while doing battle with the critical voices in her head? What made her take a chance on Tom? How did he and Penny handle Madonna the provocateur? How did Geena master the physics of catching a pop fly behind her back?

This book is the untold story of a time before the internet, when filming on location was a traveling circus and untamed behavior went unchecked. When a filmmaker and her motley collaborators, throwing vanity out the window, got some dirt in their skirts and hit one out of the park.

*First Inning*

# AN UNDERDOG AND INSIDER

CHARLIE WESSLER TREMBLED AS HE PREPARED TO TELL PENNY THE COLD, hard truth.

They smoked outside the stage at Paramount Studios while she taped the last episode of *Laverne & Shirley*, the mega-popular, critically panned ABC sitcom that made her a household name. In 1983, the show—which centered on two women roommates who paid the rent by capping bottles at the fictional Shotz Brewery—was ending its seven-year run. The ratings had dwindled. Cindy Williams, who played the bubbly Shirley Feeney to Penny's deadpan Laverne DeFazio, had walked off in protest, pregnant with her first child. The suits in charge, patriarch Tony Marshall included, refused to write in a pregnancy for Shirley, which would have been an easy solution to a happy problem, right? Right. But things were different back then; different and yet the same. Penny did the final season solo, then the suits pulled the plug.

After all that backstage drama, Penny was ready to leave Laverne behind. Laverne, however, wasn't done with Penny. The two characters—one real, the other a heightened version of the real—were inextricably linked. Penny loved drinking milk with Pepsi, and so did Laverne. Penny knew how to tap dance, as did Laverne. Both spoke with a lethargic Bronx accent and eviscerated fools in their midst with a withering look. Where did Penny end and Laverne begin? The lines blurred. People saw Penny on the street, even in Paris, and yelled, "Laverne!"

Given this deep-seated association with her alter ego, Wessler doubted whether she'd be able to land major roles playing not-Lavernes. He had met Penny through his friend Carrie Fisher, with whom he attended Beverly Hills High School. While Wessler aimed to become a movie producer, he realized that reaching his goal could take time. He decided to try his hand at managing talent instead. Actress Arleen Sorkin, who was Wessler's girlfriend, and improv comic Julia Sweeney were his first clients. He wanted Penny to be his third. It was time to make his move.

"Look," he told Penny. "You understand that when you leave this show, no one's gonna hire you as an actress. All they know is you're Laverne. And that's the only thing they're gonna be able to remember and know about you." He predicted the rejections: "No, we don't want to hire her to be in our movie because she's Laverne."

Penny's reaction to the truth-telling? She gave a lackluster "*eh*." Deep down, she knew her limitations as a performer. "I'm not gonna be doing Shakespeare in the Park," she joked later. To keep her life interesting and stay relevant in a creative community filled with smart, funny, successful people—particularly the smart, funny, successful men whose company she craved—then she had to do something different. What was that something? An open door. The promise of fun around the corner. Sure, Penny liked to complain. But she also liked fun.

"I think you should be a director," Wessler stated. The pivot made sense: she'd helmed four episodes of *Laverne & Shirley*. She was already a proven commodity. If they looked past Laverne and took Penny seriously, the suits would see her potential to punch up comedies, to make the laughs louder. "People don't understand," he said. "They don't realize that you know where all the jokes are."

Penny agreed that directing was a great idea. She hired Wessler as her manager on the spot and opened a door for him—straight to a desk in her office at Paramount, which boasted a thrilling perk: Xerox machines. This was the big time. He felt like a real player. A professional. He had made it, thanks to her.

Penny had contemplated a switch to the director's chair for years. She directed the 1979 pilot for *Working Stiffs*, a short-lived sitcom starring

Jim Belushi and Michael Keaton, and in 1982, she was in talks to lead her first feature, *The Joy of Sex*, an erotic comedy vehicle for *Saturday Night Live* icon John Belushi. The project drew inspiration from Alex Comfort's best-selling illustrated sex manual of the same name. It fell through when John, her close friend, died from an overdose of heroin and cocaine. Blindsided by the tragedy, she back-burnered her ambitions and turned her full attention to ending *Laverne & Shirley*, minus Cindy.

Wessler's enthusiasm reignited her interest at the right time. She had enjoyed her directing gigs, and unlike acting, her physical appearance mattered less. She was dreadfully insecure about her nose, her teeth, and the sound of her voice. Auditions were traumatic. But working on the other side of the camera, she could be admired for her humor, intelligence, and resourcefulness.

"I'm insecure mostly because of my looks," she told a journalist in 1976. "I keep thinking that they'll comb my hair, put on lipstick and I'll turn out to be Liz Taylor. I just cannot bring myself to accept that the homely person on the screen is me. I grew up believing that an actress is supposed to be beautiful. After I saw myself in a *Love, American Style* segment, I cried for three days. I've had braces put on my teeth twice, but they did no good."

THE BRONX, 1956. PENNY, A GIRL OF THIRTEEN, WAS CRUSHING HARD ON THE boys in her neighborhood.

"I hit Ronnie and ran and he ran after me," she wrote in her diary. "I think I love him. And Jeffrey and Gene and Joel and David."

The self-described tomboy swooned over anyone who noticed her. She flirted with objects of her affection by hitting and running and making them chase her. She'd race Ronnie Kestenbaum and win, leaving her crush in the dust. Ronnie didn't appreciate losing to a girl (how embarrassing), but Penny relished her victory. She liked being one of the guys. They allowed her into their orbit, not as a sidelined cheerleader but as a teammate. "I wasn't pretty so I played ball with them," she explained.

Penny's athleticism created social opportunities. In a working-class, Jewish-Italian slice of New York, the concrete playground was more level than the fields of the grassy, upper-crust suburbs. A girl could join a box-baseball or stoopball game without much of an argument. Had Penny come of age in a wealthy town with wide, open spaces and white-picket fences, the boys might have laughed her off their baseball diamonds. Her father might have belonged to the country club and paid for private lessons in tennis, a respectable sport for well-bred ladies. Off the court, Posh Penny might burn further physical energy swimming in the club pool or taking her horse out for a ride. I imagine her sitting in the bleachers at school games, cheering on the boys, blindly accepting that she'd always cheer on the boys. Girls in the bleachers; boys on the field. That was the way it was.

But baseball.

In the city, baseball was democratic. You didn't need to be rich to play it. You didn't need a fancy house, or a fancy car, or the fanciest equipment. All you needed was a bat and a ball, and preferably a well-broken-in glove. You could play in the street (but watch out for the neighbors' windows).

Baseball was in Penny's backyard. She and her friends cut class to watch Mickey Mantle and Roger Maris break records at Yankee Stadium. Mantle and Maris weren't boys; they were gods. They were as close to the sublime as one could get. She wanted to bask in their glory. She also wanted a piece of it for herself. She dreamed of becoming an Olympic runner and sprinting toward a gold medal. But dreaming that dream was impossible. Her mother, Marjorie, discouraged a future in sports, which meant crossing gender lines into men's territory. She told her daughter: *Boys don't like it if you're better than them. If you beat them.*

"I wasn't even thinking about that," Penny said later. "I just wanted their attention. I didn't want to be better. It wasn't a contest. I just wanted to be part of them."

Unacceptable. Who was going to marry Penny if she acted like a man? How would this unruly child—who climbed into the gutter if you cautioned her not to—ever learn to behave? Penny tested Marjorie's patience, pushing for more time outside:

"Five more minutes. Please?"

"It's dark."

"No, it's not."

"Yes, it is."

"But I can still see the ball."

"How can you see it in the dark?"

"Just five more minutes."

Marjorie Marshall had other plans for her youngest child, whom she called "the bad seed." She owned a dance school where she taught tap, ballet, jazz, and acrobatics to local kids; her husband, Tony, directed industrial films and "had the personality of a lamppost," Penny said of her dad. Yet he was smart and sporty, easy on the eyes. He had studied advertising at New York University, changing his name from Masciarelli to Marshall to hide his Italian Catholic heritage and improve his career prospects. The Marshalls had a son, Garry, and a daughter, Ronny, before welcoming their third-born, Carole, at St. Vincent's Hospital on October 15, 1943. She was named after Carole Lombard, Marjorie's favorite actress, but soon became known by her nickname, Penny. Before her arrival, Garry and Ronny had pooled pennies together, hoping for a pony. Instead, they got a sibling. (Better "Penny" than "Pony," no?)

They lived in an apartment on the Grand Concourse; Marjorie ran her school in the building's basement. Marjorie and Tony bickered often. One day, Garry called Ronny and Penny together.

"Listen, we're not getting much help here," he said. "I think it's shaky. So, I suggest that the three of us stay together. Our strength is in the three of us together and that's what we should do."

They held hands. But Garry's protection had geographical limits. Staying together was easier said than done. Garry left for Northwestern University in 1952, when Penny was eight years old, with Ronny enrolling at the Chicago-adjacent higher institution several years later. Penny found herself all alone. She felt like an only child and coped with her loneliness by getting out of the house. "There was always some lady hanging out the window," she recalled. The busybody would report back to Marjorie that Penny—who began smoking cigarettes in junior high—was up to no good, lounging on the roof or the fire escape. She was a smart kid, real smart, but schoolwork held little interest for her. She was drawn to the social energy of the streets: she could fit in anywhere, within any crowd. (Except the local girl gang, the Magnets, who rejected her. However, the boy gangs, the Falcons and the Sharks, approved of her presence.)

When Penny was a teenager, her mother announced that she planned to divorce Tony. She put Penny on the spot: *Which of us do you want to live with? Choose one.* (Penny wouldn't have to. The unhappy marriage remained intact.) Around that time, Marjorie informed Penny that she'd bled while pregnant with her and had hoped that she would die in the womb. "You were a miscarriage," she said, "but you were stubborn and held on." Marjorie kept a suicide jar in which she deposited one pill from every prescription she received over the years just in case she became blind and helpless like Penny's grandmother. With savage sarcasm, she mocked her daughter's overbite. *Those buck teeth*, she said, *could open a Coke bottle*. Years later, on Johnny Carson, Penny did just that, spinning her biggest insecurity into slapstick comedy.

Marjorie's constant critiques—"Oh, you're going to wear *that*"—punctured Penny's self-esteem. As she got older, Penny found herself needling others without realizing she was doing it.

Maternal influence extended beyond the cutting remark. For Penny, Marjorie modeled an independence that was unusual for a mid-century American wife and mother. She wore pants. She seemed to be the only mother on the block who worked. She took a lot of pride in her small business and pushed Penny to follow in her footsteps. She hoped to raise a dancer, and Penny was her last hope. And while the bad seed would have rather been doing anything else, she satisfied Marjorie by performing as part of her all-girl dance troupe, the Marshallettes. She hated it. However, she had little choice in the matter. If Penny didn't dance, Marjorie threatened, then she'd have to spend Saturday cleaning the house or doing the grocery shopping. In an act of rebellion, Penny unzipped her fellow dancers' leotards during kickline numbers.

"This was her life's work, and she approached it with an obsessive, missionlike zeal," Penny wrote in her memoir, *My Mother Was Nuts*. "She believed every child should know what it feels like to entertain. It didn't matter if they were short or tall, talented or just a kid whose mother dropped her off to get her out of her hair for an hour. She felt it was important to have the experience of hearing applause and making people happy."

Marjorie boldly pursued television gigs for her junior Rockette project. In 1952, the troupe was invited to perform live on *The Jackie Gleason Show*. Soon before hitting the stage, the dancers learned that their white tap shoes were the wrong color for the broadcast. Marjorie, calm amid the crisis, directed them to paint over the white with rose-colored stage makeup. Problem solved. All the while, Penny was suffering from a nasty flu. Her backup dancer waited in the wings to take her place.

"Do you want her to be in the show instead of you?" Marjorie asked, to which Penny shook her head, rising to the occasion.

"OK, I'll dance," she said.

The show must go on. And off it went, without a hitch. It was a miracle that Penny hadn't vomited all over the floor.

Her TV appearances continued. The Marshallettes won *The Original Amateur Hour* three times and booked appearances everywhere from charity galas to a psychiatric hospital to a lesbian club in Manhattan's West Village. "Keep close," her mother cautioned. "Keep close."

Penny kept on tapping through adolescence. At that point, she was no amateur. She could most certainly call herself a pro. She went out there and did her thing and did it well. She heard applause. She made people happy.

But the tap life wasn't for her. After graduating from Walton High School in 1961, she flung off her dancing shoes—those symbols of parent-induced agony and unexpected pride—and headed west, as far from the Grand Concourse as she could get. She enrolled at the University of New Mexico, in Albuquerque of all places, majoring in recreation, of all majors.

(As a high school senior, Penny had looked inside the crystal ball of her future and envisioned being a secretary. She took a typing course to prepare herself, knowing a working woman's limited prospects. In a grim reminder, Ronny signed up for secretarial school after graduating from Northwestern. "If that was the case," Penny asked, "why did I need to give a shit about grades? If my choice was boys or books, I picked boys.")

If Penny had been forced to declare her true major, chances are she would've chosen Sports Groupie Studies. Once on campus, Penny immediately gravitated toward the football players. They were tall and Waspy, different from the guys she knew back home. "I was in heaven, but it would have killed my mother; for 12 years she had sent me to kosher summer camps, even though we were Protestants, because she insisted Jews made the best husbands," Penny once remarked.

By surprise, she became pregnant. "I got nailed," she said later. "Thank you. A one in a million chance. What are you going to do? You make your bed, you sleep in it."

She married the father, six-foot-four Mickey Henry, who played football on scholarship, and dropped out of school her junior year. In July 1964, she gave birth to their daughter, Tracy Lee Henry. The child was a living doll, with a cute, chatty personality and dark brown hair and eyes like Mickey's.

Penny, who changed her last name to Henry, worked as a secretary to pay the bills. When Marjorie encouraged her to teach dance in Albuquerque, she didn't brush off the suggestion as she normally would have. She got a job at the area's best dance school and smoked cigarettes while choreographing routines. The good news: it paid better than typing seventy words per minute. The bad: her marriage was on the rocks. Two years after welcoming Tracy, Penny and Mickey decided to divorce. They'd gotten married too young. They parted after she returned from playing Ado Annie in a month-long production of *Oklahoma!* in Durango, Colorado. She got the gig thanks to her undeniable stage presence as a chorus girl in *South Pacific* at Albuquerque's opera house. Originally, she was asked to choreograph the show. She said no. The idea sounded overwhelming; after all, she had a kid. She did agree, however, to perform in the background, demonstrating the confidence she gleaned from her childhood training.

In Colorado, she stole the spotlight. It was a high point amid domestic ennui; Penny had been in her element, surrounded by actors and creatives who came alive at night.

Mickey's mother and grandmother did not take well to the news of the breakup. They tried to hide Tracy, fearing that Penny would take her to New York. When Marjorie showed up in New Mexico, she and Tracy's paternal grandmother obtained joint custody of the toddler in court—or so she told Penny, who thought Marjorie might have made up the story. If so, perhaps Penny and Mickey deserved their parents' shady power move, the rudderless single mother came to believe, thinking, *I'm no good. He's no good. So we're fucked.*

Dating was impossible where she was. Her low status as a divorcée made her damaged goods to judgy moms with dateable sons. She had no future in the desert. And if she moved in with her parents, she'd be treated like Tracy. Like a child. She needed a new life. Where could she go? What would she do?

She picked up the phone and called Garry, now a successful TV writer and producer in Hollywood. He had left the Bronx and never looked back. She barely knew her brother anymore. Could he help her?

THE CALL FROM HIS BABY SISTER, A STRANGER, CAUGHT GARRY MARSHALL OFF guard. He and Penny were related by blood, but to him, she'd become just a name on a birthday card. A distant relative with whom he'd lost touch.

Remember his pact to keep the Marshall kids together? Ah, yes. That. Another older brother might have hung up the phone and let the verbal contract expire. Not Garry. He felt an obligation toward helping family. Penny, though. *Yeesh.* She seemed to be a lost soul, potentially even a lost cause. So young, already so much baggage.

She showed up on Garry's doorstep without her daughter, who remained in the care of the Henry women while Marjorie returned to New York. If she wanted his brotherly wisdom and support, then she'd have to explain her motivations for coming to LA, a working town fueled by passion for showbiz, cutthroat ambition, and simmering revenge. (Could she survive?)

"What do you have in mind?" he asked.

"I don't know; I'm not good at anything," she said, sounding like Eeyore.

Oh, *come on.* Garry was too preoccupied to hold her hands this time. He was moving and shaking and trying to make things happen. He couldn't be dragged down by directionless dead weight.

"Well, we could have dinner and we could talk," he said, "but we're already talking in circles here, so go away. Look, I can't do anything until you come and tell me that there's something you like. I give up on something you love. You're not a person who loves something at this point, but you must tell me something you like or I'm not talking to you anymore."

She came back two days later with an answer.

He watched her frowning face almost light up as she told him about Ado Annie.

"But you don't sing so good," he said, an echo of Marjorie in his remark. Marjorie always told Penny she couldn't carry a tune.

"No, that was the thing; I was petrified, but I sang Ado Annie, which is not so much singing as acting," he later quoted Penny as saying. "I did Ado Annie, and they laughed, and they applauded, and I felt good."

"That was it?"

"That was it. When I felt good."

*A-ha.* At that moment, he understood exactly who she was: an actress!

The glint in her eye was a sign. Garry decided to pull some strings. He was in a cushy position to do so, having written for *The Dick Van Dyke Show* and *The Lucy Show.* He opened a door for her to join the 1968 big-screen comedy *How Sweet It Is!* starring James Garner and Debbie Reynolds as a husband and wife flirting with infidelity during a trip to France. Garry and his creative partner Jerry Belson cowrote and produced the film. Penny's role: School Girl.

It was rough out there for a Nobody. Even one related to a Somebody. On her own, Penny had trouble landing auditions. She lacked the pep and perky charm of ingenues like Farrah Fawcett, with whom she starred in a Head and Shoulders commercial. They played roommates sharing a bathroom. Farrah popped her head out of the shower, asking to borrow Penny's shampoo.

"I know it really works against your dandruff," she chirped. "But what about my gorgeous hair?"

"Your gorgeous hair will love it," Penny deadpanned.

While the crew lit the set, Penny witnessed a humiliating sight that deflated her morale: Farrah's stand-in wore a sign around her neck that read "PRETTY GIRL," with Penny's stand-in labeled "HOMELY GIRL." Farrah, trying to remedy the situation, had someone cross out "HOMELY" and write "PLAIN."

Penny went home that night and cried. She thought about quitting but had no fallback plan. Despite her setbacks, she kept tapping along. LA overflowed with fellow neurotics; it was beginning to feel like home.

Later, she snagged a part in an episode of a new NBC series called *Then Came Bronson*. On the set, she met Jack Klugman, who played Oscar Madison in Neil Simon's *The Odd Couple* during its hit Broadway run. Garry asked Penny to ask Klugman if the actor would consider reprising Oscar in a small-screen adaptation he had cooking at ABC. When pitching famous strangers, Penny lacked fear. What's the worst Klugman could say: *No*?

She did Garry's bidding, and Klugman agreed to resurrect Oscar the slouch to Tony Randall's uptight Felix Unger in 1970. The sitcom became a critical darling, with Garry casting Penny in a small but scene-stealing role as Oscar's gloomy secretary, Myrna Turner. She started out shaky—her anxiety was such that Klugman had to carry her to her mark—but she quickly mastered the assignment. Nevertheless, Paramount Television, which bankrolled *The Odd Couple*, penalized Penny for her ties to Garry.

While the show's supporting actors earned raises of $100 per week, Penny was excluded from the cash rewards.

Accusations of nepotism (not untrue) would dog Penny throughout her career. The chatter, laced with resentment, undermined a gifted entertainer. It created the feeling that she hadn't deserved her fame. That more than anything, her connections and last name—changed from Henry back to Marshall—had led to plum gigs for which an aspiring Lucille Ball would kill.

First, Penny was known as Garry's sister. Then, at age twenty-seven, she became Rob Reiner's wife. She married the actor in April 1971 after he taped the first thirteen episodes of his CBS sitcom *All in the Family.* They served Chinese takeout at the reception in Beverly Hills. She kept her surname.

"I'll always be your best friend," he vowed.

"I'll try not to make you nervous," she vowed.

Marjorie could not have dreamed a rosier match for Penny: Rob boasted a Jewish background but wasn't raised with religion. As a boy, he had lived across the street from Penny for a time, although they never met. He adopted Tracy as his own, and when she came to live with them in LA, the pretty, precocious girl changed her last name to Reiner. Rob was funny and honest, abrasive and driven. His father, Carl, a living legend in the comedy world, created *The Dick Van Dyke Show* and directed clever movies like *Oh, God!* and *The Jerk*. Rob, an aspirant director, yearned to step out from under Carl's outsized shadow. Inside the Reiner-Marshall home, he fostered a salon of sorts for men who told jokes, wore lots of sweaters, smoked pot, and schemed to make a mark in the business. Regulars included Albert Brooks, Jim Brooks, and Richard Dreyfuss. Sometimes women came over, though they were girlfriends-of and thereby accessories to male ambition.

"The girls weren't encouraged to talk," Penny said. "I knew how to do needlepoint. Anything to keep my hands from my throat. Rug hooking. I would roll the grass. I listened. I could say a line here and there from the kitchen."

Rob praised Penny's skills in front of the camera to Carl, but Carl raised an eyebrow. She was so quiet. "The way she schlumps around, you forget she's a trained dancer," he said.

When *The Odd Couple* ended in 1975, Penny sank deeper into a funk. She would often lie in bed during the daytime, letting the hours pass until the sun slipped behind the horizon. (Then she got out of bed and acted as though she had been up and about all day.) She began seeing a therapist and scored a promising job: in preparation for the Bicentennial on July 4, 1976—the 200th anniversary of the Declaration of Independence—Penny joined a hip collective of performers writing sketches for a TV spoof that Francis Ford Coppola was producing about the patriotic milestone. Her assigned writing partner, the up-and-coming Cindy Williams, had starred in the popular teen movie *American Graffiti*. On the outside, Penny and Cindy seemed as different as night and day, milk and Pepsi, Oscar and Felix. Penny projected a misleading low energy; Cindy bubbled over like uncorked champagne. Penny, even as she was intensely neurotic, appeared droll and laid-back, the sort to hang in the back of the class, passing notes and cracking jokes; that made Cindy, with her sunny Sally Field patina, the Homecoming Queen sporting her boyfriend's letterman jacket over her shoulders. Few would think to put those two together, opposing life forces and all, yet their chemistry crackled.

"We had the exact same sense of humor," Cindy told me in 2022. In one sketch they wrote, "The Salem Witch Trials," the duo lampooned the absurdity of the accusations against innocent women and men in colonial Massachusetts. Cindy played a man accused of witchcraft because he always kept his hands in his pockets. She and Penny busted up laughing when Penny suggested his courtroom defense: "I have paper hands."

One day, Garry invited them to appear on an episode of *Happy Days*, his top-rated ABC comedy set in the 1950s. They were to ham it up as Laverne and Shirley, a pair of gum-chewing, boy-crazy Pink Lady types who double-date with Richie and The Fonz. "*Hookers*," Cindy recalled thinking. "This will be fun." Their schtick led to a spin-off, *Laverne & Shirley*, in which Garry toned down the characters' insolence and transformed them into virginal blue-collar heroines. The set designers at Paramount, which coproduced Garry's shows, tried to make the girls' apartment look middle-class chic, like that of Mary Tyler Moore, adding a lovely wall-to-wall sofa, cherry wood furniture, and porcelain tchotchkes. The costars balked, redecorating the set with a lot of junk, including Penny's vintage record collection. *These girls are poor*, Penny argued. *They can't afford the finer things. They can't wear fancy clothes*. The costume department, which dressed Audrey Hepburn in her heyday, threw up its hands as the stars did the unthinkable: they repeated the same articles of clothing over different episodes.

*Laverne & Shirley* debuted in January 1976, airing Tuesday nights after *Happy Days*. They were a ratings smash. Critics pounced, savaging the show as dumb and unsophisticated, but in flyover markets where a coastal critic wouldn't be caught dead, viewers fell in love. They saw adorable goofs who made do with little. Who wiggled out of unfortunate situations through pluck and teamwork. Who mirrored themselves or the girls next door. Who reminded them of happier days when the world wasn't so damn crazy.

Garry purposely staged his family-friendly sitcoms in the '50s to avoid addressing the economic and social upheaval of the 1970s. Nostalgia offered an escape from chronic inflation, the threat of job loss, and all those pushy broads asking for a bigger piece of a small pie. Fine, Laverne and Shirley had big mouths, but they weren't trying to climb the corporate ladder or divorce a husband. Their world was small, cozy, and safe. They always landed on their feet, no matter what.

Inside soundstage 20, tension charged the atmosphere. The actors, including David Lander and Michael McKean, battled the writers over the scripts. "We wanted it better," Penny said of the show. "And sometimes we didn't do it so nicely." As one of the show's directors, Alan Rafkin, explained, "It was an asylum. And I was there to see if I couldn't calm the patients down just a hair."

In contrast to the happier *Happy Days* cast and crew, who went home at 3 p.m. every day, Laverne and company stayed late, sometimes junking a script entirely and starting from scratch. At one point, Cindy tried to fire Lowell Ganz, a writer on *Laverne & Shirley*. Penny put her foot down; she trusted Ganz to know what was funny. Cindy and her manager worried that Penny's family ties offered an unfair advantage, and it was easy to see why they felt that way: Garry had hired Tony Marshall to help manage his company, Henderson Productions, named after a character in his first TV script. Garry disliked confrontation; he preferred writing to managing. He needed a father figure to impose authority, so he empowered Tony to hire and fire, negotiate with Paramount, and control the budget. On one occasion when Penny angered Tony, he withheld her paycheck. "Pop, she's a star," Garry pleaded, defending his sister.

Penny and Cindy yelled at each another, pulling no punches. "We were like sisters," Cindy told me, adding, "I wouldn't call it rivalry." Their approaches differed. Penny expected a lot, perhaps too much, from Cindy and those around her. She'd have her lines memorized and ask why Cindy, who had dyslexia, didn't know hers by heart. And if she didn't like what someone was doing, she'd grit her teeth.

"Are you gonna get that time step?" she asked Cindy during a tap dance number. "Stand back, and I'll show you!"

Penny could be obsessive. She'd wear Cindy down. "That's the best it's gonna be," Cindy would tell her, matching expectations with reality.

Penny's detail-oriented perfectionism annoyed Cindy. Many times when blocking a scene, she directed the movements with rigid precision, saying, "This goes there, that goes there." Sometimes Penny incorporated too many props into a sequence, overcomplicating things and losing sight of the joke.

"That's not funny," Cindy would say.

"Shut up," Penny would snap back.

Often, though, the badgering pushed Cindy to make her acting crisper. While Penny considered Cindy the better actress of the pair, Cindy deemed Penny brilliant. She moved fluidly, her inventive physicality recalling *I Love Lucy*. She made rigorous physical comedy appear effortless. In an early episode of *Laverne & Shirley* called "Angels of Mercy," Laverne—volunteering as a candy striper—makes a hospital bed with the patient still in it. "During rehearsal, instead of following the script, I simply tried to make the bed," Penny wrote later.

> At one point, I tugged on the sheets, lost my footing and slipped under the bed. A light went off in my head. I realized that I could take the bit even further. The next time I practiced it I asked the prop man to powder the floor. When I did it again, I slid almost all the way under the bed. I heard the crew laughing, and even better, I saw my brother wiping tears from his eyes. I knew I couldn't get a bigger compliment.

By season three, *Laverne & Shirley* was the most-watched TV show in America, besting *Happy Days* as well as the Emmy-winning *All in the Family* (which featured Penny's husband Rob, and dared to tackle topical issues like racism, abortion, and Vietnam). "Not *one* award," Penny griped to Cindy of their lack of recognition. (Correction: Not for nothing, they did win honors from the brewery workers' union and the Stuntmen's Association of Motion Pictures for doing their own stunts.) The critical gatekeepers' hauteur rankled them. It insulted their hard work and loyal viewership. While both women earned Golden Globe nominations (Penny three and Cindy one), the Emmy Awards turned up the proverbial nose.

The indignities continued in the workplace. Through the grapevine they discovered that two actors from a rival Paramount program made double their salaries. When confronted with the discrepancy, Paramount pushed back. "Yeah, but they're men," Cindy said, summing up the studio's response. The Powers That Be threatened to drop the show.

"We actually believed that," Cindy said. "Penny did too." Cindy asked herself why Garry, who possessed the clout to make things happen, didn't advocate on their behalf.

Penny, by now the most famous Marshall, accepted the status quo. "That's where she would not have confidence in the show," Cindy said.

She worried that a bigger salary could disrupt her marriage. What if she upstaged Rob, replacing him as the household breadwinner?

*Boys don't like it if you're better than them. Let them win.*

All the better to blend in with the boys than repel them with a feminist cause. In those days, Paramount resembled a bustling college campus. Actors and writers shared meals in the commissary and blew off steam between tapings. It was exciting. Penny played first base on the *Happy Days* softball team, which counted Tom Hanks, an affable whippersnapper in his mid-twenties, among the players. An indefinable charisma seeped through his pores.

Outgoing and self-assured, cute but not conventionally handsome, Tom was a fleeting fixture on the Paramount lot. Though his two-season ABC sitcom *Bosom Buddies* succumbed to low ratings in 1982, he and costar Peter Scolari cultivated a reputation for offbeat humor and improvisational hijinks. Their characters, cash-strapped corporate underlings, conspired to dress in drag so they could live at the affordable, women-only Susan B. Anthony Hotel. Tom knew firsthand what living paycheck to paycheck was like, barely making ends meet to support his wife and their young son. He loved having TV money and sharing a spotlight with Scolari. But he grew tired of the cross-dressing conceit and the network's control over him. "I was an asshole for six months, and no one would tell me I was an asshole," he admitted later. "When you're the star of a series, you magnify trivial things. 'I can't say this! I won't do that!' You live in this airplane hangar, and you think you're important when you're not. You're really not."

At the time, he wanted off the show. He envied Tom Selleck of *Magnum, P.I.* for landing magazine covers. Where was his big *People* moment? Stage 25 was a prison; *Bosom Buddies* dimmed his light. When Paramount finally hit the cancel button and he returned to the hustle as a free agent, Tom realized that he had it good for a while. He just didn't know it. Nor could he have known then how his life would change in explosive ways to create celluloid permanence. How one day Penny Marshall—yes, *Laverne*—would open all the right doors.

## *Second Inning*

# FIRST STRIKE

Rob moved out in August 1979. He and Penny decided to separate after nearly a decade of marriage, and suddenly, Penny found herself alone in an empty house. She looked at the other side of her bed, where Rob once slept, and felt his absence. In these moments, she harbored second thoughts.

"Why exchange an imperfect husband, whose failings I can deal with, for an imperfect stranger?" she pondered.

The split was inevitable. The power couple, who once graced the cover of *People* (the headline: "Meathead & His Missus"), had grown apart. *Laverne & Shirley* eclipsed *All in the Family*'s popularity, creating an imbalance that caused Penny to feel apologetic and ashamed. "I didn't want to make more money than he did because I knew it would be a problem," she recalled. "So I negotiated lower and he said, 'What, are you crazy?'"

Rob's departure from *All in the Family*, and his role as Archie Bunker's liberal son-in-law Meathead, widened the gulf between them. She was red hot; his star was cooling. He should have known. In this business, one day you were up and the next day you were down, and then another guy—or even your wife—took your place.

The headache of renovating their home in Encino didn't help matters. They squeezed temporarily into the guesthouse, which was hell. But they never fought or argued. Instead, they asked each other, *Is this it? Are we happy?* No, they weren't.

Twilight was the loneliest time for Penny. She preferred to have a man on the property—a relief at night—so she leased the guesthouse to Richard Dreyfuss, then Tim Matheson. She moved out, hopping from rental home to rental home. Finally, in the early 1980s, she put down roots, buying a mid-century estate in the Hollywood Hills with sweeping views of the city below. At night the lights twinkled like stars. Tracy occupied a wing, and Penny invited friends to fill the empty spaces. Jim Belushi stayed two years and Joe Pesci three, overlapping with *Saturday Night Live*'s Jon Lovitz. She made her houseguests pay their own phone bills and forbade their girlfriends from sleeping over. (She wasn't into making small talk with the women.) When not working, traveling, or partying, she liked to hunker down in bed with her cigarettes and remote controls. She kept the curtains drawn. One friend called her bedroom "The Cave."

By the time Penny and Rob made their divorce official in 1981, Penny had dived into a bicoastal social scene where drugs flowed freely. She forged an instant bond with *Star Wars* heroine Carrie Fisher, a loyal friend during the highs and lows, and spent time in New York dating actor David Dukes and musician Art Garfunkel. She befriended director Steven Spielberg, who cast her in a minor role in his John Belushi comedy *1941*, a big-budget flop. "I tried to get a Quaalude in him," she reminisced in her memoir. "They were my drug of choice." Spielberg, a "square," didn't dabble in recreational sedatives, though he couldn't avoid the ubiquity of such substances in the circles in which he moved. When Penny brought him to John's thirty-first birthday in LA, there were partiers freebasing cocaine—cooking it, then inhaling it. Penny took a hit. "My neck and chest froze," she said. "I left the bathroom with my upper body temporarily paralyzed. That was fun?"

Another time, she and Carrie tried LSD while visiting John and Dan Aykroyd in Chicago, where the actors filmed *The Blues Brothers*. The women rode up and down the elevator at the Ritz-Carlton, dissolving into giddy laughter. Shortly afterward, Penny suffered a distressing anxiety attack. She and Carrie were due in Albuquerque the following day to play baseball in a *Happy Days* charity game. Penny phoned her straightlaced brother to let him know what was going on.

"Well, I think you just need to get through it," Garry said.

When they met on the diamond hours later, he rubbed her back and asked, "So tell me, that was fun for you?"

As Penny lived it up, reclaiming the years she lost to domesticity, her work ethic remained unshakable. And by the time she began thinking about directing as a safety net, a way to survive after Laverne and keep playing with the boys, she embodied a rare case: a woman who didn't have to claw and climb and bust down doors to make a movie. Penny's powerful network of male supporters rallied around her. Spielberg admired the way Penny validated needy men with artistic temperaments, really listening to their problems. "Directing is babysitting," he told her. "You do it for free. Why don't you get paid for it?"

He paid attention to how easily she put complicated jigsaw puzzles together—*that, right there, was editing.* He talked her up to Mike Ovitz, her agent at Creative Artists Agency.

On the set of *Laverne & Shirley*, "She used to cut film in her head while she was acting," said Jack Winters, one of the show's seasoned directors. "When I directed, I'd go, 'Oh, god, we've got 12 new pages out of 26 and they'll never learn it!' And Penny was out there, and not only had she learned her lines, and was doing something new to get a laugh, but she was already going, 'OK, we've got C camera on this, so we can cut that and go to closeup and then cut to the master.'"

As a concession to keep a restless Penny on ABC's lineup, Paramount approved her taking Winters's place on occasion. "This [show] isn't worth me doing, unless I can direct," Todd Smith, who handled Penny for Ovitz at CAA, quotes her as saying.

When Paramount dangled *The Joy of Sex* for Penny to direct, she doubted her ability to juggle Laverne and a lowbrow side-hustle. *Would Marty Scorsese do this film?* she wondered. *Would De Niro act in a film like this?* The responsibility. The potential to fail. It scared her. She and her shrink would have a lot to discuss.

*The Joy of Sex* made John Belushi nervous too. While Paramount envisioned an irreverent crowd-pleaser akin to *Airplane!*, this project specifically conjured carnal lust. That meant Penny could witness John in various racy and vulnerable positions. He thought *Laverne & Shirley* was garbage and told her so. At *Saturday Night Live*, he undermined women performers and writers, demanding the show fire them. In rehearsals he intentionally sabotaged sketches written by women so that they never got a chance to air on primetime. He said, "Women are just fundamentally not funny."

Given John's hostility, Penny stood to become another target of his swaggering chauvinism. Yet she saw promise in John Hughes's script for *The Joy of Sex* and hosted a reading at her home with Ed Begley Jr. and Carol Kane acting the roles and Spielberg on hand to snap photos. The night before John was to meet with the studio about boarding the Penny train, he overdosed. *Had she been with him, would he still be alive?* Once, she had flushed John's heroin down the toilet, saying, "Don't fuck with that stuff." (She'd tried the drug and it made her nauseous.) His death waved a red flag for Hollywood's libertines and addictive personalities: *what happened to Belushi could happen to me.*

In December 1983, Marjorie Marshall, who'd long ago traded the Grand Concourse for Southern California, the family's adopted coast, died after battling Alzheimer's. Seven years earlier she had flubbed a line while making a brief appearance on *Happy Days*; the memory loss resulted in her diagnosis. "Maybe it's good—she won't know who I am and will like me better," Penny joked. The matriarch had been in a coma when the Marshalls gathered at Northwestern University to dedicate the Marjorie Ward Marshall Dance Center, their $1 million gift to her. Penny cried, thinking, *I wish Mom could see this.* Months later, with Tracy in tow, she opened a window in *Saturday Night Live* creator Lorne Michaels's Manhattan office and fulfilled Marjorie's wish: she sprinkled her ashes in the air above Broadway.

That was also the year Penny buried *Laverne & Shirley*. She took exciting trips abroad, touring Australia and New Zealand with Simon and Garfunkel and crashing Carrie and Paul Simon's honeymoon in Egypt. She and Art Garfunkel had a quirky off-and-on romance that ran its course in the early 1980s.

On April 9, 1984, Penny attended the Oscars as a guest of Larry Gordon, who produced *Terms of Endearment* along with her friend Jim Brooks, also the director of the five-hankie melodrama. It swept the awards, winning Best Picture and Best Director in addition to Best Supporting Actor for Jack Nicholson. Debra Winger lost Best Actress to Shirley MacLaine, who played her prim, overbearing mother in the movie. The actresses famously clashed during the filming, and in one unscripted episode, Debra lifted her skirt to fart in Shirley's face. The offscreen friction generated authentic sparks between their warring characters. In her acceptance speech, Shirley praised Debra's "turbulent brilliance." Then she said, "I deserve this."

Later that night, Penny ran into Debra at an after-party, thinking she "must have felt like shit." She and Debra sat together and smoked for a while. Debra mentioned the next picture in her queue, a high-concept comedy-drama called *Peggy Sue Got Married* about a grown woman who wakes up as her seventeen-year-old self. A teenager again, she reconnects with her high school sweetheart, the younger version of her husband from whom she's estranged in the future. The flame is rekindled. As it happened, Penny had read the script for *Peggy Sue*. She found its premise intriguing, even profound. It had a Frank Capra quality that touched her heart.

"Why don't you direct?" Debra asked Penny.

"I don't direct," she answered, seeming to forget the time she nearly helmed *The Joy of Sex*.

"Well, maybe you will," Debra said.

When debating whether to do a movie, Debra could turn commitment-phobic; she was opinionated and demanding, a popular actress unafraid to make enemies. *Peggy Sue*'s first director, Jonathan Demme, walked away after a conflict with Debra, leaving a convenient hole for Penny to fill. Debra encouraged producer Ray Stark to hire her. He did so begrudgingly. As soon as the light turned green, Penny launched into casting mode and approached Tom Hanks and Sean Penn about roles. She had spent nearly a month prepping the movie when Stark and his producing team fired her without notice. *LA Weekly* reported that Stark thought *Peggy Sue* was too big, too important, for a novice like Penny to screw up. In a rare gesture, he threw his support behind the screenwriters—typically the lowest in the filmmaking hierarchy—who resisted changes that Penny and Debra wanted to make. The women departed *Peggy Sue*, and Francis Ford Coppola stepped in to take the reins with Kathleen Turner in the lead.

Penny couldn't seem to catch a break.

The boys were winning. She lagged as her peers, the boys, flourished in the film world. Spielberg was Spielberg, a generational talent. A wunderkind. He was always going to win. Garry navigated a smooth transition from TV showrunner to movie director with the coming-of-age comedy *The Flamingo Kid*, and Ron Howard, who played Richie on *Happy Days*, ditched acting to embark on a lofty second act behind the lens. His romantic comedy *Splash* turned Tom Hanks into the leading man he wanted to be. After *Bosom Buddies*, Tom took a recurring role on *Family Ties*, playing Michael J. Fox's alcoholic Uncle Ned. (As the saying goes, there are no small roles! Only small actors. But thanks to *Splash*, Tom made the permanent leap to the medium that, for more than a century, carried bigger clout, prospects, and paydays.)

Rob Reiner also sprinted ahead of Penny. His directorial debut, the rock mockumentary *This Is Spinal Tap*, became an instant cult classic. *Laverne & Shirley*'s Michael McKean costarred alongside Christopher Guest as members of the pretentious heavy metal group Spinal Tap. They improvised dialogue that the movie's superfans quoted to each other like inside jokes that flew over the heads of the uninitiated. ("He died in a bizarre gardening accident some years back," McKean says of a former drummer. Guest replies, ". . . the authorities said, you know, best leave it unsolved, really.")

While Penny held social advantages over lesser-known woman filmmakers—none of whom could say their joint birthday parties with Carrie Fisher were triple-VIP events—she ranked low on the long list of directors who got their first crack at A-list projects. To get the ball rolling, she set up a development deal at Warner Brothers, following the trend of big-name actresses like Goldie Hawn, Jane Fonda, and Jessica Lange who hatched studio deals, leveraging star power for a modicum of control within a patriarchal system.

Penny understood well that unlike Hawn, she'd have a harder time parlaying TV celebrity into movie stardom. With that in mind, she accepted leads in movies designed just for the tube: the romcom *Love Thy Neighbor* paired her with John Ritter, and in the feel-good story *Challenge of a Lifetime*, she played a divorced single mother who enters a triathlon and regains her confidence. *Challenge of a Lifetime* capitalized on the fitness craze that swept the nation during the Reagan Era, when Fonda incited millions of women to "Feel the burn!" in her workout videos. While suburban housewives tried to harden their figures and look as lean and lithe as Jane, the track phenom Florence Griffith Joyner, known as FloJo, offered another ideal: that of the woman athlete as superhero, all strength and speed and swagger, a human bolt of lightning. FloJo, the fastest woman in the world, wore brightly colored outfits and long hair and nails in competition, bringing style and flair to the field. She reveled in her athletic excellence. Her body didn't exist to squeeze into pre-baby Calvin Kleins. To please men. Her body belonged to her—and look what it could do.

If Penny never fulfilled the Olympic-runner fantasy she dreamed in girlhood, which FloJo lived out in spectacular ways, then at least she had the opportunity to cross the finish line on a Thursday night special. Both the actress and the Olympian helped pave the way for movies about athletic women, laying the groundwork for *A League of Their Own*.

But overall, "I wasn't anxious to work," Penny said of that time. "I'm happy to be in love more than I am to work." Her career responsibilities took a personal toll, and she got complacent. She wanted a fuller life with steady romance. In the fall of 1985, she decided to buy an apartment in New York, where cynicism reigned supreme. New Yorkers read the *Daily News* and the *Post*, not *Variety*. They also walked everywhere. Penny, who didn't drive, felt at ease on the lively streets she used to call home. In New York, she heard thick accents like hers. Having a thick accent was a unifying trait rather than a casting or dating dealbreaker.

While touring homes on the Upper West Side, she bumped into Debra, whom she loved, on the set of the crime caper *Legal Eagles*. Interpersonal drama plagued the production, which costarred Robert Redford and Daryl Hannah. Debra had been slow to leave her dressing room. Frank Price, the Universal Pictures chairman who green-lighted *Legal Eagles*, pegged Hannah as the source of Debra's issues. "I had concluded that Debra has a problem when there's another attractive woman cast in the picture with her," he says. "There's something competitive there."

All told, Redford was no shrinking violet either. "The movie did fine," *Legal Eagles* director Ivan Reitman said later. "It turned out to be more expensive than it should have been because it was the only time I went over schedule shooting, and that was because the two stars got to fighting so much that neither of them wanted to come out. Debra was just probably the worst person I've ever worked with in 40 years of making films with all kinds of stars and all kinds of actors. Ironically, she was the one who got all the best reviews when that film came out."

Within days, Penny found new digs on West End Avenue. She went out to dinner with Whoopi Goldberg, another smart cookie who spoke her mind. Whoopi was shooting *Jumpin' Jack Flash*, a comedy from 20th

Century Fox, in the city. Her star was on the rise. Her one-woman Broadway show, which aired on HBO, had captured Spielberg's attention, leading him to cast her as Celie in *The Color Purple*, a drama slated for release that December. Meanwhile, an aura of doom enshrouded *Jumpin' Jack Flash* as key crew members dropped like flies.

The movie's producers, Larry Gordon and Joel Silver, soon phoned Penny with an urgent request. Whoopi and director Howard Zieff weren't getting along, and Zieff had fled the picture eight days into filming. Could Penny jump in there and get the job done? They knew she knew Whoopi—they knew about the friendly dinner—so perhaps Penny would have the magic touch to smooth over difficulties going forward.

"Can I read the script?" Penny asked.

"What do you need to do that for?" Silver said.

Under Gordon and Silver's tight schedule, Penny would get just one week to prepare—not nearly enough time. The script was such a mess, even earlier versions penned by Nancy Meyers and David Mamet hadn't panned out. The job made Penny the captain of the freakin' *Titanic*, attempting to steer the ship after it had already hit the iceberg. Who the hell wanted that responsibility?

"I don't know," she told her manager, Charlie Wessler, of the offer. "It's like picking up somebody else's trash."

Wessler agreed: *Jumpin' Jack Flash* was not the right movie to be her first. But with that said! Why turn down a paid scholarship at a major motion picture studio? Laverne had made Penny rich. She didn't need the money. But she needed the *experience*. "You're going to learn," he said. When she consulted Garry, he echoed that sentiment, saying, "Just don't fall down. And finish." Spielberg reminded her to take the lens cap off the camera.

Thirty-six hours later, Penny arrived on set in LA, where *Jumpin' Jack Flash* relocated with a newly hired director of photography, Matt Leonetti, replacing Jan de Bont. At 5 a.m., a cruel hour for a night owl, Penny had messy hair and red-rimmed eyes. She introduced herself to the men on the crew. "I ask only one thing," she said. "When I make mistakes—and I will make them—please don't go behind my back and make faces. Just come up and tell me."

She lacked know-how about lenses and lighting and blocking scenes using one camera as opposed to the three that surrounded Laverne and Shirley's bachelorette pad. Every night, Leonetti, whose credits included *Weird Science* and *Poltergeist*, helped Penny map out daily shooting schedules. Sometimes she had him act out a scene so she could visualize it better. She got little sleep. Worse still, she suffered cramps on the job. "That wasn't too pleasant," she recalled. "At one point, I said, 'I'd much rather act.' Actors get treated better. Actors get babied."

Penny lamented the slow pace of filmmaking: waiting on the lights, the angles, the master shot. She thought, *Kill me now.* On the second day of the shoot, Whoopi invited Penny into her makeup trailer to get freshened up—a small act of kindness that pleased Penny but irked the abrasive Silver, who went looking for her.

"What are you doing?" he said, walking into the trailer.

"I felt that really I needed to get made up," she answered.

"Penny, you're the director of the movie."

"I can still look good. I just need to feel better."

"Penny, get the fuck out of here and get to the set."

"When I'm finished being made up then I'll go to the set."

The actors, the *performance*, that was what Penny knew best. On a personal level, she connected with Whoopi's character, Terry Doolittle, a lonely IT employee at a Manhattan bank who becomes an unlikely asset for an international spy. The plot spins into motion when a cryptic message flashes on Terry's computer screen. "I'm in trouble," it reads. "I need you." Penny, the reluctant captain of a sinking ship, could relate to such a left-field request.

Whoopi, her most important passenger, voiced concern about working with Penny. "She is a television actress," Silver quoted her saying. "What does she know about comedy?"

Whoopi often resisted Penny's suggestions. Penny liked actors to improvise and feed her options for the editing suite. But Whoopi hesitated to go off-script and invent new comic material if she wasn't feeling it. "Do you know what it's like doing something stupid over and over again?" she complained. She was game one day and uncooperative the next. She'd sit at the computer with her lines visible on the monitor and say, "I don't feel so good."

On *Jumpin' Jack Flash*, Whoopi was loath to leave the comfort of her trailer. She refused to do a stunt that made her nervous, throwing her shoes at a producer in protest. Her agent at CAA, Ron Meyer, advised her to make the best of the situation. *The Color Purple*, which starred a predominantly Black cast, had been a delight. It was difficult to go from *that* to sets where, as she observed, "all they could really see is what I look like." She added, "I was Black, but I also thought that I was an actor, because that's what I'd always been. And suddenly people were touching my hair, saying, 'What are we going to do with it?'"

Penny felt for Whoopi. In part, her anger came from frustration—namely, weathering two directors and a thousand script revisions. And she was getting famous. When that happens, "Everybody gets crazy," Penny said. "Everybody wants you. They're blowing smoke up your ass like you know something, and you start to behave in a certain way that's stupid, but you don't know what else to do."

Penny tried to lighten the mood. She solicited the crew's opinion on Whoopi's takes, collecting a vote. "OK, how many think that's good? How many don't? There you go. We voted. *Democracy*."

Leonetti sought to break up the tension between Penny and Whoopi by teasing the latter. "Just a touch," he says. "I remember one day I teased her a little bit and she started to chase me, so I ran out of the set in a joking way."

While visiting the set, Wessler noticed the DP placing his hand on Penny's shoulder and giving her a massage. *He's treating her like she's a child-woman, a girl*, Wessler thought. He didn't like what he saw. Penny was smart. She knew her shit. Why couldn't these guys see that?

It was the way she spoke, the question marks in her whine. She came off as helpless and insecure. That combination made a cameraman want to help her out. Perhaps it made him feel useful, like a knight rescuing the damsel in distress. Penny often weaponized her vulnerability to get the boys to do what she wanted without reminding them of their bossy mothers. Or an aggressive girl in the schoolyard sandbox, playing with *their* toys. On *their* turf.

Not everyone warmed to her unorthodox leadership style. Soon her cameraman, doubting her abilities, would revolt.

## *Third Inning*

# ANOTHER SWING AT BAT

Harrison Ford threw a script at Wessler. He ordered him to read it and give his opinion. (When Indiana Jones makes such demands, one must do his bidding.) Wessler, a guest at Ford's home in Wyoming—where the outdoorsy actor intended to teach the Angeleno how to fly fish for trout—happily complied.

Out on the porch, Wessler sat down in a couch swing and cracked open the screenplay for a movie called *Big*. The writers, Gary Ross and Anne Spielberg, Steven's sister, had invented a fantastical hook:

> A 12-year-old boy, Josh Baskin, visits a Zoltar machine at an amusement park and makes a wish to be older, so that a girl he likes at school might like him back. The next morning, Josh awakens in horror to discover that Zoltar fulfilled his request overnight, transforming the preteen into a thirtysomething adult. Older Josh escapes the cozy suburbs for gritty Manhattan and bumbles his way into a dream job testing products at a toy company. While his guileless innocence confuses colleagues, it charms the boss as well as a female colleague for whom he develops feelings. As Josh learns the ropes of adulthood, and the grown-up responsibilities it entails, he yearns to go home and be a kid again.

Wessler loved the story, and his excitement grew as he flipped the pages. On the back of Ford's script, he saw a list of six or seven potential directors, none of whom were his number-one client.

*Fuck Spielberg*, he thought. *Penny should direct this movie.* Luckily, she had an in: Jim Brooks, whom Penny considered a mentor, was the producer.

Brooks envisioned a Spielberg-Ford collaboration not involving a globe-trotting archeologist, stolen religious artifacts, and venomous snakes. The power pair were a package deal. While scheming on Penny's behalf, Wessler genuinely felt that his friend was a bad fit to play Older Josh. "He's too cool for that shit," he says.

He leveled with Ford.

"I just don't see how this is you," he said of the juvenile role.

Ford listened and seemed to agree. Wessler got the sense that he wasn't too excited about Brooks's offer. Offscreen, Ford was understated and bohemian. But as Indy and Han Solo, he loomed larger than life: earnest, wry, smirking, vulnerable. Nobody, not even Cruise, played a better action hero. Nobody would believe him as a man-child obsessed with robots. One might argue that Ford came out of the womb a fully grown man.

As soon as possible, Wessler phoned Penny. He had no idea how close Brooks was to making the movie, and they needed to act fast.

"Look," he told her. "I can't do this—it's kind of mean, it's probably not right—but you need to call Jim Brooks and tell him that you read the movie *Big* and that you wanna direct it," he said.

"What?" she said. "I can't call him and lie."

"Well, *lie*. It doesn't matter."

Penny got her agents to send her the script and liked what she read, Wessler remembers. Memories conflict as to how *Big* landed on her desk in the first place. Other accounts detail Brooks popping into Penny's office during post-production on *Jumpin' Jack Flash* and handing her a manila envelope.

"This is your next movie," he said, according to a recollection in the January 1991 issue of *Playboy*.

"Huh?" she responded.

"This is the movie you're doing next."

Proving Wessler right, Ford had given Brooks the thumbs-down, paving the path for Penny to take over. What Brooks failed to mention in approaching her was that lots of bigwigs passed on *Big*—not just Spielberg but Ivan Reitman, Charles Shyer, and John Hughes. He also didn't inform Penny that the movie had kicked off a trend of body-swapping comedies in development, including *Vice Versa* and *Like Father, Like Son*, which meant *Big* had lost its novelty. A perfectionist, Brooks spent a year retooling the script, then many months waiting on Ford. It impressed him that Penny had managed to complete *Jumpin' Jack Flash* amid the chaos. The movie hit theaters in October 1986, grossing nearly $30 million on an $18 million budget. Was it the greatest thing ever made? Hardly. But still, it earned a profit. And that was not nothing.

The reviews? Dismal. Both Roger Ebert and Vincent Canby of the *New York Times* agreed that Whoopi had been wronged, her talents squandered. Canby pinned the blame on Penny. "Miss Marshall directs *Jumpin' Jack Flash* as if she were more worried about the decor than the effect of the performance," he wrote. "Even potentially good gags somehow go unrealized, as when Miss Goldberg manages to get the skirt of a blue-beaded evening dress caught in a paper shredder. The idea is funnier than the execution."

Of course, neither critic had known the headaches behind the scenes, how Penny had swooped in on short notice, how Whoopi had been miserable. She and Penny made the best of the cards they were dealt. They crossed the finish line, grumbling along the way, but *Jumpin' Jack Flash* would be labeled a dud.

"Hey, hey, lay back!" Penny said years later, defending the effort. "Whoopi was cute in it. She was warmer than in the next six films she did. But I'm a failure. Thank god I didn't know it at the time."

(A correction: Whoopi oozed much more warmth in *Ghost* and *Sister Act*.)

Even with Brooks's blessing, 20th Century Fox, which released *Jumpin' Jack Flash* and gave *Big* the green light, cast a wary eye in Penny's direction. The studio had cleared the throne for an experienced man, not *Laverne*. "It took literally like a month of beating the crap out of Fox, who didn't want Penny to do it, to let her do it," Wessler says. "And what does Penny do? She's in New York, she's having dinner with Robert De Niro, and she says, 'You know, Bob, you should do this movie I've got called *Big*.' And he *agrees*. And I'm like, *What? No! Please, no*."

He told Penny, "No one's gonna give you money to make a movie with Bob De Niro as the little kid. It's creepy. *The little murdering kid*."

But Penny fixated on casting the thespian she nicknamed "Bobby D." following rejections from the irreverent Tom Hanks, the puckish Dennis Quaid, and the charming Kevin Costner. Tom, her first choice, was unavailable, filming one movie after another. He'd be perfect for the part; that much was obvious. But De Niro? An unexpected selection. The legendary brooder set the gold standard for actors. He was the opposite of milquetoast. Fine, he screamed "dark" and "edgy" and "Method." So what? If Bobby immersed himself in Josh Baskin, he'd throw moviegoers for a loop. *Who? Him? Raging Bull?* With a batch of *Big* copycats headed toward the theater, Penny needed her movie to stand out from the pack. Bobby offered the element of surprise.

"Let me take it a different way," Penny told Fox executives. "Let me take it to someone you never expect would behave this way."

While De Niro was attached, Penny held a casting call in New York for eleven- and twelve-year-old boys to play Young Josh. The candidates sat on the carpet of a community center as she peppered them with questions.

"Where are you from?" she asked David Moscow, who looked more like Tom than Bobby.

"I'm from the Bronx," he said.

"Which baseball team?"

"The Yankees."

(Correct answer.) Penny approached Debra about playing Josh's love interest, Susan Lawrence, his fabulously brittle coworker at MacMillan Toys. Debra thought *Big* should flip genders with an actress in the leading role instead. "Why isn't this about a girl?" she asked, overlooking the controversial aspects of replacing the concept of a virginal boy in a grown man's body with a female parallel. In any case, she turned Penny down. Debra, expecting her first child with husband Timothy Hutton, recommended Elizabeth Perkins, a twenty-five-year-old New Yorker who possessed luminous skin, liquid brown eyes, and a maturity beyond her years. She debuted on Broadway in *Brighton Beach Memoirs* and onscreen in the 1986 ensemble comedy *About Last Night*, garnering positive reviews. Brooks considered Elizabeth for the female lead in *Broadcast News* but ultimately cast Holly Hunter. He and Elizabeth remained friendly, and he also suggested her to Penny.

While auditioning for *Big*, Elizabeth read with De Niro. "He was more moody," she later confessed to Andy Cohen on *Watch What Happens Live*. "It was a little bit of a horror movie. It was Robert De Niro wandering around the streets of New York."

Wessler decided to make a move. "Penny really knows what she wants," he recalls, "but she was 98 percent wrong about that one." He admits that he "kind of colluded with her agents to get rid of that guy."

All told, Fox CEO Barry Diller was 100 percent wrong about Warren Beatty, his suggested candidate for Older Josh. He asked Penny to meet with the actor-director, then pushing fifty, old enough to be Elizabeth's father. "I asked if he would listen to me if I directed him," she recalled in *My Mother Was Nuts*. "In the nicest way, he said no. Well, that was thrilling. Why bother? At least Warren was being honest. That's all I ever ask. Just tell me the truth. I'll deal with it."

Penny told De Niro the truth: that Diller had pushed Beatty on her. The disclosure surprised De Niro. Adding to his disappointment, Fox intended to pay him $3 million—half of the $6 million he felt he deserved. Penny offered her salary to Bobby as a concession. He declined and dropped out of the picture.

Enter Tom Hanks. De Niro's fleeting attachment sparked renewed interest from actors who had rejected *Big*. Tom was as busy as ever, but back in the mix. Faced with a choice between Tom and Jeff Bridges, Penny followed her instincts. Her heart said: *Choose Tom*. She liked him personally, which certainly didn't hurt his chances at winning the part. They connected to talk *Big* while Tom, who had just turned thirty, filmed the LA-based buddy cop comedy *Dragnet* alongside Dan Aykroyd.

"Do you want *The Nutty Professor* or *Being There*?" he asked.

"*Being There*," she said, aligning her movie with the Peter Sellers satire about a simple man who lucks into a career as a respected business and political adviser.

She and Tom: they were on. She waited for him to stop working so he could work some more.

Tom feared that he would never work again. That feeling, a gnawing dread, crept into his brain and infused him with a sense of urgency. He lined up movies, back-to-back-to-back, wringing out as much of his luck as possible before his fifteen minutes were up and the opportunities vanished. What if they caught on and shelved the imposter? What if he stopped working for a minute? He might be forgotten, or worse: replaced with someone younger, funnier, more talented, more handsome, The Flavor of the Month, the next Tom Hanks. He didn't want to be a passing fad. He wanted to make this last. He was like a wind-up toy. He couldn't stop moving.

His production schedule was rather insane. With *Dragnet* wrapped, in March 1987 Tom pivoted to *Punchline*, sinking his teeth into his juiciest role yet, a bitter standup comedian who confronts internal demons onstage and off. He wasn't an actor living the part day and night, night and day; he walked on a firm foundation and knew how to compartmentalize characters and snap back to form when the director yelled, "Cut!" But for *Punchline*, Tom pulled a De Niro in his immersive preparation, hitting comedy clubs to practice his tight five. He spent two months looking foolish. "I was really terrible the first 15 times," he recalled.

If acting is about self-revelation, then Tom's character, the spiky Steven Gold, revealed the darker corners of his glib yet genial persona. Up there in the limelight, bracing for tomatoes or applause, Tom unearthed an uneasy truth about Steven and many performers like himself: the stage is addicting; attention is a drug. "That kind of power corrupts," he said, "walking into a room of 400 people and taking them wherever you want for 20 minutes. Steven is god of his universe as long as he's got a microphone in his hand. You can't help taking that home with you."

He invented a backstory for Steven: a cold, isolating childhood. An unsupportive family. An unfillable void. "I felt sorry for the guy," he said. "He's not a good human being, but he's an excellent standup comedian. I always viewed him as being trapped by this ability. It was never going to make him happy. If he goes on the Carson show and becomes a success, he is going to be just as vile and unlikable."

Of course, Tom personified likability, a quality that helped soften Steven's cruelty. While he and his alter ego existed on opposite ends of the kindness spectrum, Steven "probably has the worst aspects of my worst aspects," Tom told *Playboy* in 1989. "He is extremely competitive, for one thing. He is unable to balance his daily existence so that real life and what he does for a living have equal weight. I've certainly had those problems;

I think any actor has: The only time you really feel alive is when you're working."

He and Steven also shared a worldview that, in Tom's case, was surprisingly downbeat. "I'm constantly reminded of how unfair the world in general is," he revealed during the *Punchline* promotional tour.

What an odd thing to say for the guy who had everything. And yet, if you really knew him, it made sense.

When Tom was five years old, his parents divorced. His father, Amos, nicknamed Bud, took Tom and his older siblings, Larry and Sandra; his mother, Janet, stayed behind with six-month-old Jim, then went on to marry three times. "I just felt lonely; I felt abandoned, in the dark," Tom said of that time, when he learned how unfair his world could be. "No one is telling you the why, just the what: Pack your bags, get the stuff you want, and put it in the back of the station wagon."

With Bud in the driver's seat, chasing restaurant and catering jobs in different California towns, Tom never stayed in one place too long. Bud married and divorced a second wife, finally settling in Oakland with the third Mrs. Hanks, Frances Wong. "I read all the time 'Tom Hanks is the product of a broken, tragic childhood,'" he has complained, making light of a skewed narrative. "Horseshit! My childhood was wonderful. It wasn't a Disney movie, but so what?"

Tom grew up funny and shy, the student cracking wise in class yet always avoiding detention. He played baseball, a sport that obsessed him, in Little League, though he spent much of his time indoors watching TV. (His favorite show: *Then Came Bronson*, which featured Penny Marshall in one of its first episodes.) Several other experiences shaped the man he would become: seeing *2001: A Space Odyssey* in the theater, where he learned about magic; reading *The Catcher in the Rye*, where he learned he wasn't alone; and learning about the Holocaust in elementary school. A photograph of Nazis forcing a Jewish boy out of a Warsaw ghetto haunted Tom, who discovered that the wider world was unfair. That documenting history, in books and in movies, could be important.

At Skyline High School he found his tribe: theater kids. They loved to laugh. They understood him as the jocks could not. He donned a grass skirt to perform "There Is Nothin' Like a Dame" in *South Pacific* and penned a letter to George Roy Hill, the director of *Butch Cassidy and the Sundance Kid*, touting his untapped potential for movie stardom: "Mr. Hill," he wrote. "I don't want to be some big-time, Hollywood superstar with girls crawling all over me, just a hometown American boy who has hit the big time, owns a Porsche, and calls Robert Redford 'Bob.'"

After graduation, Tom entered community college and then transferred to California State University at Sacramento, studying theater production. He began dating a classmate, Susan Dillingham, and he honed his craft over three summers onstage at the Great Lakes Shakespeare Festival in Ohio. For Tom, Cleveland was good living. On warm nights, he brushed up his iambic pentameter in *The Taming of the Shrew* and *The Two Gentlemen of Verona*; afternoons, he sat in the right field section at Municipal Stadium, observing Indians games. *Bliss*. He would remain a diehard Indians (now Guardians) fan long after leaving Cleveland. The 1980 season seemed to resonate with him. That year, the team ranked second to last in the American League's eastern division standings. Center fielder Rick Manning remained many months away from his career highlight: catching Ernie Whitt's fly ball, the final out of pitcher Len Barker's flawless game against the Toronto Blue Jays. Power slugger Joe "Super Joe" Charboneau, the Dennis Rodman of his day, came out of nowhere to win Rookie of the Year, captivating the city with his dyed hair and madcap habit of drinking beer through his nose. Unfortunately, he injured his back during a headfirst slide in 1981, ending his stint in the Majors before it really began. The highs, the lows, the sweet victories, the jarring disappointments. Super Joe lived it all over two short years.

"Baseball is the perfect metaphor for life," Tom told GQ in 1988. "Football is a metaphor for war and basketball for struggle, but baseball is life."

For him, baseball closely resembled acting: players hung out in the dugout, an equivalent to backstage, before the big performance. When they emerged on the field, they had to focus on the game. Like making movies or playing Proteus to a packed house, professional ball promised more fun than nine-to-five drudgery. (If only Tom could hit a curveball.) He resented the pressure to strategize a grand professional plan for himself. Life zigzagged; it didn't follow a straight line. It contained too many unknowns. How can you predict the route from A to Z? He threw the map out the window, as his dad had done. Tom preferred to play things by ear and see what he picked up along the way.

In the years after Cleveland, he rarely took a breath: Susan got pregnant, giving birth to their son, Colin, in 1977. The couple married and moved to New York City. They struggled to pay the rent as Tom chased his dreams, landing a minor role in a low-budget slasher movie filmed on Staten Island. Then, *boom*, it happened: one lucky audition led to his *Bosom Buddies* break. The dominos fell, one by one: *Splash*, *Bachelor Party*, *Volunteers*, *The Man with One Red Shoe*, *The Money Pit*, *Every Time We Say Goodbye*, and *Nothing in Common*, a father-son dramedy directed by Garry Marshall and costarring Jackie Gleason. Tom cried real tears on camera, which delighted Garry, who disliked using "spritz" to fake emotion. "The film tries to show that life is funny and life is sad—all at the same time," Tom said, describing the Marshall Method. That happy-sad tone colored the universal epiphany in *Nothing in Common*: those "times when we look at our parents," he added, "and say we're not like them, we never will be, and we won't make the same mistakes—and then we come to the shocking realization that we've all made the same mistakes our parents made and we're exactly like them."

Tom and Susan split up in 1985. Susan mostly cared for Colin and their daughter, Elizabeth, while Tom jumped from one movie set to the other. He maintained that his consuming job didn't ruin his marriage; it simply fell apart.

"In some ways, I guess I've been like a classic absentee father," he admitted to *Cosmo* in 1987. "My work has taken me away a lot—and certainly being separated, even more so."

While his family unraveled, Tom kept his problems out of the workplace. "He's one of the few young actors," Garry observed, "who doesn't believe that the set should revolve around his personal life."

Tom gave his director grief on occasion. He approached Garry one day, asking, "But what if people don't care about this movie?" Garry being Garry, he responded with an avuncular pep talk. Privately, however, Tom's words stung. "You know," he told Tom later, "I lost a whole night's sleep over what you said. I kept thinking that whole night—so what if they *don't* care?"

Tom cared what the people thought, and he worried that Garry would drop a bomb on his resume. Following *Splash*, his track record at the box office had been spotty; he'd yet to carry a film over the $100 million mark. He felt he was an avatar for nerdy male screenwriters who desired to have more sex. He wanted to move away from that, to stretch himself past others' expectations. (You could only fall in love with a mermaid so many times.)

*Nothing in Common* opened in eighth place on August 1, 1986, behind *Aliens*, *Top Gun*, and *Howard the Duck*. Right down the middle. Critical reviews were mixed, though Tom and Gleason moved the ticket-buying public to tears, making them feel less alone in their own familial relations.

As he grew famous, Tom pulled the curtains close, guarding his privacy with an iron fist. He drew the line at questions about his kids. In interviews with nosy journalists, he deftly changed the subject toward baseball. He romanticized the game—the real grass fields and the extra innings that allowed him to linger a while longer.

He wanted to be a movie star without being treated like one. He wanted to sit in the stands, not in a private box alongside the team's owner. Baseball was normal. Baseball was as far removed as he could get from the synthetic experience of LA and the celebrity-industrial complex that required him to confess his innermost thoughts to promote his movies. Screw that. Baseball was life, and at the ballpark, his life belonged to him.

"When I go to sleep, one of the ways I nod out is the little-boy fantasy of imagining I'm a ballplayer," he told a reporter during a break from filming *Punchline* in the Big Apple. "And I always play for Cleveland. Center field. That's where the grace is."

On the night of August 9, 1987, Penny lay awake, her mind racing. The next day, *Big* was to begin filming at Rye Playland in Westchester County. The exits had closed, the gate locked behind her. Too late to turn back now. The sleepless nights continued the next two months, with Penny lying in bed at the end of the day and thinking, "Oh, shit, I should have done it *that* way."

Penny's on-site producer, Bob Greenhut, had forged a reputation for running a lean, boutique operation. With a dry sense of humor and a twinkle in his eye, Greenhut supervised Woody Allen's productions from his headquarters on Fifty-Seventh Street; between *September* and *Another Woman*, he took on *Big*. Penny wanted to hire Matt Leonetti, her DP on *Jumpin' Jack Flash*, but Greenhut nixed that idea. He needed a guy based in New York, not Hollywood. Barry Sonnenfeld—funny, talented, and local—fit the bill.

A graduate of New York University Film School, Barry shot industrial films, documentary footage, and even porno movies prior to working for Joel and Ethan Coen on *Blood Simple*, *Raising Arizona*, and *Miller's Crossing*. He boasted a distinctive visual eye and treated the camera as his paintbrush. His elegant, studied aesthetic complemented the Coen brothers' precise approach to filmmaking: the siblings pre-planned everything from wardrobe to set design to the position of the camera. They framed shots with a wide lens, creating extra interest, each frame a painting that could be hung in the MoMA. Barry, who would eventually go on to direct, valued efficiency. He connected the dots ahead of time so that he knew exactly what he was going to shoot. He disliked wasting film, a precious and expensive commodity. At NYU, he learned to save hundreds of dollars on a shoestring production budget by making choices in advance. He quickly grew frustrated with Penny, who threw maps out the window, perpetuating chaos over order.

"Penny didn't like to make decisions and wanted as many options as possible," he wrote in his memoir, *Barry Sonnenfeld, Call Your Mother*, adding, "Penny wanted a million different angles and would shoot many, many takes of each."

At Rye Playland, her indecision caused headaches. The scene involved Josh and Susan going on a carnival date. The frost around Susan melts as she rediscovers her inner child. Though the park was only booked for a limited time, Penny had yet to decide whether Elizabeth should be a blonde or a redhead. "Barry didn't do a good job shooting the tests," the cinematographer heard Penny complain to Greenhut. The parties opted to double Elizabeth's shots.

"So, the first night of *Big* we filmed every angle of the scene with Elizabeth as a blonde and then a redhead," Barry recalled. "Because of the time required to switch out wigs and change her makeup for each hair color—for every camera angle—we decided it would be faster to film every shot of Elizabeth as a blonde, then go back and refilm every single setup except for Hanks' close-ups as a redhead. We had a million tape marks on the ground with notes for where the camera was, where each light was, so we could quickly redo every shot."

According to Penny, Barry lacked patience lighting Elizabeth, which involved taping white cards around the actress's body so that unflattering shadows would vanish. "He was coming from the Coen brothers, and I had to make it look nice," she told journalist Rachel Abramowitz in the book *Is That a Gun in Your Pocket?: Women's Experience of Power in Hollywood*. "To light her properly takes time and he didn't want to waste the time."

Penny preferred Elizabeth as a redhead, and back at the studio, the brass viewed the dailies with relief. An establishing shot of Rye in its neon-lit nostalgia combined technical beauty and lump-in-throat emotion: it had no words, just a feeling, the perfect blend of Penny and Barry. *This is really smart*, thought Fox executive Susan Cartsonis, blown away by what she saw. Together, the director and her DP had settled doubts about how Penny would handle the picture. The subsequent footage, Cartsonis remembers, was fantastic. Later, studio heads phoned Barry after viewing *Big* in its final form, assuming he shadow-directed it.

"I'm not a film expert—I can't even work a Betacam!" joked Penny, deploying humor in self-defense. She favored taped television over photographic film, a format she previously critiqued as having no depth. The crew's burdensome equipment offered a sitcom veteran less room to improvise. To mess up and try again, brainstorming better results. Not that Penny communicated her unspoken strategy—more, more, more!—on the set of *Big*. "I think my problem is that I have a massive insecurity complex combined with a very huge ego," she observed. "If I could just trust my instincts, which I'm told are good, I'd be all right. But I never say, 'Do it this way because I want it this way.' I just mumble and make people keep asking me for my opinion until they get it out of me."

David Moscow was trying not to freak out.

He had one job—to take out the garbage—and he kept screwing it up. Or so he thought. Penny, who cast the twelve-year-old rookie as Young Josh, made him repeat the scene again and again. Somewhere in the fiftieth take, he thought, *I'm gonna get fired*.

Tom, watching from the sidelines, pulled David aside.

"Look," he told his mini-me. "I did forty takes yesterday. Penny just likes to have everything in the edit bay so that she can go and make four movies. She wants to know that she has every possible thing to make the movie she wants to make."

In hindsight, Tom "probably saved my career," David says. "I could have gone home that day and been like, 'I'm never doing another movie ever again.'"

Tom's first take could be broad. Penny tried to keep him from overplaying the part. She needed Tom to become what he wasn't: innocent and shy, or "insh," as she called it. "I knew that took away one of his favorite weapons—his verbal assurance—but I had to convince him that he had to *be* 12, not play at being 12," she told the *LA Times* in an unfiltered interview over which Tom and Barry commiserated privately. "So I surrounded him with dramatic actors, like John Heard and Robert Loggia, hoping that their presence would keep him in check. And whenever we'd try a new scene, I'd let Tom get comfortable and try different approaches—then I'd tell him, 'Bring it down, bring it *down*.'"

Tom, quick on his feet, mined memories of his own preadolescence when he had been naive and clueless. Penny spoke to him in code, giving a nonverbal cue or saying a single word like "insh," and he'd understand her. She let him go off and experiment. They worked hard to improve the sequence where Josh hides in the bathroom and perceives his growth spurt for the first time. Penny beheld a full metamorphosis as Tom sprinted out of Josh's house and grabbed a bike on which he no longer fit, a sight gag at once hilarious and horrifying. (*That poor kid! What will he do now?*) Cut to Josh spending the night in a seedy hotel, sobbing alone on his bed. (*Well, drop an anvil in my stomach, why don't you.*) Fox wanted Penny to cut that heart-tugging vignette, thinking it slowed down the pace of the movie, but she left it in.

The first week of filming, Tom showed up at a Midtown screening room to watch the dailies from the day before. Often, an actor avoids viewing his work in progress—that's the domain of the director, her producers, her DP, her hair and makeup team—but curiosity got the better of Tom. *I'm the star of the movie, I have status, therefore I am entitled*, he thought.

He'd seen the screen tests and the wardrobe tests. Why not the daily rushes?

Penny beelined toward him in the theater.

"What are you doing here?" she said. "You can't be here! You can't be here. You don't get to watch dailies."

"Ah, I think I *do*," he answered.

"No, no, you don't," she said. "You don't get to see dailies because in this room we have to talk uncensored. We are going to say *terrible* things about *you*. And the lighting. And the props. And the dolly moves. And *you*." Things like: "I hate this take, let's not use it." "His hair looks stupid." "Why does he have those folds in his neck?" "Why is his voice so squeaky?"

Enforcing her no-actor ban, Penny explained, "We have to say all these things, and if you're here to hear them, it's really going to screw you up."

Her words took a while to sink in, but he came to realize that she was saving him the psychological torture. The dailies were like the dugout: a safe space to speak off the record. He wouldn't make the same mistake again.

Penny teased Tom, nicknaming him "Popo the Mute Boy," and sometimes he heard her groan through the sound system. He took her quirks in stride. While Penny treated comedy seriously, her humor leaned toward the adolescent: take the scene in which Josh, an awkward bystander at the office Christmas party, loiters at the food table, nibbling an ear of baby corn. Penny noticed the corn in a prop salad and plucked it out, as though inventing a bit on *Laverne & Shirley*. She gestured to Tom, who read her mind. "There was no, 'Oh, let's cut and discuss the eating of the corn.' There was just shorthand," recalls Elizabeth, adding, "She couldn't stand Method acting. She just wanted you to go out there, have a good time, and nail it. And you wanted to do that for her."

When Penny asked Barry to zoom in on Tom eating the corn, he flinched.

"You have to be in at least waist high," she said, wanting the gag—and her movie in general—shot straight on and up close.

"I'm not going in," he said.

"It's too wide," she said.

"I disagree," he said.

He backed down, trying it her way.

Early on, Penny complained about Barry to Charlie Wessler.

"Well, let's fire him," Wessler offered.

Penny declined, saying, "We'll make it work."

Greenhut blocked Barry from getting the ax. His overscheduled coproducer, Jim Brooks, busy directing *Broadcast News*, phoned him one day and said Barry must be replaced. Greenhut persuaded Brooks to keep Penny's nemesis, prioritizing the crew over her complaints.

"They don't like me, they're pickin' on me all the time," she told her brother, knowing that her gender made her a target—the lone girl in the locker room.

"You're right, and there's nothing to do about it," Garry said. "Let's just find out who they are and have them killed."

Wessler never saw a DP and a director squabble as Barry and Penny had. "I think he just didn't like her," he says. "I think he was one of those men who didn't like that she kind of came from nowhere and was directing a big movie with Tom Hanks."

Nah, it went deeper than that. The two repelled each other in part because they were too much alike. Combined, their quirks and anxieties and self-loathing produced toxic fumes. Barry wanted to do his job his way, not *hers*. Yes, she annoyed him, but then again, Barry was annoyed by most people.

The second week of filming, Penny—smoking a Marlboro and munching on a White Castle hamburger—let Barry know that she had wanted him gone.

"I tried to fi-a you this weekend, but they wouldn't let me," he recalled her saying, mimicking her accent. He replied, "If you don't want me, you should get someone else. I'll understand."

At one point, he defied the pecking order and yelled "CUT" when Penny left the camera going too long. Such insubordination could be grounds for punishment, but Barry had immunity on *Big*. In his defense: Penny never called cut, so perhaps he did her actors a favor by taking matters into his own hands.

"Sometimes, you'd still be rolling and you'd hear her turn to one of the writers or to the DP and [say], 'I don't know. Do you think she should walk over to the window?'" says Elizabeth. The actress would wonder: *Are we still rolling?*

Penny didn't care. She trudged forward, digging for gold. Later, Barry praised her "self-confidence to keep shooting when everyone is telling her not to."

Sometimes lightning struck on the twentieth take. While filming the scene in which Susan soothes Josh after his office bully picks a fight, Penny suggested that Elizabeth dab Tom's wounds with alcohol, then blow on his face. ("It's such an intimate thing to do," Elizabeth says.) The sweet nothing made all the difference.

Around lunchtime that day, Penny asked her associate producer, Tim Bourne, to drive her to the gynecologist. Her period was lasting longer than usual. At the doctor, she was told that she had miscarried. The news stunned Penny, who turned forty-four that autumn.

"I had no idea that I was pregnant," she wrote in her memoir. "And as for the father—I don't know. We were shooting. You don't have time for sex." She ignored the doctor's advice to rest. Instead, "I had Tim take me back to the set, where I finished directing the scene while lying on the floor."

The studio wanted Penny to make clear that Older Josh and Susan consummated their relationship. But Penny kept it relatively PG-rated, as when Josh kisses Susan and cops a feel. It's implied that Josh lost his virginity, an innuendo that has aged poorly over time.

"In defense of the movie, it's ambiguous," Elizabeth says. "It probably wouldn't be shot today, but I feel like it was important to their love story for them to kiss. For him to sort of have that moment."

Penny desired an interlude in Josh's tricked-out Soho bachelor pad that showed the couple at play. She spent hours filming Tom and Elizabeth jumping up and down on a trampoline, acting like crazy kids.

Another lightning strike.

"I know what we're gonna do," she said. "We're gonna push the trampoline right up against the window. I'm gonna go outside."

Her bright idea: take a camera into a building nearby and point it, *Rear Window*–style, at the chaste lovers bouncing in the dramatic wide windows.

Greenhut thought the extra coverage would cost too much, and according to Jim Brooks, Barry "ridiculed Penny like crazy." Eventually, at around 4 a.m., the DP grasped the movie inside Penny's mind, the reel she couldn't fully articulate. He and Penny circumvented a sleeping Greenhut and went about creating a frameable work of art. From a low angle, the camera gazed upward.

"You know what? That shot makes the whole scene," Elizabeth says. "I'm sorry, but it does."

Across the street, Penny used a walkie-talkie to direct Tom and Elizabeth, who were both tired. She kept saying, "You need to be closer to the window." They'd bounced so long, the two felt as though they were going to fly *out* of the windows.

Elizabeth secretly crushed on Tom. He kissed her every morning on the forehead. She thought he was adorable, though off the market, totally devoted to the actress Rita Wilson. Tom met Rita on *Volunteers* in 1984 when she played his love interest. A year after his divorce finalized, and months after *Big* wrapped, they married in LA with Penny among the witnesses.

Neither Tom nor Elizabeth had a clue how *Big* would turn out, or what it would be. They certainly didn't predict a hit. Says Elizabeth, "Tom and I used to joke that we were going straight to video."

In the spring of 1988, Tom and Rita showed up fifteen minutes late to the Zanuck Theater on the Fox backlot, where the studio hosted an advance screening of *Big*. He apologized to Penny and Brooks, explaining that they got stuck in traffic driving his kids to the airport. (The Hanks progeny lived primarily with their mother in Sacramento. They visited their father often and on schedule.) This was Tom's first time seeing the finished product. Both he and Rita wept. Elizabeth cried too.

"It was so sad," Rita said afterward.

"It's just a movie, hon," Tom told his bride-to-be. "You'll get over it." He honked his nose. "What a sweet movie, I didn't expect to cry."

Penny considered *Big*, in its initial rough cut, to be a failure—a jumbled, incoherent mess. "I went into a depression," she once recalled. "My editor said, 'Go home. You're depressing me.' . . . It got to where I'd take Prozac as soon as I'd yell 'wrap.' I'd start the Prozac so the first assemblage wouldn't put me in the toilet. I could edit on it, but I can't cast and shoot because your feelings are numbed. It takes the bottom end off so you don't cry."

While unveiling *Big* to her cast and crew, she seemed confident that she'd made a good thing.

"I know you guys didn't think I knew what I was doing," she said in her opening remarks. "Just watch the movie."

When the lights came up, "Everybody was like, *Wow*," Tim Bourne says. "*She knew what she was doing.*" It suddenly clicked: she had a thread in her head that only she could see.

Her naysayers silenced, Penny joined Tom and Rita in Brooks's production bungalow at Fox. "And here's Penny!" Tom intoned. "She's a *genius*, a *genius*!" She shot him a look as he threw his arm around her shoulder. "Wonderful film! Delightful!" he enthused. "Much better than the other kids-switching-bodies-with-adults movies! What if we called it *13 Again*? Think about it."

Penny, eager to escape the Hollywood fishbowl, traveled to Russia on vacation following *Big*'s premiere in June 1988. She met a "very cute guy" who was married and thus unavailable, and in Red Square, she encountered a child wearing a *Big* T-shirt, an odd display of Western movie merch in the Eastern bloc. (As it happened, the youth belonged to a Fox employee also visiting Moscow.)

*Big* remained in theaters for months. By September, it surpassed $100 million in ticket sales. Penny became the first woman director to reach that milestone. That made her happy. More importantly, she loved that it made audiences happy—if she had one mission, that was it.

Penny's focus shifted to her next endeavor. She hotly pursued the rights to tell a little-known story about a professional women's baseball league that existed during World War II. Modern sports history had erased the league and the athletes who played in it. That bothered Penny. Her credentials failed to impress the overlooked ballplayers, a high-spirited group with a low tolerance for bullshit. They saw right through these slick movie people. Penny had to earn their trust and prove that she wouldn't turn them into a laughingstock.

She had no idea what she was getting herself into.

## *Fourth Inning*

# THE HALL OF FAMERS

HELEN CANDAELE WAS DIFFERENT FROM THE OTHER MOTHERS. She raised five boys under one roof in Lompoc, California, about 150 miles up the coast from LA. She played catch with her sons in the backyard but seldom talked about hitting home runs as a scrappy young ballplayer. In a previous life, she'd been so good that one journalist dubbed her "the feminine Ted Williams."

Helen's sporty side hadn't really fazed her son, Kelly, until the time he witnessed her participate in a powderpuff game that some Little League dads planned for laughs. Every year they chuckled watching the Little League moms strike out, botch their throws, drop the ball every which way, and play like girls. And girls knew next to nothing about baseball, their wives especially.

Kelly beamed with pride as Helen put them to shame. Off the field, she was quiet and soft-spoken, but on the grass and the dirt, she breathed fire. Jaws dropped behind home plate. Little Leaguers and their parents swarmed Kelly, demanding answers.

"Where did your mom learn to play?" they'd ask.

"She played professional baseball in the 1940s," he'd say.

"You mean softball."

"No, I mean hardball, overhand, stealing, sliding, real baseball."

Years later, he would gaze at a black-and-white photo of Helen at bat and wonder, *Why didn't I get her swing?*

"It's the kind of swing you associate with Ted Williams or Will Clark; smooth and sweeping, arms extended, weight shifting from back foot to front at just the right moment, supple wrists that snap the head of the bat through the ball," he wrote in a 1992 column for the *LA Times*. "I imagine the line drives she sent screaming through the middle or deep into the alleys in left or right center."

A photographer snapped the image in 1945, Helen's first year with the Fort Wayne Daisies, then one of six teams that comprised the All-American Girls Professional Baseball League. That season, she batted .299 with a thirty-six-ounce Louisville Slugger, ranking first in the league for hits, extra-base hits, doubles, and homers. Her teammate and older sister, Margaret, averaged a moderate .196 but excelled at third base, flaunting a fast, fierce arm. Together they reached the playoffs but lost the pennant to the Rockford Peaches.

The league expanded to fourteen Midwestern cities during its heyday, which lasted from 1943 to 1954. In the beginning, the women played a combination of baseball and softball, but by the end, they conformed to baseball's longer geometry, overhand pitching, and smaller ball size. The league's founder, chewing-gum magnate Philip K. Wrigley, owned the Chicago Cubs and viewed female ballplayers as human buttresses, their duty to provide an entertaining wartime diversion. To keep spectators in the bleachers, and a storied American sport—more important: his business—afloat while baseball's major and minor league players joined the war effort overseas. Joe DiMaggio became a sergeant in the air force and Ted Williams a second lieutenant in the marines. The boys in the minors, barely out of their teens, were being shipped to the front lines. What if they didn't return? And on a larger scale, what would happen to baseball, to Wrigley Field, if the best and brightest came home in flag-draped coffins?

The Office of War Information issued a stark warning: Major League Baseball's 1943 season could be scrapped due to a lack of men. Wrigley hedged his bets. He dispatched scouts to pluck talent from organized women's softball leagues throughout North America. A scout for league trustee Branch Rickey—the Brooklyn Dodgers boss who recruited Jackie Robinson in 1947, breaking the sport's color barrier—discovered Helen and Marge Callaghan, twenty-one and twenty-two years old, just fifteen months apart in age, at an amateur softball tournament in Detroit. The sisters Callaghan, of Vancouver, had traveled across the border with their team, the Western Mutuals. They grew up working-class Irish Catholic, the fourth and fifth of six children born to Hazel and Albert Callaghan, and played softball, baseball, and lacrosse with the boys in the neighborhood. In high school, Helen ran track and joined Marge on the Young Liberals, a hometown sandlot softball team sponsored by a political party and later renamed the Mutuals under a new backer. The girls' mother, Hazel, died when Helen was eight and Marge was nine. Their father, Albert, a truck driver and machine operator, remarried and had three more kids. He worried about losing headstrong Helen to the All-American startup. (*What if she didn't return?*) The pay was good, though, sweetening the deal. "Heck," Helen said, "we could make $60 a week. That was a lot of money for me. I didn't see 60 pennies in a week at that time."

Mostly, though, the Vancouverite craved the experience. She was just as good as those other girls. She was a hard worker. She would hit the ground running.

Alongside a third sister, Helen and Marge previously rolled up their sleeves on the home front, joining other Rosie the Riveters in a Boeing production plant. Marge, sporting coveralls and a bandana, monitored women as they branded identification numbers onto bomber equipment. Somewhat reluctant, Marge followed Helen into pro ball and the promise of a pot of gold at the end of . . . who knew?

"Helen was more forward than I was," she said. "She was more of a flamboyant type of ballplayer. . . . I was more reserved. I wasn't going to go down and play in the league at first, but Dad wanted me to go because of Helen. He wanted me to keep an eye on her. That's what he told me anyway!"

But she *was* excited. Playing ball was a lot better than working inside all day.

The rookies entered the league in its second year, playing for the Minneapolis Millerettes, an expansion team that quickly folded due to low attendance. Small fish in a bigger pond—that is, a larger city with more than one game in town—the women lost fans to a rival men's double-A team. The rumors of baseball's demise proved untrue. The pastime outlasted world wars, unnecessary wars, the draft, the Cold War, and so on. As the Allies cornered Hitler, the major leagues held on to their ballparks, continuing games even with depleted ranks. In smaller markets, however, Wrigley's girlie experiment found success. The league shipped several erstwhile Millerettes, including the Callaghans, off to Fort Wayne, Indiana, the summer that World War II came to its blessed end.

Standing five feet, three inches tall, Marge threw and batted right-handed while the tiny dynamo Helen, two inches shorter and 105 pounds, was a lefty. Helen, a self-professed tomboy, hit the best out of the two and boasted more speed. "My reflexes were faster than hers, and I got started faster, but she always beat me," Marge told the women's baseball historian Jim Sargent. "She finished faster by about a step."

Both had dark brown hair and large, expressive eyes. Though Marge, with her high, movie-star cheekbones, arguably projected more of "The Look" that Wrigley and his public-relations deputy, Arthur Meyerhoff, tried to enforce at the league's outset. Many players—blue-collar and rough around the edges, of rural countryside and gritty city—did not fit the polished, traditionally feminine image they wished to sell to the masses. Some looked more like men than women. An underlying fear of lesbianism fueled the mission to transform Babe Ruths into babes who played like men, and sprinted the bases in spiked cleats, but fit the mold of what the businessmen believed a woman should look like. A sporty beauty queen, they wagered, could attract devotees to the All-Americans' ballfields in quaint towns dotting the Midwest.

As a prerequisite, the Wrigley operation ordered its test subjects to attend Helena Rubinstein's charm school during spring training. They learned how to walk, how to apply makeup, and how to behave at fancy luncheons. The men imposed strict rules: No shorts or slacks in public, despite the popularity of women's pants with Katharine Hepburn at the forefront of the trend. No drinking, no smoking, no short hair, no visible curlers sticking out of one's hair, no colorless lips. (Absurdly, The Look even required lipstick.) On game days, the women emerged from their host family homes, hotel rooms, and team buses parading the short-skirted, one-piece uniforms designed by the Cubs' art director, Otis Shepard, and Wrigley's wife, Helen. The mogul and Meyerhoff, obsessed with publicity, solicited journalists to cover the manufactured glamour in magazine articles with cutesy headlines: "Diamond Damsels." "The Belles of the Ball Game." "The Girls of Summer." "To me, it was just funny," Helen said of the focus on feminine appearance. It was the price they paid to play the game they loved. "The girls got big strawberries on their legs because we were sliding with skirts on," she added. "We all played injured—with pulled muscles and bruises."

Violations were cause for dismissal. When Josephine "JoJo" D'Angelo got a short haircut, her team manager expelled her from the South Bend Blue Sox. The firing caught her off guard. JoJo's hairdresser suggested a face-framing bob, and she went along with the advice, not thinking it would get her in trouble. Before the forbidden trim, she did everything right. She obeyed the dress code and avoided the league's "gay crowd," she later told sports historian Susan K. Cahn. JoJo, who came out as a lesbian in the early 1940s, returned to her native Chicago, rattled to her core.

JoJo's case no doubt frightened her lesbian teammates. For them, the league had been liberating, a rare chance to form intimate bonds outside of their stifling hometowns. As homophobia rose within the culture, with the federal government removing gay people from its halls and offices, the ballfield offered community and belonging, a safe space to be themselves. Even so, the league's founding fathers formed a cage around lesbians, pushing players deeper into the closet. To survive, and remain living their happiest lives, they operated by a rule of their own: *play it, don't say it.*

Straight women didn't have to live with such fears. Helen married amateur hockey player Bob Candaele during her tenure with the Daisies, taking center field in her pink-and-burgundy uniform. She kept her maiden name professionally. In 1947, she gave birth to her first child, Rick, and sat out the season. "My husband became the woman of the house, and my sister helped him take care of the baby," she told *LA Weekly* in 1991, referencing her elder sibling, Pearl. "We all lived together the summer after Rick was born so I could continue to play."

Earlier in her All-American days, Helen caused trouble from time to time. Once, she and other rule-breakers snuck out past curfew to socialize at an army base, "but the chaperones caught us there and gave us a slap on the wrist," she recalled. Wherever they were, "guys used to hang outside our hotel, hollering up to us, and we'd throw our bras down at them."

Practical jokes abounded. "We did a lot of short-sheeting," Marge confessed to the journalist Tom Hawthorn. "We'd hide brassieres or slip a rubber snake into a chaperone's bed. We were always sneaking out on dates. How could they keep track of 19 girls at once?"

They were kids having fun, blowing off well-deserved steam. The All-Americans soldiered through eight games a week over a four-month season, sometimes in unbearable, 110-degree heat. The Daisies would travel ten hours by bus, singing and playing cards, then go out and play a doubleheader. During the league's eleven-year existence, millions of fans, women included, bought tickets to watch the teams duke it out.

"I think men liked the way we wore short skirts, socks up to our knees, and the fact that we could still play ball," Helen recalled to the *LA Times* in 1991. "They may have initially come out to see pretty legs, but when they saw us play, they kept coming back because we played damn good baseball."

Helen tuned out the folks who insisted that women shouldn't play ball. She took the game as seriously as any of her male counterparts. In her words, she was "aggressive" and "intense," needing alone time to focus. No one, she said, "could talk to me before a game."

After proving her mettle, Helen, a star, was earning $125 per week. She treated herself and bought a fur coat. Later, she would wonder, *What did I need with a fur coat?*

The league gave its players three dollars a day for meals on the road. In Chicago, Helen, new to dining at restaurants, balked when her teammates put cash on the table. She began to pick up the server's tips, asking, "Why are you leaving all this money?"

Besides proper restaurant etiquette, the Canadian had not been exposed to Black people or racial segregation. It stunned her to see places where Black residents weren't allowed to walk in front of white people and dine in the same restaurants. She witnessed the racism while traveling down to Pascagoula, Mississippi, deep in the heart of the Jim Crow South, for spring training. Up north, the league excluded Black players, a freeze-out that shunned talents such as Mamie "Peanut" Johnson, the first woman pitcher to play in the Negro Leagues.

Marge, in comparison to Helen, was vivacious and talkative, supplementing her sister's intensity. She liked bunting and would tap the ball to the infield so that Helen could run the bases, stealing second or third.

When Helen fell ill in 1948, collapsing at home plate, Marge rushed to the rescue. Helen suffered an ectopic pregnancy, in which an embryo grows outside a woman's uterus, most often in a fallopian tube. The fertilized egg can't survive, and if the tube is ruptured, the woman needs emergency surgery to stop the bleeding. Doctors couldn't reach Bob Candaele for permission to put his wife under the knife, so Marge gave her blessing—and in doing so, perhaps kept Helen alive. Helen, whose batting average had plummeted to .191, went home to recover while Marge finished out the season. Scandal swirled around her: the Daisies' board members thought she was growing too close to the team's manager, Dick Bass, an attractive former minor leaguer. Engagement rumors reached the board, which axed Bass and replaced him with three female players in the interim while they found a permanent male replacement.

Marge denied canoodling with her coach. "She says they never dated and that his fault lay in an excessive interest in women, plural," Lois Browne reported in *Girls of Summer.* (Intriguing. Why, then, would the Daisies throw Marge under the bus? The truth remains locked in the dugout's inner sanctum.)

The next year the sisters were traded, Helen to the Kenosha Comets and Marge to the Blue Sox. In Wisconsin, Helen returned to form, batting .251 to place seventh in the league. She played under her married name this time. After the 1949 season, she retired and went home to Vancouver with Bob, who ran a taxi business there. Helen had no regrets.

Marge struggled. When South Bend traded her to the Peoria Redwings, she broke her ankle and her average slipped to .157. One day, she and the Redwings' manager, Johnny Rawlings, engaged in a shouting match. Rawlings stormed out of the dugout, fuming over Marge's decision not to throw to second base.

As she recalled, "I picked up a grounder, and I turned around to throw to second, and the runner was there, but not the second baseman. So I turned and threw the ball to first base, and I got the runner going down to first."

Rawlings lost it.

"What the hell do you think you're doing?" he yelled, igniting Marge's self-declared "Irish temper."

"What the hell do you think I was doing?" she screamed back.

The fans cheered her on, making Rawlings even madder. The ex-major leaguer had spent five years managing women's baseball, once leading the Grand Rapids Chicks to a championship victory. He didn't like the Callaghan girl giving him lip.

"I was always taught if I couldn't get two outs, get one," she explained.

"You should have thrown to second base."

"It would have gone out between center field and right field, and the run would have scored."

"You should have thrown it anyway."

Marge, incredulous, sat down on the bench. She had never, ever talked back to a manager before. But Rawlings was wrong. Why did he have to confront her out in the open like that? Why not pull her aside in the privacy of the dugout?

Within three weeks, she was traded to the Battle Creek Belles. She'd met her future husband, Merv Maxwell, and decided that 1951 would be her last year in the league. She went out with a bang, raising her average to .236. Though one might call Helen the Serena to Marge's Venus in terms of slugging, Marge enjoyed her moments of glory. During a Daisies versus Blue Sox matchup in 1947, she broke a record for hitting the longest ball in league history. That ball soared over a rival's head and into the bleachers.

After eight seasons and more than seven hundred games, Marge relocated to Canada and had two sons with Merv, whom she later divorced. She looked back fondly on her All-American adventures. She would never forget them.

Women regressed in society by the time the league shuttered. Soldiers streamed back into the post-war workforce, injured and traumatized and itching to lead normal lives, supporting their families as their fathers had done and their fathers' fathers before that. The snapshot of the perfect nuclear family—breadwinning dad, homemaker mom, 2.5 kids, and the white-picket fence—projected into the nation's living rooms. So did men's baseball, televised in color for the first time, affecting the All-Americans' bleacher turnout. Wrigley had long since sold off the league to Arthur Meyerhoff, who faced difficulties managing embittered team owners. As crowd numbers fizzled, the clubs slashed the budgets for publicity, scouting, and training. Marilyn Jenkins, a bat girl with the Grand Rapids Chicks, received her pay in single dollar bills: *Who did they think she was? A waitress?*

She saw the writing on the wall. Concurrently, Chet Grant, a former manager, blamed "indecorous femininity" for the league's demise, pointing a finger at players who rebuffed the Rubinstein rulebook enforcing ladylike presentation. "Avoid noisy, rough, and raucous talk and actions and be in all respects a truly All-American Girl," the manual cautioned. Could you blame them for blowing off those stupid regulations? The mode of play kept changing. Who had the time to act like a lady?

At the start, the league resembled softball, using a twelve-inch ball and underhanded pitching. But each season, the goalposts edged toward baseball, fulfilling Wrigley's original vision. The ball shrank in size, resulting in harder hits, while the distance widened between bases and the pitcher's mound. Three years in, overhand pitching was introduced in part to muzzle accusations that the All-Americans played softball, not baseball. To their discredit, ownership leaned too heavily upon veteran athletes who became local celebrities at the expense of cultivating the beginners needed to keep the league going.

Helen and Marge, both wives and mothers, reteamed on fastpitch squads around Vancouver. In 1956, Helen and her brood moved to California. She and Bob eventually divorced, with Helen marrying her second husband, Ronald St. Aubin, in 1973.

Helen's righteous competitive spirit resurfaced while parenting her athletic sons. "You can beat them, they're overrated," she'd say of an opponent. Or: "You can hit that pitcher." "You're as good as he is, no problem." "You just have to go out and do it." And: "Try bunting. When I was in a slump, I always bunted."

At times, her youngest, Casey, ran inside the house crying. His brothers would roughhouse, picking on him as they played street football. Helen nudged him back into combat. "It's not that she was insensitive," he told the *LA Times* in 1987. "She just wanted me to learn that you can't always cry."

Casey, small of stature but big on willpower, internalized her toughness, then traced her footsteps down an unusual path: that of a son who imitated his mother, wanting to be what she was, a professional baseball player. From 1986 to 1997 he was a utility player for the Montreal Expos and the Cleveland Indians as well as the Houston Astros. His nickname: "Mighty Mite."

"Casey didn't get my mom's swing either," his brother Kelly wrote in the *LA Times*. "He got something more important: her determination. He has got that something that makes a guy who is 5 feet 9 inches in boots, who doesn't hit the long ball or run like Tim Raines, ignore the legions of advice-givers who say, 'Give it up, kid,' or 'Start a real career,' or 'You'll never play in the big leagues.'"

While attending Casey's games, a nervous Helen would look away as he took his turn at bat. She'd ask a fellow spectator, "Did he do good? Did he get a hit?"

Casey appreciated her maternal anxiety.

"It meant she was out there playing with me," he said.

His teammates poked fun when they discovered that back in the day, Helen had the better batting average. But he didn't mind the teasing. She made him proud. Later, when the sports journalist Alyson Footer asked if he got his baseball skill from Helen, Casey answered, "No, I got it from my dad. If I got it from my mom, I'd be in the Hall of Fame."

Los Angeles, mid-1980s: Kelly Candaele, a labor union organizer working with air-traffic controllers, went out to lunch with a reporter from Channel 4, an NBC affiliate station.

The reporter, Mary Wallace, was interested in stories related to the controllers and air safety. Kelly was a source.

At the end of the lunch, she mentioned her love of sports and baseball. He told her about Helen, and she dropped her fork.

"What?" she said.

There were others out there, many living in California, in total obscurity, he explained.

Never mind the airports. "I want to do a story on this," she said.

Back at Channel 4, Wallace produced a three-part series on the All-American Girls Professional Baseball League, focusing on the players who hailed from the Golden State. After the segments aired, Kelly and his partner, Kim Wilson, brought the footage to LA's public television station, KCET.

"This league existed," Kelly recalls saying. "These women are amazing. They're having a reunion in Fort Wayne—it'd be a great documentary."

For Kelly and Kim, it had been a long time coming. The two met in 1984 through mutual connections: Kelly's twin brother, Kerry, dated Kim's friend. They began dating. Kim adored Kelly, a true intellectual who would spend three hours reading after dinner at night. "He didn't even own a television set," Kim recalls. He was handsome and principled, with dark brown hair and blue eyes. He resembled a young Wilson brother—Luke, not Owen. Kim had gone to film school and aspired to become a producer. At the time, she was working as an executive assistant to Eileen Berg, who produced ABC's movies of the week.

Kim loved Helen, along with her whole family. At first, she couldn't believe that this good-natured, simple woman—the kind who sat at the kitchen table with coffee and donuts, basking in her sons' love; who made an honest living on staff at a convalescent care center, cleaning the bathrooms, among all else—had once played pro baseball. The more she and Kelly talked about the league, the more fascinating it became. Like Mary Wallace, her antenna raised: *this was a good story*. An important story. And Helen had lived it. They wanted to immortalize her, to unearth a slice of overlooked Americana. For the next few years, the pair embarked on a labor of love that consumed Kim. They combed through vintage reels at the National Archives in Washington and collected players' memories.

"I was completely obsessed with it," she says. "It's all I could talk about. It's all I wanted to talk about. And it's all I could think about."

She tried to interest her work colleagues with little success. As she tells it, "We had no money. It came out of our blood, sweat, and tears. It became a joke at ABC." When people saw her coming, they'd "look down at the ground, or, like, walk across the street, or go take the elevator," she remembers, "'cause they knew if they made eye contact with me, I was gonna be like, 'Have I talked to you about *A League of Their Own*?'"

The enterprise gained momentum when KCET stamped its approval and dispatched Kelly and Kim to Indiana, where Helen, Marge, and more than a hundred All-Americans reunited in September 1986, traveling from near and far to remember the good old days. The producers' skeleton crew included Wallace, on hand to conduct interviews, and a USC film major to record it all.

"The highlight of the reunion was the old-timers game in which my mom took the field once again," Kelly remembered. "For five innings I watched her. The snap in the wrists was still there. She still got great jumps on balls hit to the outfield. She made a final lunge while crossing first base to beat out an infield hit. The fire was still there."

Helen and Marge sat side by side on a couch for a joint interview with the documentarians, and while Helen spoke softly about her lack of nostalgia for the distant past—her boys were her deeper priority—Marge appeared slightly uncomfortable, her body turned away from her sister. (It was also a weird angle that positioned Helen more fully in the frame.) At a larger gathering, the camera caught Helen kissing Kelly's cheek as he gushed that she was the league's best ballplayer. Helen had left the organization earlier than Marge and many of their peers, but her legacy in baseball endured with one dashing son in the Majors and another literally broadcasting his reverence for her.

In loose, candid moments, the camera captured the sisters laughing and marinating in the bonhomie among their graying league-mates. Friendships sparked anew. Memories from thirty-five years ago came roaring back.

"It's the second-dearest memory in my heart—and the first one would be my son, my daughter, my grandson," said Lavonne "Pepper" Paire Davis, a former Daisy, her voice on the edge of cracking. "AAGPBL ranks right up there. Awful close to it. Close enough to be warm."

Kelly and company had competition. Another crew, led by Northwestern University PhD Janis Taylor, was in town to gather material for a rival documentary on the league. Taylor heard about the reunion through Katie Horstman, an ex-Daisy with whom she played softball. The subject was too good to be true. Too good to resist.

A steady buzz had snowballed since the fall of 1980, when the All-Americans reconnected through a monthly newsletter. Two years later, league vets held a national meetup in Chicago. Newspapers, sniffing a hot human-interest angle, began printing articles and player profiles. The flurry of media coverage culminated in the dueling documentaries: while Taylor's film, *When Diamonds Were a Girl's Best Friend*, received warm reviews following its premiere at Northwestern in May 1987, Kelly and Kim's *A League of Their Own* found a bigger platform and audience. Their thirty-minute tribute brimmed with heart and sass as the elders, unleashed, swapped stories and waxed nostalgic. It aired locally on KCET that March and nationwide on PBS in September with the *Today* show inviting Kelly and Helen for an interview with Bryant Gumbel. It was Helen's first time in New York. Kelly took her to the Elizabeth Arden Red Door Salon to get her nails done, and to her first Broadway musical, *Les Misérables*, which blew her away. The attention never went to Helen's head. Says Kelly, "She was not saying, 'What show can I go on next?'"

*A League of Their Own* won awards on the festival circuit. Kelly and Kim hoped to turn the passion project into a feature film or a TV movie-of-the-week. Kim wanted to prove to Kelly that she could make it happen.

"Don't be ridiculous," he'd say. "You're not gonna be able to make a movie out of it."

*Yes, we are*, she would respond, manifesting, putting energy into the universe. "He thought it was silly, you know?" she says with a laugh. "Because he doesn't think that way."

The partners prepared a script treatment and planned to continue the Hollywood hustle, knock on some more doors, and hope for the best. One day, in a very promising plot twist, they heard from Charlie Wessler, who managed Penny Marshall, asking to see *A League of Their Own*. Wessler's friend, the Washington-based journalist Lissa August, had phoned him, suggesting that he give it a watch. Kelly and Kim sent Wessler a copy on VHS. "Oh my god, this is fantastic," Wessler said. "This would be great for Penny."

The next thing they knew, they were being summoned to her home in the Hills. Kelly never watched *Laverne & Shirley*, but Helen had. She loved the show. Of course, she knew who Penny Marshall was. Kelly wasn't familiar with her at all.

Penny opened the door wearing her bathrobe, her hair wrapped up in a turban, and her face covered in a green face mask.

"Oh, hello," she said.

They introduced themselves.

"Go sit out at the pool," Penny said, pointing toward the backyard. "I'll be right with you."

She left the door open and scurried away. Kelly looked at Kim, saying, "You know, she's kind of eccentric."

When Penny emerged on the terrace, serving iced tea, she listened with interest as they shared their vision for a fictional film adaptation. The subject affected her on multiple levels. She immediately grasped the league's importance to the unsung tomboys who sharpened their swings well before the government passed Title IX, the watershed 1972 civil rights law prohibiting sex discrimination in federally funded schools. Resources gradually flowed into women's sports, yet in American high schools and colleges, baseball would remain a male-dominated institution with athletics offering competitive softball for girls and women, decreeing it an equivalent game that was more acceptable for womankind. Female baseball players knew better than this; still, around twelve years old, they were outright discouraged from playing hardball. Often, it was softball or nothing, and they took what they could get, feeling strange in a different game while the boys got to stick with baseball. Penny, who wasn't even offered softball in the Bronx, pre–Title IX, knew what it was like to feel different, *other*. She could imagine what a gift it was for a girl to play baseball and get paid for it.

Kelly and Kim realized their baby was in good hands. "It was like Zen archery," Kelly said. "We hit the target without even aiming for it."

In October 1987, Penny invited them to her birthday party, which dripped celebrities from corner to corner. Bruce Willis and Demi Moore were there. And Robert De Niro. Even Massachusetts senator John Kerry. Over by the pool, Kelly spent most of the time talking baseball with Lowell Ganz, a rabid Yankee fan and nerd for the sport. Ganz, you'll recall, weathered the turbulent writers' room on *Laverne & Shirley*. Since then, he and his writing partner, Babaloo Mandel, had become Hollywood's most in-demand comedy team. They cowrote *Splash* and doubled the success with *Parenthood*, excelling at clever dialogue and warm humor while humanizing imperfect characters. Ganz and Mandel socialized less than the industry's status-chasing movers and shakers; respectively, they resembled the comedian John Oliver and the journalist Carl Bernstein. At Penny's parties, Mandel jokes that he and his wife would hide behind a bush and observe the wild scene from a safe distance.

*A League of Their Own*, the Penny Marshall version, was the first movie that she developed on her own. As *Big* proceeded to gross $151 million worldwide on an $18 million budget, Fox offered Penny a permanent office. Like Ganz and Mandel, she was hot, hot, hot.

"My first instinct was to find a woman to write it, but none of the female writers I approached wanted to do it," Penny recalled, saying of the

*Parenthood* scribes: "Even though they wrote guys better than girls, I had confidence in them."

In her office, "I sat on the couch between Ganz and Mandel and listened as the writers literally shouted potential storylines at [Penny] on the other side of the room," Kelly wrote later. "Nothing seemed to be exciting [Penny], so after about 20 minutes I suggested that perhaps there should be a 'big game' toward the end of the movie that resolves some central conflict. It was not for nothing that I've watched 20 years of Hollywood movies. There was dead silence. This was clearly Ganz and Mandel's meeting."

Kelly and Kim knew they were getting a story credit, but perhaps she'd invite them to join her on set, possibly as producers. The pair tinkered with a plot that heavily influenced the film. It involved a climactic championship game and the complicated love between two spirited sisters not unlike Helen and Marge, who shared a "natural sibling rivalry," he says. He drew dramatic inspiration from the Oscar-nominated 1977 drama *The Turning Point*, costarring Shirley MacLaine and Anne Bancroft as frenemy ballerinas whose lives take different paths: one chooses family, the other career. (When MacLaine gets pregnant, Bancroft encourages her to leave ballet to have the child. Bancroft's hidden agenda: to replace her rival as the lead in *Anna Karenina*.)

Kelly drafted a character outline describing a catcher named "Helen Callaghan," a petite, twenty-one-year-old wife and mother: "When she first comes into the league, she made sure her less talented sister was given a try-out and recruited as well," he wrote. "She's very close with her sister but they have a competitive relationship. . . . Conflicted by her love for her child and husband and guilt about not being with them enough, she is eventually pressured by [her] husband to quit the league and move to California."

Kelly gave Helen a younger sister, Snookie, nineteen years old and "single with no boyfriend in sight," he described. "She's an angry young girl, mad at the death of her parents when she was growing up, and jealous of her older sister's superior athletic ability. Her motivation is to be Helen's equal—on the ballfield and off. Subconsciously, she wants to be loved by her sister but feels inadequate. She is a pitcher with a hard fastball but not much in the way of off-speed stuff. She's got a great sense of humor, although cynical, and is very friendly with her brother-in-law. She conspired with him to get Helen to quit the game."

Kelly christened Helen's husband Bobby Wilson, a name twin with his real-life father. "He's jealous of his wife's success, but the deeper issue for him is control over a world that has always seemed beyond his reach," he sketched. "He goes off to [World War II] at the beginning of the season but comes home early because he's wounded in battle. He can't find employment in Indiana but lands a job in California and pressures Helen to quit baseball."

In his outline, he based several characters on real people, including Pepper Paire Davis and Faye Dancer, the Callaghans' brassy, funny fellow Daisies, and Hall of Famer Jimmie Foxx, who managed the team for one season in 1952. Foxx befriends Snookie, becoming a mentor.

Like all writers, Kelly put himself in his work: he mocked up a cerebral stand-in, Crystal Thompson, "the only ballplayer who voted for socialist Norman Thomas for President. . . . She helps some [teammates] to read and do math. She's the only self-conscious feminist and Emma Goldman is her hero. Crystal finds out there is talk of ending the league when the war ends and rallies the players in opposition to the plan."

Ultimately, Penny and her cohorts would take over, making *League* snappier, broader, and less overtly political. But the bones remained intact.

November 5, 1988. The day had finally arrived. The crowd gathered in the hundreds, collectively pinching itself with excitement. A dream that, for decades, they didn't even know they wanted was coming true. There they were, at the Baseball Hall of Fame in Cooperstown, New York, staring at the dream realized: a special exhibit recognizing their achievements within the same hallowed halls as tributes to Babe Ruth, Joe DiMaggio, and Ted Williams.

The "Women in Baseball" installation was compact, measuring just eight feet by eight feet atop a second-floor stairwell. When All-American alums lobbied the Hall of Fame, yearning to see justice served, museum curator Ted Spencer cleared space in their honor. He had a personal connection to the league: Mary Pratt, his physical education teacher when he was growing up in Massachusetts, had played in it.

Penny lurked in the background during the league's celebratory Cooperstown festivities, doing her best to remain incognito. A month before the museum unveiled the exhibit, she phoned its publicist asking for a ticket. She wanted to network with the women and, hopefully, receive their unified blessing for her movie. When she arrived, her presence was unmistakable. Observers suspected that something was up; Penny, the most famous woman in the room, "was asking a lot of questions and taking a lot of notes," noticed Dottie Collins, once the league's star pitcher and "Strikeout Queen." Spencer spotted Penny chain-smoking, "always sneaking into the merchandising guys' office to have a smoke, always with sunglasses on and a hat pulled down to hide her face. The only time she seemed really relaxed was when she was with the ladies at the private events and everything."

Penny bought a pass to attend a reunion banquet at the Sportsman Tavern, but when she arrived, Collins took it away from her. The tavern was at capacity, forcing players' friends and families to give up their tickets and go elsewhere. The sight of Penny offended Karen Kunkel, a former Grand Rapids Chick who cofounded the nonprofit AAGPBL Players Association. Kunkel "came up and asked me why Penny Marshall should be at the dinner and not Harvey, since Harvey was one of the ones we shoved downtown to eat at one of the restaurants there," Collins recalled, referencing her husband. She let Kunkel, a no-nonsense talker, handle the situation. Penny left the premises without argument. Later that night, the Sportsman set sang the old "Victory Song" cowritten by Pepper Paire Davis and Nalda "Bird" Phillips during their overlap in the league. (Bird joined only for the 1945 season, but Pepper stayed for ten years.) The melody was full of pep, and the lyrics were rallying. The opening line: "We are the members of the All-American League, we come from cities near and far." It goes on to acknowledge the players of Irish and Swedish descent, and even the Canadians! They were "all-Americans," Pepper and Bird wrote, celebrating the athletes of European heritage who comprised the league (and embodied male overlords' whitewashed view of what an "American" woman was supposed to look like).

Pepper simmered with anger on Penny's behalf. She recalled Penny explaining that the "All-American board had refused to talk to her. They even went so far as to tell other All-Americans not to talk to or associate with her and called her a bad influence."

Days beforehand, Penny reached out to Pepper, who lived in Southern California, with two requests: Could she use her song in the movie? And would Pepper care to join Penny for dinner at a Cooperstown steakhouse?

Yes, and *yes*. Pepper managed to corral her close friend, Faye Dancer, among a few other All-Americans, to dine with Penny, her producing partner Elliot Abbott, and her writers, Ganz and Mandel, as well as Helen St. Aubin and Marge Maxwell.

"We didn't say a word," Abbott, then an executive at Penny's newly minted Parkway Productions, tells me. "It was like being with an Air Force squadron who fought in World War II, telling war stories. They were filthy. They were wild. Absolutely wild. And at the end of the meal, you love them."

Afterward, Abbott asked Ganz and Mandel, "Do you have what you need?"

"Oh yeah," they said. "We've got it."

Over the weekend, the board of directors revealed why they snubbed Penny. "The reason they gave," Pepper reported, "was that they had signed options with another company and for some reason, god only knows why, they labeled Penny an outsider."

Two relative unknowns, Bill Pace and Ronnie Clemmer, ran the rival Longbow Productions. The producers had worked as journalists in Detroit before launching Longbow in California. After reading an article about the league in the *Boston Globe Magazine*, the newsmen, who knew a good hook when they saw one, hopped on a plane and pitched board members over beers. "We were not Hollywood types," Bill says. "We were not schmoozers." The board responded to their regular-guy-ness. According to Kunkel, slicker opportunists had courted them over the years. Fiercely protective of the league's legacy, she worried that in the wrong hands, the AAGPBL would be demeaned as a punch line, the butt of an infantile joke. Bill and Ronnie secured the board's trust and acquired the rights to the Players Association and the story of the league. In Bill's view, it would be "immoral" not to sign a contract with the women.

The news frustrated Penny. She didn't want other movies competing with hers. In a meeting, Abbott, a shrewd, pro-Penny supporter with light blue eyes and a receding hairline, complained to Kelly and Kim: "What did we option from you? We optioned air."

They took a moral stance, insisting that the league wasn't for sale. *It's public domain*, they felt. *That was like saying you want the rights to the Vietnam War. You can't have the rights to the Vietnam War.*

Stricken, Kim watched her hard-fought dream suddenly fade away. She and Kelly would have little to do with the movie from then on.

Penny phoned Bill and Ronnie and negotiated a deal that pleased them. Penny, as it happened, had topped their list of potential directors. They'd gotten what, and *who*, they wanted.

Like Penny, David Anspaugh, the Indiana-born filmmaker known for the bighearted basketball drama *Hoosiers*, viewed the PBS documentary and glimpsed a lot of potential. He'd once rooted for the Daisies in Fort Wayne—a young boy, sitting in the stands, watching women play baseball. Who else in Hollywood could say that? He targeted the league as his next movie, but then he heard Penny had something cooking and gave up. He'd lost what he wanted.

Brenda Feigen was another interested party. The prominent feminist and attorney worked alongside Ruth Bader Ginsburg at the ACLU in the 1970s, supporting the passage of Title IX. As the second-wave women's movement reached its apex, she wrote for Gloria Steinem's *Ms.* magazine, interviewing tennis phenom Billie Jean King for a cover story on women athletes.

Sometime in the late 1980s, Feigen collected a bunch of material on the AAGPBL, including, she said, videotapes given to her by "the girlfriend or friend of the son of one of the players." (The former Kim Wilson, now Kim Southerland, does not recall meeting Feigen back then.) Feigen had pivoted to a career as a talent agent and movie producer and shared a Midtown office suite with Penny. She didn't really know her, but she knew that she smoked constantly. Feigen hated cigarette smoke, so she avoided a closer connection. But one day, documents in hand, she thought, *What the hell? She's a producer. A director. A woman. Why don't I mention it to her?*

She entered Penny's smoky headquarters and pitched her on directing a women's baseball picture that Feigen hoped to produce. "At her urging," Feigen wrote in her memoir *Not One of the Boys*, "I told her all I knew about [the league]. We agreed that I would check out interest in Hollywood, so on my next trip there, I pitched the project to Amy Pascal," an executive at Columbia Pictures. "She watched the videos, got all excited, and told me that she thought they'd really want to make the movie. She just had to run it by Dawn Steel, who was then head of production at Columbia. I was delighted that all the decision-makers were women."

A few days later, Pascal called Feigen to inform her that the studio rejected the pitch. Feigen arranged more meetings, including one with 20th Century Fox, for which Penny was making *Big*. Those meetings went nowhere. Later, Feigen heard that Penny and Fox were reteaming on a movie about women ballplayers. She was stunned, seeing red. She hired an attorney at the LA-based firm of power lawyer Tom Girardi and filed a complaint. "I am happy to tell you this because it's so disgusting," she says. "I settled for $50,000." Feigen, who had a family to support, accepted the money with a heavy heart. She, too, had lost what she wanted.

GANZ AND MANDEL WERE TAKING THEIR TIME ON THE SCRIPT.

They disliked doing research, but for Penny, they studied up, poring through a seven-hundred-page master's thesis on the All-Americans written by a woman who had played in the league. Penny was a stickler. She didn't want anyone to look at the movie and go, *Oh, that's a pile of crap*. And so, the writers drowned themselves in the history: the bus trips, the chaperones, the hijinks, the home runs, the first tastes of freedom.

They put their own spin on the siblings at the center of the plot, renaming the eldest Dottie Hinson, an exceptional, self-possessed athlete who overshadows her kid sister, Kit Keller, a feisty pitcher with a colossal chip on her shoulder. While Dottie's husband, Bob, is off fighting the good fight, she maintains her parents' Oregon homestead and lords over Kit as her superior on Lukash Dairy's amateur all-girl softball team. When a wisecracking scout sees Dottie dominate a game, he attempts to interest her in trying out for a brand-new, too-good-to-be-true, women-only league funded by Walter Harvey, the Candy Bar King of Chicago.

At first, Dottie turns the scout down. She's *married*. What kind of war wife runs away and takes up *professional* baseball? But Kit, aching to ditch farm life, begs him to take *her* to the Windy City tryouts. The scout relents on one condition: Dottie must come along for the ride. Dottie, however, won't budge. She tries to talk some sense into Kit.

**DOTTIE:** Hey, you remember that girls semi-pro team from Portland that came out here a few months ago?
**KIT:** Oh yeah. They all looked like Uncle Ted.
**DOTTIE:** Remember, how everybody looked at those girls. You want everyone to look at us like that?

**A desperate Kit pleads:**

Dottie, I gotta get out of here. I mean . . . I'm nothing here.

The next day, Dottie gives in, and they hop aboard the moving train to Harvey Stadium.

"This will sound weird," Ganz tells me, "but Babaloo and I saw ourselves in the sisters." Once upon a time, the scribes took a leap of faith and left their native New York behind, journeying cross-country to LA where they hoped to make it big as comedy writers (not ballplayers). "It felt very real to us," he adds of Dottie and Kit's trek. "It felt kind of like something we had done."

Both were the Dotties of their families, the ones who did the best. When Ganz and Mandel arrived in Hollywood, they kindled a friendship outside The Comedy Store on Sunset Boulevard, "making fun of people who had jobs," Ganz recalls. "We were already completing each other's sentences before we started writing together."

They agreed that Dottie and Kit would play for the Rockford Peaches, the league's most winning team in real life, and they wrote the women a sneering, leering, self-loathing slob of a coach—Jimmy Dugan, whom they loosely modeled on famed slugger Jimmie Foxx, a heavy drinker who fell on hard times. Another apparent muse: Hack Wilson, a colorful, combative character who drank himself out of the Majors.

Ganz and Mandel shared a desk and sat at opposite ends, writing every single word in the same room. Together. Unlike other Hollywood writing teams, they didn't divide up the work and tackle scenes solo. Instead, Ganz bounced off Mandel, so to speak, improvising, getting into character, the air filling with words. As they spit-balled, they wrote on paper using ballpoint pens.

One day, they conceived a rant in which Jimmy rages at right fielder Evelyn Gardner for missing the cutoff person on a throw. The true-life inspiration: a woman director (whose identity remained secret) weeping during a story meeting in which the duo participated. They heard a producer mutter under his breath, "What is this crying? Did Howard Hawks ever cry at a meeting?"

On the page: Evelyn starts sobbing hysterically, and Jimmy explodes even further, unleashing an earful. Ganz and Mandel concocted dialogue on the fly and acted the scene out loud. They scratched out words and revised in tandem, writing:

> "Crying? There's crying? There's no crying in baseball. No crying. **(getting angry again)** When Rogers Hornsby was my manager he once called me a ~~steaming~~, talking pile of pig shit. And that was in front of my parents who had driven down ~~to~~ from Michigan for the game. Did I cry? No. There's no crying!"

The Peaches' sisterhood appalls Jimmy. He hates that he's managing a bunch of chicks. They offend his fragile, toxic masculinity. *Who do these gender-bending lightweights think they are?* (*What the hell had he become?*) As Jimmy rips Evelyn apart, it is possible that he would subject a male crybaby to the same needless verbal abuse. Do men cry in baseball? Oh yes, all the time. And despite his titanic show of anger, Jimmy Dugan is *definitely* weeping on the inside. His attack on the emotional Evelyn is a projection of the contempt he feels toward himself—for the shameful tears he's holding back, and that he can't show because to do so would make him less manly in society's eyes. As crafted by Ganz and Mandel, his tirade was hilarious because of its exaggerated specificity and the truths it contained about men and baseball. Jimmy was like those pissed-off, helicoptering Little League dads who live vicariously through their sons and are always yelling over the slightest mistake. (If you've ever been to a Little League game, then you know exactly what I'm talking about.) The right actor could take the bit and run with it.

That scene, and Jimmy's one-liner ("There's no crying in baseball!") would eventually be the most-quoted in sports movie history. Scratch that:

In *sports* history, period. For a couple of baseball junkies, that was like winning the World Series.

While Ganz and Mandel tinkered with their draft, every studio, every producer in town, rolled out the red carpet for Penny. They wanted her to recreate the magic of *Big*, but she wasn't interested in the high-concept elevator pitches they tossed her way. Stuff like: *A horse is your next-door neighbor. A dog turns into who-knows-what. Yeah, no thanks.* Then, quite mysteriously, a promising script appeared on her desk without a cover letter attached. It was titled *Awakenings*. Penny flipped through the pages, consumed by the story: a Bronx neurologist, experimenting in 1969, uses the drug L-Dopa to resurrect catatonic survivors of the global "sleepy sickness," or *encephalitis lethargica*, outbreak that spread between 1915 and 1926. When his star patient reverts to a passive state, the doctor discovers that the breakthrough is fleeting. That waking life is precious, and you only get one. (Carpe diem.)

Penny cried. She felt guilty for complaining as much as she did. She thought of her mother, and how Alzheimer's made her unresponsive and faraway, a shell of her former self. As Marjorie diminished, awake but not *there*-there, Penny had wondered if she could still understand her. *Awakenings*, adapted from Dr. Oliver Sacks's 1973 memoir, grabbed Penny by the shoulders and made her pay attention to it. She appreciated the way screenwriter Steven Zaillian handled chronically ill characters as though they were human beings, worthy of respect and humanity. The script inspired her to get out of bed and do the damn thing. No one expected her to direct a drama, and that was a blessing. Taking on a new genre released Penny from the intense pressure to repeat *Big*'s success with another hit comedy.

The scientific subject matter intimidated her, though.

During a bout of insecurity, Penny lamented to Carrie Fisher, "What do I know about any of this?"

"What do you know about anything?" Carrie said. "You'll read a book."

Sacks admired Penny's commitment to researching the medicine behind the miracle. "She's extremely bright," he recalled, "with huge energy and enthusiasm. I think that woman works harder than anyone I've ever seen."

She opened her Rolodex and called Robin Williams and Robert De Niro directly, bypassing agency gatekeepers. The actors signed up to play the doctor and the patient, with De Niro sinking his teeth into the latter role. Penny had finally caught her big fish, Bobby D.

When Barry Diller, the picky czar of Fox's film studio and companion TV network, passed on the project, he gave Penny permission to solicit Columbia Pictures, where Dawn Steel, the studio's first-ever woman president, waited with open arms. Penny pitched *Awakenings* to Steel (nickname: Steely Dawn) in a room filled with men. Tension permeated the atmosphere.

"Don't trust any of these guys," Steel told Penny in private. "They will fuck you over."

"Do you want to do it?" Penny asked.

"Yes," she said.

"Are you going to be here still while I make it?"

"I hope so."

Steel, relatively new in the job, had inherited her predecessor's spotty film slate and green-lighted clunkers of her own, like *Casualties of War*. Her head was on the line, and a changing of the guard was underfoot. In her previous tenure as a production executive at Paramount Pictures, Steel shepherded such hits as *Top Gun*, *Fatal Attraction*, and *Flashdance*. She pushed the button on *Awakenings*.

In January 1989, Diller dialed Penny at Santa Monica's Pritikin Longevity Center, a medically supervised health and wellness clinic. She was trying to "get healthy and clean and stop smoking," she explained. "It was cheaper than the Canyon Ranch in Arizona, where I had gone a few times with Carrie, who would sneak in food and defeat the point of being there."

Penny advised Diller to talk fast because speaking too long on the phone made her want to pull out a cigarette and smoke it right there and then. Old habits die hard. Diller cut to the chase: his friend, the mega-rich Revlon owner Ron Perelman, wanted Penny to direct a series of TV commercials for the cosmetics company. She took the money and filmed a who's who of boldfaced names, from Gregory Peck and Lauren Bacall to Lakers coach Pat Riley and NFL quarterback Joe Montana, as they answered the question, *What makes a woman unforgettable?*

On March 29, 1989, a sheepish Penny shrouded her eyes while the ads aired during the sixty-first Academy Awards. She watched the broadcast at the home of writer Jerry Belson and his wife, Joanne. *Big* had nabbed two nominations—Best Actor for Tom Hanks and Best Original Screenplay for Gary Ross and Anne Spielberg—with Penny snubbed in the directing category. The Academy recognized Barry Levinson for *Rain Man*, Martin Scorsese for *The Last Temptation of Christ*, Alan Parker for *Mississippi Burning*, and two comedy directors: Mike Nichols (*Working Girl*) and Charles Crichton (*A Fish Called Wanda*). Levinson won Best Director while *Rain Man* claimed Best Picture. As expected, Tom lost the golden statuette to Dustin Hoffman, but thanks to Josh Baskin (and Harrison Ford for saying no, and Penny, of course, for saying yes), he stood on top of the world, a future king among kings. He had a great life, a great wife, and one shining Oscar nod to his name. He navigated the horde of TV cameras, a well-wisher asking a benign but loaded question to which he already knew the answer: "It's gonna be hard to live this year down, isn't it?"

That evening, Geena Davis accepted the trophy for Best Supporting Actress, her voice shaking in a sign of nerves. Her winning role: an eccentric dog trainer in *The Accidental Tourist*, a romantic drama starring William Hurt as a travel writer whose life falls apart after the death of his son. Geena's character helps him pick up the pieces. The actress, bashful socially yet bold in her style and career choices, had carved a niche for herself channeling quirky sidekicks: a ghost in *Beetlejuice*, a Valley Girl in *Earth Girls Are Easy*, and in *The Fly*, a devoted girlfriend to a scientist who morphs into a human-sized insect. *The Accidental Tourist* pushed her into more serious territory. At the Shrine Auditorium, she exuded Golden-Age glamour in a Cinderella gown, dripping with diamonds. She kept her speech short and sweet, thanking her husband, Jeff Goldblum, a.k.a. The Fly, who smiled in the audience. Afterward, she sashayed into the wings while presenters Melanie Griffith and Don Johnson walked behind her. She looked like a queen, and they, her court.

Ganz and Mandel submitted their script for *A League of Their Own* before *Awakenings* began production in October 1989. Penny never told them out-and-out that she loved the result, but she did: she loved it. In fact, she loved it so much that she got angry when Diller's direct report, the newly anointed Fox studio chairman Joe Roth, wanted to make the movie right away, without Penny. Rather than wait until she finished *Awakenings*,

Roth hired director David Anspaugh, who jumped at an opportunity reclaimed. Penny stayed on as a producer.

"You had to make it so *good*," she complained to Ganz of the screenplay.

Perhaps it was for the best. Penny preferred to direct men over women. With men, "I get a better reaction," she told a journalist in 1991. "Because sometimes when I'm directing, since I'm not the most articulate person, I'll say [the line] or I'll do it; I'll act it. And I'll say, 'Don't do what I'm doing; just get my intent.' Guys don't think they're going to sound like a woman or look like a woman, or anything like that. But if you do it for a girl, they seem to feel like you're trying to act their part—which I'm not."

Actresses were tricky, especially with a woman in charge. Penny had to be extra careful not to step on toes, or trigger memories of critical mothers. She had to play mommy and daddy all at once, a delicate dance. Maybe Roth was doing her a favor and helping her avoid excruciating headaches. Maybe the girls needed a father figure in the dugout. In relinquishing her *League* to a guy, Penny sucked it up and took one for the team.

## *Fifth Inning*

# THE TRYOUTS

SCENE: DEDEAUX FIELD. FEBRUARY 1990. ACTRESSES AS FAR AS THE EYE could see.

Hundreds upon hundreds of hopefuls converged on the diamond at the University of Southern California to try out for the women's baseball movie, the talk of the town. Many were very famous. Others not so much. One actress, Glenne Headly, showed up in ballet slippers. Another, Sean Young, of *Blade Runner* and *Dune* fame, walked onto the grass in an antique Yankees uniform. Marla Maples, a former beauty queen and future wife of Donald Trump, wore full-glam makeup and a sash that read "Rockford Peaches." Of Maples, Penny would remark, "She wasn't bad."

That winter, actresses booked every LA-adjacent batting cage in anticipation. *A League of Their Own* felt once-in-a-lifetime, the Halley's Comet of jobs. A refreshing antidote to the stock female sidekicks on the call sheets: Supportive Wife. Nurturing Mom. Hot Girlfriend. Third Babe from the Right. While Anspaugh advised agents to send only their best, the very worst tried crashing the audition anyway. Penny, who was wrapping *Awakenings* in New York, refused to coddle the athletically challenged. She told Ganz, "You could bring me the greatest actress in the world—if the coaches say they're not trainable, they have no chance of being in this movie."

Team Penny divided prospective Peaches into three categories—Athletes, Trainable, and Hopeless—and brought Rod Dedeaux out of retirement to score the women on hitting, catching, and fielding. Dedeaux, who coached the Trojans to eleven national titles during his forty-five-season tenure, patrolled his namesake stadium alongside USC assistant baseball coach Bo Hughes, grading the women on a scale of one to five, worst to best. He loved the ladies. The septuagenarian had his eye on one woman, a stunner, who couldn't swing a bat to save her life. Frowning, he asked in his New Orleans accent, "Is she trainable?"

Among the auditioners: Courteney Cox, Cindy Crawford, Sarah Jessica Parker, Tatum O'Neal, Kelly Preston, and Brooke Shields, not to mention Elizabeth Perkins, who failed the test. Penny leveled with Elizabeth over the phone. "You throw like a girl," she said.

Daryl Hannah requested a private audition, as did Mariel Hemingway, Laura Dern, Jennifer Grey, and Guess jeans model Carré Otis. Demi Moore, Penny's ideal Dottie, was the first contender to practice with Dedeaux and Hughes. In July, Moore's supernatural romance, *Ghost*, would top the worldwide box office, besting Garry Marshall's *Pretty Woman*, a charmer starring Julia Roberts as a hooker with a heart of gold and a megawatt smile. "I had run into [Demi] prior to *Awakenings* and asked if she could play ball," Penny said. "It turned out she could. She was coordinated—and a strong actress."

Unbeknownst to Penny, Tracy Reiner entered the competition so that her cousin, Wendy Hallin, wouldn't have to try out alone. Wendy, the daughter of Penny's sister Ronny, who produced the TV sitcoms *The Hogan Family* and *Family Matters*, had played in an amateur softball league, giving her a leg up, but "was afraid to be around two thousand actresses," Tracy tells me. She reassured Wendy: "Don't worry, it's actresses."

Tracy, then twenty-five, a doe-eyed beauty with thick raven hair, didn't go in cold: she was naturally athletic and dabbled in recreational sports with her musician friends. And yet, she felt awkward, like "I wasn't supposed to be there," she recalls. She tried to remain inconspicuous and stay off to the side. As she threw a ball to Moore's agent, she heard Dedeaux say, "Damn, that girl's got an arm."

Afterward, Tracy and Wendy drove back to the Hollywood Hills. Tracy, recovering from an earlier surgery to remove her wisdom teeth, had "popped" the stitches in her mouth. "I took a whole bunch of aspirin," she says, "and then threw up black [blood]." *I'm getting in so much trouble when we go home*, she thought to herself. *I gotta tell Mom about my teeth.*

When they walked inside, Penny paid no mind to her stitch-less predicament. She was already in the know. She demanded answers to how the cousins had tested within the top twenty highest scorers at Dedeaux Field. The feat blew her away. She got excited and encouraged Tracy to keep auditioning as Anspaugh narrowed his cast roster. "You gotta do this," she said. In conversation with her director, Penny addressed the persistent elephant in the room: nepotism.

"I don't want you to think just 'cause she's my daughter. . . ."

"I know, Penny," Anspaugh said. "She earned it."

While household names vied to impress the coaches, with varying degrees of mediocrity, the real athletes came out swinging.

Rosie O'Donnell, a standup comedian and VH1 veejay, flew in from New York for the occasion. *If I don't get this part, I'll quit show business*, she thought. *If there's one thing I can do better than Meryl Streep, it's play baseball.*

(As it happened, *A League of Their Own* was said to have interested Meryl, who loved a physically demanding role, though perhaps hardball was a challenge even she could not master.)

Rosie, on the other hand, grew up like Penny, playing with the boys. In the early 1970s, Title IX had yet to take effect in Rosie's hometown of Commack, New York, so Little League remained off-limits to her. She'd sit on the margins at her brothers' games, waiting to dive for foul balls. When her agent alerted her to the *League* casting call, Rosie knew she held a competitive advantage.

"I went to LA to the batting cages and saw lots of actresses there trying to learn to hit and learn to be athletes, but you could tell the ones that naturally *were*," she says, adding, "There were just some players that knew how to play and had played their whole life. And it was very familiar to them."

She counted herself among them.

THE NIGHT BEFORE HER TRYOUT, FREDDIE SIMPSON, A TALL, BLONDE MODEL-actress with a pert, January Jones nose and a supporting role in a TV movie to her name, taught herself how to hit a fastball. Freddie's agent told her that Anspaugh wanted to see pretty girls who could play baseball *and* act. Well, then she fit the bill to a tee. Growing up in Kentucky, Freddie played baseball with her father, a multi-sport athlete and former college basketball player. She eventually switched to softball because that was what her school provided, and she also played volleyball and basketball. "Even though I got a scholarship for volleyball to college, I would say baseball was my best sport," she says.

One day, a non-sporty fork in the road materialized, and right there and then, she decided to take the path unknown. Scouts from John Casablancas discovered her at the mall, and pleasing her sister, Freddie signed a contract with the modeling agency. Like a scene out of a movie, she jetted off to Paris, passport in hand. "I don't think I ever even wore a dress," she says. "I mean, I was really a tomboy."

After her time abroad, she decided to give Hollywood a try. She moved to LA and began working with Roy London, the famed acting coach whose clients included Brad Pitt, Sharon Stone, and Geena Davis—none of whom could outplay Freddie on the diamond.

"It was one of those magical days where you leap into the air and catch the ball," she recalls of passing the Dedeaux test. "I hit amazing."

Neezer Tarleton, a non-famous stuntwoman, was another fierce competitor.

"I killed it," she recalls of her triumphant tryout, sharing a memory she'll never forget: walking past Helen Hunt, a gifted actress who had starred in *Project X* and *Peggy Sue Got Married*. Neezer recognized Hunt from the CBS movie *Quarterback Princess*, in which she portrayed a teenager fighting for a spot on her high school football team. She prevails in her efforts, winning both the state championship and the title of Homecoming Princess.

Neezer had made Hunt feel insecure.

"Don't worry about her," she overheard a man telling Hunt. "She's a nobody."

On February 2, a fellow nobody, twenty-nine-year-old Megan Cavanagh, had the most inspired baseball audition of her life. She wasn't a great fielder, but she compensated in batting skill. She, like Tracy, crashed the tryouts, in Megan's case tagging along with a friend, not a cousin. She had read the script and wanted to be Marla, a plain Jane with a killer swing, the third most important Peach in the movie. Every day she repeated positive affirmations, including, "I am the greatest baseball player" and "This or something better now manifests for me in totally satisfying and harmonious ways for the highest good of all concerned."

Her hazel eyes, large and round, flashed with mischief. She was a sketch comedian with the Second City touring company and did not have an agent. Two years beforehand, she made the move from Chicago to the City of Angels, paying the bills as an office manager at Rodale Press as well as a hostess at Ed Debevic's. Staff of the '50s-style diner got into snarky character, frequently teasing patrons, but Megan channeled a sweet alter ego named Gladys Kolacki. *You can call me Glad*, she told customers.

Baseball was a religion in Megan's childhood home outside Chicago; her father, Jim, loved the Cubs, passing down his devotion like an heirloom. Her athletic journey began earlier in her twenties, when she covered second base for her theater group's coed softball team using no gloves.

Rod Dedeaux made her very nervous, but when he pitched her the ball one-on-one, she showed him what she was made of. "I got into my game face," she says.

Lori Petty looked at Marla Maples, all dolled up, and thought to herself, *You know we're playing baseball, right?* She understood Maples's thirst, though. "When you see a movie in which all the leads are women and all the men are supporting parts, of course you want to be in it," she explained, "because you get to be a whole person, not just a type."

At the time, Lori starred opposite Richard Grieco in the one-season Fox crime procedural *Booker*, playing his tough, quirky sidekick. The short-haired, twenty-six-year-old gamine had also filmed the Robin Williams black comedy *Cadillac Man* (her role: his mistress), Lori's biggest break following appearances in the failed sitcom *The Thorns* and other series in which she surfaced as a "Female Punk" or "Hooker," among other unsavory background characters.

Intensity radiated from her core. She had a rough upbringing. She was born in Chattanooga, Tennessee, the eldest of three sisters, and raised in Iowa. Her father was a Pentecostal minister who always wanted a son. "So ever since I picked up a ball, I played baseball," she said, comparing herself to Tatum O'Neal, the lone girl ballplayer in *The Bad News Bears*. "Like, I was the pitcher on the all-boy baseball team. I hit it out [of] the park and all that stuff. But once you hit puberty, something terrible happens and they make you play with a big mushball."

Lori's mother left an abusive marriage and became hooked on drugs and booze, turning to prostitution to support her family. In her teens, Lori was sexually abused by someone she knew. The aspiring actress moved to New York at age eighteen and waited tables between auditions, crashing on friends' couches and at the YMCA, sometimes in Central Park. Her exquisite, wide-eyed beauty was her ticket out of poverty.

Lori had made it this far, against all odds.

She wasn't some pageant-queen dilettante; she was there to win.

"I was like, 'Nobody's better than me at baseball,'" she says. "I mean, it's not being an asshole—it was just being real."

DAVID ANSPAUGH MADE LITTLE ATTEMPT TO HIDE HIS HEART.

He wasn't hip or cool or a comedy whiz. He possessed the faith of a point guard hurling a half-court shot with seconds on the clock. *Hoosiers*, his directorial debut in 1986, made grown men cry. It boasted the right ingredients for a sacred sports classic: Gene Hackman as the flawed but inspiring coach of a high school basketball team in 1950s rural Indiana; a heartbreaking Dennis Hopper as a player's alcoholic father, whom Hackman recruits to be his assistant; riveting, action-packed shots on the court, featuring local kids rather than actors. *Hoosiers* had a sentimental '80s score, redolent of the era, but it cut through the sap with elegant cinematography that conjured Andrew Wyeth, the camera lingering on the austere heartland landscape with its open roads and sleepy intersections. Within this heightened sense of place, a melancholy rippled like a quiet wooded creek. These folks, in this part of the country, had been forgotten. When Hackman comes to town, the outsider faces hostility for his gruff, relentless coaching style. (It is discovered that his former employer, a university, fired him for assaulting a player.) But day by day, he earns the respect of his young, disaffected underdogs, teaching them to hustle and score with newfound confidence. In the satisfying finale, they take the state championship and Hackman is redeemed. A question hovers: Does the coach swoop in and rescue the boys, or do they rescue him? The last shot is a black-and-white photo of Hackman, the improbable champions, and their trophy. "I love you guys," he gushes in a voice-over.

Anspaugh, a son of Hoosier country, graduated from Indiana University and traveled westward, first to Aspen, Colorado, where he worked as a substitute teacher and ski instructor, then to LA, where he enrolled in USC's film school. He made a mark in television dramas, producing *Hill Street Blues* and directing *St. Elsewhere.* While he traded the Midwest for the sun-soaked Pacific coastline, he kept returning to his roots. *A League of Their Own*, like *Hoosiers*, offered Anspaugh a storybook script based loosely on actual events, a bevy of underdogs, and another chance to go home. In the spring of 1990, the filmmaker, whose warm smile and crinkly George Clooney eyes made him look like a breezy Midwestern minivan dad, scouted Indiana locations, on the hunt for stadiums and train stations, and took Elliot Abbott to a high school basketball game. Their crew narrowed down the search to Evansville, a city that hugged the Ohio River. Its vintage ballpark, Bosse Field, which opened in 1915, was the perfect mothership to film baseball scenes. (The Peaches' true home, Beyer Stadium in Rockford, Illinois, had been neglected over time and paled in comparison to Bosse. Preservationists have since restored its original field.)

Fox, budget-conscious, kept Anspaugh on a tight leash. *A League of Their Own*, if left unsupervised, could spell the kiss of death for a studio. Indeed, writing big checks for a period baseball picture—*this* one in particular—went against conventional wisdom. Baseball wasn't popular in Europe, a major global market for Fox, already limiting the movie's box-office receipts. The green-light process terrified the suits in the corner office. If the movie bombed, Diller could fire whoever pressed the button.

Still, Sara Colleton, an executive who oversaw *Big*, had managed to persuade Joe Roth's skeptical predecessor, Leonard Goldberg, to let her option *A League of Their Own*. Goldberg gave the thumbs-up well before *Field of Dreams* hit theaters in April 1989. That fantasy drama, directed by Phil Alden Robinson, headlined Kevin Costner as Iowa farmer Ray Kinsella, who hears a voice in his cornfield that whispers, "If you build it, he will come." Ray gets a vision of a baseball diamond and Shoeless Joe Jackson, his dead father's favorite vintage major leaguer. He mows over the corn and builds a ballfield, summoning Jackson's ghost, then Ty Cobb, among other mythical figures, all the while bleeding money from lost crops. When the farm is on the brink of foreclosure, the divine intervenes: Ray's dad appears, and the two—long estranged—have an overdue catch at dusk. Twinkling in the distance, cars beeline toward the farmhouse.

"They'll come to Iowa for reasons they can't even fathom," James Earl Jones, playing a visionary writer, tells Ray in an earlier monologue. "They'll turn up your driveway, not knowing for sure why they're doing it. They'll arrive at your door as innocent as children, longing for the past. 'Of course, we won't mind if you look around,' you'll say. 'It's only twenty dollars per person.' They'll pass over the money without even thinking about it. For it is money they have and peace they lack."

Jones stands in front of the field, urging Costner not to destroy it.

"America has rolled by like an army of steamrollers," he continues. "It has been erased like a blackboard, rebuilt and erased again. But baseball has marked the time. This field, this game: it's a part of our past, Ray. It reminds us of all that once was good and it could be again."

*Field of Dreams* opened to warm reviews, scoring $84 million internationally and an Oscar nomination for Best Picture. Raved Roger Ebert: "This is the kind of movie Frank Capra might have directed, and James Stewart might have starred in—a movie about dreams."

General rule: a good baseball movie is *never* about baseball. The acclaimed *Bull Durham*, also starring Costner, is about second chances. *The Natural*, based on the Bernard Malamud novel and starring Robert Redford, is a morality tale. *Field of Dreams* is wish fulfillment: the dream of reconnecting with an emotionally distant father through the common language of baseball.

While Colleton developed *Field of Dreams* at Fox, the studio's president of production, Scott Rudin, withdrew his support and put her project into turnaround, clearing the path for Universal Pictures to pick it up in 1987. Colleton's colleagues thought the movie wasn't commercial enough. After Rudin slammed the brakes, one of her supporters saw Colleton sobbing in her office. A tall, glamorous brunette, the woman had vision and taste. Colleton was like a character, a *dame*, out of the 1940s, with an affectation. She advised a female mentee to wear lipstick to meetings even if she was tired. Other advice: *just do your job like you're not afraid to be fired.*

She understood how a purportedly niche baseball movie could have broad appeal, even crossing gender lines, and it seemed that the industry was catching up to her. Roth, her new boss, had produced the Paramount comedy *Major League*, in which Charlie Sheen pitched for the Cleveland Indians and Margaret Whitton, fulfilling the she-devil trope, played the team's sabotaging owner. *Bull Durham* and *Major League* each made around $50 million in 1988 and 1989, respectively—not too shabby for a pair of so-called uncommercial genre flicks.

The first major actors cast in *A League of Their Own* were men who had both lived in Penny's home: Jon Lovitz, who naturally spoke with an old-timey voice, was to provide comic relief as scout Ernie Capadino while Jim Belushi filled Jimmy Dugan's grouchy shoes. At thirty-five years old, Jim resembled an athlete past his prime, complete with a thinning hairline and a whiff of Dad Bod. He'd stepped out from underneath brother John's shadow and carved a nice nook in Hollywood headlining lighthearted movies such as *K-9*, *Mr. Destiny*, and *Taking Care of Business*. He was boyishly handsome in a way that appealed to women but did not threaten their husbands. Whereas Ordinary Joe might think twice about inviting Robert Redford to a backyard barbecue, he'd happily summon Jim to crack open a couple Miller Lites and shoot the breeze. Jim had the goods to portray a believable crank, the kind you loved anyway. "I mean, he *was* that character," Anspaugh says. "It was so exciting to have him onboard."

Assembling the Rockford Peaches proved far trickier. Anspaugh cast a wide net, holding baseball auditions in New York, where Gina Gershon and Joan Jett were seen, as well as Evansville, tapping into raw regional talent in *Hoosiers* tradition. In LA, he reviewed the ingenues who showed the most promise at USC. Téa Leoni, a striking blonde with seductive intelligence, made an immediate impression upon Anspaugh.

"Well, you work at a garage or something," he said, observing her utilitarian ensemble.

"No, I'm a welder," she answered.

Anspaugh added Leoni to his team along with Rosie O'Donnell, Megan Cavanagh, and Freddie Simpson, whom he praised by saying, "You are a beautiful, talented actress trapped in a baseball player's body."

He chose Tracy, who could cry on cue, to play Betty Horn, nicknamed "Betty Spaghetti," the Peach who breaks down in the locker room after receiving terrible news about her soldier-husband.

Fox pushed the production's start date from April to July, giving Anspaugh extra time to juggle the moving parts: The location wrangling. The costume design. The screen tests, which he thought were "so good." There were delays in casting Dottie and Kit. With Demi Moore temporarily out of the picture, readying to film the Chevy Chase comedy *Nothing but Trouble*, Daryl Hannah and Laura Dern topped the list of leading ladies. So did Helen Hunt, Mariel Hemingway (a marvelous presence as a bisexual track star in the 1982 drama *Personal Best*), and Sean Young, who would pull an infamous stunt in 1991 and show up to Warner Brothers dressed as Catwoman in a desperate but amusing grab for *Batman Returns*. As Anspaugh learned, she was "pretty good" in her private baseball session. "And so," he says, "we decided to read her." He flew out to London, where she had gone to film the erotic thriller *A Kiss Before Dying* with Matt Dillon. He liked Young even though her kookiness became a red flag for others in Hollywood.

While Anspaugh ran what he considered a smooth operation, Ganz and Mandel felt the train going off the rails. They missed Penny's guiding spirit. They looked at screen-test footage and couldn't figure out why it wasn't working. Insecurity edged into their brains: Was it *him*, or *them: the writers*? One day, Penny joined Ganz and Mandel in a screening room. They cringed watching scenes that involved Hunt, who wasn't funny at all, and looked at one another, wondering, *Did we stop being funny?*

"I don't understand what's going on here," said Penny, concerned.

"We can't go ahead with this," they told her.

It was him. Anspaugh had to go.

"His movie was great," says Mandel, referencing *Hoosiers*, "but he and humor are not meant to be."

Penny and Abbott, her producing partner, took the writers' side.

*"Look, we're begging you,"* Abbott recalls Ganz and Mandel pleading. *"Don't let him direct the movie. Convince the studio to not make it right now. Wait 'til you guys are done with* Awakenings, *and make sure that you and Penny are involved in it. They didn't want another director. Normally, you wouldn't afford writers that much say, but like I said: they're dear friends and they wrote a great script. And we said, 'OK.'"*

On June 2, 1990, the showbiz trade magazine *Screen International* reported that Anspaugh was on track to begin shooting the next month, with Hannah and Dern as Dottie and Kit. Then, eleven days later, *Variety* reported a head-spinning update: the actresses were out, and Moore was in—well, at least for a hot second. She withdrew within days of rehearsals and a baseball clinic, throwing Fox a curveball.

The studio was having trouble attracting talent. "Actors don't want to embarrass themselves," says Bill Pace, the liaison between the fraught production and the AAGPBL board. Sure, a film editor can make the strategic cuts necessary to turn a fake into a professional, but "you still gotta look and do the part," he adds.

Anspaugh was in Indiana when he got word that he'd been fired. The message dropped like a Baby Grand atop his head, sounding notes of discord and disbelief. He was blindsided. *You gotta be kidding me*, he thought. *Why?* No one came forth and told him the reasons. He heard nothing from Penny. In an earlier meeting with her, he had expressed discomfort in filming the more cartoonish aspects of the shooting script that Penny ultimately approved. *I can't have Rosie O'Donnell diving into the crowd after a foul ball and coming up with a hot dog in her mouth*, he thought. *That's not gonna happen in my movie.*

"You work with Lowell and Babaloo," she encouraged. "I like where you're going with this." In hindsight, she recalled of Anspaugh: "I didn't think he'd get the comedy, but to me the heart was more important."

Anspaugh's efforts went nowhere. The writers weren't getting the vibe he wanted, and scene by scene, page by page, he could feel it. He was taking their jokes out.

He exited *A League of Their Own* without clear answers. One year later, Joe Roth heaped unnecessary salt on the wound, telling the *LA Times* that he'd jumped the gun and made a "fatal error" by hiring Anspaugh. "I loved the material, but I soon lost confidence in [the director]," he told the paper. Plus, he lamented, the studio wasn't drawing "the caliber of actress I had hoped."

As *League* fell apart, the budget—around $18 million—climbed higher. Roth called a meeting in his office. He allowed Penny to smoke despite Fox's restrictions on cigarettes indoors.

While she took a drag on her Marlboro, exhaling the fumes, Roth vouched for Sean Young.

Penny stood up.

"Are you out of your mind?" she argued. "This is an ensemble piece. Sean Young is difficult."

She spoke her mind to studio guys. They weren't used to a woman speaking like that, putting her foot down and saying, "You're crazy!" Saying *no.* But Penny treated everyone the same way, and even directed her blunt feedback at power brokers like Diller and David Geffen.

Roth put *A League of Their Own* into turnaround, which meant that he had decided not to go forward with the movie. Parkway Productions was free to shop it elsewhere. If another studio was willing to pick up the tab, Fox would sell off the rights and recoup its investment. Roth liked emotional sports movies, so he should have kept the Peaches on his roster. Yet the risks mounted: skittish men dreaded the uncertainty of casting nobodies. They also feared Diller. What if the movie flopped? What would happen to their heads? Their kids' college funds? Their tables at Spago? Even more ominous, Penny made decisions in an old-school Hollywood fashion and paid little mind to budgets and time management. Roth's head of production, Roger Birnbaum, side-eyed a spendy filmmaker as spoiled. A former Fox executive recalls that Birnbaum and Penny had "frenemy energy," and he wasn't going to fight for *A League of Their Own*, which belonged to Penny loyalist Sara Colleton. The movie was a genre-breaker; nothing like it had been done before. "Original is hard to get made," the executive says. "It's terrifying for decision-makers because there's no model to compare it to."

After Penny completed *Awakenings*, Jon Peters and Peter Guber, who ran Sony Pictures Entertainment, offered her a production deal.

"If you come with us, we'll even let you do that girls movie," she recalled them saying. The cochairmen assumed the throne at Sony's movie division in late 1989, when the Japanese electronics conglomerate acquired Columbia Pictures from the Coca-Cola Company for a whopping $3.4 billion. Dawn Steel was replaced by Frank Price, whose conservative demeanor masked a curious, creative spirit. Penny liked Price, and Price liked Penny. While *Awakenings* went over-schedule and over-budget, hovering near $29 million, the studio never yelled at Penny—not directly, at least. Michael Nathanson, the production chief, did protest when she requested a wrap party at the end of filming.

"You can't make Penny pay out of her own pocket," said her agent, Todd Smith, twisting Nathanson's arm. Columbia underwrote the wrap party.

Peters and Guber, eager to get projects off the ground and moving, hadn't shown much enthusiasm for *A League of Their Own*. Collectively, the hitmakers had produced *Rain Man* and Tim Burton's *Batman* blockbuster. Now what? *Bat Girls*? They'd call down to Nathanson, asking, "Are you sure you wanna make a period baseball movie? Is Frank really considering this?"

"Nobody wants to do a baseball movie," Penny recalled. "No one wants to do an all-women movie. No one wants to do a period women's baseball movie, but they wanted me to sign with Sony."

Diller did not match Sony's offer. He urged Penny to accept and switch studios. At Columbia, Price, Nathanson, and Amy Pascal, who survived the Sony acquisition, caught *A League of Their Own* in their mitts.

"I remember telling Frank that it was a nightmare making [*Awakenings*]," Nathanson says. "Even though it was a nightmare, at the end of the day it came out great. I used to joke sometimes that if Penny were on the Titanic, and you're handing out orange life preservers, and you got to Penny, she'd wonder, 'Do you have a green one?'"

Columbia paid a staggering $7 million to release *League* from Fox. The industry stood back in awe. That Penny Marshall, she might be worth the expense.

"DON'T YOU WISH WE HAD A COMEDY?" PENNY ASKED ABBOTT AS THEY PULLED up to the Sony lot.

Folks were lined up outside the theater for the very first screening of *Awakenings*. They held beers and umbrella drinks because, hey, *this is a Robin Williams movie. It's going to be a gas.*

Penny ventured inside with Abbott and braced for a letdown. As the moving images projected onscreen, the drama unspooled at a brisk pace, each scene teeming with quiet emotion: Williams, toned down and understated, brings his sleepy-sickness test subjects back to life. They catch the tennis balls he pitches at them and respond to the rock music that the nurses play. They thrive on Williams's radical drug treatment and let loose on the ballroom dance floor during a rare trip outside the hospital. In a devastating act of immersion, De Niro struggles to stay lucid as the drugs stop working. The last ten minutes are a doozy: a kind, beautiful woman pulls De Niro close for a dance, his first and last. The camera closes in to capture the layered expressions on his face: the joy, the sorrow, the coming loss. The moment is deeply felt, but never corny. It's showing without telling. It's Penny Marshall at her best.

Afterward, Abbott heard people crying and blowing their noses. He told the theater manager to wait some twenty seconds until turning on the lights. *Give the audience time to gather itself,* he said. When the darkness lifted, "they were just destroyed," he recalls. "They stood up and applauded."

*Awakenings*, which Penny trimmed from six long hours down to two, premiered in twelve theaters on December 22, 1990, grossing $417,076 its opening weekend. Three weeks later, it opened wide and went on to collect $52 million in total ticket sales. The reviews ran the gamut. *New York Times* critic Janet Maslin hated the movie, calling it sentimental, oversimplified, and overly jokey, while the *Washington Post*'s Rita Kempley praised De Niro and Williams as well as Penny, writing that she "masterfully plays our strings without becoming either melodramatic or maudlin."

Awards momentum swirled around her. At the height of Oscar campaign season, when the studios release their most prestigious fare in a heated battle for nominations, Penny promoted *Awakenings* amid another stint at the Pritikin Center. During an interview with *Us* magazine, she blew up a balloon, a trick she used to curb her relentless hankering for a cigarette. She had suffered a health scare within her first week on set at Brooklyn's Kingsboro Psychiatric Center: a tooth infection caused her foot to swell, and she wound up in a wheelchair those first few days. "I have these strange diseases," she said. "No one has what I have." Directing from her seated position, she rallied the crew: *let's keep going.*

"Why do you want to be in a hospital for four months?" her friends said of the film's dreary location.

"I was depressed in a toy store," she answered, "what difference does it make?"

In a post-detox sit-down, this time at her home, she told the *LA Times* that she couldn't break her worrisome smoking addiction. Gum surgery was on the horizon.

"I stopped smoking for three weeks," she revealed. "I took the shot. But I got a report from New York there was a sound glitch on reel five. A cigarette flew into my mouth, OK?"

Tracy brought her a Diet Pepsi while Penny juggled the reporter's questions and a stream of effusive phone calls. On the line: Joe Pesci. Bob Greenhut. Mike Nichols. All admired *Awakenings* and wanted to say so.

"People said it was so brave to do a drama," she said. "I didn't think it was bravery. I figured I had an excuse: If it didn't work, I could say, well, 'That's not my strength.'"

Almost ten years had passed since she divorced Rob Reiner, yet the exes continued to orbit each other in cringey ways. Columbia wanted to release his horror film, *Misery*, on the same day as *Awakenings*. Penny picked up the phone and called Rob.

"Hi," she said. "Do you really want to come out the same night? Do you want to be looking at your [ticket] lines when I'm looking at mine? I think not."

*Misery* debuted in November 1990, garnering $61 million and critical acclaim, especially for Kathy Bates's turn as a deranged fan who kidnaps a bestselling author. One of Penny's nieces snapped a photo of *Misery* and *Awakenings* side by side on a theater marquee in Chicago. Penny was amused. Though she insisted in public that she felt no rivalry with Rob, those who knew Penny sensed some underlying competition. Rob married his second wife, photographer Michele Singer, in 1989; Barry Sonnenfeld had introduced them. But still, his first divorce continued to make headlines: a June 1990 edition of *People* magazine reported that CAA, which represented both Penny and Rob, mistakenly seated them together at a Madonna concert. Rob switched seats to dodge the potential awkwardness.

When the 1991 Oscar nominees were announced, neither earned Best Director nods. And yet, the Academy named *Awakenings* among the Best Picture hopefuls. De Niro, naturally, made the Best Actor list.

The directing snub infuriated Team Penny. Garry Marshall rightly blamed the sexism ingrained in Hollywood while Penny wondered why Williams hadn't been nominated.

"The Academy screwed Penny," Todd Smith says. "They did the same thing to Randa Haines." Haines's *Children of a Lesser God* competed for Best Picture in 1987, without recognition for its director. "It was disgusting," Smith, still stewing, adds of the institution's failure to acknowledge Penny. (But unlike Haines, Penny often escaped the suffocating "female director" label used in the media and beyond. When describing the grumbling force formerly known as Laverne, many observers simply called her "a director.")

On March 25, 1991, she invited friends over for a non-nominees party. On the menu: fried chicken and macaroni and cheese, comfort food to nourish the deflated soul. Martin Scorsese showed up after losing to first-time director Kevin Costner, whose white-savior epic, *Dances with Wolves*, triumphed over *Goodfellas*. Scorsese leveled with Penny about the odds of her winning a shiny gold man.

"Look, first of all, you're Italian: *fuhgeddaboudit*," he said. "Second of all, you're a woman: *fuhgeddaboudit double*. You don't got a chance in hell."

That night, Barbra Streisand presented Costner the gold man for Best Picture, then flocked to Penny's house. The Academy snubbed Streisand the following year. Her romance, *The Prince of Tides*, captured seven nominations but not a one for its director, Streisand. In his opening monologue, host Billy Crystal crooned, "Did this film direct itself?" (Babs laughed in appreciation.)

"I loved seeing her walk through the door, looking comfortable and ready to have fun," Penny recalled. To her, Streisand modeled what truly mattered: "doing work you loved, not winning awards."

PENNY DUSTED OFF THE DEFEAT AND STEPPED UP TO THE PLATE. SHE WAS ready to get back on a film set: no, not a psych ward in autumn. A ballpark in summer.

She phoned Anspaugh's location manager, Dennis Benatar, to see if the venues were still available. Bosse Field wasn't going anywhere. Booking Wrigley Field, however, required plenty of advance notice.

"Let's do the baseball picture," Greenhut told Penny. "Sets are already built and in storage somewhere."

Penny, fulfilling Ganz and Mandel's wish, would helm *A League of Their Own*, earning a salary of $3.75 million for directing and producing. She dove into casting, and as usual, she spent untold hours underwater, hunting for pearls. Unfortunately, Dottie frontrunner Demi Moore, her number-one draft pick, was expecting her first daughter, Rumer, with husband Bruce Willis. "She literally got fucked out of the part," Penny said. While her deeper involvement drew welcome buzz and sparkle to the resurrected endeavor, Penny's actress hunt netted lackluster results: on the set of *My Cousin Vinny*, Joe Pesci tried to teach Marisa Tomei some baseball basics in hopes of landing his future Oscar-winning costar an audition. Tomei sent Penny a tape of herself playing ball, but the footage left Penny unimpressed. Meanwhile, Farrah Fawcett was trainable, but at forty-three, she had aged out of the part. Other Dotties considered: Kyra Sedgwick, Robin Wright, Elizabeth McGovern, and Melissa Leo.

In March 1991, Penny crowned a winner, choosing Debra Winger, whom she nearly directed in *Peggy Sue Got Married*. The friends were finally working together after all these years, and Debra proved an inspired choice to perform gritty greatness as the Rockford Peaches' MVP. A double threat, a celebrated actress with Helen Callaghan's iron will, she was more than up for the challenge.

For Kit, Penny needed an actress who could withstand Debra's force of personality. A physical resemblance helped too. She liked the idea of Moira Kelly, and as usual, her casting instincts were spot on: Kelly not only looked like Debra, with her expressive light eyes and brunette smolder, she also possessed the acting chops to equal her power. The daughter of Irish immigrants who raised six kids on Long Island, Kelly, twenty-two but an old soul, projected attitude and humor. At the time, she was filming a role as a wealthy, entitled Olympic figure skater in *The Cutting Edge*, a sexy, romantic spin on *The Taming of the Shrew*. "Don't quit your day job," she snarked, eviscerating her new skating partner (D. B. Sweeney), a washed-up hockey player who worked construction to pay the bills. Whenever Sweeney fell on the ice, she skated circles around him, taunting, "Toe pick!" That catchphrase reverberated through middle school hallways in 1992 as girls used it around boys who had no clue what the word meant. "Toe pick!" traveled within girl groups like an inside joke, a note passed in class, a cheeky way to get a boy's attention—or drag him down to size.

Penny figured that Kelly—sugar and sporty spice and everything right—could film *A League of Their Own* after wrapping *The Cutting Edge*. But reality threw a wrench into her plans: Kelly broke her leg on the ice rink, forcing Penny to bench the idea of her.

She scouted other would-be, could-be Kits: Sandra Bullock, four years from her breakthrough in *Speed*; Ally Sheedy; Marcia Gay Harden; Justine Bateman; Catherine Keener; Patricia Heaton; Teri Hatcher; and Ashley

Judd, the twenty-two-year-old daughter of country singer Naomi Judd. In her notes, Penny's casting director, Ellen Lewis, described Judd as "so beautiful." On April 8, 1991, Lewis listed Geena Davis as a "no" for Kit. Later that month, she scribbled "Laura Dern—check again." In May, she noted that Helen Hunt was returning to read the part.

Penny zeroed in on Lori Petty.

"They flew me to New York to audition for, like, the eighth time," Lori says, recalling how she sat upon a little wooden bench outside Penny's door, waiting to be called into her spacious uptown apartment.

"Scrappy, athletic, confident, she was the only actress who stood up to Debra Winger when they read together," Penny wrote in her memoir. "It ain't easy to read with Debra, either. She'll fuck with you. She'll throw in extra lines or add asides. It flusters some people. Which is why she does it. You have to stay together, and Lori did. She was also a hell of a player."

Lori, at last, scored Kit Keller, ending six months of torture. "I was young, I was grateful, I was thrilled," she said. Not to mention, going places: in recent months she'd played Keanu Reeves's surfer gal pal in the thrilling *Point Break*, slated to make waves that summer.

Tom Hanks, who often surfed to clear his restless mind, read *A League of Their Own* a couple of times over the course of its development. Once Penny and Debra teamed up, the prestige factor doubled: Columbia, hoping to catch a bigger fish, placed Jim Belushi on the back burner. Tom, hoping to spend a summer in baseball nirvana, tossed his hat into the ring. He was dying to play Jimmy Dugan.

"Can I have it?" he asked Penny.

He needed it. He had taken a break from the movies following a chain of duds: *The 'Burbs*, a forgettable dark comedy; *Joe Versus the Volcano*, an underappreciated gem costarring Meg Ryan; *The Bonfire of the Vanities*, which gained infamy as a major critical and commercial disappointment, embarrassing everyone involved. Director Brian De Palma's maligned adaptation of the Tom Wolfe bestseller was a cautionary tale in miscasting, with Tom an ill fit for Sherman McCoy, the Wall Street bond trader whom Wolfe characterized as a "Master of the Universe." McCoy wasn't Everyman; he owned fancy real estate on Park Avenue.

Peter Guber, a *Bonfire* producer, had championed off-brand Hanksian decency above suitable McCoys including Tom Cruise, a persuasive

White-Collar Professional with a Big Ego and Bigger Problems. (See: *The Firm*, *Jerry Maguire*.)

"You look at this arrogant rich guy and you know that somewhere in his past he was a likable kid," Guber told Julie Salamon, whose book *The Devil's Candy* chronicled the unfolding disaster. "Tom Hanks brings that to it."

It amazed Tom that Guber wanted *him* rather than an actor with a patrician bearing, like William Hurt. *The Bonfire of the Vanities* was his fifteenth film, and by far his most controversial, analyzing race and class and New York City's heady culture of money and power, forces that collide in McCoy's explosive hit-and-run trial for the death of a Black man. In contrast to Tom's mostly safe repertoire, *Bonfire* had currency and a hot-button, contemporary edge, not to mention the capacity to launch The Nicest Man in Hollywood™ higher into the stratosphere among the serious movie stars who played against type. Tom understood the gamble and rolled the dice. "Maybe I'm perfect, maybe I'm absolutely wrong," he said.

The gamble backfired. *Bonfire*, made for $47 million, collected only $15.6 million. It opened on December 22, 1990, the same day as *Awakenings*. One crashed and burned; the other prospered.

Tom stepped away. It was time to breathe and start anew. While he never became a town pariah—its operators still kissed his ass—his flop era had done damage. Inside Columbia Pictures, over which Guber, a Master of the Universe, presided, pessimists viewed Tom through a lens of caution. The studio "didn't jump up and down and clap their hands when they heard 'Tom Hanks,'" Lowell Ganz recalls. "They weren't actually *ecstatic*, like we were." Instead, knowing baseball had limited popularity outside America, Columbia hoped to hire a Jimmy Dugan who had "an international presence" and might broaden *A League of Their Own*'s global reach. Says Ganz, "Penny, surprisingly, had a little bit of a wrestling match to get Tom in the movie. I remember they kept talking about *Europe*. They kept wanting somebody who was popular in Europe."

Tom wasn't that person. The studio talked about Michael Douglas and even Paul Newman since Jimmy, on paper originally, was intended to be an older man. William Morris agent Frank Frattaroli recommended these names to Ellen Lewis in a note dated February 12, 1991: Patrick Bergin, Harvey Keitel, Armand Assante, and Eric Roberts. Truth be told, none in that bunch screamed hilarity. Neither did Pat Riley, who had recently stepped down as the Lakers' head coach. Penny, like Jack Nicholson, was a Lakers superfan. "She dragged [Riley] in for a long, videotaped audition, which was perfectly fine but didn't have any real comedy," says Bob Greenhut, calling her obsessive approach to casting "painful." Throughout all the auditions, Penny "basically went through the entire script," he adds, testing "to see what was funny, what wasn't funny, what worked, what didn't work. It was rude to the actors we brought in, but it was a way to experiment."

Team Penny had not set out to make a big-budget, sprawling movie, though *A League of Their Own* began to move in that direction. The studio pushed for *lighter, starrier*—in other words, a mainstream comedy. Ultimately, they hoped to bait someone juicy for Jimmy—if not an international star, then a force of levity to balance Debra's gravity.

On May 5, 1991, Lewis sent a memo to Amy Pascal, mentioning only one non-American actor, the Irish Gabriel Byrne, a thinking woman's heartthrob, on a shortlist including Bill Pullman and the backburnered Tom and Jim Belushi. The tall, good-looking Pullman, who auditioned for Penny on the Columbia lot, "played best romantically," Lewis noted. In the shooting script, Jimmy and Dottie had an illicit flirtation. (More on *that* soon.)

When Fox put *A League of Their Own* on ice, Jim still got paid for acting work that he never did. In the second go-round, Columbia lacked the zeal to retain him as the Peaches' grumpy leader.

"They didn't want Tom either, to be honest," Penny revealed later. "And Tom came to me and said, 'I want this part. I need this part.'" But Columbia, she recalled, "didn't want to pay millions of dollars to an actor who had just had five flops."

Tom was an expensive risk. His salary had climbed to $5 million. Penny went to bat for him anyway.

"I thought he was wrong for the part," she said. "But he's a great guy and gets along with everyone. I just couldn't let him look the way he looks. He would seem like a distraction to the girls. They would be thinking he was cute. So I tried him in glasses, messed with his hair, and finally I said, 'Eat! You've got to eat. Get fat.'"

In an email, Jim tells me, "I had the role on Saturday, and then Frank Price gave it to Tom Hanks on Monday."

Columbia announced Tom's casting in June, just a matter of weeks before the movie was to begin shooting in Chicago. Much of the crew was already there, prepping *A League of Their Own* inside a lofty building on historic Prairie Avenue. According to David Dumais, a costumer in the wardrobe department, Jim sent over his gym equipment ahead of time because he wanted to exercise on location. When Tom edged him out, the gear sat in a corner, unclaimed.

"Tom wanted to hide in the movie, not star in it," says Babaloo Mandel, who worked with Ganz to remold Jimmy into a younger, thirty-five-year-old wretch. The character is a washed-up ball of nasty: he's a sloppy drunk. He takes history's longest pee in the locker room as the women watch, astonished. He chews tobacco and spits it upon a friendly league official's nice leather shoe. He treats his team like manure; he is so lazy and entitled that Dottie, a grown-up, must step up and coach the Peaches herself. Jimmy, the anti-Dottie, grits his teeth, spewing venom at her fans: "You can all kiss my ass," he seethes.

Jimmy hates everyone, himself most of all. He is a surlier reflection of Jimmie Foxx, one of the greatest hitters of all time, right up there with Babe Ruth and Hank Aaron. Foxx, nicknamed Double X, played for the Philadelphia Athletics, the Boston Red Sox, the Chicago Cubs, and the Philadelphia Phillies from 1925 to the end of World War II. "He was built like a Greek God, with bulging biceps and [a] sculpted physique," wrote baseball historian Bill Jenkinson in *The National Pastime: From Swampoodle to South Philly*. "His rounded face was marked by handsome features set off by a full head of brown hair and bright blue eyes. His joy was infectious, hustling on the field with a spontaneous smile and boundless enthusiasm."

At thirty-two, Double X slugged his 500th home run on September 24, 1940, becoming the youngest major leaguer to do so and join the hallowed ranks of Ruth. But the following year, his career took a sudden nosedive. He suffered chronic pain and blurred vision that was possibly the result of a concussion he received in 1934 when a ball clocked him in the head. As his pain intensified, he turned to the bottle, and his performance weakened. Double X retired in 1945 after one season with the Phillies. While facing the Pittsburgh Pirates at Forbes Field, he "blasted his final two major league homers by launching a pair of 420-footers into Schenley Park," Jenkinson noted. "When it was all over, [he] had accumulated 534 home runs, an impressive total, but far from the 714 predicted just a few years earlier."

What happens to a hero who loses his powers? Flash-forward seven years:

> Foxx, a shadow of what he once was, accepts a job in Indiana managing the Fort Wayne Daisies. The team makes the 1952 playoffs, but Jimmie could care less. He dozes in the dugout, pulling a hat down over his eyes as the players lead the team. He lasts only a single summer with the All-Americans. Several years later, he does two seasons coaching baseball at the University of Miami and just one as the hitting instructor for the minor league Minneapolis Millers. His drinking habit impairs his ability to show up the way his bosses need him to. Off the diamond, he takes other jobs, certainly respectable jobs: He sells sporting goods in a Cleveland department store. He works as a car salesman and a coal truck driver. In 1967, at the age of fifty-nine, he collapses during dinner with his brother in Miami and cannot be resuscitated at the nearest hospital. Afterward, an autopsy reports that he choked to death.

"Jimmie was a great guy but he was very unhappy about being out of organized baseball," Pepper Paire Davis, the Daisies' catcher, said of her former manager. "He found it very hard to deal with the 'women' ballplayers. He just couldn't understand it." Yes, "he had a drinking problem, but a lot of ballplayers did at the time," she defended. "Jimmie was not alone. Jimmie was also neither vulgar nor rude. He was a quiet, classy, polite man. He had a heart that was hurting from being out of baseball sooner than he should have been."

With that in mind, Ganz and Mandel crafted a meaty redemptive arc that, in some ways, pulled focus from the central sisterly struggle. While Jimmy grows from a royal pain in the ass to kind-hearted curmudgeon, he becomes deeply invested in the women's success, making the still-recovering misogynist much more enlightened than Foxx and other subpar AAGPBL coaches phoning it in. Dottie's dignified example inspires Jimmy to find purpose and a calling. To finally try and clean up his act.

"I just think he's a guy who knew that he blew it," Tom said. "He had it great. He didn't realize he had it great when he was playing baseball, but now he knows that he had it great. And it was only through his own stupidity and bad behavior that he took himself out of the game. Because he blew out his knee in a stupid kind of accident, and it was all because of his drinking."

The torment within Jimmy's soul intrigued Tom at a professional crossroads when, if he made another *Bonfire*, his ambitions could meet an early grave. (Then, back to network television.) Tom understood the guy's anger on a cellular level. As a star from a working-class background, he did not have the cushions of nepotism or family money to provide a firm foundation, and so he had worked himself to death, concerned that if he stopped job-hopping and proving his worth, Hollywood would stop calling. That stress made Hanks salty, not sweet. It gave him edge, and hustle. It made him deeply grasp how someone like Jimmy Dugan, a once-great ballplayer, could become such a jerk.

He also liked that Jimmy was not the main story, and that Penny urged him to gain weight. His handlers, however, questioned his judgment. *He wants to play* what? *An unlikable loser? He's not even the focal point of the movie. This is how he plans to end his two-year hiatus?*

Hey, if *A League of Their Own* bombed, Tom's so-called secondary character role all but ensured that he'd escape the blame, even as Jimmy underwent a transformation as vivid and powerful as any male hero's journey in the movies. In 1991, Tom—who once preferred to wing it—was making strategic moves and putting himself back together again, piece by piece. He left William Morris and signed with CAA. He bought a beachside home in Malibu. He dabbled in screenwriting, including a stab at *Significant Other*, a Walt Disney Studios romance about an alcoholic and her husband. He and Debra Winger were set to costar, though the project stalled with the departure of director Alan J. Pakula. According to a report in *People* magazine, the actors jointly lobbied to remove Pakula, rejecting the script he wrote for the movie.

On *A League of Their Own*, Debra tried to oust Ganz and Mandel too. "She wanted to bring in some New York buddies to rewrite the script," Mandel says.

But Penny, nothing if not loyal, refused to let that happen. She aimed to keep her team together, through thick and thin. While Debra seemed to have fun diving into baseball training with Lori, her little movie sister, she was a pot on the verge of boiling over, the bubbles rising to the surface with gathering speed.

As Penny assembled the Peaches, she brought Tracy back to play Betty Spaghetti. "She started to practice and would come home happy," Penny said. "In a way, I saw in her what I wanted to capture in the movie: empowerment and pride. Don't be ashamed of your talent."

Rosie O'Donnell never expected *A League of Their Own* to be pulled out of turnaround. She was delighted to reaudition and read for Marla Hooch, but Penny didn't see Rosie as Marla. Instead, she gave her another part: Doris Murphy, a bawdy infielder.

"I told her not to eat," Penny said. "To this day, she says that I'm the only director that ever told her to lose weight. Well, I say those things if they need to be said."

Did they, though? Nobody told The Babe to shed pounds. If you enjoy moving your body, then you can be an athlete—at any size and shape. Penny's mindset reflected the warped thinking of the times: that thinness signified good health and athleticism, which is simply not true. And yet, many women starved themselves to get skinny, the aesthetic goal. Rosie would maintain her curvy figure, modeling self-acceptance on her future daytime talk show. *This is who I am*, she conveyed to her viewers, many of whom looked at Rosie and saw themselves.

At Megan Cavanagh's reaudition, she read with Debra, Lori, Tracy, and Rosie, who followed her out of the building and said, "You're the best Marla that I've seen so far."

Megan focused on the "so far."

Deflated, she phoned her friend Amy, and during their conversation, the operator interrupted with a call waiting. Her new agent Pat Brady was on the other line, screaming, "You got the part! You got the part!" Megan cried and screamed back. The next day, she reported to Dedeaux Field for baseball rehearsals, which were unpaid. She would not earn a paycheck until Chicago, and until then, she continued her shifts at Ed Debevic's.

One day, Lori walked into the diner with an entourage. Megan, working the hostess stand, tried to play it cool. Maybe, fingers crossed, her Gladys Kolacki gimmick would render her unrecognizable to Lori, saving her the embarrassment.

*Ah, too late.*

"Megan?" Lori said. "Oh my god!"

And that was how Megan earned a new nickname: Do You Want Fries with That?

Penny drafted Freddie Simpson to play Ellen Sue Gotlander, a beauty queen and shortstop, and Lindsay Frost, a Meg Ryan lookalike, for "All the Way" Mae, a firecracker from California. Others added: Anne Ramsay as Helen Haley, first base; Ann Cusack as Shirley Baker, left field; Renée Coleman as Alice Gaspers, left field; and Bitty Schram as Evelyn Gardner, right field. Bitty, a spirited, New Jersey–born blonde of twenty-four, had studied at the University of Maryland on a tennis scholarship, graduating with a degree in advertising design. Yet acting was her true passion, and that spring she'd filmed a minor part in the crime drama *Fathers & Sons* starring Jeff Goldblum. Bitty missed the big baseball tryouts but managed to audition for Ellen Lewis in New York, as did Parker Posey, who would've made a great Peach. Lewis wanted Bitty to read a Kit scene. Bitty sat in the hallway, thinking, *I am not right for this role.* She told Lewis what she felt, so Lewis handed her Evelyn's emotional meltdown in response to Jimmy's "No Crying in Baseball" hissy fit.

"That was up my alley," she says. "I knew that was in my wheelhouse."

Bitty nailed it and Lewis sent the tape off to Penny. Weeks later, her agent delivered the bad news: she didn't make the cut.

"Oh no, I'm gonna get this role," Bitty said. "I just know it."

Lo and behold, within a month, minds changed and Bitty was on an LA-bound flight to train alongside Debra and the gang.

At the time, pilot season was underway. The Big Four networks were commissioning new series and pulling actors into long-term contracts. When Fox picked up *Stand by Your Man*, a short-lived sitcom featuring Rosie and Melissa Gilbert, Penny asked Diller to adjust the taping schedule so Rosie could film *A League of Their Own*. Meanwhile, Penny lost Lindsay Frost to an NBC sci-fi serial, *Nightmare Café*, which meant she had to recast "All the Way" Mae. She needed a triple threat who could play ball, dance, and, ideally, act.

Penny approached Madonna, the most notorious woman on the planet. She had read a magazine article in which the shape-shifting pop star expressed her greatest ambition: to be a movie star. She wanted that for herself from the time she was a performative, motherless girl growing up in suburban Detroit—well before she took MTV by storm and remolded it in her image. Before the Jean Paul Gaultier cone bra and her stormy first marriage to Sean Penn. Before "Like a Virgin" and "Like a Prayer." She had made headway toward her dream: she dazzled as an East village bohemian in Susan Seidelman's 1985 dramedy *Desperately Seeking Susan*, where her wooden line readings somehow made sense for her character, a jaded downtown punk-princess. Her tepid follow-ups, *Shanghai Surprise* and *Who's That Girl*, did nothing to help her goal of Hollywood domination, though her sparkling cameo in *Dick Tracy* (the role: underworld chanteuse Breathless Mahoney) drew positive reviews. In an apparent effort to keep production costs down, Warren Beatty, the movie's director and her then-boyfriend, persuaded Madonna to work for scale and accept minimum wages. She brought considerable value to the stylized crime comedy, including the slinky number "Sooner or Later," written by Stephen Sondheim. In March 1991, Sondheim won the Oscar for Best Original Song, which she performed during the live broadcast. (She brought rival pop phenomenon Michael Jackson as her platonic date to the show—because she disliked attention of any kind.)

"Do you want to see me pitch?" Madonna asked Penny when they met to discuss *A League of Their Own*.

"No, I already have a pitcher," Penny said, referencing Lori. "But I do have to see if you can play."

Madonna wanted a part bigger than Mae; Penny was direct with her.

"I don't think you need to carry a movie right now," she said.

For all her experience in front of cameras, Madonna still required a cushion of skilled actors around her—and she seemed to accept it. She was eager to pass the baseball test, to prove herself worthy of the ensemble, and she visited Queens, New York, for a three-hour session with St. John's University coach Joe Russo.

"Take your stance," Russo said.

"What's a stance?" she asked.

She had no clue how the sport worked, and no interest in organized sports generally, but toward the end of her crash course, she began to hit the ball. "A very strong and compact girl," Russo declared. "Great potential." For the love of White Castle sliders fresh off the grill, Madonna was *trainable*. After impressing Russo, she traveled to the Cannes Film Festival to screen her raunchy documentary, *Truth or Dare*. At a seaside dinner party, she encouraged guests to participate in the game of the same name, and they obliged: Madonna French-kissed French actress Anne Parillaud on a dare, and filmmaker Roman Polanski confessed that his first sexual experience was with a "boy."

Besides movie stardom, breaking taboos was on Madonna's wider agenda. She courted controversy wherever she went. She delighted in giving conservative society the middle finger. She embodied sin and desire, the forbidden fruit that branded her a wanton temptress in religious hot zones from the Bible Belt to the Vatican. Her carnal sexuality electrified her young fans, many of whom came from sheltered backgrounds. They weren't supposed to like her, yet they couldn't take their eyes off her. Her detractors hated her power over the youth. But they, too, could not look away. The more they attacked her, the mightier she became.

In *Truth or Dare*, a revealing look at her blockbuster Blond Ambition world tour in 1990, she gave director Alek Keshishian unprecedented access to her life on the road. He exposed her for who she was: a type-A workaholic with an insatiable competitive drive and thirst for the limelight. Her mother, also named Madonna, died of breast cancer when she was just five years old, creating a void of love to be filled by millions of strangers. While she showed a loving, maternal side to her male dancers, most of whom were openly queer, she also lacked a sensitivity chip: She mocked a dorky Kevin Costner during a backstage meet-and-greet, sticking her hand down her throat after he called her concert "neat." She humiliated her brother, who struggled with alcoholism, and a childhood girlfriend who asked her to be the godmother of her unborn child. She laughed while gossiping about a tour makeup artist who was drugged and assaulted after a night out dancing. She disapproved of people whom she perceived as lacking control over their lives. Her exhibitionism was calculated to shock: she fellated a bottle on camera and feigned masturbation onstage. In an amusing sequence, Toronto police threatened to arrest her before a show. Madonna, leading a group prayer backstage, referred to the city as the "fascist state of Toronto." She was funny, mean, warm, cold, self-absorbed, insolent, trailblazing, and unabashedly political.

When Penny told Rosie that Madonna might join the cast, "I was like, *holy shit*," Rosie says. "I couldn't wrap my head around [it]."

Penny instructed Rosie to bond with the Queen of Pop.

"Rosie," she said, "tomorrow Madonna's coming in here. If she likes you and likes me, she'll do the movie. Don't mess up."

How intimidating. Madonna was one of the most famous tabloid fixtures in the world, possibly second to Princess Diana. As a veejay in New York, Rosie wondered how a fellow esoteric comedian, Sandra Bernhard, had managed to crack Madonna's inner circle. Wasn't that strange? Madonna was so iconic and inaccessible. Yet Sandra broke through the ice and forged a close public friendship. Would Rosie be able to pull that off and fulfill Penny's extraordinary request?

Before meeting Madonna, Rosie watched *Truth or Dare*. In the exhibitionist she recognized a common origin story: they both came from big Catholic families, and both were named after mothers who died young, from the same disease. Rosie had never met another adult woman who lost a mother that way.

"Hey, I saw your movie last night," Rosie told Madonna.

"You did?"

"Yeah. And I'm named after my mother and she died of breast cancer, and I'm the oldest girl in the family."

*Boom*. From then onward, they were like siblings. Penny dubbed them "Ro and Mo," a moniker that stuck.

"You're going to be best friends," she ordered. "Mo, you teach her how to set her hair, and Ro, you teach her how to play ball."

Ganz and Mandel got to work, beefing up their script with comedic Ro and Mo bits. With Mo onboard, Mae became brassier, more streetwise.

On June 9, 1991, the *LA Times* dished the unsourced news that Columbia Pictures hoped Madonna would play Kit to Debra's Dottie—a sign that within the studio, Mo supporters thought she should have a bigger role. A subsequent report corrected that she was just one of the girls.

Debra was livid. She threatened Penny, saying that if she hired Madonna, "it would be a long, hot summer," according to Frank Price. Debra made it clear that she was going to be very difficult. Penny had blocked her from hiring new screenwriters, but Madonna was worse. Madonna was the last straw. She resented what she viewed as shameless stunt casting, a cheap and cynical betrayal of honest filmmaking. That made Penny, the betrayer, a sellout. "You're making an Elvis movie!" she complained. When Debra agreed to do *A League of Their Own*, she hadn't asked for cast approval, which she usually got. The perk was a sore subject. CAA represented both Debra and Madonna; in the mid-'80s, the former briefly left the agency to protest how it stuffed *Legal Eagles* with fellow client Robert Redford.

While Price surmised that Debra was jealous of Madonna, nobody mentioned Madonna's interview in the May 1991 issue of *The Advocate* in which she dissed Debra's dramatic performance in Bernardo Bertolucci's epic *The Sheltering Sky*, a financial failure for Warner Brothers the previous winter.

"Debra Winger was so wrong," she told the magazine. "Oh, it was so wrong, so wrong. It was so unsexy. It was horrible."

If Debra felt disrespected, that article certainly might have fueled her anger.

In any case, Penny didn't want to spend a long, hot summer dealing with her. "No one tells me how to cast my movies," she griped. She asked Price for help. "Let me take care of it," he said.

Price notified Debra's agent, Rick Nicita, that he planned to replace her and wanted to settle her out of her deal. Debra requested a meeting to plead on her behalf. She entered Price's office alongside Nicita and her lawyer, Barry Hirsch. Price listened as she spoke with very little interruption.

"Debra, I've heard you for an hour," he said. "And all I've heard is self-justification: how right you were in what you did. And I don't happen to think you were right. Neither does Penny. And we can't take the chance of bad behavior on the set."

Columbia paid Debra about $3 million to go away.

"Are you crazy?" Peter Guber said in a phone call to Michael Nathanson. "Have you just paid an actress off for a movie?"

"Well, contractually, that's what we had to do," Nathanson explained.

As Debra recalled to *The Telegraph*, "It was the only time I ever collected a pay-or-play on my contract. In other words, I collected my pay even though I did not play, and that's very hard to get in a court."

Before Debra's departure, Geena Davis phoned Ganz and Mandel about punching up the script for a movie she had in the works. They couldn't accept the job, they said, because they were too busy prepping *A League of Their Own* for Penny Marshall.

"I read that movie," she said. "I love that movie."

Regrettably, she told them, Penny had already cast the only part that interested her.

Did Geena mean Dottie? Of course, she meant Dottie. The buzzers went off in the writers' heads. They'd heard about the drama with Debra and Madonna.

"Don't go anywhere," they said.

They phoned Penny and Elliot Abbott. *We just had an interesting conversation with Geena Davis*, they relayed. *As you fight through what appears to be a Debra Winger war, just have this information.*

Geena was outstanding in *Thelma & Louise*, which had hurtled into theaters, causing a commotion, just before Memorial Day. As Thelma, a neglected housewife outrunning the police with her best friend, Louise (Susan Sarandon), who shoots and kills Thelma's attempted rapist, she smoked up the screen, radiating grit and sex appeal, vulnerability and strength. The female buddy film got people talking and established Geena as a bona fide movie star rather than just a whimsical Oscar winner. Overnight, she joined Madonna in a place she'd never been before: the cultural zeitgeist.

But could she throw a baseball?

Years before, Geena had played catch in New York with her first husband, Richard Emmolo, during their short-lived, early-1980s union. "I was sure that with training I'd be able to learn good-enough 'movie baseball' to pull it off," she wrote in her memoir, *Dying of Politeness*.

Penny summoned Geena to her house on La Presa Drive, and in preparation for the encounter, the actress wore a miniskirt and high heels by design. There was no way Penny would test her throwing skill in *that* outfit, right?

"This meeting is simply about your ability to play the role, not play sports, so don't go near a baseball," her agents told her. "And she *will* ask you to throw a ball, so be prepared."

As they prophesied, Penny put her to the test.

"OK, less just see you trow da bawl," Geena remembered her saying in her nasally Bronx brogue.

The actress, still learning to stand up for herself at that point in her career, said no. But Penny kept prodding.

"Come on, just for one second, come on, just trow."

With disappointment, Geena gave in.

"Fully five minutes went by before I was out on the fucking lawn, throwing a fucking baseball," she wrote, adding, "I later wondered if trowin' da ball was less about my skills than Penny trying to see if she could *get* me to throw it, even though I'd been ordered not to, because then she'd know I wouldn't be a problem when we made the movie. Or she simply wanted to see me throw a ball and was going to make it happen no matter what anyone said. Bottom line, she rolled right over my fledgling badass."

Penny recalled: "Her agent said not to play ball with her, but I took her out in the backyard anyway and discovered she was a natural. I had my new Dottie."

Weeping, Debra told the Peaches, "I'm not going to be able to do this part, you guys. I'm gonna have to leave." They were "devastated," Megan Cavanagh said. "Captain, oh my, Captain. Gone."

The abrupt shift from Debra to Geena unsettled Lori Petty. The movie was supposed to start filming soon, and she looked nothing like Geena. Would Penny pull Lori off the team too?

## *Sixth Inning*

# CHICAGO

LORI BRACED FOR BAD NEWS. SHE WAS SO SCARED AND NERVOUS. IF Debra got fired, that put her next on the chopping block.

*Well, then, fuck, I'm outta here,* she told herself. *Because we both have sparkly light eyes and dark hair, and I'm a package deal with this lady.*

Then Penny Marshall called, asking, "Will you have dinner with Geena Davis?"

"I'm like, 'Yeah! I'll have dinner with Geena Davis!'" Lori recalls responding. "Jesus Christ, yes, I will. Yes, yes!"

Geena and Lori came face-to-face for the first time in the thick of June 1991. "Maybe Geena got to see if she liked me or if I was an asshole or what? I don't know," says Lori, who deferred to the six-foot-tall strawberry blonde and describes that meeting thusly: "Hi, please say I can be your sister," and "What do you want me to do? I can do that."

Afterward, Penny informed Lori that she was bringing Geena onboard.

"Does that mean I'm still in the movie?" Lori asked.

"Of course, you're still in the movie," Penny said. "What are you talking about?"

Penny always intended to keep Lori, yet Lori could not read Penny's mind, so how could she have known?

The shoot was scheduled to commence July 10, giving Geena some space to play catch-up. In the meantime, the cast descended upon Chicago, where the actresses' boot camp resumed at a new location, the Illinois Institute of Technology, the Sears Tower looming in the distance. USC coach Bo Hughes joined the production as a technical adviser, a title also given to Karen Kunkel, the serious but fun-loving AAGPBL board member who once booted Penny from a reunion gathering. She was less of a steady presence than Hughes, an affable yet hardcore mentor in his thirties. Coach Hughes wanted the women's movements to appear clean and fluid on camera, as though they really knew what they were doing. He observed their skill sets: Rosie was advanced, well ahead of others. Lori had a solid windup. Geena was supposed to be the Rockford Peaches' virtuoso, but she lacked even the basic training. The amateur would have to start from scratch and fake excellence as much as possible. She grabbed a vintage 1940s glove and began drills, trying to pick up the essentials within a matter of days. Thankfully, Geena had a dedicated body double—a substitute who knew how to play ball—but she couldn't rely on her double to perform every single stunt, not with the camera pointed directly at Geena's chiseled visage, not with the camera judging Geena's catching stance. Dottie Hinson was a superhero, and Geena had to look like one at least. *No pressure at all.*

"I crouched down into position and tried to catch the ball, and when I missed [the catch], the ball hit my shins," Geena tells me. "They didn't have me in shin guards yet, and I ended up having these polka-dot bruises on my shins—like, covered with round bruises from the ball. One of the coaches said, 'You know, it's a lot easier to catch the ball with a glove than your shin.'"

Coach Hughes, who brought on a young assistant, Abe Flores, to help, once told Tom Hanks, "She doesn't even know that she's got to take the mask off." The judgment, the whiff of locker-room hazing, motivated Geena to try harder.

She was thirty-five years old and freshly divorced from Jeff Goldblum. In the fall of 1990, after wrapping *Thelma & Louise*, she filed to end their three-year marriage on amicable terms. "Ultimately it had been my decision to end it, but I also regretted it terribly," she said in 2022. "We still saw each other quite a lot at first, which eased the transition a bit. But I feel now that I was too hasty; I should have given us more time." Back then, she was becoming her own woman, a leading lady who modeled authority and self-respect. On *Thelma & Louise*, Susan Sarandon had shown her how to be assertive. Geena gravitated toward acting roles that allowed her to be bolder than she was in real life, but Susan was totally comfortable in her own skin. Her confidence was not an act. Geena watched in awe as Susan critiqued the script without apology, saying, "On page one, I don't think I would do that" and "Maybe we could take out this line or move it to a later scene."

As Susan said what she wanted, the director, Ridley Scott, didn't fight back. He absorbed her feedback. Geena took mental notes. *People can be like her? God, what a way to be.*

On *A League of Their Own*, she worked within her physical limits. Without endlessly apologizing. At the same time, she felt a loss of the exhilarating power that she had filming *Thelma & Louise*, Sarandon her Alpha ally. In a script meeting, Geena asked Ganz and Mandel to make Dottie funnier. The character was so *stoic* compared with the others who clowned around her. Geena wanted laughs too.

"They happily agreed to punch it up for humor for me," she recalled in her memoir. "A few days later the script came back with some additions—but in each case, it seemed like my new line teed up a new joke for Tom Hanks's or Jon Lovitz's characters."

Often, women were the butt of the men's jokes. She confronted the writers.

"It can't be that hard, guys," she said.

"No, it *is* hard," they replied. "It's actually pretty hard to come up with jokes for women. . . ."

"Why not imagine I'm Billy Crystal—just pretend you're writing funny lines for *him*, but then it will be me who says them."

That advice didn't seem to sink in, but no matter. She leaned into Dottie's position as the straight man, the boss Peach who kept a cool head, the one future fangirls wanted to become. Finally, "I'd decided I was going to become Gary Cooper. Someone with quiet strength, someone who when a job needed doing, would get it done."

Well, Geena had big cleats to fill.

"The funny thing is, I was really *not* athletic as a kid—at all," she says. "Everybody wished I was. The girls' basketball team in high school was like, 'Please join!' I'm like, 'I don't know how to play.' They're like, 'Just stand there!'" Until her sophomore year, she was the tallest kid in her class. "But I was very shy, physically. I didn't want to try anything and have people laugh at me or look at me or something."

And yet, she managed to embrace her height advantage on the track team, leaping over the high jump—an adrenaline rush. She was also an honor student and fluent musician, playing the piano, the organ, and the flute. She grew up middle-class in Wareham, Massachusetts; her father was a civil engineer and her mother a teacher's aide. She had one older brother and a healthy imagination: hence, her early interest in acting. While playing outside, young Geena and a girlfriend pretended to be the rugged ranchers in *The Rifleman*, a Western series on ABC.

"It never occurred to us that there were no female characters we wanted to perform," she told the author Becky Aikman. "There was *Bewitched* and *I Dream of Jeannie*, where the women had superpowers, but every episode was about them having to sit on their powers so the man in their life wouldn't get upset or feel emasculated."

After graduating from Boston University, she took her drama degree and her bee-stung lips and moved to New York. She waited tables and worked as a salesclerk for Ann Taylor, amusing herself by posing as a mannequin in the store window. She captivated passersby: *Was she real? Was she fake? Wait, did she just move?!* Eventually, Henri Bendel hired her to pose in its Christmas window.

Geena figured that modeling was her fastest route to Hollywood. She signed with the Zoli agency, which sent her to audition for director Sydney Pollack, who needed a real model to spice up his comedy *Tootsie*, starring Dustin Hoffman in drag. She nailed it, landing a small but memorable role that required her to wear a bra and panties. On set, she was relaxed and natural, impressing the men ogling her. Geena's pleasant, unaffected quality translated on film, and the gigs kept coming. Within three years, she was headlining her very own TV sitcom, *Sara*, projecting intelligence as a San Francisco lawyer. The show got the boot after four months, but Geena rebounded in the movies, building up a portfolio of sweet-natured eccentrics. Art imitated life: at the home she and Goldblum once shared in LA, the couple installed a life-size cow sculpture in the backyard. She confessed her wish for their love nest to "resemble a carnival ride with bumper cars, firemen's poles, and an office like a fun house," *Elle* magazine reported in 1989.

Geena bristled at the word most often used to describe her characters: *kooky*. The adjective was a misunderstanding, an insult to ordinary women in extraordinary, sometimes fantastical circumstances. Yes, she starred in some unusual pictures: *The Fly*, for instance. But, she argued, "I was the center of the storm in that movie."

That centeredness trickled down to *A League of Their Own*, a chaotic pressure-cooker with nonstop fires to put out. Her costars viewed Geena as a grounding force. A professional who liked to joke around but kept her eye on the ball.

"She was a love," Renée Coleman says. "She was just complete love and seemed like one of us because she was awkward and didn't know how to play ball." She didn't put on airs. She was simply Geena, the glamazon goof next door, "this funny, self-deprecating, adorable nut."

She brought a different energy than Debra.

"Like, Geena is severely laid-back," Lori says. "It's wonderful. I don't know what it is: I don't know if it's a cool confidence. I don't know if it's shyness." For the most part, she kept a cordial distance. "She was always there, always ready, always knew her shit, you know?" Lori adds. "And then, she'd go back to her room. While we were, like, playing pranks at the local Denny's, she's, like, sleeping. Like a grown-up. She's so sleek."

Geena commanded a grown-up salary in the vicinity of $2 million, roughly the same as Madonna's *League* paycheck. Lori, the second lead, pocketed about $175,000, equal to Jon Lovitz, who only appeared in the first half of the film.

Lori's first big action movie, *Point Break*, had yet to hit theaters. Nobody had seen her holding her own opposite Keanu and Swayze and looking amazing on her surfboard. Nobody really knew who she was. *Point Break*'s director, Kathryn Bigelow, had glimpsed her potential and how to use it. Penny Marshall saw Lori too. Still, surrounded by a constellation of known quantities, Lori couldn't help but feel outshined.

For Lori, "it was very, very easy to feel like the lesser-than, the overlooked sister," she says. "It wasn't true, of course, on set. But here [Geena] is, an Academy Award winner, and she's six feet tall and she's drop-dead gorgeous and she was in *Tootsie* and she's a movie star. . . . And I'm just this person who's in this movie."

When Lori felt intimidated, she would make the inferiority complex work in her favor. She would pour her deepest insecurities into Kit.

MADONNA'S ARRIVAL TRANSFORMED THE SHOW INTO A THREE-RING CIRCUS.

Freddie Simpson didn't recognize her at first. Her hair was dyed brown, and she seemed smaller in person. Madonna changed her look at the speed of light, though her "Material Girl" video, in which she impersonated Marilyn Monroe, cemented the chameleon's image as a sexy platinum blonde. Throughout her evolution, the thirty-two-year-old persisted in pushing buttons. *A League of Their Own* presented fresh targets. She kept her costars on their toes. What outrageous thing would she say next? Which truths would she point out?

At Dedeaux Field early on, Madonna dished snark when Anne Ramsay's partner visited practice. Ramsay had not made David Anspaugh's cut, but Penny brought her back and gave her a "life," a word Garry used when hiring newcomers. Ramsay's character, Helen Haley, did not have the biographical depth of Dottie, Kit, Jimmy, or Marla Hooch, so Penny concocted a backstory for Helen, a compassionate brunette who helps the illiterate left-fielder Shirley Baker (Ann Cusack) find her name on the list of girls who made the team. *You're on the intelligent side*, she told Ramsay, who studied theater at UCLA. *A lot of the original players used the money they made in baseball to start their careers. Helen is gonna go to medical school and become a doctor.*

Ramsay, a day player on TV, knew the movie would change the course of her life. "It was the beginning of my career and I was scared shitless," she says. As a gay actress in 1991, she had to decide whether to come out on set or keep her sexuality hidden. Coming out was risky back then. To be out and proud in America was to be Other. While gay executives, agents, and artists worked in Hollywood, the industry took the nation's temperature and sustained a culture of caution among the talent. In the past, its publicity apparatus set up sham heterosexual couplings to fake out the public. To be out and proud in Hollywood was still to be a liability. It all came down to money, as everything did, and it was presumed that openly gay stars would empty out movie houses. For an actress on the up and up, coming out meant that you might lose out on all sorts of roles: the leads, the love interests, the man-crazy best friend, basically any character who identified as straight. And, hell, that was most of them.

"Carol, here's Madonna; Madonna, my roommate, Carol," said Ramsay, introducing her girlfriend to her costar.

"Roommate, huh? *Yeah, right*," Madonna said.

Ramsay started laughing.

"She can see that we both have rings on," she recalls. "We weren't married, of course. She put it right there, Madonna. And I was like *You're so fucking right* in my head. *What am I doing*? Like, I'm not fooling *one* person here."

In Chicago, Madonna worked harder than anyone her castmates had ever met. She rose at 4 a.m. and jogged eight to ten miles, then trained with Coach Hughes from eight to noon, then headed to the dance studio to rehearse Mae's jitterbug number, the highlight of a complicated set piece at the fictional Suds Bucket nightclub. On the practice field one day, she told the actresses: "If anybody stays and plays until we can't see the ball anymore, then I'll take you to dinner."

Megan Cavanagh, the fourth lead, did not know how to act around Madonna. And Lori felt awkward just saying her name.

"What are we supposed to call you?" she asked. "Because calling you 'Madonna' is like calling you 'The Empire State Building,' and I can't do that."

When Madonna brought a boom box on the premises, she set it down and said, "Any of you girls break it, you're buying a new one!"

"You're richer than most third-world nations," Rosie told her. "Don't ask these little twenty-year-olds to pay for your boom box."

If Mo was Queen Bee, then Ro was court jester, unafraid to razz her in good fun. Mo liked to push her body to the brink; Ro hid under the proverbial bleachers when Penny made them run three laps around the field's perimeter. While Penny wasn't watching, Ro would stop running and then join back up for the third lap. Penny, knowing Ro was cheating, would place her hand on Ro's back. No sweat? She'd make Ro finish the dreaded drill.

"Penny was always screaming at me that I was playing baseball like a dancer," Mo recalled later. "But I couldn't help it."

As Tom Hanks observed, "In the early goings, her throwing technique was pretty much, *step, step, step, fling*—like it was choreographed—*step, step, step, fling*."

Coach Hughes mentally moved the human chess pieces to where they belonged on the diamond. Madonna, originally positioned on third base, could neither hit nor throw, despite her trainability. Hughes put her on center field, a move that allowed her to glide upon the grass with a dancer's grace—the camera would love that.

Injuries abounded. When the actresses switched from modern gloves to real-deal period mitts offering less protection, Ramsay broke her nose. Coach Hughes had thrown the ball that hopped out of her mitt, smashing her bone.

"Hey, Anne, don't worry if it's not healed by the time we start filming," Penny reassured. "I'm gonna write it into the script."

For a sliding tutorial, Coach Hughes asked a production assistant to procure a Slip 'N Slide. "You're kidding me," the PA said.

Megan embraced her teacher's methods. "I'm first! I'm first!" she said. "Watch out: *Thunder!*" She ran, slipped, and whacked her head on the ground, sustaining a head injury. When asked where she was, Megan replied, "USC." (They were at ITT.) She heard someone say, possibly to Coach, "We gotta stop doing this. They're dropping like flies." Then Tracy and Bitty banged their heads on the slide of death, joining Megan at the hospital for hourly monitoring. Megan called them the "Concussion Triplets."

Another time, after a long day of baseball, Megan, a vegan, ate a hot dog and was hospitalized for dehydration. "I had five saline bags before I peed," she says.

From Coach Hughes's vantage point, these girls did not care about the risks of getting hurt. They worked hard, like hungry minor leaguers; they were warriors. They were back on the field in no time.

Before Geena's arrival they'd picnicked in Skokie, a northern suburb, with AAGPBL elders, who played a game while they watched. Dolores Dries, nicknamed Pickles, taught Rosie how to throw two balls at once. Pepper Paire Davis shared a helpful batting strategy for women ballplayers: "You need to bend your knees," Renée Coleman recalls her saying. "Everything that they've told you to do, do exactly that—[and] bend your knees."

With Pepper's advice, their hitting improved. The Californian was sixty-seven and struggled with walking. While her playing days were over, her love for baseball blazed eternal. "She was so open and smiley and everyone's grandma," says Megan, adding, "She could pound the Budweiser."

The meet-and-greet served a dual purpose: to recruit able-bodied All-American vets for the movie's finale, a meta-reunion in Cooperstown. About sixty seniors tried out and forty were chosen, including Mary Moore, an infielder whose stint as a Battle Creek Belle ended after she sliced two fingers in her off-season factory job. (Helen St. Aubin, formerly Callaghan, was ill with breast cancer and unable to participate in the making of the movie.)

In the evenings, the rookies disappeared into the glittering skyline. The two tallest scrapers, the Sears and the Hancock, pierced the heavens, conducting an elegant symphony of steel, glass, and light that stole your breath every time you looked. The biting winter wind had gone dormant, and as the city thawed, it became very, very hot, the air thick with humidity. It came alive for three months, maybe four, and what a time it was to be alive in the summer of 1991. Chicagoans took their boats out on Lake Michigan and grilled meat in their backyards, where squirting ketchup on a hot dog was pretty much verboten. (A cookout's star condiment: mustard, in school bus yellow.) Every weekend, the neighborhoods threw block parties with loud music and beer—Old Style if you were a diehard Cubs fan. Chicago was a sports town divided along class and racial lines: the North Side, whiter and more well-to-do, was home to Wrigley Field; the blue-collar South Side, where redlining and housing discrimination marginalized Black residents in the middle of the century, rooted for the White Sox, although mostly white fans attended games at Comiskey Park, streaming in from bungalows below the Loop. The baseball rivalry ran deep. Sometimes a Cubs fan married a Sox fan, though the latter wouldn't be caught dead at Wrigley. *Yuppies? Thanks, but no thanks.*

Only one athlete could unite the factions: Michael Jordan. On June 12, His Airness led the Chicago Bulls to the team's first-ever championship title. Two days later, several hundred thousand Bulls superfans flowed into Grant Park to celebrate Jordan, Scottie Pippen, and coach Phil Jackson. The crowd was diverse, the fashion normcore: loose-fitting, basic, from the mall. Bulls merchandise was everywhere: on heads; on bodies; on feet sporting Air Jordans. Onstage at the Petrillo Music Shell, the Bulls' half-time dancers, the Luvabulls, bopped in sync to a hip-hop routine, tossing their manes of thick, curly, up-to-there hair.

John Rusk, Penny's second assistant director, had never seen a city go that crazy. The fandemonium rubbed off on Lori, who requested Jordan's jersey number, twenty-three, on her flared peach uniform.

Madonna was having none of it.

In a handwritten letter to fashion photographer Steven Meisel, she complained, "I cannot suffer any more than I have in the past month learning how to play baseball with a bunch of girls (yuk) in Chicago (double yuk).... I have a tan, I am dirty all day and I hardly ever wear make-up. Penny Marshall is Lavern [*sic*]—Geena Davis is a Barbie doll and when God decided where the beautiful men were going to live in the world, he did not choose Chicago. I have made a few friends but they are athletes, not actresses. I hate actresses, they have nothing on the house of extravaganza. I wish I could come to N.Y. and visit."

She told Meisel that she'd love "to do this book thing" with him. Off the set, she began planning their collaboration: *Sex*, a collection of erotic photographs for the coffee table spotlighting Madonna and friends in highly sexual poses.

If Madonna decided that she liked you, then you felt lucky, *chosen*. In rehearsals for the Suds Bucket dance sequence in which the Peaches cut loose, she didn't get to choose her partner, Eddie Mekka, who had played Carmine "The Big Ragoo" Ragusa on *Laverne & Shirley*. Penny hired Mekka, of whom Madonna disapproved. *He doesn't know how to partner*, she griped to Lou Conte, their scene's choreographer. *He's breaking my hands.*

She was a tough critic. She also told Conte: "Geena Davis is the most uncoordinated person I've seen in my life. I don't know how she's gonna do this."

At five feet, three inches tall, Eddie stood about an inch shorter than Madonna. He'd performed on Broadway, earning a 1975 Tony nomination for Best Actor in a Musical for his leading role in *The Lieutenant*. Good, steady gigs were hard to get after *Laverne & Shirley* went off the air; the work dried up. Penny, bless her, was giving him another life, but Madonna made him nervous. She much preferred the gifted Tony Savino, who led a jitterbug workshop for extras at the movie's Prairie Street offices. When the principal cast arrived without advance warning, Savino found himself teaching dance steps to Geena and Rosie and, *holy shit: Madonna*. She disappeared behind a column, then reemerged, barking, "WHO'S IN CHARGE HERE?"

The room went silent. Nobody moved. Karen Frankel Jones, an original member of Chicago's elite Hubbard Street Dance Company, pointed a finger at Savino. "He is," she said.

Savino had jitterbugged his whole life. The jazz dancer came up through the disco era, winning lots of money in dance contests and appearing on *Dance Fever* in 1980. Based in the Midwestern metropolis, he performed in musicals, commercials, and *Ferris Bueller's Day Off*. He was confident and Italian-American, just like *her*. He grabbed Madonna by the hand, and they moved in rhythm. At one point, he stepped over her legs and spun her around, a nifty move they would later recreate on camera. "You're very brave," she told Savino.

Conte, who founded Hubbard Street in 1977, wasn't crazy about what they were doing. But he thought they looked natural together. When he informed Penny that Madonna would rather partner with Savino, she responded, "No. Eddie has a little part called Guy in Bar. They make out after the number. If you want to put this other guy in [the jitterbug], that's fine, but we have to focus on Eddie."

Conte forged a compromise: Mekka would start off dancing with Madonna, then grab Rosie for a spin while Madonna and Savino took the floor. At the end of the night, Mae would canoodle with Guy in Bar, to whom Penny remained loyal.

Madonna and Savino started hanging out. She invited him to a birthday dinner for her assistant, Melissa Crow, at the Rosebud, an Italian restaurant on Taylor Street. He sat next to Madonna and Shep Pettibone, who produced her hit songs "Vogue" and "Express Yourself." When Madonna excused herself to go to the restroom, it seemed that all the surrounding women diners followed her inside: that annoyed her. Melissa, an unpretentious sweetheart, opened gifts from Tiffany, and they headed to their next stop, the Baton, a nightclub north of Wrigleyville where drag queens performed. Savino knew the Baton's owner and alerted him that Madonna and her entourage were on the way there. Rosie, Madonna's newest wing-woman, and Coach Hughes, whom she teased for being "boring," were along for the ride. As they took their seats on the upper level, the show began: Mimi Marks, a legend in her own right, started to perform "Vogue," dressed as Madonna. Hughes advised the real Madonna to tip her.

Mo looked at Savino. "Do you have dollars I can tip?" she asked.

*Are you kidding me?* Savino thought. *You're the richest woman in the world and you're hitting me up for money?*

"I'll pay you back," she said as he handed her about $10 in cash. She walked down the stairs and toward the stage and tipped Mimi, who cried, "Oh, my god!" When Madonna returned to her seat, the audience glimpsed her heart-shaped face and screamed.

*What is my life at this second?* Savino wondered. *This is unbelievable.*

The lovely Ann Cusack, whom the girls affectionately called "Annie Cue," brought her famous younger brother, actor John Cusack, to the Baton. The Cusacks hailed from Evanston, home to Northwestern University, on the city's North Side.

"He showed up and he was, like, sitting with Madonna and hitting on her," Savino recalls. "I'm, like, *dude, really? This is not gonna happen.*"

Another night, on July 7, Madonna wanted to go dancing—for fun, not work. She asked Savino to pick her up at the Zebra Lounge, a retro piano bar in the upscale Gold Coast neighborhood. Tracy was celebrating her twenty-seventh birthday there. Savino went inside and extracted Madonna and a sexy companion, who was very likely the model Tony Ward, having appeared in her racy music video for "Justify My Love." Earlier that year, *People* magazine reported that she and Ward, her boyfriend since 1990, had called it quits. Whatever their relationship status, "He was stunning," Savino says.

The three piled into Savino's Toyota Tercel.

"You need to get a car with stronger air-conditioning," she said.

He drove them to a Black gay bar on Halsted Street, but when they arrived around 8 p.m., the place was empty. It was still early. Madonna and Savino freestyled on the dance floor; he cringed as the DJ started to spin "Vogue" in too-obvious homage. Her fellow actresses left the Zebra Lounge and followed them there, taking over the bar. Later, Savino drove Madonna back to her hotel, the Four Seasons, where Penny also stayed along with Geena, Tom, and Jon Lovitz, who used the code name "Edna

Poopaleedoop." Mo (who used "Louise Oriole") wanted a frozen yogurt, so Savino made a pit stop at a yogurt shop on busy Rush Street. While people recognized her, she wasn't mobbed. Chicago knew when to leave a diva in peace.

THE CAMERA DEPARTMENT OCCUPIED A HOTEL A FEW BLOCKS NORTH OF THE Four Seasons. One night late in pre-production, Penny's cinematographer, Miroslav Ondricek, had a sudden epiphany: he would film *A League of Their Own* in 35 mm using an anamorphic lens, a widescreen format that required new, expensive equipment—the right cameras and magazines to hold the film stock, not to mention heavier lenses. With the changes, Steadicam operator Craig DiBona would have eighty-five pounds of gear attached to his body.

Ondricek was from the Czech Republic; he loved soccer and hockey but understood nothing about baseball. "It's like an American picnic," he once observed. He rode film's Czech New Wave during the 1960s, beginning a long collaboration with director Milos Forman that included American productions such as *Hair*, *Ragtime*, and *Amadeus*. Penny loved Ondricek and hired him on *Awakenings*. Unlike Barry Sonnenfeld on *Big*, he accepted Penny and her visual taste: up close and personal, story before style. The fifty-six-year-old had a gray goatee and a thicket of gray hair atop his head. He walked with a cane from an accident earlier in his career. It was an extension of his personality, and he used the instrument as a long arm, pointing at things and unintentionally bruising crew members. When he was happy, he tapped his cane; when he was upset, he'd rap someone's ankle.

"I could look in his eyes and know exactly what he thought, and if he didn't like a shot he walked in front of the camera," Penny said. "But his thick accent was impenetrable. I couldn't understand a single word he said. Milos said he couldn't either—and he was Czech."

During Ondricek's anamorphic flash of insight, he summoned Gary Muller, his first assistant cameraman, to his hotel suite in the middle of the night. Ondricek wore a big, white robe and sat next to a stack of baseball books. He showed Muller a photograph that squeezed a pitcher, batter, and catcher into one frame, and said he wanted to recreate that effect.

"Mirek," Muller said, using the abbreviation for Miroslav. "We're shooting in two weeks. When are we gonna get these lenses?"

"Oh, you go back to New York," he said.

Ondricek directed Muller to relay the message to Penny and her production managers. He was too afraid to do it himself.

The next morning, Muller stepped into the producers' hub, greeting Greenhut, Abbott, Joe Hartwick, and Tim Bourne.

"I gotta talk to you guys," he said.

Their immediate response? Teasing but not: *What's the matter? We're paying you enough money. You want more money already?*

"This is nothing about money," he said.

He showed Ondricek's baseball book to Greenhut, who tossed it across the room.

"What, are you nuts?" Greenhut said.

"Don't kill the messenger," Muller said. "It's from Ondricek."

"Where is he?"

"He's in a hotel, hiding."

Then Penny walked in.

"What's going on here?" she asked.

Muller explained the situation.

"OK," she said. "You go back to New York, and you get what he wants."

The producers notified Columbia of the switch, which added at least a million dollars to the budget. The charges went up and up, but the picture looked better.

By early July, the studio was on Penny's case to start filming—time was money, and every minute lost would cost them. On the Fourth, she threw a party at the old Comiskey Park, the White Sox's historic South Side dominion. A private stadium celebration came with conditions: since Columbia was paying, Team Penny had to film *something* to warrant the expense. They shot the girls catching fly balls and turned off the cameras for a cast and crew softball game.

On the morning of the tenth, the circus moved to St. James Lutheran Church in Lincoln Park for the first official day of principal photography. The scene: Marla's wedding to her beau, Nelson, played by Alan Wilder, a local actor from the prestigious Steppenwolf Theatre Company. In the movies, scenes are often filmed out of order, and so Penny began not at the beginning but in the middle of the script. Megan and Alan stood on the church steps as their real spouses observed the action across the street. The day was surreal.

"Madonna. Geena Davis. All these people are my bridesmaids?" Megan thought, feeling nervous. "How crazy is this?"

Another bridesmaid: Robin Knight, an athlete with a wide smile and dimples in her cheeks. Robin tried out for *A League of Their Own* in LA but didn't crack the Peaches' core lineup. She flew to Chicago anyway and talked her way onto the team, bunking with a different actress every night until the producers finally paid for her to have a hotel room. "How do you say no to that kind of effort?" said Penny, who made Robin a background Peach, one with her own name: Beans Babbitt. ("Beans" because Robin couldn't sit still.)

Outside St. James, Penny approached Robin, concerned that she wasn't filling out the bosom of her blue dress. "Could we get some more stuffing for Robin?" she shouted into the street. That was Penny: no filter, getting the job done.

Later, inside the church, Penny pivoted to the scene where Mae walks out of confession, leaving the priest hot and bothered. Between takes, Tom walked toward the altar and genuflected, making the sign of the cross. "Please forgive me for *Joe Versus the Volcano*," he said. Everyone cracked up laughing. "Please, god, make this movie a hit."

The next couple days, the Peaches got dolled up for charm school at the South Shore Cultural Center. "Gracefully and grandly," intoned actress Ellie Weingardt, channeling Helena Rubinstein, as they glided in unison across the floor. "Sip and *down*," she sing-songed during a teatime tutorial, and when modeling the proper way to sit on a chair, she cautioned, "Legs always together. A lady reveals nothing." Lori, like the All-Americans of yore, could hardly keep a straight face; Penny used her genuine laughter in the final cut.

When Weingardt lined up the girls, assessing their appearances, she grimaced at the sight of Megan, who resembled a deer in headlights.

"What do you suggest?" she asked the actress playing her assistant.

"A lot of night games," the assistant replied.

The joke would not age well. Neither would the icky treatment of Marla Hooch as a visual gag: Go ahead and call me humorless, but what's so hilarious about mocking a person's looks? Dehumanizing an adorable character? Do better, writers! Don't sink that low, Penny! And yet, in the early 1990s, such crude jokes were blindly accepted in popular comedies. If you rewound back fifty years, you could imagine the league's male masterminds smiling in agreement: *night games. Ha. Good plan.*

"You know, you really are a good-lookin' girl," a guilty Lovitz told Megan. "You're really not ugly!"

"Jon, I don't care," she said. "I'm laughin' all the way to the bank."

Penny gave her actresses ample space to be really funny. To riff and see what stuck. Megan would put spit in her hair and do everything she could to look her worst. Penny kept rolling as Weingardt flitted away from Megan, who squirmed and popped her large saucer eyes, her expression communicating, "Can I go now?" Like a comic seamstress, she buttoned the scene.

"I don't call 'cut' because you never know what's gonna happen," Penny argued. "And I need the ends of scenes. People will call 'cut' on the period of a sentence. It's stupid."

In the row of Peaches, you see Weingardt judging Tracy ("The hair: soften and shorten") and Renée ("The eyebrows: thin and separate, there should be two"), then giving no criticism to Téa Leoni, whom Penny cast as a Racine Belle, or Geena, Lori, and Freddie. The absent Madonna and Bitty Schram were meant to appear in the vignette as objects of the etiquette instructor's ire, not specimens who met with her approval. Bitty wanted to have a black tooth, "and so she put some black stuff on her tooth," Freddie says. However, Madonna copied Bitty, stealing her bit, which meant Bitty couldn't do it. The bit-stealing was a pattern for Madonna: if she liked someone's idea in rehearsal, she would often take that idea for herself.

When Freddie went to retrieve props that she had selected for the scene, the prop man told her that Madonna took them.

"What? And you let her?"

"Well, it is Madonna," he said.

*OK, I see how it is,* she thought. "We had a shoot, and I got a lot of attention, and she didn't because, of course, they were making them all look as bad as possible. And she couldn't stand that moment."

Freddie and Madonna had struck a lopsided friendship. At one point, Madonna sent Freddie a bunch of clothes because she said she "dressed like white trash." But it wasn't until the props incident that Freddie began to distance herself.

One-on-one, Madonna could be sweet and caring, but at charm school, a group setting, she was *Madonna,* the star who did what she wanted. She messed with Mollie Mallinger, Ondricek's lone female camera assistant. As Mollie crawled on the filthy floor, moving the actress's marks, Madonna refused to step off hers so that Mollie could move it.

"Excuse me," she said, looking up at Madonna. "Could you please step off your mark?"

Madonna slammed her foot down on the mark, grinding into it.

Mollie wasn't about to beg. *Fine,* she thought. *I'll leave it and you'll be out of focus.*

The day *Point Break* opened, on July 12, a contingent organized an outing to support Lori and see the movie in the theater; afterward, they played Truth or Dare. Among the participants: David Strathairn, the handsome and fun actor whom Penny chose to play Ira Lowenstein, a suit based on Arthur Meyerhoff, who took over the league from Wrigley back in the day. (Penny wanted Christopher Walken for Wrigley stand-in Walter Harvey, but he was too pricey. She cast Garry instead. "My brother's cheaper," she explained.) Penny had a crush on Strathairn, who was no stranger to baseball movies, having played real-life pitcher Eddie Cicotte in John Sayles's sepia-toned indie drama *Eight Men Out.* A bit of a hippie, Strathairn preferred to sleep in his trailer rather than a hotel. He went to jazz clubs. He could really *hang,* even more so than Tom Hanks. For weeks he had no clue that Tracy was Penny's daughter. One day, he approached her to compliment her great attitude on set, and how she got along with everybody. "Oh my god," she said. "You don't know Penny's my mom."

Bobby D. happened to be in Chicago doing research for his role in the gangster comedy *Mad Dog and Glory.* He was staying at the Drake Hotel on Lake Michigan. "Tracy got involved with his personal trainer, Dan, who she knew from *Awakenings,*" Penny recalled. "Bobby corralled me into going to crime scenes with him. He knew the cops would talk to me while he wandered around and observed. After a couple of field trips, though, I told him that I couldn't go with him every time a body turned up."

Sixty miles northwest of downtown, in the small village of Union, the Illinois Railway Museum provided the antique Zephyr train that transported Dottie and Kit from Oregon to the Land of Lincoln. Penny's masseuse and part-time driver, Gary Tacon, played the attendant helping the sisters aboard. While filming a scene inside cramped quarters, Lovitz's asthma ignited as the train suddenly caught fire—there were no flames, just a lot of black electrical smoke, and it filled his lungs. He couldn't breathe. They stopped the shoot, and Lovitz threw up outside. Once the fire was put out, the company loaded back into the Zephyr and finished what they started.

The next day, Megan used up all her tears while filming Marla's emotional farewell to her father, Dave (the wonderful Eddie Jones), at the East Union Depot. Penny handed Megan ammonia tablets to make her eyes water, advising her to "pop them." The tactic worked. "She was an actor's director," Megan says.

On the second week of shooting, all hell broke loose. The location: the Robert R. McCormick House, a Colonial Revival mansion in the western suburb of Wheaton that once belonged to the publisher of the *Chicago Tribune*. The grounds surrounding the home were lush and green, like something out of *Pride and Prejudice*. But this was not Mr. Darcy's Pemberley estate; it was the property of Mr. Harvey, who summons the down-and-out Jimmy Dugan in a successful effort to sell him on managing the Peaches. Against the old-money backdrop, Garry and Tom walked and talked and delivered one of Ganz and Mandel's funniest bits from their script:

> Harvey pushes a button and doors slide out revealing a bar with a bartender in uniform. Jimmy is amazed. The sight of this makes him thirsty.
>
> **HARVEY:** This is Pee-Wee. He's a big fan of yours, Jimmy. You were his favorite player.
> **JIMMY:** Oh, thank you, uh . . . Pee-Wee.
> **PEE-WEE:** Get you something, Mr. Dugan?
> **JIMMY:** (tempted) Uh, no thanks.

**HARVEY:** Pee-Wee and I are old friends. We came out from New York together when we had nothing. I was supposed to work for him. Life.

**Harvey pushes a button and the doors slide closed.**

In the end, Penny dropped the wacky bit on the cutting-room floor. It felt closer to a Monty Python sketch than one of her films.

When the time came to film inside Harvey's conference room, where the Candy Bar King pitches business associates on his newfangled girls' baseball scheme, it was getting late. Tom had gone home, and Garry remained on standby as technicians installed a large, wooden lighting grid above the long table around which actors were to sit. The grid seemed to cover the entire space, stretching about eighteen feet wide and twenty-five feet in length. At 9:05 p.m., the wood made a loud cracking sound, buckling under the weight of the hot lights. The structure crashed down on the crew, striking Greenhut in the head and Ondricek in the ribs. At least fifteen ambulances showed up. Greenhut and a gaffer, Peter Donoghue, were taken to DuPage Hospital, treated, and released. Greenhut wore a neck brace for several days. An on-site first-aid nurse treated Ondricek, Tim Bourne, and camera assistant Eddie Effrein for minor injuries.

"That was the ugliest, *ugliest* accident I've ever seen in forty-four years on a movie set," says Billy Kerwick, the best boy grip on *A League of Their Own*, who got hit on the shoulder but wasn't hurt. The sconces that lined the walls stopped the grid from falling flat on the floor and potentially causing more destruction. The mansion's wallpaper, imported from China in the 1920s, was destroyed. "I'm surprised they let us back into the place because there was a lot of damage," Kerwick adds.

Penny jumped right into the shipwreck, handling debris. Kerwick and his comrades spoke of her valor during the van ride back to the hotel, where they decompressed over lots of beer. "She didn't run," he says. "She could have just walked away, like, 'You stupid assholes,' whatever. But she was right in there with us, helping us clean out the mess."

Out on the porch, Garry ate a sandwich while chatting with John Rusk, the second AD. Both men managed to dodge the calamity. The production designer, Bill Groom, tried rescuing the most notable nonhuman victim:

the wallpaper. He flew in museum-caliber art restorers from New York to fix it; they wore magnifying glasses on their heads. Several days later, the circus returned to the disaster zone and filmed the business meeting as if nothing had happened.

Next, they took over FitzGerald's, a watering hole in suburban Chicago whose interiors passed for the Suds Bucket saloon. Fans gathered behind barricades, watching the cast trickle inside. Megan, who grew up nearby, spotted a former high school classmate named Barb, who shouted her name. "I am 'hometown girl does good,'" she thought. Outside, temperatures reached one hundred degrees; inside, the crew turned off the air-conditioning because it made too much noise. Actresses huddled around a large studio fan blowing cold air in the back of the sweaty bar. With all the bodies and equipment packed indoors, it was hotter than Hades. Penny sat in the director's chair as her masseuse worked her neck and shoulders. Filmmaking was a slog; the sixteen-hour days made her muscles ache.

"First of all, I'm jealous that you're getting a massage by that hot guy," Tony Savino recalls thinking. On second thought, "it's kind of excessive," he felt. To Savino, they looked like a couple at a party.

Originally, Geena was supposed to participate in the swing dancing, but given her lack of experience, she sat out the choreographed performance. Instead, Dottie busts up the revelry to warn the girls—who broke curfew after Mae poisoned their chaperone—that Lowenstein is on his way. "He catches us and we're outta the league," she says.

Unlike Mae, Dottie would *never* resort to such twisted pranks.

Unlike Dottie, Geena possessed an impish side. She took Oreos from the craft services table and replaced the cookies' frosting with mayonnaise. Then she walked around FitzGerald's, offering the tainted treats to her unsuspecting victims. Joey Slotnick, who played one of Doris's groupies, bit into one and made a face.

Lori out-pranked Geena when she tricked Madonna into making out with Eddie Mekka for hours, for no reason.

"So Madonna really wants to do great," Lori says. "She's really, really into it and she's really wanting to be professional and she wants to do it well. And she's very sincere." As she and Eddie flirted, "the camera's pointed toward her," Lori remembers. "Then they turn the camera around on me, and she goes, 'So Lori, so the camera's on you. So, like, what do you want me to do?' And just because I'm an asshole, I said, 'Well, Madonna, you have to do what you did on your side of the camera. You have to make out with him all the time.' So I made her make out with him for, like, another hour and a half."

The jitterbug went smoothly otherwise. "We're shooting into it," Penny explained to Lou Conte as they watched the monitors with Elliot Abbott. For a take involving a handheld camera, "Penny was holding on to the cameraman as he's twirling around, and I was holding on to her," says Conte, who ensured the footwork was on point.

As Savino pulled Madonna through his legs and gave her a twirl, she flashed the white bicycle shorts she wore underneath her black vintage Hawaiian-print dress.

"Tell her to keep her legs together," Abbott told Conte, who passed the message to Madonna.

"Story of my life," she quipped.

Team Penny shot a series of scenes that she never used: in one, a cute guy (Stephen Mailer, son of Norman Mailer) hits on Kit and dares her to try to strike him out, removing his shirt for the occasion. Before she wins the dare, Jimmy shows up and tries to talk her out of it. "Maybe this is a decision you should make with a few less beers in you," he tells Kit, his tone mildly condescending. "Or maybe not."

In another deleted scene, a tipsy Marla accidentally yanks off Dottie's overcoat, revealing her nightgown underneath. Jimmy ogles Dottie the hottie and clocks Lowenstein over the head with a whiskey bottle, knocking him unconscious. Dottie is shocked, and rightfully so. The gag, a misguided effort to protect the Peaches from getting in trouble, did nothing to advance Jimmy's progression into a responsible adult. In post-production, Penny excised Tom and Strathairn from the Suds Bucket.

She allowed Alan Wilder to stay.

Megan had spoken highly of Alan to Ellen Lewis. Out of all the actors up for Nelson, including Alan's Steppenwolf cohort Tracy Letts, only he displayed warmth. He'd walk Marla to her doorstep and kiss her hand and cheek if she let him.

"He maybe thought of himself as not that attractive," Alan says of Nelson. "And then when someone seemed to be gaga about him," his confidence blossomed. It was love at first sight—for Marla too. "She saw his sweetness," says Megan, who spent two days serenading Alan with "It Had to Be You," the jazz standard also used in *When Harry Met Sally* and *Annie Hall*. She hunched her shoulders, as Penny instructed, and wore a little microphone in her ear so she could hear the music that accompanied her off-key singing. Onstage, she unleashed Marla's dormant vamp: gone was the clueless naïf. In her place crooned a woman in lust, belting her heart out to a man who made cheese. It wasn't just bad karaoke; it was character-driven comedy on the level of *Saturday Night Live*, but with heart and soul.

"I'm singing to Nelson," she protests as Dottie tries to pull her away. "Ain't I, baby?"

"You sure are," he replies, swooning.

When the circus wrapped the Suds Bucket, having gotten everything it needed, a background saxophonist was flirting with Lori.

"You wanna go to a gig with me?" he asked.

"Hell yeah," said Lori, who didn't have to work the next day.

"It's a private gig," he said.

"Great."

The saxophonist took her to an office building that had a stage area. That night, he was backing up none other than Aretha Franklin. They sat with Aretha and the rest of her band in a teeny-tiny dressing room before the concert.

A man walked into the room to fetch the Queen of Soul, who was eating fried chicken. "You ready, Ms. Franklin?"

"Where's my money?" she asked.

"Oh, I'm sorry," he said, handing her a check.

"No," she said. "I told you that I want my money in cash."

The man was flummoxed. "Where am I gonna get however-many thousands of dollars?" Lori quotes him as saying.

"Well, that's not my problem now, is it?" the singer answered.

They waited until the wee hours of the morning. Finally, the man returned, proffering a paper bag filled with cash. Aretha went out there and gave it all she had.

Afterward, Lori hopped in a taxi as the sun came up. *I really like this acting thing*, she thought. *I really do.*

◇◇◇

On July 29, Wrigley Field opened its gates to Penny and her caravan.

The Cubs were away that week, playing the Cincinnati Reds and the New York Mets. The Major League Baseball season was becoming more dramatic than anything Hollywood filmed at the ivied ballpark. At a July 23 home game, umpire Joe West benched Andre Dawson after the outfielder argued a strike-three call, and Dawson, stewing inside the dugout, lost his cool, hurling seventeen bats onto the field. The crowd went wild and dumped cups of beer and pop from the bleachers. It took a while to clear the detritus, and when the game resumed, the Cubs wound up defeating the Reds, eight to five.

To make 1991 look like 1943, Bill Groom and some one hundred others worked overnight to cover Wrigley's skyboxes with canvas so that the modern structures receded into the background on film. Retro billboards were also installed in the back of the stadium.

"They hated the fact that we were on the grass," Abbott says of the Cubs' front office. "The grass at Wrigley is sacred."

The franchise set strict ground rules: cast members and cameramen could walk on the field, but everyone else had to stay off. Plastic mats were to be placed underneath equipment. Dolly shots—in which the camera rolls along a track, ensuring smooth, fluid movements—were forbidden.

"I mean, you got a major league team," Craig DiBona, one of *League*'s two union camera operators, says in defense. "If you destroy the infield, and the ball bounces all over the place, when a guy hits a ground ball, that'll totally screw him."

Miroslav Ondricek's limited baseball knowledge had concerned Abbott, who phoned Michael Nathanson at Columbia, explaining, "When we say to him, 'Go to first base,' he doesn't know what base that means." Nathanson called in reinforcements: his father, Ted, who filmed MLB games for NBC Sports, spent about a month in Chicago giving the DP the play-by-play. "He just didn't know what to do," Nathanson says of Ondricek, "so he was willing to do whatever he could to get it right."

For the Harvey Stadium scenes at Wrigley, the backdrop of the women's baseball tryouts, Penny recruited dozens of regional women to fill up the diamond, sporting dusty pants and jerseys and coveralls. Some recruits partook in a scene or two. Others stuck around, joining *A League of Their Own* for the long haul. Besides Robin "Beans" Knight, Penny added several new faces to the Peaches' roster, including Neezer Tarleton, the LA stuntwoman who intimidated Helen Hunt in the Dedeaux trials; Patti Pelton, an actress, athlete, and social butterfly who lived within walking distance of Wrigley; and Kelli Simpkins, Connie Pounds-Taylor, and Sharon Szmidt of Indiana and Kentucky, each of whom Penny picked because they were tall. She could place them near Geena so that Geena would not appear to tower over everyone.

After a mid-June trial in Evansville, Connie was originally chosen to play outfield for the Racine Belles, a team composed of some twenty-five women, notably the actresses Téa Leoni and Janet Jones, whose claim to fame was her public role as the wife of hockey great Wayne Gretzky. In Chicago, Penny sized up the lanky twenty-seven-year-old nonprofit worker and traded Connie to the Peaches, for whom she warmed the bench.

"I had a baseball mentality," Connie said. "My first response was: 'I don't sit the bench.' I was on the bench most of the time—it hurt my soul because I couldn't play ball."

That said, positioned next to Geena, Connie (player name: Connie Calhoun) was in a prime position to be seen in the movie—you can spot her behind Geena in the locker room, on the bus while Dottie talks to Jimmy, and on the field during the "No Crying in Baseball" scene. The actresses' body doubles, by contrast, mostly disappeared into the scenery. (Penny called them her "fakes.") While the crew set up the shot, a double stood upon her actress-doppelganger's mark, and when the camera rolled, she sometimes performed her stunts or filled out the opposing teams, throwing on uniforms for the Kenosha Comets and South Bend Blue Sox. On *A League of Their Own*, the doubles were among the movie's young ringers—the girls from primarily Midwestern cities, towns, and rural pastures who were aces on the diamond. While many played softball, Anne Ramsay's double, the talented twenty-year-old Julie Croteau, had defied the long-standing pattern that divided school-age girls and boys into separate camps, softball and baseball, with coaches enforcing an accepted conviction among adults: That girls were physically inferior to boys, and therefore unable to keep up with them. That it was shameful and emasculating to even include girls who bested the boys. Who didn't "throw like a girl"—an offensive phrase to this day—because they had spent their formative years practicing technique.

"For young boys it is culturally acceptable and politically correct to develop these skills," Linda Wells, longtime coach of the Arizona State softball team, told *The Atlantic* in 1996. "They are mentored and networked. Usually girls are not coached at all, or are coached by Mom—or if it's by Dad, he may not be much of an athlete. Girls are often stuck with the bottom of the male talent pool as examples. I would argue that rather than learning to 'throw like a girl,' they learn to throw like poor male athletes. I say that a bad throw is 'throwing like an old man.' This is not gender, it's acculturation."

When she was seventeen, Croteau and her parents filed a sex discrimination lawsuit against her high school in Manassas, Virginia, accusing the varsity baseball coach of violating Title IX and cutting Croteau from the team because she was a girl. In school, Croteau, who grew up playing tee-ball and Little League, made the junior varsity squad but didn't get much playing time—that coach replaced her on first base with a boy teammate she had defeated for the position. She was bumped to second string. She believed that he'd been embarrassed by her presence. As the 1988 suit made headlines, she refuted the adults who told her to play softball like the other girls, even though she loved baseball the most.

"Softball is an entirely different game," she told the *Washington Post* at the time. "In baseball, the ball is harder and you learn to catch it because if you don't, it hurts."

Croteau lost her case. She felt that with prejudiced eyes, her coaches had seen her as lesser than, and the boys as faster and more skilled. Classmates gave her the cold shoulder. She'd stood up for herself and they resented her for it. Did the court's verdict dampen her love for baseball? Not a bit. If anything, it strengthened her resolve to keep going, through the peaks and valleys and loneliness of being the first woman to regularly play men's NCAA baseball as an undergraduate at St. Mary's College of Maryland, where she batted .222 her first season. The philosophy major, who hit .171 in seventy-six at bats with the Seahawks, quit the team her junior year due to sexual harassment from teammates and the athletic department. In June 1991, she publicly detailed a toxic environment that included a teammate telling her she did not belong, opposing pitchers throwing at her, and a bus trip in which her fellow players read aloud a *Penthouse* magazine article that described women's body parts. Baseball had stopped being fun for her; rather, it triggered pain. After hanging up her uniform, Croteau left St. Mary's with plans to transfer elsewhere and sent an audition tape to Columbia Pictures, which contacted her out of the blue about *A League of Their Own*, a welcome jolt of hope and excitement.

*Would she be interested in playing ball on the big screen?* Yes, of course!

*Would she send over pictures of her legs?* Huh?

Soon, the odd request made sense: the filmmakers were matching Croteau and Ramsay's bodies. Both women were lefties and five feet, seven inches tall. It was a dream job for Croteau, who bore a passing facial resemblance to Ashley Judd (if Judd were a natural blonde). When she set foot on Wrigley Field, she felt lucky to be there. She also observed improper slides and other wrong moves, worrying the movie would turn women ballplayers into a joke. *Oh, no,* she thought. *This is gonna take us backward.* The spectacle recalled the late nineteenth century when entrepreneurial men hired female burlesque troupes to perform professional baseball for entertainment. The actresses barnstormed with bravado, behaving rebelliously in a macho sphere. With team names like the Blondes and the Brunettes, "They put on a show for fans—mimicking male players' mannerisms while adding their own feminine twists," author Debra Shattuck wrote in *Bloomer Girls: Women Baseball Pioneers*. "They 'kicked' at empires, stopped on the base paths to fix their hair, caught balls in their skirts, formed 'bucket brigades' to relay balls from the outfield, and even downed glasses of beer while seated on the bench during games."

The traveling performances offended polite society but titillated the working class in the years after the Civil War. Baseball as we know it derived from rounders, an English bat-and-ball game that had been played as far back as the reign of monarch Elizabeth I. Rounders was a hit with both men and women, boys and girls, and was sometimes called baseball. Jane Austen referenced the game in her 1817 coming-of-age novel *Northanger Abbey* while her teenage protagonist, Catherine Morland, reflects on preferring "cricket, base ball, riding on horseback, and running about the country at the age of fourteen, to books." By the mid-1800s, American women had launched intramural baseball at single-sex colleges such as Vassar and Wellesley, and toward the end of the century, played the sport professionally on teams that were women-only or blended women and men. In the 1880s, John Lang, a white barber from Pennsylvania, founded the Dolly

Vardens, two Black women's teams that donned short, showy, and colorful calico dresses. Together, they were "the first professional women's baseball team in the United States," Jennifer Ring reported in her book *Stolen Bases: Why American Girls Don't Play Baseball*. Lang, trying to capitalize on a growing appetite for "novelty" games, subjected the Black ballplayers to racist mockery and media coverage—his stunt lasted only one season.

Around the turn of the century, white athletes with authentic skill started to make headlines, notably pitchers Maud Nelson, who played for women's organized baseball teams including the Boston Bloomer Girls and the Chicago Stars, and Lizzie Arlington, the first woman to sign a contract with a men's minor league team. Arlington's successors, hurlers Alta Weiss and Jackie Mitchell and first baseman Elizabeth Murphy, competed in men's minor and semi-pro teams in the decades preceding World War II. Famously, Mitchell—brought on to the Chattanooga Lookouts as a publicity ploy—stunned spectators when she struck out Babe Ruth and Lou Gehrig during a 1931 exhibition game against the Yankees. But like the vaudeville Blondes and Brunettes, Mitchell and other real-deal trailblazers were treated as curiosities without a serious future in the profession. After Mitchell's feat on the mound, Commissioner of Baseball Kenesaw Mountain Landis voided her contract, declaring that "life in baseball [is] too strenuous for women."

Telling her story in the *LA Times* seventy years later, journalist Brian Cronin wrote, "Mitchell continued to play baseball as a barnstormer, but eventually grew sick [of] the circus-like atmosphere of the games (like having to play an inning while riding a donkey) and retired at the ancient age of 23 in 1937 and took an office job working for her father's company. She refused to un-retire when the All-American Girls Professional Baseball League was formed in 1943."

In Chicago in 1991, Lita Schmitt, Rosie's double, did not share Croteau's grave concerns about whether Hollywood was going to present the AAGPBL as a Big Top act. Schmitt had auditioned at Evansville's Harrison Baseball Field after reading in the newspaper that Penny was looking for female baseball or softball players under the age of twenty-eight. Schmitt, who worked in technology at a pharmaceutical company and grew up playing softball with her sister in their small Kentucky town, was patted down and judged a physical match for Rosie in terms of height, hair color, and calf muscles. Penny tapped Shelly Adlard, the first women's basketball player inducted into the University of Evansville's Athletic Hall of Fame, to double Lori, and Brenda Watson to double Madonna. The actresses adored Brenda, who radiated an endearing positive attitude and got the job after a girl from Madisonville, Kentucky, rejected it, complaining, "I don't want to be Madonna's double." A deal-breaker, apparently.

"I think she was religious, real religious," Schmitt recalls.

DeLisa Chinn-Tyler and another Black woman were the only players of color to try out for *A League of Their Own* in Evansville. DeLisa, a FedEx driver, had once been a star center fielder on the Evansville Express, the revered women's softball team that won tournaments throughout the area in the 1970s and '80s. Penny, standing by the fence with a clipboard, pulled DeLisa aside and explained that the AAGPBL had excluded Black players.

"Yes, I know," DeLisa said. "Well, I figured that I'm fair-complexioned enough. Maybe you could put makeup on me."

They both laughed. Penny told her that she conferred with Lisa Beasley, who led extras casting in Indiana, and wanted to write in a special non-speaking role for her. DeLisa remembers her saying that she'd earn $750 with royalties and her name in the credits.

Earlier in production, Lori Petty had urged Penny to acknowledge the league's racist history.

"Suddenly I feel uncomfortable about this: Black women weren't allowed to play in our league," she said. "We can't just pretend that's not true."

"You're right," Penny agreed.

Ganz and Mandel were always adding things. Why not that?

At Wrigley, Geena snapped right into character. She scribbled copious notes in the margins of her script, and yet she was loose on set, not seeming to overthink or over-rehearse or go all Daniel Day-Lewis. For her favorite scene, the one in which Dottie snatches Doris's hostile throw with her bare hand, Geena caught a ball made of foam material. From a short distance off-camera, the crew repeatedly threw it at her until Penny got the Money Shot, the one that makes you go, *Damn, she's a badass.*

Sam Hoffman, a production assistant in his twenties, subbed in for Geena in the catcher's position when her regular double, a stuntwoman, couldn't make a throw to second base.

"Let me try," Hoffman said.

"Go put the wig on," Penny told him. He did seven throws in a row from behind the plate, the camera aiming at his back.

Madonna, not to be outdone, dove on her stomach into a base, a tough stunt to pull off. It would, of course, be seen in the movie, but still Mo felt inconsequential, just like everyone else showing off.

"I used to be a star," she lamented to Penny. "You're making me an extra."

While Lori and others within the cast and crew never witnessed Madonna behave like a cliché prima donna, a term that spelled out her very name, at least one production assistant, Lew Baldwin, a college student from Texas, arched his eyebrow as she demanded Evian over ordinary water and took her time filming takes. Was she *that* much of a princess, or was she parodying quote-unquote *Madonna*, the artistic creation shaped from her blood, sweat, and DNA, or were perfectionism and stage fright causing diva-like delays? All the above, perhaps? With Madonna, the lines smudged like yesterday's eyeliner.

Penny, her equal in meticulousness, was busy gathering threads that showed the entertainer, and the women at large, being awesome. In her final edit of the sublime, electrifying tryout montage, which mimicked a brisk wartime newsreel, she overlaid disapproving narration from an anti-feminist radio hostess: "Careers and higher education are leading to the masculinization of women, with enormously dangerous consequences to the home, the children, and the country," she sneers. "When our boys come home from war, what kind of girls will they be coming home to?"

It's a sequence that makes you want to stand up and cheer—for the ballplayers rather than the spoilsport.

◇◇◇

TOM HANKS WASN'T SCHEDULED TO BE THERE, BUT HE SHOWED UP ANYWAY TO revel in the ballpark's nostalgic glory and hit some bucket-list balls with his thirteen-year-old son, Colin, and Lovitz.

"What are you doing here?" Abbott asked him.

"What? Are you kidding?" he said. "Throwing the ball on the grass at Wrigley Field."

Tom had a solid grip on Jimmy from the get-go, but Baldwin, who assisted the camera department, sensed Lori's struggle to find her footing and her character amid all the commotion. She was receiving a lot of notes from Penny and the producers. In Lori's recollection, she ran around like a little puppy with "all the energy on the planet," too preoccupied to soak in her rarefied surroundings.

Tom and Lori played catch during one of her breaks.

"Petty," he said.

"What?" she said.

"You know when people say, 'Remember when? Wasn't it cool when . . . ?'"

"Yeah."

"This is *that day*. Right now. It's not always going to be like this. This isn't always how it is. You're gonna remember this."

For Megan, Wrigley was also a heightened experience. She brought her father to the set, and they sat in the dugout; she watched him revert into a giddy little kid.

"None of my sons made it into the major leagues, but my daughter did," he said later.

In early August, days after the circus had moved on, the Cubs played the Mets at home. The teams complained that balls were taking weird hops on the grass. They blamed *A League of Their Own* and the metal spikes on the women's cleats for ruining the grounds—even more evidence that there *was* crying in baseball. The tears would trickle down to the Ohio River Valley.

## *Seventh Inning*

# INDIANA

GLORIA MALLAH PULLED UP TO A RAMSHACKLE WHITE FARMHOUSE IN Saint Philip, a sleepy community nine miles west of Evansville. Without a cooling Great Lake breeze, the landlocked cornfields and dusty backroads that flanked the American Gothic abode and its companion barn baked in the sticky, late-summer heat, thermometers ticking toward ninety-five degrees for too many days. When Gloria set foot on the *A League of Their Own* base camp, wherein platoons of crew members busied themselves among gear-filled trucks, makeup trailers, and craft service tables, she came face-to-face with her new boss, Penny Marshall, who shook her hand and said, "Welcome to hell."

Penny's loyal personal assistant, Bonnie Hlinomaz, needed a break from working seven days a week, so Gloria, who previously assisted a prominent Indianapolis family, was hired as Bonnie's replacement on nights and weekends. Her friend in Indiana's film office, which aimed to attract Hollywood to the Hoosier State, recommended her for the job, and she picked up and moved downstate for three months. On that first day, Team Penny showed Gloria inside her boss's trailer.

"This is where we keep her sake," the tour guides said, opening a refrigerator.

Penny liked to sip the Japanese rice wine cold, and at the end of a long day on set, some alcohol might wind up in her cup. Adult beverages flowed within the work-hard, play-hard, after-hours culture of *A League of Their Own*. While prepping the movie on Prairie Street, Penny would open a bottle of Santa Margherita white wine and serve it to the crew. (Greenhut preferred Dewar's Scotch whisky.) She loved being around the men—they got things done, they gave her attention, and they knew how to have a good time. One late night, she drank sake with Bill Groom and "lost her Penny accent," speaking clearly about the craft of acting in a way that made the designer respect her on a deeper level, Groom says. It was the way that she spoke to Tracy and Carrie, when perhaps she could be Penny Marshall without amplifying "Penny Marshall," and leaning into self-parody as a defense mechanism. She wasn't a morning person and sometimes napped during pre-production, but once filming kicked off, a dutiful focus took over. Bonnie, who had long, blonde hair and "cool clothes," as one former production assistant observed with admiration, was good about getting Penny up and going and anticipating her needs. Penny loved doing jigsaw puzzles in her trailer during lighting setups to calm her mind. Bonnie would sort the pieces by color, making it easier for Penny to assemble a puzzle as people walked in and out, talking shop. Several years later, on *The Preacher's Wife*, Penny promoted Bonnie to associate producer, yet seemed to miss her thoughtful methods. She'd grab someone's walkie-talkie and put in a jigsaw request, saying, "Bonnie. Puzzle." On *A League of Their Own*, if she wanted to reach Greenhut, she'd look at Bonnie and say, simply, "Bobby." That meant: get the producer on the phone.

"Penny, what do you want? I'm going to craft services," says Tim Bourne, the unit production manager, while recreating a common scenario on set.

"I'll have a coffee. No, maybe tea. No, maybe both," he drones, impersonating her voice. He adds, "I mean, that's how she was. She just could not make up her mind."

Even on scorching days, fielding a gazillion questions, Penny seemed in her element. Bernadette Mazur, who headed the makeup department and worked on *Awakenings* and *Riding in Cars with Boys*, Penny's fraught final effort, recalls, "This was her favorite movie. This is where I saw her in the best head, the happiest."

She wore baseball caps, with her hair pulled back in a ponytail, and a headset around her neck. Her style was athleisure: T-shirts, tank tops, and basketball shorts, and what seemed like a different pair of sneakers every day. Sometimes she sported tube tops that exposed her shoulders, drawing a side-eye or two, but she could care less about decorum or looking like a quote-unquote "lady." She'd run around in a terry cloth tube top and a pair of shorts, demanding, "Get me another meat rocket!" That meant, "Get me a hot dog!" For breakfast, she'd eat a giant plate of bacon on the ballfield. ("You couldn't even believe that she could eat that much bacon," Sam Hoffman marvels.) She didn't adhere to a healthy, plant-based diet like Madonna, a vegetarian who told the movie's caterer that she refused to eat anything that "takes a shit." Penny liked junk food. Comfort food. Other people's food. If Bourne had a piece of chicken on his plate, Penny would grab it and eat the skin, the most delicious part. (Such was her comfort level with Bourne.) She buckled a fanny pack on her waist that contained cigarettes, a lighter, and cinnamon-flavored toothpicks, and when she finished shooting a scene, she folded the pages of her script in half, increasing the document's bulk. The folding gave her a sense of satisfaction, like checking items on a never-ending to-do list.

Into this colorful, frenzied environment, Gloria entered fresh. She had never worked on a movie before, and while she wasn't needed on set, she stuck around after touring Penny's trailer to watch Geena and Lori race each other outside the farmhouse belonging to the fictional Keller family. The scene at the top of *A League of Their Own* doubles down on Dottie's dominance and Kit's sense of inadequacy, illustrated earlier when Dottie swats a winning hit during a ballgame, effortlessly one-upping her sister, who ignores her advice to lay off the high ones. A verbal catfight ensues:

> KIT: I <u>like</u> the high ones!
> DOTTIE: Mule!
> KIT: Nag!

As Kit strikes out, Ernie Capadino cackles in the bleachers. Later, she and Dottie walk home through fields painted green to brighten up sunburnt crops, Kit venting to her number-one frenemy.

"Did you ever hear Dad introduce us to people?" Kit asks Dottie, the former's shoulder-length copper wig a bedhead mess compared with the latter's flawless mane, every soft curl in its place. "*This is our daughter, Dottie,*" she mimics, gesturing emphatically. "*This is our other daughter, Dottie's sister.*"

When Kit starts walking ahead of Dottie, then breaking into a sprint, Mr. Keller's favorite daughter cannot help but outrun her. An athlete through and through, she wants to win, never mind that she makes Kit feel even worse about herself.

In truth, Lori was faster than Geena, and it proved a challenge to slacken her pace on purpose. Weeks before, while Penny filmed the two running toward the Zephyr, Lori complained that Geena was too slow. The director instructed her to fake it and settle for second-best. "If you watch the scene," Penny remarked, "Lori's feet are going faster than she is moving forward."

As for Geena, the cameramen thought she ran like a duck, and rather than film her legs and feet, they tried framing her from the waist up.

Neither woman had ever milked a cow, so Mike Haley, the first assistant director, showed them how for the scene inside the barn, in which Capadino tries luring a reluctant Dottie to Chicago. During Lovitz's closeup, a bovine background extra dropped to the floor and began giving birth, unscripted. Lovitz, in the moment, didn't notice. He went forth, saying his dialogue.

"Cut!" Penny yelled.

"What?" he asked.

"Didn't you notice the cow behind you just fell over?"

"Oh," he said.

Penny paused filming. While onlookers delighted in watching Mother Nature do her thing, Hoffman looked on in disgust. "*Have you ever seen a placenta come out of a cow?*" he asks, the sight still haunting his memory. Yes, the unexpected delivery was a goopy mess, but the calf could not have been cuter: its owners named it Penny. As rain began to fall over the fields, the cast on call—as well as Tom, a welcome if unnecessary presence for scenes he wasn't in—entered the barn to take pictures with the adorable, gangly beast, who'd been cleaned up. Penny picked up her namesake and grinned.

Outside the barn, a second adult cow sabotaged Lovitz. The animal, making a sound ten times louder than any plane flying overhead, mooed behind him as he tried to get out his lines without success.

"Why are you stopping?" Penny asked.

"Because the cow," he complained.

"Well, then tell it to shut up," she said.

"All right, fine," he said, craning his head toward his nemesis and ad-libbing, "Will you shut up!"

Penny, rolling camera of course, kept the outtake in the movie. She also cleared room for the line he nailed while dropping Dottie and Kit at Harvey Field, announcing with a blasé affect, "Yeah, I'm just going home, grab a shower and a shave, give the wife a little pickle tickle and then I'm on my way."

It never failed to get a laugh. Hours after completing his duties one day, Lovitz remained in full costume inside his individual trailer, which Teamsters attached to a pickup truck, thinking its inhabitant had gone home. He popped his head out of the camper, making his presence known quickly before the truck hit the road with him in the back.

Hoffman, an affable talent wrangler promoted from PA to additional second AD amid the production, insists that it was "much harder to get Lovitz out of hair and makeup than any of the ladies." He teased the comedian, whom he found "so fucking funny," joking that he could stay in the makeup chair all day long but still not turn into a leading man. "Shut up, shut up!" Lovitz retorted.

Around dinnertime, base camp shut down for the night. Penny and some twenty-five crew members (never, ever actors) would later convene at *League*'s Evansville HQ to watch the dailies as a group. When digital video dethroned 35 mm film in the decades to follow, forever changing the way movies were made, the collective practice of viewing daily rushes inside a projection room disappeared. In the 2020s, a veteran set hairstylist reviews her handiwork alone on a computer screen or handheld device.

Flashing back to 1991: largely exhausted, Team Penny ate good food and drank wine while their leader yelled at the screen. The dailies would go on and on and *on*. Editor George Bowers and his assistant, Doron Shauly, logged ninety to one hundred hours each week splicing and dicing and perusing thousands of feet of film, sometimes sitting with Penny and Miroslav Ondricek at 2 and 3 a.m. Shauly had never worked for a filmmaker who showed dailies that late, yet the editors catered to her night-owl schedule, with Bowers always in a good mood. Penny adored Bowers, one of the few Black lead editors working in mainstream motion pictures. An insider-outsider like Penny, he hailed from the Bronx and crucially benefited from the support of mentors who found success within the industry. His mentor, the pioneering Black editor Hugh Robertson, helped lift Bowers up the ladder earlier in his career. He eventually edited movies such as *Sleeping with the Enemy*, *Shoot to Kill*, and *Harlem Nights*, and he was an associate producer on *Jumpin' Jack Flash*, later cutting Penny's *Renaissance Man* and *The Preacher's Wife*.

"He was so patient," Bourne says, recalling that "Penny drove him crazy because she liked options." She "was a great director for actors and a terrible director for us," he adds, and though she exasperated Bowers, Bourne remembers his "very sweet relationship with her. I mean, he would complain and bitch, as we all did. He'd roll his eyes, but he was into the story." Bowers, who died in 2012 of complications related to heart surgery, understood Penny's gooey marshmallow center, and turned up the emotional volume to a level that pleased her. At times, the raw footage moved viewers to tears. Garry's daughter, Kathleen Marshall, a PA, cried during the heart-wrenching takes of Ann Cusack's Shirley not knowing whether she made the league. (In addition to Kathleen, Penny also hired nieces Wendy and Penny Lee Hallin, her sister's daughters, as a PA and an apprentice editor, respectively.)

As one hour stretched into three, "You fake going to the bathroom or you slide off the couch and crawl out on your hands and knees," cameraman Gary Muller recalls. "It was so funny—a couple of times the lights would go on and there would only be, like, three people in the room." *How many times*, he mused, *can we watch Bitty Schram try to hit the ball?*

On occasion, Penny got tired and only lasted about forty-five minutes. Gloria, whom she called "Glor," would show up in a Volvo 740 and drive Penny to her rental home, fetching snacks and hanging out for a bit. On Sundays, Penny sat and chain-smoked near the pond in the backyard, where she did the crossword puzzles in the *New York Times* and the *Indianapolis Star* as well as Evansville's local newspaper. Penny relished collecting antiques, so Gloria accompanied her to the area's bountiful storefronts selling old treasures and curios. She was crazy about reverse-painted Tiffany lamps, owning hundreds of them, and gravitated toward rough-hewn tables, duck decoys, quilts, and hooked rugs. Once she bought a rug on which a woven deer smoked a cigarette—if an item induced smiles, she'd add it to her collection. (At her Hills haven, she stored birthday and Christmas presents within a room she christened "The Mall.") In Indiana, Penny's antique-hunting fervor rubbed off on Tom's wife, Rita, and Columbia's field executive, Amy Pascal, each of whom snapped up homespun blankets. While Penny collected gems ranging from priceless heirlooms to kitschy crafts, she drew the line when she shopped at a store in Petersburg, a small town where she had scouted filming locations with Bill Groom and Dennis Benatar. The owner sold American flags, which were dusty and dirty and thrown in a corner. Groom asked the man if he had any from the 1940s.

*I got something really special I can show you*, Benatar remembers him telling Groom. Then, Benatar says, "He goes behind the counter, and he pulls out two Nazi flags in pristine condition, in plastic bags. I thought Penny was going to run out of the place."

She looked at Groom and remarked, "Bill, I think it's time to go now."

Besides decorative objects and art, true-crime artifacts captivated Penny. One day, Gloria, packing drawers in her boss's bedroom, stumbled upon large photographs that measured around 8.5 by 11 inches and depicted grisly scenes from the Jeffrey Dahmer murders in Wisconsin. Apparently, Penny had ties within the Milwaukee Police Department, or knew people who knew people, and somebody mailed her the disturbing material. She kept her sleeping quarters dark and goosebump-cold, the room temperature seeming arctic, just the way she preferred. Says Gloria, "Looking through these black-and-white photos of things in the freezer and heads in the meat freezer, I mean: it was a trip."

"What is this place?"

So remarked Rosie O'Donnell as she gazed out the window of the chartered plane that flew the cast to Evansville. Down below, the flatlands unspooled in an endless patchwork quilt, rolling out greens and browns, forests and meadows, siloed farmsteads, and residential sprawl. If you lived there, or once did, then the land pulled your heartstrings, evoking the pastoral brushstrokes of a Van Gogh; it was in your blood. But if you surveyed it for the first time, you might as well have landed upon a different planet.

"Even though it's the third-largest city in Indiana, I think it felt for the coastal people very much like a sleepy town," Kelli Simpkins, who played Rockford Peach Beverly Dixon, an outfielder, says of Evansville, her hometown. It's "not a shape-shifting fashion center," she adds. "They went to a place that is incredibly Republican, incredibly conservative, incredibly heteronormative. I don't know that I would have said *that* at the time. Because I was from there, and I was inside of it."

In that era, the city had a Democratic mayor, Frank McDonald, who held office from 1987 to 2000. Its politics are a mix of blue and red, and the redness builds as the terrain becomes more rural, ultimately coloring the whole state. Evansville's location on the Ohio River, bordering Kentucky, had made it a rich manufacturing hub for automobiles, appliances, and construction equipment, and during World War II, its factories flourished. One factory built more than six thousand P-47 Thunderbolt fighter planes; another turned out "bullets by the billions." At a river-adjacent shipyard, Rosie the Riveters made up a sixth of the labor force—Uncle Sam needed the women, so much so that Indiana used government funds to set up day-care centers to accommodate working mothers.

While the city's west side retains a blue-collar reputation, the east side, characterized as more white-collar and suburban, is home to the University of Evansville, a private college with a respected theater program. Anitra Larae Donahue, who worked as a PA on *A League of Their Own* during her high school summer break, describes the dynamic way back when the population numbered 126,272: "You had the east side, which was kind of bougie, upper middle class. You had the west side, which is redneck, even though we're north of the border." There was "a mall and a half," Anitra says. "There was a twenty-four-hour Denny's, and the football rivalry was fantastic among people who cared." In the middle of the warring school factions sat magnificent Bosse Field, the third-oldest American ballpark still in regular use for professional baseball, ranking behind Fenway Park and Wrigley Field. The wide-brimmed stadium, a sea of photogenic, jungle-green bleacher seats, is partly surrounded by industrial buildings and single-family homes that evoke a John Mellencamp song, as does the

Hickory Pit Stop, a mom-and-pop barbecue joint across the street. Since 1995, Bosse has hosted the hometown baseball team, the Evansville Otters, a club within the independent Frontier League.

For a time, there was talk of building a brand-new facility that would attract luxury amenities, but "people like the old way of doing things, and so the ballpark prevailed," Jeff Lyons, the longtime meteorologist for the 14 News station, explains. Though Lyons could not care less about celebrities, their arrival in 1991 electrified the populace: before the internet exposed the mundane, hidden lives of the rich and famous, an aura of mystery hovered over movie stars, especially Madonna, the biggest sideshow at the circus. On a drizzly morning in May 2022, the Otters practiced among the ghosts of Tom Hanks, of Geena Davis, of Hollywood veterans, of virtual unknowns, of the girls who traveled from near and far for a taste of what it would be like to have a league of their own thirty years earlier.

"Everywhere we looked, everywhere we went, there were signs: 'Welcome, A League of Their Own,'" makeup artist Paul Gebbia says. "The bars: 'League of Their Own—Come in, Free Drinks.' We never felt this before in New York City, where there's a production on every other corner."

They felt so welcomed. Initially, there was some culture shock as the well-represented East Coast crew adjusted to their new backdrop. Gebbia and his coworkers in hair and makeup moved into temporary apartments along Green River Road, a main street lined with dozens of fast-food restaurants. During an outing to the supermarket, they convulsed in laughter when they saw an aisle devoted to corn dogs. He recalls, "We were like, 'Corn dogs: What the hell is that?'"

In a Chicago nightclub, *Sun-Times* columnist Bill Zwecker asked Tom whether he was excited to leave America's third-largest city. "Well, no," he answered. "I'm sure Evansville is a nice town, but it's certainly not going to have all the excitement Chicago has."

Once he arrived, Tom fully embraced a folksier way of life. He devoured Dairy Queen and pork ribs and lived with his family in a beautiful ranch-style home outside Evansville. Tom and Rita's rental rested on five acres and had a long driveway and a small pond where security guard Mike Duckworth, a Vanderburgh County sheriff's deputy, hooked a fish as a Town Car was taking Tom to set.

"Come here!" Duckworth yelled to Tom, who got out of the car and walked over. Duckworth handed him the rod and reel. ("You'd think that I had given the guy a million dollars," he remarks.)

"What do I do?" Tom, a novice fisherman, asked. Eventually, he reeled in a three-quarter-pound bass, declaring, "I wanna eat it!" He was "tickled to death," Duckworth says, after the guard cleaned the fish and delivered it to him.

Geena kept a lower profile in Indiana. She was dating Gavin de Becker, a prominent security expert who advised *A League of Their Own*, and she took his concerns seriously, even declining to share her address with a studio-approved chauffeur back in LA. But people talk, and people told the *Evansville Courier* that Geena's home away from home included a swimming pool built specifically for her. People, though, mostly left her alone. "I think it's my height," she joked to a fellow Peach.

Madonna temporarily moved into a single-story, white-picket-fenced refuge in McCutchanville, an affluent township north of Evansville that has rolling hills. There, she invited her costars and makeup artists to celebrate her August 16 birthday, for which she made Rice Krispies treats. There, she hosted a special visitor, rapper Vanilla Ice, whom she dated and later spotlighted in her scandalous *Sex* book. "We had fun everywhere we went, and we would go just the two of us," Ice (real name: Robert Van Winkle) told journalist Ethan Alter. "It's funny because we had disguises, so you'd never know it, but we were in public with everybody. We went shopping at the malls, we ate at Chili's and Waffle House. I had a mustache and this crazy wig and glasses, and we would go to the movies and stuff. People did notice us. I remember she didn't like to be noticed. And I didn't care. And she didn't like it that I didn't care. And if they asked her for an autograph, she would say no. And the same person would come to me, and I said, yes, no problem. And she would get so mad at me for that. So mad at me. She's like, 'How dare you undermine me.'"

While Madonna wanted to dine out in peace, Ice was happy to make a fan's day, advising his reluctant paramour: "Spit the food out. Get up and take that picture. Shake a hand and make a friend." (But was he aware that highly targeted women pop stars can't easily make friends in normal society? As it were, stranger danger lurked around every corner.) Madonna's dedicated staff, assistant Melissa Crow and a personal trainer, completed a minimal entourage, and one night, guard Mike Duckworth was assigned to monitor the house. Around 5 a.m., the trainer approached Duckworth's car and said, "You need to get her paper."

"I'm not her paperboy," he answered, refusing to leave his post and fetch the day's news at the mailbox located an eighth of a mile away. "You want her paper? You go get it."

A couple days later, on duty at Bosse Field, Duckworth received orders to retrieve Madonna from her trailer. As she opened the door, almost knocking him down, she snapped, "Fuck you."

If someone despised her, perhaps she could sense it. Perhaps she deployed cuss words as a shield to protect her privacy around strangers. But rather than say, "Leave me alone," she zinged unwholesome, four-letter words, like a no-bullshit New Yorker stuck in traffic. De Becker thought she needed a decoy to fake out fans and potential stalkers—in at least one instance, her double went undercover. In nearby Huntingburg, the site of *League*'s second stadium location, police caught a deranged man who ran around his house naked, brandishing a knife and threatening to kill Madonna. "What they ended up doing," says Dale Payne, Huntingburg's Parks and Recreation superintendent, "was just taking him to the mental hospital in Evansville. They didn't actually arrest him, and they just kept him there until the movie was over. Then they released him."

On the call sheet, Madonna was M. Smith and Geena was G. Smith. Tom never changed his name, though he did have to hire guards to keep unsolicited autograph hounds from ringing his doorbell. One guy made an unexpected visit, driving thirty people on a hayride up to the front door. He was a bit offended when Tom declined to ride along. Setting boundaries fostered some resentment. "Every now and then," Tom said, "people would drive by and flip us the bird."

The non-stars among the cast either stayed at a hotel or used their per diem to rent an apartment. Columbia Pictures, flush with cash, offered a per diem, or a daily allowance covering living expenses. Who wanted to crash in a depressing hotel room? Tracy and Lori opted for a house with a pool. "Francis Ford Coppola sent us cases of his wine," Lori said. "It was just awesome." Toward the end of filming, she found $20,000 in tiny yellow envelopes that she had thrown in her Nike bag and carried around without knowing it.

MEGAN CAVANAGH AND HER THEN-HUSBAND RENTED A STUPIDLY CHEAP apartment for $150 a month and filled it with furniture they bought at Walmart after she earned her first big paycheck. On August 17, she reported for duty in nearby New Harmony, a town on the Wabash River in Posey County and the site of two failed utopian communities in the 1800s. Entering Ribeyre Gym, a handsome pile of bricks dating from 1924, she prepared to ace Marla's baseball audition.

"All right, bring out [her] double," Penny said, referencing stand-in Shelly Niemeyer, with whom Megan got along well.

"Wait, wait, wait, wait," Megan said. She explained that she'd been "working on this for a really long time. I'm batting eighty miles an hour on both sides. You gotta give me a chance."

Penny allowed her to try. The scene: as her nurturing father cheers her on, Marla bats both right-handed and left-handed, at one point breaking a window. "It's OK, honey, that was good form," Dave Hooch reassures, directing the sheepish savant to hit leftie. Megan decided that Mrs. Hooch had died in childbirth, leaving Dave to raise Marla on his own with no other women around. She wore a gold cross necklace throughout the movie and pretended it once belonged to Marla's mother. In the gym, Megan held the necklace in her hand and prayed that she could do what Penny asked her to do.

As Coach Hughes pitched to Megan out of the camera's view, she hit high and low, making as much contact as possible.

*Please, god, please let me get through this*, she thought. She kept going until the film ran out. And when it ran out, everyone clapped for her.

"We're not gonna use any of your double's footage," Penny declared.

For her efforts, Megan was awarded a batting champion trophy that later broke, unfortunately. Did she break that gym window? No, that's what they call movie magic. That was all Hughes, hurling a ball through six different windows at different angles.

The following weeks were devoted to baseball scenes at Bosse Field and Groom Stadium, later renamed League Stadium, an hour's drive northeast. Connie Nass was the Republican mayor of Huntingburg, a quaint, picturesque village with German Catholic heritage, and, according to 1990 census data, a population of 5,242 residents, 99 percent of whom were white. Mayor Nass hoped to lure Penny to her storybook dominion and pump money into the economy. She crashed a meeting between Evansville officials and the Indiana Film Commission related to *A League of Their Own*, her ambitious methods annoying her rival, Mayor McDonald, whom she says refused to speak to her for a year. After getting the producers' attention, she met Penny and Bill Groom underneath Huntingburg's rickety grandstand, which was built in 1894 and worse for wear. While Nass watched ballplayers there as a little girl, the grounds had since turned into a multifunctional stage for horse racing and the county fair. In May 1991, she struck a deal: if Columbia Pictures paid to expand and renovate the bygone cluster of wood, a sparkling diamond in the rough, then the Rockford Peaches would have a custom-made home base. From there they would travel to Bosse Field for away games. Nass demanded the structure be permanent—Hollywood's parting gift to Huntingburg.

Team Penny took the bait, and Groom redesigned his namesake stadium from scratch, dispatching union set builder Harold Collins to supervise its construction. Collins's workers hustled twelve hours a day, six days a week for two months to make the mid-August deadline. The makeover cost about $800,000, and the big reveal dripped nostalgia, conjuring balmy summer nights, salted peanuts and cold beer, scorecards and mosquitoes, the sharp crack of a bat, and hearty applause. The architecture was cinematic, with elegant visual symmetry that would please Wes Anderson. A blond wooden ceiling towered above rustic green bleachers, a retro press box perched in the middle of it all. Groom installed old-fashioned subway turnstiles from New York, and near the scoreboard, billboards advertising Coca-Cola, Budweiser, and Harvey Bars. (The chocolate bars' tagline: "Healthful. Satisfying!")

Megan got emotional when she first laid eyes upon Groom Stadium, and the level of detail astounded Ann Cusack, who felt as though she'd stepped back in time. Even the trash was historically accurate. "They had period *garbage*," Cusack marvels, and when the players and extras were in costume, it was easy to lose track of what year it was.

The Peaches arrived the week of August 18, bright and early. Penny had enforced an egalitarian call time: she wanted the women there by 7 a.m., regardless of who went where in the hierarchy.

"It's just too many people," she said. "It's just too many. You're all coming at seven, you're all going home at seven. That's the end of it."

Anne Ramsay was in heaven. "I was there to do a job and be ready for it, whenever she wanted," she says. "And I loved it." While waiting to film one day, Megan spent eight hours idle, her bone-straight hair in curlers—and when she finally removed them, her locks stuck straight out. Madonna, for whom idleness was borderline sinful, used her downtime to jog with her trainer on country roads, or stalk Hughes in the lunch tent for private practice on the side field.

"We need to go work out," she said.

"I want to eat," he said.

Geena would find a shady spot and read a novel while Tom, a good-natured troublemaker, sought out Robin Knight to play catch and goof off. People envied Robin's easy friendship with Tom, saying, "He doesn't come to get me!" The two played "stupid little games," she recalls. "We put Madonna's chair in center field and played 'hit the chair.'" On occasion, a Peach's empty workday dragged on for eighteen hours without camera time—still, as Columbia hemorrhaged money, she got paid to sit there. All the while, the filmmaking apparatus, including cameras, racked up daily costs of about $140,000.

Renée Coleman, otherwise known as superstitious left fielder Alice Gaspers, who warns her teammates to cross their fingers as they drive past a cemetery, compares *A League of Their Own* to a war movie in which they were members of a platoon. The production was "too big for the people involved to know what was going on," she says. "The Peaches were just props that talked."

All the moving parts, all the *waiting*, enhanced the confusion. "Is this going straight to video?" Megan wondered, not knowing how Penny was going to piece everything together. And Penny, true to form, wore her doubts on her sleeve. Megan watched her roll around, complaining, "Why am I doing this movie?" In the stands at Bosse Field, Alan Wilder approached Penny and inquired how she was doing. "Don't ask," she lamented. "The ballplayers can't act, and the actresses can't play ball."

Penny Marshall and Cindy Williams as *Laverne & Shirley* in 1976. (*Bettmann Collection/ Getty Images*)

Marshall talks to Tom Hanks on the set of *Big*, the film that made her the first woman director to gross more than $100 million at the box office. (*Brian Hamill/Getty Images*)

When chewing gum magnate Philip K. Wrigley founded the All-American Girls Professional Baseball League in 1943, he required players to attend charm school. (*Courtesy of The History Museum, South Bend, Indiana*)

An AAGPBL player slides during a night game. (*Courtesy of The History Museum, South Bend, Indiana*)

The Fort Wayne Daisies celebrate a victory during the early 1950s. The league ended in 1954. (*Courtesy of The History Museum, South Bend, Indiana*)

The fictional Rockford Peaches strike a pose on the set of *A League of Their Own*, Marshall's big-screen tribute to the women who played in the AAGPBL. *(Courtesy of Adina Goldman)*

The ringers hired to double the actors and fill out opposing teams sit on the dugout at League Stadium in Huntingburg, Indiana. Julie Croteau, the first woman to regularly play men's NCAA baseball, looks directly at the camera. *(Courtesy of Adina Goldman)*

Marshall meets with cinematographer Miroslav Ondricek, camera operator Craig DiBona, and her star, Geena Davis. (*Courtesy of Ondrej Kubicek*)

Ondricek surveys the scene, holding the cane that was an extension of his personality. (*Courtesy of Ondrej Kubicek*)

Off-camera, Rosie O'Donnell goofs off in a golf cart. (*Courtesy of Alina Martinet*)

Madonna studies her script alongside makeup artist Francesca Paris. (*Courtesy of Francesca Paris*)

The busy pop star, who said she had "an empire to run," talks on the phone during a break in filming. (*Michael Ochs Archives/ Getty Images*)

In Chicago, Madonna, O'Donnell, and *League* dancer Tony Savino pose with The Baton Show Lounge owner Jim Flint and his fabulous performers. (*Courtesy of Tony Savino*)

In Indiana, *League*'s cast and crew pose outside Marshall's rental home. Zoom in and spot: Hanks, his wife Rita, and their infant son, Chester. (*Courtesy of Ondrej Kubicek*)

Davis and Lynn Cartwright, who played Older Dottie in the film, at the Los Angeles premiere. The former wore a baseball-themed dress designed by Nicole Miller. (*Corbis Historical Collection/Getty Images*)

Madonna and Rosie navigate a swarm of paparazzi at the New York City premiere. (*Michael Ochs Archives/Getty Images*)

Jon Lovitz embraces Marshall inside Tavern On the Green, the site of *League*'s glitzy afterparty. (*Robin Platzer/The Chronicle Collection/Getty Images*)

Tracy Reiner and Megan Cavanagh reprised their characters for a short-lived TV spin-off in 1993. (*CBS Photo Archive/Getty Images*)

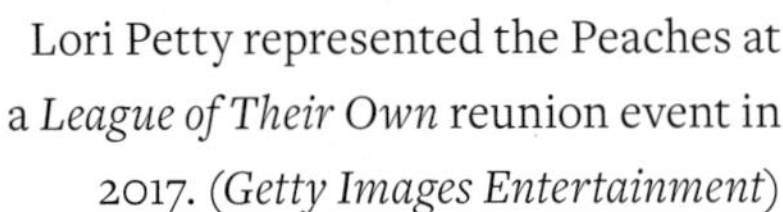

Lori Petty represented the Peaches at a *League of Their Own* reunion event in 2017. (*Getty Images Entertainment*)

And at the ESPY Awards in 2002, Marshall flashed a T-shirt with the film's famous catchphrase. (*Michael Caulfield Archive/WireImage*)

Occasionally, she would turn to someone and say, "My next film is going to be two men in a room."

Like many men in her crew, she "thought that she was gonna go off to Indiana and have a relaxing summer in the sun, playing baseball," Tom said. He added, "It's a logistical nightmare."

Three cameras shot on the field, tripling the amount of film. Even in close-ups, the lenses' wide frame showed folks in the background acting or doing their thing—for script supervisor Mary Bailey, who tracked continuity, the added activity made her work three times trickier. Not to mention that dozens of volunteer extras were needed to occupy seats any given day. As the blazing heat baked bodies, seat-fillers fainted, and worse: One elderly couple suffered double heart attacks, requiring immediate medical attention. Others accidentally swallowed bees that fell into their sodas.

The producers doubted the movie's chances for broad commercial success.

"They thought, *Oh, this is a small thing, really,*" says Tim Galvin, *League*'s art director. "*You know, it's just a bunch of these women out in the countryside and not fancy.*" There weren't car chases or explosions. Given the dearth of glamour and violence, they asked themselves: *How could this cost so much?*

A small, expensive city of campers and tents clustered around the ballparks. Geena and Tom and Madonna and Lori inhabited individual trailers while the supporting Peaches shared three Honeywagons. Menstrual cycles began syncing up. "I got everybody else's period," Tracy says. "I got Rosie's period." The Teamsters made exaggerated complaints that menstrual blood had clogged the bathrooms, making it impossible to pump the fluid out of a Honeywagon.

The first thing in the morning, the Peaches reported to hair and makeup. With Penny's full support, Francesca Paris, the head hairdresser, mostly avoided the stylized '40s-style pompadours that aged certain actresses. While Geena was given a youthful look, her tresses simple and gathered back, Francesca thought Bitty Schram, twelve years her junior, could get away with an exaggerated lift. Madonna, inspired by Hedy Lamarr, had her dark curls parted down the middle, and stylists dyed Lori's black hair red, attaching a half-wig to her existing pixie cut since Penny disliked full wigs. Lori, who favored boyish streetwear, looked like a different person with her character's Prince Valiant pageboy. When she wasn't in costume head-to-toe, she could be seen wearing boxer shorts, dark circles underneath her eyes.

The wigless Geena required constant color maintenance. The production couldn't find a top-level colorist in Indiana to refresh her bright coppery shade, so expert instructions were sent to Francesca's cohort, Anthony Cortino, who protested, "I'm a hairstylist, not a fucking chemist!" As she got a rinsing, unnatural-hued water trickled from her portable salon into the parking lot. Her steady makeup man, Joe Campayno, was low-key, just like her. Geena belonged to Mensa, the organization for people with high IQs, and "was on a different plane than everybody else," says Paul Gebbia, who did makeup in the camper next door where Penny—giving her quiet Dottie some breathing room—placed higher-key extroverts like Rosie, Madonna, and Lori.

"You're going to share a makeup trailer with [Mo]," Penny informed Lori early on.

"Why?" she said.

"'Cause you can handle her."

During lunch breaks, Lori and Madonna were "joined at the hip," caterer Tom Morales says, recalling, "Everything about Madonna was shock treatment, man." One day, "She was pantomiming giving a blow job and Geena just went like, '*Oh, my fucking god*,' and ran." In one of Morales's first encounters with Madonna, he asked her if she'd had breakfast and she responded sarcastically, testing his reaction. "Well, I sucked James Woods's cock in the elevator," she said, to which he replied, "Well, I thought you didn't eat anything that took a shit." (They were friends from that point onward, and she hired his company to cater a stop on her world tour.)

Madonna harassed Sam Hoffman, the new assistant director, in a way that would not fly today. It was a challenge to extract her from her trailer, as she'd say, "Sam! Don't you understand I have an empire to run?" When he would ask her to come outside, she'd say, "In your mouth." He was having the time of his life, being around baseball and beautiful new female friends, and he dealt with her inappropriate behavior in stride. She had power, and he did not, and she flexed her high celebrity status for sport. It was a good thing, then, that he was comfortable around actors, enough so that he mustered the confidence to give Geena a screenplay he wrote. Later,

Madonna summoned him to her trailer, putting him on the spot: "So, you gave Geena your script to read? What am I, chopped liver?"

When he asked her to sign a photo of her for his parents' friends' daughter, she griped something along the lines of, "OK, not only do I have to suck your parents' dick, I have to suck your dick and then your friends' dick?"

"All right, girls, roll in the dirt," Penny would say on the field. "Your uniforms are too clean."

Depending on which games they filmed, the Peaches alternated between clean and dirty tunics, often within the same day. There was a clean game and a dirty game, and the back-and-forth made Irene Ferrari, the wardrobe supervisor, want to quit. "Clean or dirty?" she'd ask the assistant directors, who tried to get an answer from Penny.

No actual, full-on game-playing occurred, except a few times at night with a camera running. The crew would set up and tell the women, "Just play."

Otherwise, most Peaches played fake movie baseball, banking vignettes and bits and pieces for the edit bay. Says Geena, "They had a giant slingshot that would send the ball hurling up the fence when anybody hit a home run." Or pretended to hit one. The men used the slingshot for hours and filmed the Peaches and their opponents running to catch the ball as Craig DiBona chased after them. Once, Madonna hit a pitch and froze in disbelief, watching the ball fly upward. The take was no good because she didn't run. Still, Ondricek rejoiced, exclaiming, "Put the flags out!"

Lori suffered in the humidity. "The wig, the hat, the wool socks, and the creepy spiked shoes," she said. "Fuck, it was terrible. I slid into home once and my cleat got caught in the rim of the plate. I kept going and my foot stayed there. I broke my foot early on, and if you notice one of my socks is often pushed down lower than the other one. It's to hide the plastic removable cast that I wore through half the movie."

Renée badly injured her thigh while filming an action shot in which Alice steals third and slides into home plate. Her double, Vickie Buse, was MIA, tired of sitting around with nothing to do. The crew asked several guinea pigs if they'd be interested in doing the slide, and they said no. Naively, Renée said yes. "I did it not knowing what I was signing up for," she recalls, comparing her eager younger self to The Beaver on *Leave It to Beaver.* She got bruised on the first attempt. The bump grew larger and more gruesome over five takes and by the fifth slide, it stuck out three inches, feeling like a cantaloupe duct-taped to her leg. No one, not even Coach Hughes, had seen anything like it. The blood should have been drained, but they were in the middle of nowhere, miles from any hospital. Like a good soldier, Renée continued filming: Penny, knowing the ghastly purple bruise was too good not to put in her movie, filmed Anne Ramsay icing the monstrosity as Renée grimaced in pain. "They had to put makeup on it to tone it down," she says, "because it was so hideous." It took her fifteen years to regain the feeling in her leg.

(In commentary for the 2004 edition of the *League of Their Own* DVD, Penny discussed Renée's iconic strawberry with actresses including Tracy and Megan who remained awed by its authenticity. "She also got a fish tattooed on her stomach so don't give me that crap," Penny remarked. "One drunken night.")

Though Greenhut worried about the women throwing their arms out, Ondricek just wanted to keep shooting. Sometimes it was the reverse, with the producer wanting to roll cameras while Ondricek waited for the skies to cooperate. For continuity's sake, the DP tried to keep a scene's weather patterns consistent. The cloudless blue yonder could hold things up.

"He was very slow," Greenhut says. "Penny championed him, whatever he wanted to do. I just did not have that kind of patience. I lost it one day. I was at the office in the morning, and I came to the set, and they're all just sitting around. It was a perfect beautiful day, and nothing had been shot! Whole cast is out there. Whole crew's out there. And I said, 'What's going on?'"

"Mirek is waiting for some clouds," Penny said.

"Clouds? It's a baseball movie. I mean, shoot it in the sun."

And then, Greenhut recalls, "I just went crazy." He started running around, saying, "Just set up the camera, we're shooting it." Greenhut pushed equipment over, "knocking it out of the way, and I just had a meltdown which ended with Penny tackling me. The only way she could get me to shut up and get me out of there was to tackle me. And then they dragged me off the set. But we shot. And anybody watching that movie, you know, as far as like, 'Oh gee, that shot was in the sun and that one was in the clouds,' I mean, *gimme a break*."

In Greenhut's view, striving for perfection squandered two precious resources: time and money. He put Madonna on watch after she arrived late a few times, telling her, "Hey, you gotta stop this shit. You're being an asshole. Everybody sees it. You're not helping yourself." He called Mo's agent, and afterward received an apology written on two white cards with her name in black letters at the top of each card. "I did not mean to sound beligerant [*sic*] on the set yesterday and I have never been accused of being unprofessional," she began in cheerful blue ink, her handwriting squat and hurried, "but I was caught off guard between takes and there was no way I could explain myself or answer your question properly." She wrote that she knew they were running behind schedule and was genuinely sorry for holding up the shoot. She took responsibility for regularly blowing off her call time but said she had done so with permission from the hair and makeup departments. "Yesterday was the first day I did not even bother to check in with [Bernadette] + Francesca," she said, calling her delinquency "an act of defiance and frustration." Since Huntingburg, she explained, she had felt confused, unprepared, and unconnected to both *League*'s story and Mae. She felt worthless and out of control and urged Greenhut to keep lines of communication open to her. She wanted to learn. She wanted to work. She didn't care about the money—she had enough of that. What she cared about was being a good actress and making a good movie.

While stranded in movie hell, Madonna was in negotiations with Time Warner, the parent company of her Sire record label, to hash out a $60 million superdeal to form her own entertainment imprint. She was also on the verge of losing the title role in a film adaptation of Andrew Lloyd Webber's *Evita*, which lingered in development limbo with its director-of-the-moment, Glenn Gordon Caron. When Madonna—her brain fixed on the future, the next thing and not the now—saw her current director approaching, she'd say, "Hide me, Penny's coming."

She was losing interest. In Huntingburg, Madonna wrapped herself one day, escaping in a car with her driver without Penny's knowledge.

"Where's Mo?" Penny yelled an hour later.

*Mo left*, she was told. *She went back to McCutchanville.*

Fury rose within her. "That's it," Penny announced. "I'm gonna write her out of this picture. I'll make her pregnant!"

As Gloria chauffeured her home, she put her feet up in the passenger window and fumed into her boxy, antennaed Motorola cell phone, continuing her threat to whoever was on the other line.

"I'll have her fucking written out of the script," she said.

Madonna got the message. She left a mea culpa on Penny's answering machine, vowing that she would never wrap herself again.

Bitty Schram was ambushed.

When Penny summoned Bitty to sob hysterically opposite Tom, the actress received no warning.

"They were like, 'OK, shoot this scene now,'" she says. "And I was like, *Oh my god.*"

She had been in the business just ten months. There was crying in a taped audition, and then there was crying with *everyone* watching. She couldn't understand Penny's inscrutable way of speaking. She was confused. On edge. "I took all my fears and just put it in the scene," she says. "I didn't expect it to be that way, but it was, and it helped me."

As Tom gave her a mouthful, she listened and cried every single time. They did a lot of takes as clouds drifted into the frame and messed up the shot. When the camera was angled on Tom, she tried "not to blow my wad," she says. When the camera turned to Bitty, the tears flowed. She was in the groove, in the moment. She was Evelyn Gardner, and Jimmy Dugan, not Tom, was shaming her in front of the fans. Bitty felt like she was in trouble.

"You let the tying run get on second!" Tom barked, getting in her face, giving a thousand percent, at once a cartoon and a hothead at the end of his rope. "And we lost the lead because of you! Now you start using your head! That's that lump that's three feet above your ass!"

The crew combusted with laughter. Mike Haley, the first AD, had managed to persuade Penny to cast him as the umpire in the instantly classic "No Crying in Baseball" scene. A practical joker, Haley would pull stunts like sticking his bare butt through the scoreboard. Mike Nichols, the director for whom he worked most often, had planted him as an extra in *Working Girl* and *Postcards from the Edge*, yet Haley's physical appearance—rather, his mustache—gave Penny pause. To win the role, he took an electric trimmer and shaved off his facial hair right in front of her. *OK, you're in,* she said. *Make it up as you go along.*

"Good rule of thumb: treat each of these girls as you would treat your mother," Haley scolded Tom, who snarked behind his back, taunting, "Did anyone ever tell you, you look like a penis with a little hat on?"

Haley flinched, turned around, and shouted, "You're outta here!"

The men improvised their ensuing brawl while Ro and Mo ad-libbed in the dugout.

Mo: "You're out! Have a beer!"

Ro: "I'm in charge now!"

Bitty feared getting negative feedback from the dailies. *I hope we did a good job,* she thought afterward. The next day, she learned that Penny had been very pleased. "You leave it up to the gods and, you know, I guess it's talent," says Bitty, who wasn't ashamed of hers. As soon as studio executives screened the results, they knew Tom's one-liner would help sell the movie. Sid Ganis, then Columbia's top marketing executive, celebrated early by ordering T-shirts that read "There's no crying in baseball!"

All told, in Bitty's Indiana bubble, "by no means did I think that scene was gonna be anything in a movie," she says.

How could she have possibly known? She was deep in the thick of it.

Bitty, a tennis player, initially swung her bat like a racket. For instance, Renée recalls, "If a ball came on the inside, she'd jump over the home plate and try to hit it as a backhand."

While the learning curve remained high, Geena began to show improvements while knowing what she could and could not do. Her self-aware intelligence earned Coach Hughes's respect. For the scene in which Dottie catches a ball while doing the splits, Geena filmed the setup, extending her legs in opposite directions, but ceded the actual stunt work to a male gymnast from the University of Evansville. Geena's confidence grew over the weeks. On *A League of Their Own*, she was told that she had "untapped athletic ability." When Dottie catches a fly ball behind her back, Geena figured out the mechanics of pulling off the neat trick.

"They planned to have the stunt double do it, and she was having a little trouble," Geena says. "I had an *idea*, and so I said, 'Let me try it.'" She figured, "If I looked up at the ball coming straight at my face, and then bent my neck down, it would go down my back and into the glove that was waiting at the bottom of my back. And that worked."

A competitive spirit permeated the air as Peaches jockeyed for position next to the A-listers, craving screen time, the director's approval, a moment in the sun. The competition caused some friction. Many were out for themselves.

According to Rosie, "There were little cliques that formed and reformed, and people were friends and then not friends, and we all sort of reverted to our adolescence for part of the filming."

Rosie, a popular Peach on set, and Téa Leoni, the Racine Belle at whom many gazed with cartoon heart eyes, had "this running battle for a while," location manager Dennis Benatar says, "but they made up and they were best friends after that." Leoni, who makes blink-and-miss appearances in the movie, was crass, funny, and down-to-earth. She even listened to Garth Brooks. (She had good taste in music.) She also had a few credits to her name (the soap *Santa Barbara*; The Dream Girl in the comedy *Switch*), and a bright future ahead of her, starring in movies such as *Flirting with Disaster*, *Deep Impact*, and *Jurassic Park III*. Yet over the course of the shoot, Penny underutilized her and she became increasingly withdrawn. In early June, the twenty-five-year-old had married Neil Tardio, a producer of TV commercials who was based in Chicago. More than one Peach questioned her choice to settle down so young, with so much promise, with a guy who lived outside of LA.

"I thought Janet Jones and Téa Leoni were going to leave," says Rosie's photo double, Lita Schmitt. "I mean, I'm surprised they stayed on the movie because I remember Téa Leoni in the dugout going, 'This is a bunch of bullshit. Like, why am I here if I'm not doing anything?'"

Three years earlier, Jones said "I do" to Wayne Gretzky in a grand ceremony in Edmonton, Canada, that aired live on television across the country. Soon afterward, the Great One, an Oiler for nearly a decade, was traded to the Los Angeles Kings, bringing him closer to his wife's profession. Jones, a decent athlete but an actress by trade, had previously notched roles in *A Chorus Line*, *Police Academy 5*, and Garry Marshall's *The Flamingo Kid*, but a star-making breakout movie eluded her. In *A League of Their Own*, Penny showcased a fantastic shot of Jones catching a ball and then firing it with a high-speed velocity that seemed to spark invisible flames. When her husband visited base camp, he brought their two-year-old daughter and one-year-old son and autographed a hockey stick for Ondricek, making the cinematographer's day.

THE WEEK THAT DELISA CHINN-TYLER SHOWED UP AT BOSSE FIELD, SHE spent a lot of time sitting off to the side, out of the camera's view.

"Don't you want to be in the movie?" a woman asked, unaware who DeLisa was.

"Yes, I want to be in the movie," she replied.

"Well, you need to get out there," the woman said. *There* meant Bosse's historic hunter-green seats where white extras were congregated.

DeLisa explained that Penny told her she couldn't be seen in the crowd scenes. She was awaiting something more important: her big solo, for which Wardrobe gave her a blue printed dress, white hat, and brown Mary Janes. She wasn't much of a hat person, but she liked the dress because she thought it made her waist look "very, very tiny."

The set got quiet as she shot the fifteen-second, word-free scene that would resonate for years to come. DeLisa's nameless character, watching a game in segregated seating, picks up a ball on the foul line and hurls it like a cannon over Dottie's head and into Ellen Sue's glove. The impact causes Ellen Sue to remove her mitt while Dottie, humbled, looks at DeLisa in amazement. DeLisa nods and walks away, a stirring reminder of what the league lost by keeping Black players off the field.

"They told me to throw the ball and give 'em a look, you know, as if to say, 'Black women can play too,'" she says. "And so I did. I threw the ball and I nodded my head down and I turned and walked off. They said, 'You nailed it.'"

DeLisa laughs as she remembers her friends saying, "That is *you*." DeLisa adds, "I guess that's just my demeanor."

She threw a lot, and on one of her throws, the heel of her shoe broke. Celebrities paid their respects: Rosie shook her hand and Penny signed her glove and a ball. "Nice throw," Geena wrote on the same ball. Tom Hanks handed her a ball with his signature, saying, "Nice throw, young lady." When the production asked if she wanted to meet Madonna, DeLisa answered, "Not really."

More than three decades later, many involved with *A League of Their Own* don't know DeLisa's name, despite her brief cameo gaining lots of attention as a thoughtful acknowledgment of racial exclusion within the AAGPBL. DeLisa symbolized the legacies of Toni Stone, Mamie "Peanut" Johnson, and Connie Morgan, the three women who played in the male-dominated Negro Leagues. Stone, the first barrier-breaker, joined the Indianapolis Clowns for the 1953 season, succeeding Hank Aaron on second base. (Aaron had switched over to the Majors, signing with the Boston Braves five years after Jackie Robinson integrated the league.) Stone, who batted .243 and hit one of Satchel Paige's fastballs, endured hostility from some of the Clowns and was barred from changing in the locker room. Her peers "would throw the ball to her so that she was positioned in a way to take a spikes-up slide from the opposing player coming in," her biographer Martha Ackmann said. One time, the Clowns' business manager "got all the players on the bus after the game and said if anyone ever does that again they're getting a bus ticket home." Stone flaunted her spike-induced wounds like badges of honor.

Peanut, a petite pitcher standing five feet, three inches tall, played three seasons with the Clowns, earning their respect. "She maybe weighed ninety-eight pounds wet," her teammate, Gordon Hopkins said, adding, "It was no joke. It was no show. . . . Mamie, she was good."

When Peanut was seventeen, she and her friend Rita were turned away from an AAGPBL tryout near Washington, DC. "They just looked at us, as if to say, 'What do you want?'" she recalled later, saying, "They wouldn't give us the opportunity to try out." She thought they were out of their minds. The league permanently maintained an unofficial "No Blacks Allowed" policy. Among its narrow-minded patriarchs, whiteness equaled All-American beauty, the wholesome girl next door. The frosty treatment of Peanut and Rita spoke volumes: Black girls and women were viewed with spite and suspicion because of the color of their skin. Those who yearned to play organized hardball encountered hazing within the Negro Leagues and racism if they dared tread upon white women's territory.

While traveling with twenty-eight men in the Jim Crow South, Stone was perceived to be a prostitute. The owner of a boardinghouse that hosted her male teammates once "directed her to the nearest brothel," Ackmann said. Stone thus began a habit of lodging at brothels, perhaps identifying with prostitutes' outsider status. "They were kind to her. They gave her a place to stay. They even sewed padding into the shirt of her uniform so that she could take hard throws to the chest."

When DeLisa made her acting debut, she was thirty-one years old and driving packages for FedEx. *Laverne & Shirley* had been one of her favorite shows. She used to dream of Olympic greatness as Penny had, but her mother wanted her to stay in Evansville. She grew up "kind of a tomboy," one of two girls who played on her neighborhood baseball team, and every day in the summer, she stayed in the park until it closed, revolving between different sports. She practiced hard.

"I would just take the ball, and by myself, I would just throw it as hard as I could against the fence working on my grounders," she says. "I'd flip the ball up and take my bat and smack it into the fence."

At eleven years old, she joined a women's softball team sponsored by Club Paradise on Lincoln Avenue, the only youngster on the lineup until she recruited friends of similar age. Three years later, in July 1974, their team, the Evansville Express, won a state championship. DeLisa, in center field, loved the competitiveness of softball most of all. "I wasn't much of a talker," she says. "You know how some people talk a big game? I would rather just show you."

The Express traveled all over the place, playing games in Milwaukee and Chicago, Little Rock, and St. Louis. They called their bus the "Lazy Susan." Their rivals "would say, 'look at those little girls,'" Tamara Wagner-Marion, a former catcher, told the *Courier & Press*. "I don't think there was a girl on the team who didn't think it was the best time of their life."

DeLisa talks with pride about her past achievements, including setting women's softball records at the University of Southern Indiana, which lies to the west of her hometown. In the 1979 season, she had a .410 batting average and stole nine bases in a single game against Saint Mary's College, a feat that remains unchallenged.

"My arm was so strong," she says. "If I caught a one-bounce, anybody around Evansville that knows could tell you: I could throw you out at first base."

She did not like losing. She was all over the field.

"Lisa used to take balls away from me," her teammate complained to DeLisa's husband.

"Well, you wouldn't go out far enough to get 'em," DeLisa told her.

On the Express, she brought white players to the team—if they were good, she didn't care what color they were. When one recruit expressed fear about going to a Black neighborhood, DeLisa said, "Girl, nobody's gonna bother you."

"We accepted white people in our area," she recalls, "but it was like we weren't accepted as much in the white neighborhoods." During a game in Jasper, a town north of Huntingburg, DeLisa was called the N-word. She kept her head down. "I just want to be able to get back to Evansville safely," she told her friends.

In 1990, the Census reported that Black people accounted for 9.5 percent of Evansville's residents. Black migrants fleeing violence and poverty in the South settled downtown and along the riverfront after the Civil War. The community created a vibrant residential and business district that blossomed in the middle of the twentieth century, despite threats beyond its parameters.

"Racial hostility kept the Black population of Indiana small, but it also fed the cultural and social discrimination that made Indiana the beating heart of the resurgent Ku Klux Klan in the 1920s," historian Heather Cox Richardson wrote in the *Milwaukee Independent*. "Under violent con man David Curtis Stephenson, who raped, mutilated, and murdered a female state employee, the Indiana Ku Klux Klan developed the idea of '100% Americanism,' which argued for a hierarchy of races in which the White race was uppermost. Immigrants and Black Americans, that theory said, were destroying traditional America."

Indiana's Klan established its first branch in Evansville, where Stephenson worked for a coal company. In 1923 he became the hate group's Grand Dragon and amassed tremendous political power within the state, growing Klan membership to encompass half a million Hoosiers and more than 30 percent of white males. Most members were Protestants from the middle and upper classes who feared losing their status to marginalized groups, including Catholics. By 1928, just four thousand members remained with the Klan as Stephenson sat in prison for murdering his aide, Madge Oberholtzer. Traces of his influence persist.

J. Patrick Redmond, a novelist and English teacher in Evansville, has never seen Klan activity there. "Absolutely there are members of the Klan that live here somewhere—that's going to be any community throughout the nation," he says. "The largest presence that I know of the Klan is in Madison, Indiana," two hours to the east. In 2021, the Southern Poverty Law Center tracked active Klan branches in Madison on the Ohio and in Valparaiso near Lake Michigan.

In the summer of 1991, in broad daylight, Madonna's assistant, Melissa Crow, was driving on a wooded road when she turned around a bend and saw the Klan gathered in a park. She was stunned. She looked for rolling cameras, thinking the scene wasn't real. But there were none. Just a lot of people milling about in white hoods.

On the street in Evansville, Lori Petty saw a Klan supporter collecting donations in a Folgers can. "They had to sit on me to keep me from murdering that person," she says. "We had fifty extras quit because we had a Black PA and they said they weren't taking no orders from no N-word. Fifty extras quit because a Black woman was giving them water." She adds, "Look, this is not an indictment of Evansville. This is an indictment of America."

The Sho-Bar, a gay bar in an industrial part of town, tucked away northeast of the city center, was *A League of Their Own*'s favorite hangout. Picture the Suds Bucket yet cozier and inconspicuous, with a dance floor and a stage for drag performers. It occupied the bottom level of a two-story, prewar building, and according to Patrick Higgs, an actor who once deejayed at the Sho-Bar, it was run by a former madam. "I always heard that she owned, like, a house of prostitution but was a bail bondsman by day," he says.

Inside, plastic booths lined a long wall that seemed to be "ripped out of Dairy Queen," says Redmond, whose world changed the night he stepped into the Sho-Bar in March 1993. The writer grew up in Vincennes, a former French Catholic settlement on the Illinois-Indiana border, and hiding his sexuality in his early twenties, he feared someone would recognize him inside the bar. "Not thinking at the time that whoever's in there probably feels the same way," he recalls. That first outing, he lingered in the parking lot until mustering the nerve to cross the threshold. At the Sho-Bar, his universe expanded, making Redmond feel less alone. He met kindred spirits and danced to a remix of Whitney Houston's "I Will Always Love You." On the wall he glimpsed Madonna and Lori's signatures scrawled in fluorescent ink. "That shows that they are allies within the gay community of middle America," Redmond says. "*We know you are here. We are with you. We stand with you.*" Those autographs "represent so much more and something so great, above and beyond, 'Oh, we came here and danced.'"

Second ADs John Rusk and Sam Hoffman were among the straight guys who hung out there because it was fun. Higgs spun popular music and once cued up Prince's "Gett Off" for Lori, who adored the Purple One. While celebrating her twenty-eighth birthday, Higgs says, "she was all over the floor," doing the caterpillar. Penny rented out the venue for the occasion, and during the several times she visited the Sho-Bar, she liked to hang back and watch the action. Says Higgs, "She passed out in my DJ booth a couple times." One night, Penny "drank too much," camera assistant Mollie Mallinger remembers. Ondricek's second-in-command, Tom Priestley, "took her home," she says. "She vomited all over Tom's car," a Bronco. "I had to take it to go get it clean."

*League*'s gatherings produced many hangovers, and at least one brush with the cops. "I got totally smashed [at Sho-Bar] one night and got a DUI going home," Greenhut says.

Gloria Mallah doesn't remember Penny drinking a lot or getting wasted. Her boss liked to dine at the House of Como, a fun Lebanese restaurant with the kitschiest of decor—a light-up Santa Claus. (According to rumor, if Santa was lit, that meant illegal gambling was going down in the basement.) For the most part, Gloria says, Penny stayed home. Neither Geena nor Tom made Sho-Bar cameos, and Madonna did not return after autographing the dive's wall—she'd totally blown her cover and put the bar on the map, proving a boon for business. The publicity lured "straight college kids" and "it sort of got a little less gay," Higgs says.

The attention in the local media disturbed Rosie. As Paul Gebbia tells it, she "got into words with Madonna while they were both in the makeup chairs." Ro told Mo, "I can't believe that you did that. Mo, why would you go to the only place in town where gay people have a place to be private and to congregate?"

The openly gay Gebbia, who met his long-term partner in Evansville, didn't fully understand Rosie's anger until she confided in him that she had relationships with women. During *A League of Their Own*, a time Rosie has described as her "brief hetero period," she dated a man. She came out to a *Cosmopolitan* writer in an interview the following year, but the magazine would not print her disclosure.

"Are you gay?" the writer asked.

"Yes," she said.

Rosie surmised that *Cosmo*'s editor, Helen Gurley Brown, omitted her announcement to protect her. A decade later, as her Emmy-winning daytime talk show wound down, she went public while doing standup at Caroline's Comedy Club in New York.

Ro's disagreement with Mo did not ruin their bond. Mo looked up to Ro and sought her advice, and Ro offered it solicited and not. Like Mo, she said and did what she wanted to do.

"I think Madonna was looking at Rosie as like a mother figure," Gebbia says. "I know she was."

In a tender moment, Madonna stood and stared at her reflection in the makeup mirror.

"I miss my Mommy," she said.

Rosie got up and gave her a hug.

## *The Bottom of the Seventh*

# ROCKFORD VERSUS RACINE

TOM HANKS DIDN'T MIND WAITING.

"Do you know how much they're paying me to sit in that luxury camper?" he told an apologetic AD. "Don't worry about it." But he rarely locked himself in his trailer. He liked to be around other people. He fed off the humanity of his surroundings, soaking it all in, observing everything. Madonna teased him for frequenting the lunch tent on days he didn't have to work. She thought he was cheap: after all, if he were off set, he'd have to buy his own meal.

"There was a gossip sheet that was being circulated around the set called *Peach Phuzz*," Hoffman says. It showed up each Friday on Xeroxed pages, asking playfully tongue-in-cheek questions such as, "Who was *that* person canoodling with *this* person?" As filming neared the end, it was discovered that Tom penned the *Peach Phuzz* column. "Nobody knew he was doing it anonymously," Hoffman says. "He was amazing."

Tom had plenty of material to circulate if he chose to. *A League of Their Own* spawned affairs and divorces and all manner of intrigue. Here are a few tidbits from my reporting that Tom would be too polite to repeat:

- Hungover Racine Belles dropped like flies while lined up for a pregame National Anthem scene. The Belles had mocked the Peaches for choosing to stay home the night before rather than attend a party. "They were like, 'Oh, you guys from Hollywood are little babies and blah blah blah blah,'" Lori says. At Bosse Field the next day, several Belles passed out, inducing Schadenfreude. "Take off your costume," Penny told a Belle. "Put it on someone else."

- Pepper Paire Davis, in town from SoCal and staying with Tracy, revealed a hidden "truth" about her husband as she and the girls played Truth or Dare at a Bonanza restaurant. (What did she confess? She wouldn't say.) Tracy, meanwhile, took a dare to run around the restaurant three times, singing the alphabet. Lori "wound up having to take her shirt off behind some signs right by the restrooms," Pepper reported, adding, "Suddenly, a lot of guys had to go to the bathroom. Tracy ran over and told her that she was flashing everybody."
- PA Patty Willett swooned when she spotted David Strathairn in a tractor on set, wearing a dusty purple T-shirt and jeans. *That is, like, the hottest man ever*, she thought, *just sitting there chilling.*
- We all know Penny smoked cigarettes. But Geena? Who knew?
- Madonna allegedly canoodled with a married Racine Belle as well as a crew member who was in a relationship with someone else. She was tempted, a witness suggests, by forbidden fruit she could not have.

The *National Enquirer* was invasive compared with *Peach Phuzz*. The tabloid published a photo of Madonna on set with curlers in her hair. Remembering the caption, makeup artist Linda Neuffer says, "It said 'Material Girl with material curls', walking with her security guard." She cracked up laughing as she realized that the *Enquirer* had mistaken Colin Hanks for a bodyguard. Colin, a base-camp fixture, did odd jobs for the production, like serving watermelon and cappuccinos to the cast. The middle schooler had wanted Air Jordans, and while Tom could easily buy them for his son, he made Colin earn the coveted sneakers—but not by safeguarding Madonna. In Alan Wilder's recollection, the *Enquirer* published dirt that Tom and Madonna weren't getting along. Mo brought up the story to Tom in the makeup trailer, but he had nothing to say about it one way or another. He seemed to lack interest in stoking the flames.

"She had a distinct personality and that's kind of interesting to get used to after a while," Tom told *Entertainment Tonight* in 1992, adding, "I did end up liking her. I thought she was neat. I thought she was cool."

Gossip hounds pursued silly photographs of the actresses. One image of Bitty and Madonna locking lips made the rounds on set. The studio's on-site publicist, Stuart Fink, confiscated the evidence so it didn't land in the hands of the *Enquirer*. "The tabloids came around," Tom Morales says. "They were offering big money for that picture. Like, big money."

"Man, I can make $150,000 if I sell this picture," Morales's junior staffer said.

"No, you won't," he warned. "They'll never let you work again."

*A League of Their Own* was an "awakening experience," Hoffman says, for a lot of background ballplayers who "were gay" and "this is when they came out." The women woke up, so to speak, when they got to Chicago. "So suddenly, you take all these girls—who a lot of them are closeted—and you put them together in a hotel," Jim Kleverweis, a former PA, explains. "And it could have been a reality show. Like, all sorts of pairings and couplings were happening. And then when they got back to Indiana, more pairings and couplings were happening. And there were a lot of arguments and then breakups and all that kind of stuff."

For Kelli Simpkins, who would go on to cocreate *The Laramie Project*, the play based on the 1998 murder of gay college student Matthew Shepard, "It wasn't until I got on that set and then moved to New York that I was like, 'Oh my god, there's an entire cultural landscape that I was not privy to because it was not in my backyard.'"

There was an open sexuality. While some weren't out in the public sphere, they talked freely about their partners and lovers. Madonna's "super queer," Simpkins says, and her "beautiful, queer dancers" visited base camp. She had never been around anything like it. Her mind blew open. "There were people who would come up to me and say, 'You're gay.' And I'd be like, 'No, I'm not!'" What could they see in her? How did they know? On *A League of Their Own*, she learned that it was possible to be out, to have a partner and friends, to thrive in the arts, whether you shouted your orientation from the rooftops or not. Simpkins, a twenty-year-old theater major at Indiana University, became close friends with Julie Croteau, a straight ally who'd go out dancing at the Sho-Bar. As for her fellow ringers' experimentation, Croteau says, "I don't remember any stories where it was not a positive thing for that person."

In Geena, Simpkins found a role model. She watched the star assert herself, saying, *I wanna do a different take.* Or: *Can we do this?* In total control of how she appeared on camera, Geena and her makeup artist, Joe Campayno, often conferred to execute the look she wanted. "She was a real leader on that film," Simpkins says, "in vocal ways and in just the way she carried herself. She's a very powerful figure without needing to say a lot of words." She admired the respect that both Geena and Tom showed people from Evansville and actors of lower rank. They set a tone of good humor.

Sometimes, however, things got weird. (And not in a bad way.)

"Geena's Mensa," Bernadette Mazur says. "She would do things like take a piece of paper and cut it up and it would become an organ that you could play."

Once she constructed a baseball stadium out of paper.

At one point, Geena joked in *Interview* magazine, "I just started going nuts." She had heard a song from *Jesus Christ Superstar* on the radio and thought, "Who's listened to that lately?" She began playing the soundtrack in hair and makeup each morning. Obsessed, she tried to revive the musical with eager participants: Tom performed the role of Caiaphas, the priest who appears later in the score; Campayno and Anne Ramsay each sang the part of Jesus; and Hoffman played King Herod. Says Geena, who assigned herself the priest Annas, "I had a very small but passionate part."

"We cast Madonna as Judas," she said. "I don't think she ever found out about it, because she never came to any rehearsal, and she got *canned* from our show. We were going to do it Hawaiian-style and we were investigating renting grass skirts and coconut bras." Colin, earning those Jordans, made helmets out of hollowed-out watermelons.

Penny bestowed Screen Actors Guild cards as surprise gifts to Simpkins, Robin Knight, and Patti Pelton, each of whom had yet to join the influential labor union. She "gave me some lines and said, 'Welcome to SAG,'" recalls Pelton, who played second-base Peach Marbleann Wilkinson. While Pelton's dialogue was ultimately cut, thanks to Penny she could move to LA with a golden Guild ticket in hand.

Going into *League*, a guy in the camera department warned Mollie Mallinger about Penny, saying, "She doesn't like women. Stay away from her. Mind your own business." He said that she liked to be the center of attention, with folks fawning all over her. He said it was always about Penny. But when all was said and done, Mollie came away with a different perspective. She didn't feel that Penny hated women at all. If that were the case, then why had she hired so many smart women to be around her? Women like Bonnie Hlinomaz and Amy Lemisch, her former assistant-turned-associate producer. Cynthia Flynt, her costume designer. Mary Bailey, her script supervisor. Alexis Alexanian in the production office, and so on. She also felt that Penny "actually cared about everybody. She looked at everybody as, like, a family. She was very dedicated to everybody. Like, once you broke into this group, you were part of the family."

Penny was temperamental, though. "I thought she could be really mean-spirited," Coach Hughes's assistant, Abe Flores, says. Especially as the day wore on, her New York toughness began manifesting in yelling; to Flores, yelling demonstrated a lack of control. If hair and makeup attempted last-minute touch-ups, she'd lose patience: "Hurry up," she ordered. "We gotta shoot this."

Francesca Paris was Penny's first hit. As she went in to do a touch-up, Penny grabbed her by the seat of her pants and pulled her back, declaring, "No, no, no!"

"Penny," Francesca said, "you're not gonna like it when you see it in dailies. I have to!"

Getting "hit" became a running joke, and almost a source of pride. Francesca and other targets rarely took the hits personally. "Did you get hit today?" someone would ask, to which another would reply, "Yeah, I got hit today." T-shirts were made that had bullseyes on the back.

Penny targeted Gebbia before shooting the scene in which the Peaches' bus driver, fed up with the unruly antics on board, storms off and leaves the team stranded by the side of the road. As chaperone Miss Cuthbert, played by Pauline Brailsford, runs out of the bus to confront the driver, the schmuck grabs some dirt and throws it in her face. (The violent soil strike didn't sit right with Megan Cavanagh, who knew Brailsford from Chicago, where the sixty-two-year-old British actress was artistic director of the Body Politic theater company and taught drama at Columbia College. She felt that it degraded Brailsford. "Yeah, well, something had to happen," Penny told Megan.)

While Brailsford sat in his chair, Gebbia dipped a brush in a cup filled with fake dirt and brushed the residue on her face.

"No, no, no, no," Penny said, snatching the cup. "Like this." She flung the contents in his face, as though she were the driver and he the chaperone. Gebbia's eyes closed instantaneously, and when he opened them, he had white rings around both.

"That's the look I want," she said.

Everybody laughed. After Penny's hands-on demonstration, Gebbia dirtied up Brailsford to her liking. The next day, she apologized to Gebbia.

"I wasn't offended at all," he told her. "I just wasn't expecting you to do that."

As Penny lobbed curveballs, Tom thrived within the unpredictable atmosphere she fostered. He wanted to direct in the future, so she put him in charge of directing the third camera, which shot scoreboard activity. She didn't hover over him like a helicopter parent. She let him share in the holistic filmmaking process.

"She can drive me crazy, making me do things one hundred thousand times," he told a journalist in 1992. "But Penny's passive personality gives a collective feeling on set rather than the idea that the director is God."

Tom wore another uncredited hat: he was, unofficially, a Penny Marshall translator. He filtered her direction for Peaches (not Tracy Reiner) who had trouble understanding what she was saying. Her megaphone amplified the mumbling, making it worse. In one instance, he stood up for the women, notably Freddie Simpson, as she filmed an outtake in which Ellen Sue twirls her baton and tells a story about a beauty pageant she won. When a camera operator directed Freddie to her mark, the actress did as she was told. Then Penny began to yell, "You're not on your mark!"

Tom looked at Penny.

"Are you gonna yell at us this entire movie?" he asked. "You gotta stop yelling at us."

If Tom harbored anger, he funneled it into Jimmy Dugan.

"By the way, I loved you in *The Wizard of Oz*," he told Brailsford in a scripted diss comparing her to the Wicked Witch of the West. Though Tom, not big on substance abuse, was play-acting a drinker, you could practically smell the booze on his breath. While Freddie, to his amazement, dipped Skoal, Tom disliked chewing real tobacco and substituted Tootsie rolls, Raisinets, and energy bars. In one take, he spat the crushed-up food upon David Strathairn's shoe as Lowenstein calls out Jimmy's despicable leadership.

"Now, Jimmy, you have some pretty good ballplayers here," Strathairn pleaded. "You wanna give 'em a little bit of your—"

"Ballplayers? I haven't got ballplayers!" Tom bellowed, slurring his words. "I've got girls! Girls are what you sleep with after the game, not what you coach during the game."

The spitting caught Strathairn off guard.

"I just had to be there and hold my ground and not ruin the scene by laughing," he says. "It just seemed so real, so grounded, so perfect for the character. And he just kind of took the tone of the movie in his grasp and just held it there throughout. It was just brilliant."

Tom filmed two kissing scenes, but Penny included only one—Jimmy, half-asleep on the bus, groggily embracing Miss Cuthbert. When he opens his eyes, he freaks out and chugs a flask, then spits out the liquor, a reaction that was totally over the top, Penny thought, and yet undeniably rib-tickling. The other kiss involved Jimmy and Dottie. As the coach gets to know his standout Peach, and beholds her humbling excellence, he starts taking his job seriously. His turning point occurs toward the middle of the film: he's annoyed when he notices Dottie giving signs to Marla, who's at bat; Dottie, coaching the team in his absence, triggers a nagging fear that he's useless and good-for-nothing. After all, this woman, this force of nature who is way out of his league, makes him look bad. Jimmy, motivated to assert his masculine authority, sends Marla conflicting signs, finally stepping into his managerial responsibilities. Along his path to redemption, he develops into a better version of himself, all because of Dottie. Is she the superior manager of the two? The movie suggests so and allows undercurrents of romantic attraction to zing between the unlikely work spouses, who share intimacies and affectionate gestures while sitting together on the bus. For instance, as Jimmy reaches for a bottle of beer, Dottie, looking out for his well-being, hands him a Coke instead.

The studio had wanted Dottie to help the alcoholic get sober, but Penny refused, protesting, "I ain't doing that scene." She did, however, appease Columbia executives' desire for Jimmy to crush hard on a married muse. In the shooting script, one night Dottie watches Jimmy hit off a pitching machine after a game. He practically proposes marriage on the spot:

> **JIMMY:** I love watching you play. You're like Cobb or Williams. It's like you're starving and every pitch was a meal. I love that.
> **DOTTIE:** No. I just like to play . . .
> **JIMMY:** You're an animal. You're a ballplaying animal. (using his hand to indicate three levels, each one higher than before) Food—air—baseball. That's you.

Dramatic much? Still, Jimmy's insight pierces Dottie's steely front and awakens her soul, drawing out a not-so-humble brag that contains the ring of truth.

> **DOTTIE:** You know sometimes when I'm out there, it feels perfect. Like I'm doing something perfect.
> **JIMMY:** Right.
> **DOTTIE:** And I think . . . I can do anything. I can catch everything they hit and I can hit everything they throw. And I'm the best. And I love it!
>
> **She's FLUSHED with excitement. He grabs her and KISSES her. She lets him. A moment later, she pulls back. Dottie is STUNNED. So is Jimmy.**

Oof.

> **JIMMY:** I'm sorry. I . . . tripped . . . It's my knee . . .
> **DOTTIE:** (almost crying) How could you do that to me? I thought you liked me.

She runs into the locker room and tells Lowenstein she's quitting the league. When he asks if Jimmy is the reason, she declines to confirm his accurate suspicions; and when he asks if it's Kit, with whom she has growing tension, she says, "It's not really." He offers to trade Dottie to Racine, where he sent Marla so she could be with Nelson, but soon changes his mind and sacrifices a furious Kit, not perfect Dottie. (Kit blames Dottie anyway.) In Ganz and Mandel's original order of events, Dottie remains a Peach but stops speaking to Jimmy, who's crossed moral and professional lines. As far as baseball goes, she's got her eyes on the prize at the start of Rockford and Racine's seven-game championship series, ignoring newly traded Kit and happily reuniting with Marla, who reveals that she's pregnant. Mr. Harvey, watching the women from afar, complains, "They're kissing each other on the field . . . I don't go for that." A blamey Jimmy tries to make peace:

> **JIMMY:** You know it wasn't just my fault. You were there too, you know.
> **DOTTIE:** I was tired. I was lonely.
> **JIMMY:** Oh, and I have a rich, full life.

He begs her to be his friend again, and she blows him off. The game heats up: Doris hits a grounder and Dottie, on first base, races for second, sliding straight into Marla, who flips head over heels and crashes on the dirt. For many Peaches and Belles, baseball is life, but for Marla, it is suddenly life and death, her unborn child at risk. She's taken away in a stretcher following the shocking collision, which stuntwomen performed at Bosse Field in September 1991. Dottie, horrified, insists that she didn't know Marla was blocking her path. "You knew," Kit chides, going in for the attack. "You act like nothing matters, like you don't even care, but you're so full of it. You'd do anything to win." Chiming in, Doris remarks, "Jesus, Dottie, it's only a game."

In her hotel room later, Dottie is relieved to learn that Marla and the baby are OK. Cut to a pleasant surprise: Bill Pullman, cast as Bob Hinson, walking through the door with a cane, his leg injured from a sniper attack. "Can we just hold each other for the rest of our lives?" she says through tears. When morning comes, Bob whisks her away to the Pacific Northwest, an outcome she prefers to toughing through the championship with resentful women on both sides, her sister glaring from the rival dugout.

With desperate eloquence, Jimmy seeks to change her mind before the Hinsons get out of Dodge.

> JIMMY: (softly) This is chickenshit, Dottie. You want to go back to Oregon and have a hundred babies, great. Hell, I'm in no position to tell anybody how to live . . . But sneaking out like this—quitting—you'll regret it for the rest of your life.
> DOTTIE: It just got too hard.
> JIMMY: It's supposed to be hard. If it wasn't hard everyone would do it. The "hard" is what makes it great.

In the editing room, Penny streamlined *A League of Their Own* to remove Marla's near-tragic tumble and Jimmy's improper pass at Dottie, instead focusing the suspense upon Dottie and Kit, the OG plot-stirrers. Beneath the bickering, the mismatched sisters represent different paths during a transitional time for women. Like many female traditionalists of her generation, Dottie formed her home life around a man. Even with newfound liberties, it was very hard for women to let go of centering the men in their lives, whether that was their husbands, their boyfriends, or their fathers. While Kit, an adventurer, yearns to take the road less traveled, Dottie chooses the status quo, the safest lane on the open highway. Penny understood Dottie's perspective and withheld judgment.

The day prior to her humiliating swap from Rockford to Racine, Kit goes nuclear after Dottie and Jimmy mutually decide to put her on the bench. As Kit, looking ragged, fumes in the dugout, Doris pours fuel on the fire.

"What's the matter, Kit?" Doris sneers. "You too big to finish your own games now?"

That was the final straw. Kit hurls her glove at Doris's head and attacks her, igniting a melee. (According to Lovitz, Rosie expressed genuine anger at Lori while filming the scene.) As the Peaches rush in to stop the fight, Dottie and Mae shove each other. Jimmy hoists Kit over his shoulder and dumps her hard in the locker room shower.

"You stay down there, and you cool off!" he orders, turning on the water. Penny had the girls improvise reactions. "She was in a fugue state," Helen Haley rationalizes to Doris, who explodes. "Shut up, Helen!"

Later, Kit—eye makeup smeared, voice breaking—accuses Dottie of treating her like a baby and being harder on her than other Peaches.

"I treated you like a pitcher," Dottie explains. "A pitcher who'd lost her stuff."

"I just get so mad," Kit wails, standing beside her locker. "Why do you gotta be so good?"

Geena's acting was controlled and less-is-more, a reflection of self-possessed Dottie, leading Rosie to call her "Geena the Macheena." But Lori oozed raw emotion, exposing every nerve ending within her slender frame. Her performance felt unscripted and from the gut and echoed the exhaustion of Kit's Sisyphean struggle to prove herself and receive the validation she craves from Dottie. It's frustrating to think that Dottie might just be incapable of providing the emotional support that Kit so desperately needs. Then again, Dottie is not Kit's therapist—she's the ballast stabilizing the ship and Kit the wind in the sails, blowing every which way. Kit is beyond Dottie's control.

Cameraman Gary Muller sensed strain in the way Geena and Lori moved around each other, showing an awkward chemistry that bugged Penny. They seemed happier when they were apart.

Lori's frayed nerves were visible on set. She would joke that she weighed only eighty pounds toward the end of the movie—if she did lose any weight, stress likely factored in. Lori was tired, and in her downtime, she slept, read, wrote, and watched Blockbuster videos. She was often aloof from the rest of the cast, and she seemed insecure about her looks and the role, say people close to the production. Although Lori ranked second on the call sheet, "She was overshadowed," a former PA says. And she was still young, still processing all of this, all at once. At times she misunderstood the dynamics of people's positions. "Will you go get me some water?" she asked a crew member who did not work in catering. But she showed up, knew her lines, and gave it the best she had. While Tom and Geena slipped in and out of character with a veteran actor's ease, Lori appeared Method in comparison. She could require a bit more time to get into a scene. In the championship games, "she wanted those scenes to be right," John Rusk recalls. She was extremely present, especially in the Racine dugout, fatigued and covering her head with a glove. "She was like that—on the edge of hyperventilating," Rusk says. "But that was her being the character. She was just that intense."

Penny liked what Lori was doing and directed her to keep doing it. As Lori got older, she learned a valuable acting lesson: "You don't try to milk an emotion or continue an emotion," she says. Instead, "Go outside and have a Coke. Go eat a peanut butter and jelly sandwich. Get away from it so you can go back fresh. 'Cause fresh is how you got there to begin with."

Cut to Geena, observing Lori's anxiety attack from afar. She looked concerned—as Dottie, at least. Jimmy's impassioned, spirit-lifting lecture, the verbal equivalent of Ted Lasso's "Believe" sign, had made an impact, forcing Bob to turn the car around and drive his determined wife back to Wisconsin. The contest was too important to lose, and though Dottie's heart belongs to Bob, her allegiance lies with her team. She's got to finish the job, even if that means defeating the person for whom baseball is more than a temporary diversion.

ON A SATURDAY IN SEPTEMBER, NINE THOUSAND EXTRAS LINED UP OUTSIDE Bosse Field for the Women's World Series, waiting as much as four hours to get inside. The production needed about five thousand faces to fill the stands—actual living, breathing humans, not the life-size cutouts that had been distributed in the upper levels. Team Penny worried that volunteers would get bored and leave, since word had spread that donating unpaid time to sit idle in loaned period clothing wasn't all it was cracked up to be. Sometimes it looked like nothing was happening. Lights were being strung. Sound was being tested. Actors sat on the field under umbrellas. Well, the townspeople had jobs to do too. Their lives didn't revolve around a movie shoot.

As bait, *A League of Their Own* launched a publicity campaign to get bodies in seats, dangling raffle prizes (a car, televisions, and cash) and free entertainment: Tom danced to "Tequila," Geena and Rosie performed "Bohemian Rhapsody," and Rosie belted out "Like a Virgin," prompting Madonna to bolt out of the dugout and tackle her. Madonna, who mooned Groom Stadium's bleacher-fillers in August, paused those shock-and-awe shenanigans and grinned as she threw signed baseballs into the crowds. With Fun Aunt energy, she fawned over the tiniest extra, two-month-old Kaitlyn Marie Willis, whom she jokingly renamed "Laverne." And when seventy-three-year-old Oscar Loveless won a photo with her, she hugged and kissed him on the field, saying, "Now you're no longer loveless."

The Evansville media was eager to score a big Madonna exclusive. Intrepid reporters hid in cornfields waiting for a sighting, and Dan Katz, an anchor at 14 News, broadcast an amusing segment titled "Searching for Madonna," in which an intern dressed like her and walked around town. *A League of Their Own*'s publicist, Stuart Fink, kept journalists at arm's length until it came time to promote the World Series giveaways. Usually, Fink gave off condescending airs, "like a city slicker" deigning to speak with "rubes on a cornfield," Evansville meteorologist Jeff Lyons says, adding that as Fink's attitude softened, getting schmoozier, "the people around here could see through it." They were savvy and understood how to play the game, blithely accepting the access he offered.

As Lyons reported the weather off third base, wearing a sailor costume to match the throwback climate, Fink pushed Ro and Mo on him without warning. The ambush interview aired live, with Mo hiding behind Ro and whispering in her ear.

"You look just like Pee-Wee Herman in kind of a cute, masculine way," Ro said, relaying what Mo had told her. "And she hopes that you're free to go to Haub's steakhouse tomorrow night."

"OK, well, thank you," he replied, thinking quickly on his feet. "We won't take in any movies then since I look like Pee-Wee Herman. That could be potentially dangerous, actually."

Weeks back, Paul Reubens, who played the hammy Pee-Wee on his popular children's TV show, was arrested in Florida for pleasuring himself at an adult movie theater.

"Very funny," Ro quipped, advising Lyons not to quit his day job. She then declared that Mo would put on a ballpark concert the following day. Mo, squashing the false news, shook her head back and forth. *Madonna, perform pro bono? Come on now.*

Fink placed a fedora-clad Dan Katz and his wife, Beth, in prime seating where the couple watched an airborne glove topple Justin Scheller, the five-year-old who beat out four hundred other kids to land the role of Evelyn's obnoxious son, Stilwell, a thorn in Jimmy's backside. Scheller had a tough time filming the scene in which Jimmy flings a mitt at Stilwell's head, knocking the daylights out of the little devil. "Tom Hanks didn't want to hit me hard," Scheller says, recalling how he froze while anticipating the glove hitting him. People were getting frustrated, so Rosie took Scheller aside and tried to distract him. "Look at the camera," she ordered, "and say, 'You're gonna lose!'" Then someone, possibly a grip, not Tom, did the dirty deed and the child fell over. Everybody went crazy, including Penny, who requested forty more takes. The element of surprise had worked. "Nobody likes to get hit in the face," he says, "and I was in so much shock." In a take where Scheller sat up, dazed and confused, Bitty—the only Peach to play a mother—reassured, "He's OK," while Rosie, breaking character, looked at the lens with an authentic laugh.

Scheller, sweet and well-behaved off camera, was from Saint Wendel, Indiana. His mother, Golda, who read that Penny was auditioning local boys, took him to the casting call on a lark. Amazingly, the Stilwell search came down to Scheller and a boy who looked exactly like Dennis the Menace, and in the end, he says, Penny picked "the chunky little kid instead of the skinny brat." He had a rosy-cheeked Norman Rockwell look that matched *League*'s playful tone—when you saw him, you smiled with affection. Bitty was maternal toward Scheller, coaching the neophyte on his scenes, and Ro and Mo played video games with him. Ro even let him borrow her handheld Sega Genesis.

*But now, without further ado, the nail-biter to end all nail-biters. The moment of truth. Game seven, Dottie versus Kit. As Kit steps up to the plate, Ellen Sue's on the mound. "High fastballs," Dottie advises the pitcher. "She can't hit 'em, can't lay off 'em." She shoots daggers at the embattled Belle, looking as though she could eat her alive, and fastens on her catcher's mask, her suit of armor. This is war.*

*Strike one.*

*Strike two.*

*The third time's the charm. Kit whacks a high one into right field.*

As a hidden crew member threw to her, Lori, a self-professed "competitive motherfucker," genuinely made the hit that you see in the movie. "I really like them high and outside," she said. "I ran the bases perfectly. Your foot is supposed to touch the inside of the bag with your outside foot, and I did that with no stutter steps or anything."

Lori rounded the diamond three times per Penny's orders, a Louma crane tracking her trajectory. On the third take, Lori puked everywhere. ("Because you drank and smoked," Penny reminded her later.)

"Do it again," Penny said.

"Penny, I just puked!"

"I don't care. Let's do it again!"

*Dottie registers shock as Evelyn fields the hit and throws to Marbleann. Kit rounds third, charging at Dottie like an angry bull. They collide and fall to the ground.*

Both Lori and her double, Shelly Adlard, recall separately sliding into Geena's stuntwoman to film the home-plate pileup. According to Adlard, Lori wanted to do the unadulterated stunt but was cautioned away from unnecessary roughness due to her foot injury. Penny, completing her anamorphic jigsaw, wound up using a neat shot of Lori hurtling through the air—evidence, Lori says, that she got dirt in the skirt.

"You can see my Marky Mark underwear on underneath those horrible fucking satin shorts we had to wear that just really held in the heat so nicely," Lori tells me, adding, "I had a logistical double who would be around, but I did every single thing you see in the movie."

Lori never warmed to Adlard, who was equally competitive. When they met for the first time, they raced each other, surprising Penny. Every so often, actresses would take pity on Adlard, apologizing for Lori's apparent animus.

*Oh, no! The ball has a mind of its own. It escapes Dottie's clutches, rolling off her fingers. "Safe!" yells the umpire, calling the World Series for Racine. The Belles crowd around Kit and lift the pennant-clinching victor atop their shoulders. Jimmy looks on, shaken, while Dottie's lips curl into a smile.*

To this day, the Peaches' loss remains the biggest upset in the sports film genre. The fans were deeply invested in Rockford and Dottie, their hero. They expected her to go all the way, but Kit, *that miserable striver*, had to go and ruin *everything*, stealing Dottie's rightful title: champion. There was no way, the fans believed, that Dottie Hinson, that paragon of competence, could lose her grip on that ball. That belief stoked a favorite theory among her loyalists: she threw the game on purpose as an act of love. Since Dottie intended to trade her catcher's mitt for an oven mitt, she had nothing to lose by letting Kit win, by making her year, by giving her a life.

Bitty and Kathleen Marshall, whom Penny promoted from PA to Rockford Peach for the grand finale, think Dottie dropped the ball intentionally. Geena knows the answer but prefers keeping it to herself. "Everybody has so much fun arguing about it," she says, careful not to spoil the debate with the last word on the matter. And Lori? She defends Kit as winning fair and square.

"Everybody has different life experiences," she says. "Right? So for those of us who fought and clawed and, you know, climbed fucking mountains [with] bare feet and shit, we know that Kit cut her in half and won, right? There are people who maybe have a simpler life or maybe think they control shit more than they control. And maybe they think she dropped the ball on purpose—I mean, I don't know. I don't know if I worded that correctly. I just think there's different ways of thinking."

Ponders Lori: "And then, why would you ever drop the ball on purpose in a World Series?"

Good question. Kelly Candaele takes the perspective of an academic with athletic lineage. "The biblical scholar John Dominic Crossan, in his book *The Dark Interval*, writes about the importance of games in reinforcing the ways in which [they] teach us about our own limitations as human beings," Candaele wrote in *NINE: A Journal of Baseball History and Culture.*

> The complex rules of baseball, for instance, limit what we can do on the field as players, circumscribes the area where the action takes place. The game is designed in a way to make failure one of its essential features. No one has, or ever will, [played] the game perfectly. In fact, a game that could theoretically be played perfectly would soon become boring. Thoughtful professional athletes appreciate this fact, while most fans do not. According to Crossan's reading, serious games are a practice for a life of "disciplined failure," for the inevitable limitations and disappointments that every life entails. No one can be better than the game itself, but the limitations the game imposes by its rules and difficulty is what sustains our enjoyment of it.

When Jimmy says, "It's supposed to be hard," he alludes to the sport's rigors. Even Dottie can't transcend its laws. If she cheated to lose, then she disrespected the league and its sisterhood, Kit most of all. She would have rendered Kit a fraud by design. Could Dottie even live with the guilt over the dishonor? While Penny left the ball drop open to interpretation, the shooting script carried a whiff of a suggestion that cheating occurred:

KIT: Did you drop that ball on purpose?
DOTTIE: Who me? You know I'd do anything to win.
KIT: Yeah, but you never drop the ball.
DOTTIE: You just beat me. You wanted it more than I did.
KIT: (dubious) Yeah? . . . I don't know.

After a brief hug, the sisters acknowledge their deepening rift.

DOTTIE: I really didn't get you traded. I swear.
KIT: (believes her) I know. I just get . . . so . . .

Dottie nods.

DOTTIE: I know.

They almost laugh.

KIT: But, you know, someday, I'll figure it all out. And then we'll be buddies.
DOTTIE: Yeah?—I feel like we're—drifting away. Like we're—not gonna be close.
KIT: (trying to be more positive) Oh . . . you never know.

They share one last exchange before parting for good.

DOTTIE: Lay off those high ones.
KIT: I kill the high ones.
DOTTIE: Mule.
KIT: Nag.

They board their separate buses, as Dottie stares across SADLY.

"I don't know if my mom ever thought about the ways in which competition with her sister Margaret may have contained elements of irresolvable family rivalry," Candaele said of Helen Callaghan, adding, "Some moviegoers clearly regard *A League of Their Own* as a morality tale about conflicting loyalties. I prefer a more pragmatic view. By not dropping the ball on purpose, Dottie was not choosing one set of loyalties over another—her teammates as opposed to her sister—but was simply playing the game according to the suppositions of the game itself. By doing so, it is clear my mom betrayed neither the integrity of the game—or her teammates."

MIROSLAV ONDRICEK WAS EXHAUSTED. IN OCTOBER HE TOOK A BREAK TO rest and never returned. Though he and Penny weren't buddy-buddy, they shared a mutual respect. Yet that connection fizzled as Penny grew closer to Tom Priestley, his A-camera operator. It upset Ondricek to feel his authority diminish, but nonetheless he handed the reins to Priestley, *A League of Their Own*'s unofficial DP in its ending stages. Priestley began his new post the day Geena and Bill Pullman filmed their reunion scene. Penny sat on the bed in Dottie's bedroom, giving direction and talking with her hands. At one point, someone in the crew jumped on her. "She was rough-housing in the bedroom—like, just playing while they were rehearsing or setting up lights or whatever," Erica Arvold, a tall casting assistant recruited to stand in for Geena, remembers. (Pullman did not have a stand-in; Arvold, hugging him for a camera setup, mistakenly held on too long. Pullman was a gentleman about the gaffe.)

Penny terrified Arvold. "Not because she was obnoxious and mean, but she just was herself. And she was brash," she observes. "And I come from a very gentle family. And just even her way of speaking—her enthusiasm for everything—it was not what I was used to." It felt, to Arvold, like watching fireworks. She wasn't nurturing; rather, Arvold says, she was "bold and big and opinionated and amazing."

Priestley was also brash, a strong personality from New Jersey who had assisted Ondricek on *Amadeus* and *Awakenings*. His impressive list of credits included *Network*, *Annie Hall*, and the Meryl Streep movies *Kramer vs. Kramer*, *Sophie's Choice*, *Silkwood*, and the underrated *She-Devil*. Ondricek's work was "brilliant," Priestley says, "and I learned a lot from him. He was great. I loved working with him." He appreciated the creative freedom that Ondricek gave him. "European cinematographers would basically just light and converse with the director on certain things," he says, "where a camera operator worked directly with the director to set up shots, talk about the coverage, the extra shots needed and the angles and all the different techniques." A New York–based cinematographer, by contrast, multitasked the above while his camera operator fulfilled his primary function: operating the camera. Not so on *A League of Their Own*, where Priestley, replacing Ondricek, earned an "additional photographer" credit.

Emotions ran high when the Peaches filmed the scene in which Stilwell runs up and down the bus, wreaking havoc. (Justin Scheller felt uncomfortable hitting the women with fly swatters and had to be talked into it.) The seasons were changing, and the women were burned out. (In a show of solidarity, Geena had T-shirts made that read "Free the Peaches." Penny rolled her eyes at the sight.) The team had sat on that bus for a long time. In Freddie Simpson's memory, Ondricek's substitute "was not very nice. And he was yelling at everybody all the time and it was just kind of endlessly going on."

As Scheller darted past Freddie, he messed up her hair. She reached up to smooth it, drawing Priestley's ire. "Watch out!" she quotes him saying. "You're fucking blocking Madonna!"

She says he screamed at her on the next take.

She stood up. "*You* are not *ever* allowed to speak to me this way again," she told him. "I will not stand another minute of all this screaming, all the ways that we're being treated right now. It's not OK."

Several Peaches stood up and said, "Yeah!"

He ran off the bus.

"Penny tried to talk to me," Freddie says, "and she was like, 'Well, you know, Freddie, you know, it's stressful for everybody.' I'm like, 'Hey, I'll take direction from *you* but I won't take direction from this guy.'"

Priestley was frustrated and tired. "I didn't yell at her," he says. "It was exasperation."

Penny shut down the shoot, calling it a day. Freddie was scared, thinking, "What did I do?" Later, other men on the crew called Freddie to commend her for speaking up. The next morning or so, she glimpsed Priestley sitting quietly without looking at anyone.

"Are you OK?" she asked him.

"Yeah," she says he answered. "Sorry. I've been yelling."

"Yeah, OK, it happens to everybody," she said.

From that point onward, heads cooled, and the raging subsided. The production, signaling that Freddie was in the right, pushed her call time to a later hour.

One morning, an Eastman Kodak van showed up on location, unloading cases of Champagne alongside the country road where the Peaches' bus driver leaves the team in a lurch. The New York–based company, which provided cameras and film to Hollywood, happily rewarded Penny for surpassing one million feet of film. According to Gary Muller, she shot up to twelve thousand feet each day, and eventually her grand total would eclipse two million feet. Penny's sound editor, Dennis Drummond, recalls a colleague's estimate that the film strips were lengthy enough to wrap around Manhattan "like three or four times." Overjoyed, Kodak pulled out all the stops: it sent a high school marching band in Penny's honor and arranged a lobster lunch with all the trimmings. Says Elliot Abbott of Penny, "She really attacks a lobster."

In another roadside surprise, on October 15 Garry hired a plane to fly overhead, trailing a banner that shouted, "HAPPY BIRTHDAY, PENNY." "He's a good brother," she said.

The women's boarding house scenes were filmed at the Soaper-Esser House in Henderson, Kentucky, and the bus and locker room interiors were shot inside an Evansville airplane hangar that operated during World War II. Within the hangar, Team Penny checked off the Pee Scene, a late script addition that best boy grip Billy Kerwick spotted Ganz and Mandel writing on the bathroom floor of a Radisson Hotel lobby. It marks the first time the Peaches encounter Jimmy, who stumbles drunk into their changing room and relieves himself in a urinal for a full fifty-three seconds. Penny stood off to the side with a water hose and bucket, controlling Tom's "urine" flow so that he didn't know when he would stop peeing. The Peaches reacted with varying degrees of horror and fascination, and once more, Tom translated Penny for them, saying, "OK, girls! Louder, faster, funnier!"

Rosie had just about had it.

"You need to tell Laverne that we need to get going here," Jim Kleverweis, a PA, remembers her telling the first AD, Mike Haley, who streaked the set to lighten the mood.

While Rosie loved Penny, and vice versa, the two differed in their opinions of how Rosie should approach Doris's short monologue revealing why she settled for her deadbeat boyfriend. Rosie read a queer subtext between the lines.

"None of the other boys ever, uh . . . always made me feel like I was wrong, you know?" Doris says. "Like I was some sort of a weird girl or a strange girl or not even a girl, just 'cause I could play. I believed them, too, but not anymore, you know? I mean, lookit: there's a lot of us. I think we're all all right."

"We are," Betty Spaghetti seconds.

Kit nods in agreement, and Doris takes her boyfriend's photograph and rips it up, dumping the pieces out the bus window.

"Rosie, this is not a gay thing," Penny said. "This is just, you know, that she-don't-feel-normal, now-she-does."

"Well, all I'm doing is reciting the lines, the words that they wrote, that's what I'm doing," Rosie explained. "I didn't change one line."

"No, but don't do it like that," Penny said. "Can you not do it like that?"

Rosie, who understood Doris as Penny could not, stayed true to her original delivery.

"So I did it again," she tells me, "but I did it the same way because that's what the speech meant to me: that here she was, this gay woman, at a time when you weren't allowed to be gay, completely in love with this woman, Mae—and doesn't even know what to do about it." Doris, she adds, "doesn't even really know that it means she's gay."

Penny "made a choice not to deal with the women's sexuality," Rosie says. "It was very interesting when we met them all"—the real-life players—"and they all had partners . . . some absurd statistic percentages of those women were, in fact, lesbians. And that was kept silent and out of *A League of Their Own*."

Some of those aging players had roommates, so to speak, and did not put a public label on their partnerships. Others had husbands, confusing observers who assumed all women who play baseball are gay. When Penny, angling for a broad box-office hit, chose to ignore the AAGPBL's queer history, she perpetuated a cycle of silence that muzzled athletes and actresses alike from coming out on the wider stage. It was, as they say, a different time, with Penny unwilling to push boundaries and apparently uninterested in doing so. "[She] was playing in a boy's club," Megan Cavanagh says. "She was not gay." Nor was she "making a film about gay women," Renée Coleman explains. "She was making a film about baseball players who happened to be women. If you were gonna make that film now, you would also absolutely include the fact that many of them had found a kind of safe space for the first time in their lives to actually be gay."

On the last day in Evansville, hearts were heavy. Robin Knight cried her eyes out, and Madonna wiped Patti Pelton's tears. "I loved my li'l sis, Lori Petty, and all our teammates," Geena reflected in her memoir. "I have to think we were feeling something like what the original Peaches did, back in the day—bonded by this extraordinary experience we all shared. And we're all still very close to this day." Affirms Sam Hoffman, who became a producer and director for film and TV: "When it ended, everybody was just convulsively sobbing. I've never been on a movie where, like, everybody just was so intensely connected to each other." The forced proximity forged lasting friendships. New York and LA were working towns, all about the hustle, but Indiana was like going off to college. It was really getting to know people, enough where you can be your whole self. It was bonding through hardship. It was analog, before the iPhone monopolized attention and free time. It was pure and libertine. At the October 19 wrap party inside Marina Pointe, a bar and grill on the Ohio, George Bowers danced to Santana. While there was live music, Madonna only took the floor when a DJ spun.

As parting gifts, she gave a vibrator to Lori, and for others: satin boxer shorts with the word "Peaches" on the cuff. She wrote a letter to each Peach. "Don't take any shit," she told Megan, who had newly learned that she was pregnant. By that time, Hollywood was buzzing about her. Agents who wouldn't look at her were showing sudden interest, based on early word of mouth. Megan flew home to LA with costars while Rosie hitched a ride on Madonna's private jet, which landed at Van Nuys Airport. Ro and Mo got into separate cars and rolled down the windows as they went over the hills.

"Bye, Ro," Mo said.

After four long months with a glamorous new best friend, Ro felt that moment was like a movie—one that *she*, a humble daughter of Long Island, starred in. What had her life become?

Two giant trucks hauled Penny's antiques westward, but she couldn't go home yet, nor did she seem to want to. It was Cooperstown or bust.

## *Eighth Inning*

# COOPERSTOWN

A HELICOPTER LANDED IN THE MIDDLE OF DOUBLEDAY FIELD, TWO blocks from the National Baseball Hall of Fame and Museum. Penny stepped out of the aircraft eating a piece of pizza and greeted the senior citizens awaiting her arrival. "Hi, everybody," she said.

She'd invited AAGPBL vets to appear in the movie's epilogue: a poignant reunion centered around a Hall of Fame homage to the league, an echo of 1988. While touring the museum months earlier, Penny blanched at Cooperstown's league-centric exhibit—in Penny's eyes, it was "insignificant," though former Battle Creek Belle Mary Moore defends its size, saying, "It isn't a very big display. But it *is* a display."

Ondricek gave the thumbs-down. "When it came to thinking in cinematic terms," Penny recalled, "Miroslav simply called it 'ugly.' As a result, we took over a room and decorated it ourselves, making it look more like a genuine shrine to the pioneering women who inspired the movie."

She asked Ellen Lewis to find actresses who could pass for older versions of Geena, Lori, Madonna, Rosie, Megan, Tracy, and Freddie, as well as Anne Ramsay and Annie Cue. When Peaches offered to wear old-age prosthetics and graying wigs, Greenhut overrode their youthful enthusiasm, telling Penny, "Over my dead body we're gonna sit around for a week watching these girls get made up and go through their clown makeup."

Lewis championed hiring age-appropriate doppelgangers.

"It could fail," she says, "but it could work really well, and knock wood: I think it did."

All too often in these cases, suspension of disbelief is required to willingly—and begrudgingly—accept the incongruity of two actors playing the same role within the same work. But Lewis did one hell of a job. For Older Dottie, she discovered sixty-four-year-old Lynn Cartwright, a vision of Geena thirty years into the future who possessed high cheekbones, full lips, and brown eyes. Cartwright had been in the business since the 1950s, picking up character roles in the low-budget Western *Black Patch*—opposite her husband, the actor and screenwriter Leo Gordon—as well as the cult genre flicks *Queen of Outer Space* and *The Wasp Woman*. As she aged out of ingénue parts, she and Gordon joined the Group Repertory Theatre in North Hollywood. Blink, and you'll miss her brief appearance in *The Garbage Pail Kids Movie*, one of the worst films of 1987 and, perhaps, of all time. *A League of Their Own* would be her last film before she retired.

"Do we really even have to go to Cooperstown? 'Cause, you know, that'll never be in the movie."

So pondered John Rusk, who missed his family in Rhode Island. He hoped to be home by Halloween, but with *League* days over schedule, he was stuck in a holding pattern of Penny's making.

That taxing week, Team Penny's remaining troops filmed Cartwright as she reconnected with Older Doris, Older Mae, and Older Marla, played by charmers Vera Johnson, Eunice Anderson, and Patricia Wilson. Cartwright caught a ball bare-handed, as Dottie did at Harvey Field, and learned that Helen became a doctor, Ellen Sue married a plastic surgeon, and Mae settled down after sowing her wild oats. As for Dottie, she had been widowed since Bob's death the past winter. She and Kit were no longer in touch. Cue page 119 of Ganz and Mandel's primal script:

> **MARLA:** So, where's Kit? Did Kit come with you?
> **DORIS:** Yeah, where's the old Oregon Rifle?

**MAE:** Is it true? We heard she married some real rich guy and had like a hundred kids.
**DORIS:** Is she with you?
**DOTTIE:** Um, I . . . I don't really . . . Kit and I aren't that close.

**The others glance at each other, knowingly. Dottie is EMBARRASSED.**

**DOTTIE:** See, she stayed in Rockford and we . . . I mean we wrote . . . sometimes and Christmas, we used to . . . exchange . . . but we're not . . .
**MARLA:** Let's play some ball.

Penny filmed Greenhut and Pickles Dries, who pitched three seasons with the Peaches in the 1950s, as they observed Cartwright from Doubleday's plain metal bleachers.

**GREENHUT:** Who's that?
**PICKLES:** Oh, that's Dottie Hinson. Best darn ballplayer in the league.

Greenhut volunteered to play Man in Bleachers, not wanting to pay an actor to say the dinky line. On the field, Penny pointed a stealth camera at Mary Moore and other seniors playing ball. "We didn't know she was filming," Moore says. Penny came out of the woodwork to ask, "We got any sliders?" One gal raised her hand and ran in and slid. Moore, standing on second, followed suit.

With just twenty-four hours to film inside the museum, Penny milked every second. She invited Mark Holton (Older Stilwell) to watch a baseball documentary in the upstairs theater. She hoped the film would put him in the right frame of mind to internalize the emotions of a reformed rascal who had watched his late mother do the extraordinary.

Holton heard she liked sake, so he handed her a gift: a small bottle of the sweet alcoholic beverage and a shot glass. She opened the bottle, took a few sips, and put it away. "And never really mentioned it except for a smile," he says.

There was not "a dry eye on the set," Penny recalled, as Holton held back tears reminiscing about Evelyn, telling Cartwright, "She always said it was the best time she ever had in her whole life."

Holton wanted to come close to choking up without going over the top. In one take, his jaw quivered with feeling. Penny yelled cut—yes, actually—and he filmed take two.

"Where was the quivering thing with the jaw?" a cameraman asked.

Holton did not try to recreate the quiver. That would've looked phony, he thought. (Penny wound up using one of his quiver-less takes in the movie.)

Cue Older Dottie walking past a photo of Jimmy, who died in 1987, and Older Ira cutting the ribbon to let the players—the real ones and the actresses pretending—into the exhibit. They crooned the "Victory Song" as Older Kit, portrayed by lookalike Kathleen Butler, entered the room with a large entourage of grandkids, confirming that she has, in fact, created a family and fully conformed to twentieth-century America's definition of female success. She and Dottie locked eyes and walked toward each other, embracing through teary smiles, closing the rift between them.

"I had a contingent of AAGPBL ladies who were heading back to Florida early the next morning, and I didn't want them to be delayed," Penny said. "I called them together and explained they could go back to the hotel for the night, and I'd shoot the rest without them, or they could stick around. It was their choice. But they had to know we were going to shoot late, possibly through the night. They exchanged looks. Then Pepper Davis stepped forward and, speaking for the group, said, 'That's okay, Penny. We'll consider it a doubleheader.'" In 2012, Penny remarked, "That still gets me."

The "Victory Song" burned a hole in Tim Bourne's ear. It felt like listening to "It's a Small World" on repeat, a continuation of the rousing singalong led by Freddie, whom Penny handpicked last-minute over Madonna, refusing to pull a Warren Beatty and exploit her recognizable voice at every opportunity.

The circus was relieved to wrap for good, but if Penny had her way, the show would go on. "She didn't want to say goodbye," Bourne says, also witness to her separation anxiety on *Awakenings*. "She was the captain of the boat, you know? And now it's over. Now she's gotta go to a little dark room for several months. She would say that she hated the whole process, but I don't think that was really true."

After pulling an all-nighter, Jim Kleverweis fell asleep at the wheel driving four other drowsy production assistants back to the hotel in the morning. He snapped awake just in time, avoiding a potentially tragic accident. He had never been so tired in his life.

John Rusk's wife prepared to take the kids trick-or-treating without him. She created a half-man, half-woman costume because she'd be playing the role of both mom and dad. Rusk made it home in time.

It was safe to say that Penny accumulated enough material for two sequels and a six-part Ken Burns docuseries. She put four teams of editors to work on the second floor of Columbia Pictures and hired Richard Marks as a ghost editor. Marks, whom friends called "Richie," had edited Francis Ford Coppola's *Apocalypse Now* and *The Godfather Part II*, Jim Brooks's *Terms of Endearment* and *Broadcast News*, and the Charles Shyer and Nancy Meyers collaboration *Father of the Bride*. He was highly efficient with a sharp eye for comedy; like Penny, he knew where the joke was. Bowers accepted the additional hands, though feathers ruffled when Penny tapped two editors to take turns handling the same reel. She worked with whoever was available, even if the overlap led an editor to gripe, "What the hell happened to Reel 5?"

In editing mode, Penny was lovely and gruff, and wore tinted sunglasses. She smelled of cigarettes and played poker with post-production staff as the reels loaded.

On April 29, 1992, a man walked into the darkened bubble where Team Penny scrutinized frames and mixed sound.

"Do you know you guys are the only ones here in the building?" he asked.

Hours earlier, a predominantly white Ventura County jury acquitted four LAPD officers of brutally assaulting Rodney King, a Black man. A bystander had videotaped the atrocity one year earlier. The verdict sparked six days of riots that immobilized the city and left sixty-three people dead.

Everyone got into their cars and entered traffic gridlock; Penny called Gary Muller and Mollie Mallinger from her cell phone. That spring, the camera professionals were in the area shooting *Calendar Girl*, a Parkway Productions comedy-drama that Penny set up at Columbia with John Whitesell in the director's seat. It starred *Beverly Hills, 90210* hunk Jason

Priestley as a 1960s dreamer on a quest to meet Marilyn Monroe. Tom Priestley, a name twin with Jason, was the cinematographer.

"I'm in the crew van and I'm on neighborhood watch," Penny said, apparently landing safely in the Hills. She wanted to make sure they were OK.

"Penny," Mollie said from her Malibu Canyon condo, where Muller was living platonically, "maybe you should come here because nobody's gonna find us where we live."

When LA's caffeinated grind was buzzing normally, Geena dropped by the studio's Culver City lot to dub Cartwright's voice, which proved a challenge for her since she talked faster than Cartwright. The vocal dubbing is "what really made people positive that it was me," says Geena, loving that she fooled them.

Tom Hanks, noticeably slimmer, stared at himself onscreen during a looping session and said, "Penny, where's my limp? You know how long I practiced doing that limp."

He was extremely pleased with how awful he looked.

"They'd put me in a really boxy suit for the first scene and I looked like a behemoth," he told the *LA Times*. "I had rolls of fat on my neck. And my fingers . . . I looked ham-fisted in that thing." He added, "I didn't want him to have my skinny little wrists and pipe-cleaner neck. I didn't want him to look like me."

Lori, eager to learn more about moviemaking, shadowed Penny in the edit chambers. Nearby, De Niro reviewed a reel from *This Boy's Life*, a coming-of-age drama in which he plays an abusive stepdad.

"You guys gotta come in here," he said, ushering the women to his side. Like a proud father, he bragged on the talents of his movie stepson, a seventeen-year-old rookie named Leonardo DiCaprio.

"Look at this fucking kid," Lori quotes Bobby as saying.

Leo wowed Lori. She knew a movie star when she saw one.

Meanwhile, Lori wowed Dennis Drummond, the sound editor. "She was just a badass little baseball player," he says, vocally Team Kit.

One afternoon, *New York Times* reporter Peggy Orenstein grilled Penny in her production office as a *League* art director mocked up vintage newspapers across the hall. Invoking her Oscar snubs, Orenstein solicited her take on Hollywood's undeniable gender bias—at the time, women directed just 5 percent of studio films. Penny flatly refused the bait.

"I'm a director," she said. "I'm a woman. But to classify man-directors, woman-directors—can't we just say director? I'm not trying to avoid the issue. It's just that it makes me crazy. I mean, they say, 'They won't give big-budget action movies to women.' As a woman, I wouldn't wanna *do* a big-budget action movie. It doesn't *interest* me."

That was ironic because *A League of Their Own* contained action shots galore. (The moody Kit and Jimmy provided the metaphorical explosions.)

After the *Times* interview, Penny returned to work, putting the finishing touches on the feel-good Cooperstown coda. She did not address the stunted progress for women in baseball—indeed, little changed since the league disbanded—and swept the sad truth underneath a bed of marshmallow fluff. In Penny's ending, the Peaches apparently lack bitterness toward the men who killed their unconventional livelihoods. They're grateful to have played at all, and their passive acceptance reflects a lifetime of lowered expectations: *That's just the way it was, you know? Why press for a bigger display?*

Melancholy for the glory days, the best time of their lives, washes over the wistful closing image: a black-and-white photo, a nod to *Hoosiers*, of the Peaches and their coach. Penny directed the camera to zoom in on Dottie and Kit, flanked by Betty Spaghetti and Ellen Sue, and linger there a while.

"You hold it too long," Marks told her in post-production. "I think it's a little manipulative. Let me just try this other thing."

Penny took a beat, then shook her head.

"Nahhhhh," she said. "Leave it that way. I like it like that."

SHE SCREENED HER FIRST CUT FOR TRUSTED SOUNDING BOARDS, INCLUDING her brother, Garry, her friend Randy Newman (the singer-songwriter who scored *The Natural*), and *League* survivor Joe Hartwick, who had fretted over filming delays, telling a fellow producer, "We're screwed."

When the lights came up, Penny asked, "Is it too schmaltzy?"

"Not for me, love," Hartwick said, touched by the movie's heart. "I think it works just perfectly."

Hans Zimmer, the wunderkind German composer, wrote the score. He "didn't know shit about baseball," Penny said, but she admired his music for *Driving Miss Daisy* and "knew he could do Americana." Amusingly, when Zimmer showed up in Culver City, he wore a trench coat. *Who wears a trench coat in Los Angeles?* People laughed behind his back.

One day, Penny and her editors listened to the song that Madonna and Shep Pettibone cowrote for the movie's end credits. While recording *Erotica*, her sexually charged concept album with a deep-house groove, Madonna took a two-day break to hum the melody over computerized chords and rewrite a string arrangement. The result: "This Used to Be My Playground," an atmospheric downer that *Stereogum* writer Tom Breihan accurately described as a "morose torch ballad." The brooding lyrics evoke nostalgia and regret—"This used to be my playground / This used to be my childhood dream"—as Mo pines for the past. She references the AAGPBL obliquely, asking, "Why did it have to end?"

Penny was not impressed.

"Goddamn it," Christopher Capp, an assistant editor, quotes her as saying. "No way am I putting this piece of crap in my movie."

Not two seconds later, Amy Pascal phoned Penny, asking if she'd heard "This Used to Be My Playground." Pascal thought it was brilliant, Capp recalls, and couldn't wait to use it in the movie.

"Penny had a fight with the studio because she did not want it," he says. "She didn't know that Madonna was going behind her back either. She thought she was the only one who was getting it. And Madonna was smart enough to send it to everybody. That way nobody could override her and say, 'This isn't gonna be in the movie.'"

Penny and Elliot Abbott argued about the song. He predicted that it would be a top-selling single; she disagreed. "OK, we'll see," he said.

She had asked Carole King to write something special, initially intending to use King's submission, "Now and Forever," over the rolling credits—prime placement for an original theme. King grounded the saccharine tune with her trademark gravelly rasp, a contrast that won Penny over. But an entitlement within Madonna's contract bumped "Now and Forever" out of the slot, giving Penny little choice but to prioritize her brassiest Peach. When she informed King of the situation, the singer-songwriter was bummed. Penny found a spot for "Now and Forever" in *A League of Their*

*Own*'s opening scene, a post-production add-on filmed at a home in Sherman Oaks, an LA suburb. Reprising Older Dottie, Cartwright filmed her character leaving for Cooperstown with reluctance.

"Come on, Mom," her daughter urges. "I mean, you're gonna get to see Aunt Kit! You two hardly ever get to see each other."

"We *still* won't," Dottie complains. "Kit won't be there. She'll be traveling around with that husband of hers."

"Frank: He has a name," her daughter corrects. "And he's always been very nice to you."

Dottie worries that no one will remember her. She feels left out. Plus, "It was never that important to me," she says. "It was just something I did. That's all."

Caving to the pressure, she heads out the door while her two grandsons play basketball in the driveway. She advises the older boy, the Dottie, to go easy on his sibling, and the younger one, the Kit, to "kill him."

The scene tempers the sisters' Hall of Fame hug and undercuts the premise of an estrangement. Test audiences "did not believe that the sisters would be estranged from each other," Rusk says. The feedback forced Columbia to order a rosier reshoot of Geena and Lori's post–World Series farewell. A set was constructed on a soundstage.

Penny's finished cut did not sit right with Mark Canton, Columbia's newly installed president.

"Why not end on Geena, Tom, and Lori?" he asked Penny.

"Because that ain't the end of the movie."

"Well, I don't know," he said. "These are old ladies."

*Yeesh.* To be fair, though, he did have a point: the movie stood mightily on its own without the flash-forwards into the present day. Several of the contemporary scenes now have dated Lifetime Original Movie vibes while everything in between remains propulsive, epic filmmaking.

In October 1991, the forty-two-year-old Canton replaced the seasoned Frank Price, two decades his senior, hoping to green-light films with social relevance. He was one of those self-made success stories, a hotshot who started in the Warner Brothers mailroom and worked his way upward. At Warner's, Canton oversaw the production of *Batman* and *Lethal Weapon* but was also involved with *The Bonfire of the Vanities*, which he praised as the best movie he'd ever seen before it crashed and burned. A fast talker with curly hair, he had a flair for Italian-made clothing. Supernova stars and directors bedazzled him.

"I'm not slow-moving," Canton told the *LA Times*. "I'm not going to come in walking, but I won't drive the car off the road, either."

While Price's colleagues grumbled that he moved too slowly on projects, under his watch the studio released John Singleton's *Boyz n the Hood*, a critical and commercial smash. His exit disappointed Penny, who named Older Kit's spouse after him.

The month he started at Columbia, Canton visited Penny on set in Cooperstown. She insisted that he take her antiques on the company jet and fly them back to LA. He was furious, not to mention late for a scheduled dinner with Mike Nichols.

Cooperstown "was hallowed ground," Canton says. "But I never understood why Penny felt the need to kind of explain what's going on when people were into what was going on. She over-milked the joke, you know?"

Neither did he understand her decision to cut the kiss that had AAGPBL players up in arms. *That doesn't happen when your husband's at war*, they argued, decrying Dottie's transgression.

*We can't keep the kiss*, Penny and Abbott explained to Canton. *Tom and Geena will be hated.*

"Well, Canton was batshit," Abbott says. "He said, 'What do you mean?' He said, 'We have to do it. It's the money. The two big stars. What are you talking about?'"

They told him they'd test-screen it both ways, with the kiss and without. When they collected the scores, their instincts proved correct: people hated Tom for kissing Geena.

Canton conceded defeat. Not that he had much control over the matter. Penny retained final-cut privilege, giving her the right to edit *A League of Their Own* with minimal bureaucratic meddling. The perk was given to directors whom the industry deemed bankable—think Spielberg—or artistically important, like Woody Allen.

CAA overlord Mike Ovitz was the one who informed a clueless Penny that she had final cut. "Up till then," she said, "I didn't know that I wielded such power. Who had time to wield?"

Pascal supported Penny's sentimental bookends. The executive, generous and sensitive, toed the tense line between pleasing both the studio and Penny in her requests for more time on set and in the editing suite. While *A League of Their Own* drew positive early chatter, the *New York Times* reported worry within Columbia over its ballooning budget, which the newspaper put somewhere in the ballpark (pun intended) of $45 million to $50 million. Michael Nathanson estimates the costs as "much closer to $60 [million] or $70 million." That was verging on *Batman Returns* territory. The second installment in the stylish Warner Brothers franchise was reported to have blown way past its $50 million budget—to the tune of $80 million. Still, you *knew* that hordes of wannabe Caped Crusaders were going to crowd into the theater the day the sequel opened.

Hollywood began to view *A League of Their Own* as a potential cautionary tale. Pessimists predicted financial misfortune akin to *Hook* or *Bugsy*, big-budget productions considered money-losers despite turning profits. Why? Those movies cost an arm, a leg, and countless besmirched reputations to make. Would Penny recoup Columbia's investment? And how did she expect to sell a female-led sports movie to a male audience? Didn't men recline in La-Z-Boys watching sports movies while their wives served them microwaved Bagel Bites?

Canton took a rosy outlook in the press, telling the *Times*, "It's Penny's third feather in a great-looking hat."

The feather was unusual. It stuck out among the buzzy sequels slated to open that summer. Columbia sandwiched *A League of Their Own* between two projected blockbusters: *Batman Returns*, starring Michael Keaton (arguably the best Bruce Wayne ever), and Disney's follow-up to *Honey, I Shrunk the Kids*. Each film (yes, even Tim Burton's twisted take on Gotham City) qualified as family entertainment.

At first, Columbia underestimated *A League of Their Own*'s appeal for families. Advance word of mouth revealed a passionate, if overlooked, fanbase: young girls.

When Abbott showed the movie to his two daughters, who were around ten and six years old, they said it was the best movie they'd seen since *Wayne's World*.

"Penny, that's the review," he said, relaying their reaction.

"Are you serious?" she said.

"They loved it," he said. "Absolutely loved it. And they want to be Rockford Peaches for Halloween."

He told the story to Sid Ganis, Columbia's marketing chief, who asked, "Do you think there's a big audience out there for girls?"

"I think there's a huge audience," Abbott predicted.

"Shit," Abbott quotes him as saying. "We never even thought of that. We never even went there."

The insight spurred the studio to tweak its promotional campaign, fashioning the slogan "Who says girls can't play baseball?" Columbia continued courting adult men. In a poster for *A League of Their Own*, marketers used a color palette that was either gender-neutral or stereotypically masculine, depending on your perspective. Three large baseball-card graphics—Geena to the left, Tom in the middle, Madonna to the right—graced the top of the poster's blue-sky background. Geena and Madonna wore white, not peachy-pink, uniforms. The movie's title, in teal and red, filled the center, and at the bottom, a shrunken group of Peaches hoisted Lori in the air. The *Village Voice*, commenting on Tom's position above the title, suggested the studio rename the movie *The Babes*.

An international ad featured a woman preening from the waist down, sporting a short skirt, shapely gams, and a bat behind her back. Worldwide, "baseball is a difficult subject to position in the marketplace and sell," one marketer told the *LA Times*. "The legs seemed like an attractive way to go."

Aiming squarely at women, Penny and Abbott hatched a unique deal with QVC to hawk *A League of Their Own* merch to the shopping channel's forty-two million viewers. They tested the scheme several weeks ahead of the movie's July 1 release, selling 1,200 jerseys in twenty-five minutes. In a follow-up appearance, Penny corralled Tom and Lovitz to help her peddle more than $400,000 worth of jerseys, jackets, caps, and shirts.

At least two Peaches snuck into focus-group screenings. As Anne Ramsay was out walking in Santa Monica, an audience wrangler clutching a clipboard asked if she would give her opinion on a women's baseball movie. Ramsay couldn't resist signing up. She debated whether to go, thinking she'd get in trouble, but she decided to take her chances. "I'm sweating," she recalls. "I'm nervous. I have a hat on—like, I'm hiding my face. I have my head down." She never told Penny she was there.

Megan, in the last months of her pregnancy, attended a preview wearing a long coat and coke-bottle prescription glasses—all the better not to be recognized. A friend had an extra ticket and invited her. In a harrowing turn of events, Penny and all the producers were in the theater. *I hope they don't see me*, she thought. *I shouldn't have come here*. She gasped audibly when Marla made her screen debut, revealing huge eyes that Ondricek had fondly compared to those of a cow. She cried. It disappointed Megan that Penny trimmed some of her scenes, notably in the World Series, though she didn't care *that* much. She was on cloud nine. When the movie ended, she bolted for the door, telling a guy working the exits, "I'm pregnant. I think I'm gonna vomit. You gotta let me out."

David Denby of *New York* magazine thought Penny dropped the ball, and that was putting it mildly. "After her second film, *Big*, she appeared to be a director with solid commercial instincts and a soft, light touch," he wrote in his blistering review, "but *A League of Their Own* is teeming with obvious and trite ideas. We can see every plot development coming: We know the feminist formulas (every chauvinist changes; every woman finds her self-respect)." He praised Geena's "regal" performance and suggested that Tom, in the right roles, "could become not merely likable and funny but a great actor. Hanks never forces: He slowly lets us realize the slob boozer is actually an intelligent and perceptive man."

Denby hated Kit. "She's petulant and self-absorbed, and writers Lowell Ganz and Babaloo Mandel miscalculated disastrously when they made her rivalry with Dottie the center of the movie." As for "All the Way" Mae, "Marshall coldly uses Madonna, who plays a slut and is treated like a slut—distantly and contemptuously," he observed. "I admit it's hard to get an acting performance out of this woman, but can't she at least be given a shot at creating a character? (To sell the movie with her name and then hardly give her a close-up is sheer cynicism.) Worse, the filmmakers put down sexism and then make innumerable jokes about fat and ugly people." He called the cheap shots hypocritical, writing, "Marshall has revived women's baseball, it turns out, only to condescend to it."

Half the critics agreed, with Geena emerging unscathed. Among the chief complaints: *A League of Their Own* was too superficial, too safe, too corny, too unconvincing. "None of these players is as embarrassingly lumpish as John Goodman's Babe Ruth, but most throw awkwardly and hit obvious pop-ups that we're meant to believe are extra-base blasts," opined

Lawrence Toppman of the *Press-Telegram*, while *Pioneer Press* critic Deborah J. Kunk accused Lori of overacting and suggested that Penny "may do better with male leads."

The *New Yorker*'s Michael Sragow charged Penny with giving Tom preferential treatment. "The director has bent over backward to publicize *League* as an 'entertainment' rather than a feminist statement," he jeered. "In the film itself, her defensiveness and her confusion about portraying female power reach ludicrous extremes. When Geena Davis and Tom Hanks, who are both six-footers, sit next to each other on the bus, Hanks has the height advantage." (Indeed, Penny wanted Geena to remove her shoes for a scene with Tom.) Sragow ruled, "The only semi-courageous aspect of the movie was the decision to make it."

Janet Maslin of the *New York Times* loved *A League of Their Own*. "Rarely are feminist attitudes handled as breezily and entertainingly as they are here," she wrote. "And seldom, even in baseball movies, do so many clever touches come out of left field." She lauded Penny for successfully casting Geena and Tom against type and permitting Madonna to be "very funny" without outshining the ensemble. Where fellow critics condemned the insults targeting Marla, Maslin thought Penny had made Ernie Capadino look foolish and "shortsighted" for mistreating her.

Roger Ebert, dishing out three stars and a thumbs-up, became fascinated by Dottie's willingness to quit while she was ahead.

"The ambiguity about a woman's role is probably in the movie because it was directed by a woman, Penny Marshall," he wrote. "A man might have assumed that these women knew how all-important baseball was. Marshall shows her women characters in a tug-of-war between new images and old values, and so her movie is about transition—about how it felt as a woman suddenly to have new roles and freedom."

As Penny explained to the studio, Dottie was "afraid of life" and content within her comfort zone. One night she phoned Abbott around 11 p.m. Though the movie was in the can, second thoughts swirled in her brain. Price, Pascal, Nathanson, even Peters and Guber: they gave her the freedom to make *A League of Their Own* her way. What if she failed them?

"We never should have done this baseball movie," she said. "We just never should have done it."

"You're nuts," he told her. "You're absolutely insane."

She kept him on the phone for hours. She was struggling to accept that *A League of Their Own* had turned out just fine.

On June 22, Penny gritted through the world premiere at the Academy of Motion Picture Arts and Sciences. She thought the Academy theater had "no vibe" and the screening was "terrible," recalling that "Tom and I left the moment it finished, skipping the party." And yet, press coverage proves they briefly showed their faces. The *LA Times* spotted Penny mingling on an AstroTurf parking lot made to resemble a carnival. The worrywart, "notoriously nervous for her premieres, approached the theater with the look of a condemned criminal," Bill Higgins reported. "At the party, after being mightily praised, she looked like she had gotten a reprieve." Waiters wearing T-shirts with the catchphrase "THERE'S NO CRYING IN BASEBALL" served popcorn, peanuts, and meat rockets. Nikki Finke of *Los Angeles* magazine watched Garry Marshall wrap Tom in a bear hug and asked the men to name something women do better.

Tom: "Oh, please, please, *please*, you're gonna have to get a little more specific than that. OK, I've got it. They give birth better."

Garry: "And they make much better sisters."

Geena, there with beau Gavin de Becker, was fabulously on-theme in a baseball-inspired white minidress with curved red stitching. She bought the Nicole Miller design in a store. "I wish I still had it," she says.

Alongside the red carpet, Shannon Fuhs, a high school student vacationing from Huntingburg, watched the cast step out of their limos and trickle indoors. She and her younger brother and sister wore shirts with their hometown name. Shannon had been a bleacher-filler at Groom Stadium.

"Oh my gosh, you're from Huntingburg," said Lori, pixieish in an LBD, stopping to say hello. "I loved that small town."

Special guests Pepper Paire Davis and her son, Willie, waited outside the entrance for Penny to arrive, since she had their tickets. The woman of honor was running late, worrying Tracy, who tried to reach her mom on the phone but couldn't get through. "It was getting scary," Pepper wrote in her memoir. "I think Tracy was about ready to call the police. All eyes were anxiously straining, looking down that blocked-off, barricaded street for a big black limo. Then, here comes this little *Chitty Chitty Bang Bang* Volkswagen."

The door opened, Pepper continued, "and this rear-end comes awkwardly backing out. That's the only way you could get out. Tracy gasped and said, 'Oh my god, it's my mom.' Penny turned around and said like only Penny can, 'Well, I'm here now. Let's party.'"

As Penny's limo backed out of her driveway earlier that night, its engine caught fire—hence, the delay. The Volkswagen was her last resort.

After learning that some of her teammates hadn't received invitations to the premiere, Geena wrangled tickets and sent a limo to pick up Renée and Neezer and Robin and Patti and Freddie. In the theater bathroom, Freddie ran into Penny.

"Are you OK with how much you were in the movie?" Penny asked.

"Yeah," Freddie said. "It was much more than I thought."

Before the lights went down, Babaloo Mandel overheard three male executives from other studios panning the movie's prospects.

"This is what they say: *If the league didn't work, why should this movie?*" Mandel tells me. "That's all you need to hear. And [you] go, 'Oh my god. We're dead.'"

Pepper sat in a special box overlooking the screen. She'd already seen *A League of Their Own* when Penny privately presented it to the cast and crew. "You could hear Tracy and Lori and my Peaches laughing like crazy when they saw themselves doing those things," Pepper said. At the Academy, she was riveted anew, her untamed past flashing before her eyes. "It was another ride on the time machine," she reflected.

Geena liked *A League of Their Own* the first time she saw it, though Penny's scene-shuffling surprised her. Still, she contends, "she did a genius job editing that movie." Tom appreciated that Penny axed the Jimmy-Dottie affair. The "relationship ended up being more of a combination of some degree of attraction, sexual or whatever, and also respect between a man and a woman, which sometimes can be a much more dangerous thing," he said. Penny, he felt, was right to keep the office romance unrealized and ambiguous.

*A League of Their Own* charmed Ann Cusack. But Renée Coleman, steeped in memories of Indiana, was underwhelmed. "We all hated it," she admits. "And so, we thought it was just gonna sort of die [an] ignoble death. And that would be it."

What did Madonna think of the movie? The Peaches missed her—to some, a surprise of a feeling—but back in Evansville, she was persona non grata.

The previous November, Madonna dissed the city in *TV Guide*, telling Kurt Loder, "I may as well have been in Prague." While stuck there, she had missed Paris Fashion Week, and worse, could not access MTV—mandatory viewing for a pop trendsetter—due to an issue with her cable hookup. As a result, she turned on boring old broadcast television, with its limited channels, and sat "catatonically in front of it." On location, she said, "for the first time in my life, I felt very disconnected."

Brian Jackson, a popular morning show host at the Top 40 radio station 96.1, serving the Evansville metropolitan area, noticed a decline in Madonna's popularity among her local fans. "Prior to her presence in Evansville, I would say they would've built a temple," Jackson says. "It was practically cult-like. People loved her and her music. And even though adults were slightly offended by some of it, they knew that there was a lot worse out there."

Later, Jackson received numerous calls from extras about her coldness on set. "Nobody's *that* cool—that was the consensus," he says of the complaints. The temperature dropped after she compared their home to one of Europe's most beautiful capitals. Listeners asked the station, "Why are you still playing her music at all?" Jackson defended the airplay. "Maybe she's a rat's rear end," he argued. "*OK, fine. She's a rat's rear end.* So are a lot of other people in music and we play their music, so: big deal."

The station's program director, Barry Witherspoon, wasn't offended by Madonna's remarks. Did he agree with her? No. But he understood how Evansville's slower pace could frustrate the urbane pleasure-seeker. A shrewd media mastermind, Witherspoon saw an opening to capitalize on her candor and organized an anti-Madonna protest outside Roberts Stadium, where Elvis once performed, and promoted it over the airwaves. The stunt seemed like harmless fun, a goofy thing to do on a Saturday afternoon. Three hundred participants lay down in the parking lot, spelling out Madonna's name with a line slashed through it. "Get a life, Madonna!" they chanted. Witherspoon rented a helicopter and invited the *Courier & Press* to photograph the sit-in from above. The gambit drew national attention, with tabloid news shows airing the aerial footage and interviewing haters. "She's trash, man," one guy told *Hard Copy*. On *Entertainment Tonight*, a Macaulay Culkin clone smirked, "I don't like her. She's a dork," while Indiana senator

Dan Coats, in a separate interview, invited Madonna back to his state for a peacekeeping mission.

She ignored the hoopla. The bad press was good for her brand. (Everybody wins!)

According to gossip columnist Liz Smith, Madonna mulled whether to attend *A League of Their Own*'s New York premiere. "It depends on how much energy she wants to expend pushing a film in which her screen time is not major," Smith wrote in June of 1992. She did grace *The Arsenio Hall Show* with her presence, promoting the movie alongside Rosie. The two bantered off-the-cuff, as though they'd known each other longer than a year. "We both slept with Warren Beatty," Mo cracked as Ro insulted her highbrow taste in movies. When Arsenio brought up Mo's rumored fling with Oakland Athletics power hitter Jose Canseco, Ro joked that he "coached Madonna privately" on *A League of Their Own*, and when Ro, calling *League* a "very good movie," declared that she was going to see it a second time, Mo formed the letter L with her hand and snarked, "*Loser.*"

Mo felt the movie sugar-coated history, but liked it all the same: "Oh, I think it's cute, it's not *Gone with the Wind*, it's not *Doctor Zhivago*, it's no work of art," she told *The Guardian* that September. "It's entertainment, light, there's some funny moments, it's very sweet." But it saddened her to imagine Mae running the dishes instead of bases. Were Mo the director, she'd have "made a big stink about the fact that [the league] didn't go on."

Ro and Mo reteamed June 25 at the Ziegfeld Theater, Mo the big smiling fish at the center of a school of paparazzi. She wore big black sunglasses, like Anna Wintour on the front row of a high-fashion runway. Ro donned black, as did Tom and Rita, with whom she filmed Nora Ephron's *Sleepless in Seattle* later in the summer. The funereal chic continued with Tracy (black dress) and Penny (black suit and Converse sneakers). Bitty Schram closed her eyes and covered her ears when she saw herself onscreen. Feeling self-conscious, she got up and walked out. Lovitz, who stayed put, cried during the credits, bursting with pride. "Jon, you're a big star now," Regis Philbin said at the after-party at Tavern on the Green.

Meanwhile, in America's Prague, Justin Scheller rolled up to Showplace Cinema East dressed to the nines, a pint-sized showman flaunting a white top hat and tails with a peach cummerbund. Columbia Pictures pledged

$20,000 toward the benefit screening's effort to raise money for a new roof at Bosse Field. "Anybody who was anybody went to that premiere," Scheller, who teaches high school in Indiana, says of downstate social butterflies. The movie's adult jokes flew right over his head. Afterward he signed autographs in a tent filled with the noise of Racine Belles happily reuniting. DeLisa Chinn-Tyler lingered in her theater seat, her eyes combing the credits for her name. She didn't find it anywhere, and her disappointment lasted years. Friends encouraged DeLisa to call Penny directly and fix the error; she later tried reaching her on Facebook but didn't know how to make a connection. She gave up trying.

Five hours to the north, Megan, her due date approaching, celebrated with one hundred friends and family members. She skipped the coastal premieres, wanting to be near her mother when her water broke in the days to come and she held her son for the first time.

In Lompoc, California, Kelly Candaele hosted a packed watch party that doubled as a fundraiser for the town's high school girls' softball team. An estimated sixteen million women played the sport in the US, a softball booster told the *LA Times*, and *A League of Their Own*—the story of Kelly's mother—had the potential to reach millions more. Helen, the honoree, was frail and unable to fully bask in the glow of it all. The sixty-nine-year-old cancer patient took her last breath on December 8 in Santa Barbara. At her funeral, I'm told, guests wept as her family played "This Used to Be My Playground."

THE JUNE 29 EDITION OF *VARIETY* COLLECTED ANONYMOUS PREDICTIONS ON the movie's box office: a producer said the "baseball film with no balls" would do $45 million in total, while an exhibitor threw out $90 million, remarking "Not *Field of Dreams*, but Hanks and good word-of-mouth should draw."

*A League of Their Own* opened wide on a Wednesday, claiming the number-two spot that weekend. It ranked below *Batman Returns* and above *Boomerang*, *Sister Act*, and the Ray Liotta thriller *Unlawful Entry*.

"We went to about three or four different theaters," Abbott says. "And that's when I learned that when they buy a ticket, they laugh harder, and they cry a lot harder [compared to test audiences]." He phoned Ganz and Mandel, saying, "I think we got something, boys."

Within a week, *League* had raked in $23 million and bumped Batman off his number-one perch. It clung there until *Honey, I Blew Up the Kid* knocked it to second in the middle of the month. The numbers kept climbing and climbing. On September 8, the movie transcended $100 million, prompting the studio to take out a delirious ad in the trades that exclaimed, "WE'VE GOT LEGS!!"

Penny and Tom heard the news while promoting *League* at the Venice Film Festival. In lieu of Kodak-funded Prosecco, the friends feasted upon a giant cake.

Spielberg, inspired by Penny's documentary-style outro, asked her permission to use the concept in *Schindler's List*, which closed with Jewish people saved by German industrialist Oskar Schindler paying respects at his grave. The historical masterwork deservedly won the Oscar for Best Picture in 1994, and that year Spielberg and Tom scooped up shiny gold men for Best Director and Best Actor, respectively. Tom's searing portrayal of an AIDS-stricken attorney in the courtroom drama *Philadelphia* hastened an astonishing upward trajectory that happens but once in a lifetime to an actor.

*A League of Their Own*, a mere footnote in the Tom Hanks film library, was Penny's pinnacle, even as it eclipsed her stardom. Dottie and Kit loomed larger than Laverne and Shirley. Schoolgirls in 1992 didn't know Laverne. They watched *Full House*, *The Fresh Prince of Bel-Air*, and sometimes *Roseanne* with their parents. They helped Penny collect $132 million worldwide, more than any baseball movie, more than *Field of Dreams*, *Bull Durham*, *The Natural*, *42*, and *Moneyball*. They harmonized the "Victory Song" at recess and succumbed to the angst of "This Used to Be My Playground," which topped the Billboard Hot 100 chart that August and became Madonna's tenth number-one single, proving Abbott right.

Julie Croteau and Kelli Simpkins had since moved to New York City, Croteau for a temporary internship and Simpkins to pursue acting full-time. They bought tickets to see the movie together and were touched that Penny credited their names, knowing that she truly valued them. Croteau, who worried that *A League of Their Own* would embarrass women ballplayers, was amazed by how good it was. She cried when Doris discussed feeling different than other girls. "It spoke to me as a young athlete," she says, adding, "That's what I had lived a few years earlier."

In New York, Freddie also watched *League* with ordinary folk, their standing ovation surprising her. *Oh*, she thought. *I guess it's good.* And on the opposite coast, eight little Rockford Peaches showed up at Renée's Culver City door on Halloween. "I was so completely overcome," she says. "To this day, I regret not telling them that I was a Peach."

Renée doled out candy in a witch's costume, green face paint and all. If she had revealed that she was Alice Gaspers, that the bruise wasn't fake, would the girls even have believed her?

*A League of Their Own* hit video stores in February 1993, strengthening its hold over the youth. Jessica Mendoza, a twelve-year-old athlete from Southern California, would go on to watch the movie hundreds of times. So many times, in fact, that it weaved into the tapestry of her life. The Peaches weren't cutesy beauty queens; they were scrappy and messy and imperfect. They had grit and attitude, redefining what it was to be a girl, and Jessica had never seen characters like them in the movies. She idolized Dottie, the strong hitter she aimed to be, and while the heroine veered traditionally feminine, Mendoza said, "she'd go and do something that was not characteristically female." Jessica wanted to emulate her. Sure, she'd seen Brett Butler play at Dodger Stadium, but he was a guy. She hungered for women role models. There were none playing baseball and softball on TV. There were none like Dottie.

In a lot of ways, Jimmy Dugan reminded Jessica of her father, Gil, a football and baseball coach who mentored her and her younger sister, Alana, videotaping their swings. He hung a sixty-pound punching bag on the porch and painted it with a strike zone. Jessica practiced her heart out.

She and Alana, two years her junior, played softball together and against each other. Alana was shorter and feistier. Their dynamic mirrored the love, and jocular sparring, that Dottie shared with Kit. They'd sling mud at each other, shouting:

*Stop swinging at the rise ball!*

*I like the rise ball!*

In Jessica's opinion, the movie had a fatal flaw: the hotly debated ball-drop. The implication that Dottie, her idol, cheated. Jessica felt like she knew Dottie, and the Dottie she knew would not hesitate to tag Kit, saying, "You're out." Sports wasn't about keeping the peace; it was about *winning.* But Hollywood would always be Hollywood, sacrificing reality for the sake of drama. In her heart, she knew that the real Dottie Hinson would never drop that ball on purpose.

## *Ninth Inning*

# BEYOND THE OUTFIELD

In the summer of 1992, Penny hired Gloria Mallah to house-sit while she traveled for several weeks. Gloria, who'd flown into LA from Indiana, noticed a difference in her boss. Penny was trying to kick smoking and eat healthier, and it affected her mood. She ate jicama cut up in sticks to quelch her cravings.

Penny and Gloria bickered like family. One day, the former asked her house sitter-slash-assistant to drop her off at Carrie Fisher's house, but worried she was too clueless a driver to find her way back home. She made "Glor" stick around as she and Richard Dreyfuss reminisced about the old days when Dreyfuss resided in Penny and Rob Reiner's guesthouse. Carrie, with whom Penny spent hours on the phone, had a housekeeper named Gloria, an unusual, though fitting, coincidence for friends who were like sisters. In the Hills, Penny invited Glor to Tracy's baby shower—Tracy and her partner, Dan (De Niro's trainer), were expecting their first child, a boy—and offered her pool house not to Dreyfuss but to Megan Cavanagh and her husband and new baby. Penny's household was clean, organized, and homey, with a diner booth in the kitchen. Downstairs, where Gloria slept, she displayed the Zoltar machine from *Big*. It scared Gloria, who had night terrors. Penny was "very caring when she knew I had one," she says.

That winter, Penny made a pact with CBS to turn *A League of Their Own* into a small-screen sitcom. Ganz and Mandel created the spin-off, which starred Carey Lowell as Dottie, Christine Elise as Kit, and Sam McMurray as Jimmy Dugan. Megan and Tracy were series regulars, and Garry, Lovitz, Freddie, Patti Pelton, and Pauline Brailsford popped up in one or two episodes. Penny, an executive producer, directed an episode and invited Tom to helm another in which Dottie hits a line drive and almost kills the Peaches' team mascot, Benny, a real chimpanzee. (Fret not: Benny makes a full recovery, and I laughed despite myself when he pats a Peach on her butt in the locker room.)

"Will you do it?" Penny asked Tom over the phone.

"Yeah," he said, "but it has to be [shot] between these [specific] dates."

While the production values were low compared with 35 mm Panavision, spinning off a sports blockbuster made sense: if a thing works, make more of it! Right? Wrong. "For the first time since *Laverne & Shirley*, my ulcer started up again," Penny groaned to *Newsweek*. The show, good on paper but lacking the sheen and pulse of the original, swung and missed with critics and viewers. CBS pulled the plug after six episodes. Mollie Mallinger, who assisted in the camera and electrical department, heard that Penny produced the show "to keep everybody working."

Afterward, Tracy acted alongside Tom in *Apollo 13* and *That Thing You Do!*, his delightful directorial debut, and appeared in Garry's *Princess Diaries* franchise and Penny's *Riding in Cars with Boys*. Megan notched post-*League* roles in the Mel Brooks comedies *Robin Hood: Men in Tights* and *Dracula: Dead and Loving It*, as well as the Julia Roberts romcom *I Love Trouble*. Her agent got her an audition for *Saturday Night Live*, and while she was a natural in the vein of Molly Shannon, she was wary of working with men who might not understand that she had a child to raise and couldn't be on call 24/7. Since booking Marla Hooch, she remained a steady working actress, one who held the distinction of belonging to something bigger than herself. Both she and Tracy became advocates for women's baseball, attending trade shows around the country with AAGPBL alums who very much enjoyed having fun. During a trip to Hawaii, they sang karaoke and Megan pretended she was a Russian girl named Svetlana. "You're gonna go places!" a man (not Nelson) hollered from the audience.

The Parkway production *Calendar Girl* did not earn such applause, grossing just $2.6 million in the fall of 1993. The reviews stunk, and the deaf community protested the choice to hire a hearing actor to play a deaf character. At least a thousand hard-of-hearing actors auditioned for *Calendar Girl*, yet Kurt Fuller was cast in the minor role of Arturo Gallo, a bill collector hunting Jason Priestley's character. An interpreter was recruited to teach Fuller sign language.

Penny switched studios for her next directing venture, Disney's *Renaissance Man*, a pleasant if forgettable drama in comedy's clothing. Danny DeVito starred as a divorced and unemployed businessman who takes a temporary job teaching Shakespeare to underachieving army recruits. In the process, he inspires his pupils and finds personal redemption—not unlike Jimmy Dugan. Before Penny said yes to *Renaissance Man*, Tom gauged her interest in taking the reins of *Forrest Gump*, a film based on Wilson Groom's novel about a slow-witted sweetheart of a man who witnesses significant American events ranging from Vietnam to Watergate to ping-pong diplomacy in China.

"We were offered the *Forrest Gump* project to do," Greenhut says. "And Tom wanted Penny to do it. And I read the script. I said, 'Hey, why not? This is great stuff. Classic material.' And I couldn't talk her into doing it. She was, like, afraid of it."

*How am I gonna do all those battle scenes and everything?* she asked.

*Let the second unit directors and special effects guys handle the explosions*, he reassured. *You don't have to worry about that. You'll just watch and say, "Yes, it's good." Or "No, do it again."*

Both Greenhut and Abbott tried changing her mind, but she wasn't willing to deal with the logistics involved. "That was our withdrawal-from-Afghanistan moment that we blew," Greenhut says, adding, "Her judgment went off the rails, you know? Well, as far as I'm concerned, selfishly, when she didn't want to make *Forrest Gump*." Perhaps "she felt it would be too much pressure," he thinks. "*Look, I did my two hit movies. So let me do something more formulaic and not have to worry about doing* The Ten Commandments *or something*." From his angle, "She developed some bad habits and just spiraled a little out of control. [She] and Carrie Fisher were each other's worst enemies in terms of, like, being good role models for each other."

Offering an explanation to broadcaster Larry King in 2012, she said, "One of my best friends had lymphoma, and he was very sick. . . . Sometimes life is more important than show business." She had told Tom, "I can't. I gotta stay put."

Two weeks after Tracy delivered her eleven-pound son, Spencer, in a home birth, making Penny a grandmother, Penny toasted her fiftieth birthday with Carrie and friends including Robin Williams, Jack Nicholson, and Anjelica Huston. "Despite reaching middle age," she said, "I felt as energetic as I did twenty years earlier. If necessary, I could go all night, and sometimes I did."

On Sunday, May 29, 1994, she was rushed to a hospital in the Hamptons while staying at the fifty-seven-acre estate of her close friend, Ron Perelman. Penny, who was released the next day, heard on the radio that she'd suffered a heart attack, which she denied. "I was fine," she recalled. Telling the story later, she explained that she'd been out with Perelman the night before and had only "a sip or two of a drink." She woke up the next morning with a strange stiffness in her arm. After a series of tests, "The doctors said I had Syndrome X or Prinzmetal's angina, which I thought meant I'm not supposed to listen to heavy-metal music."

She bounced back May 31 for *Renaissance Man*'s Hollywood premiere, smiling on the red carpet with DeVito and Mark Wahlberg, the rapper better known as Marky Mark, who played a soldier who learns to love the Bard. Stacey Dash was the lone woman among DeVito's students and one of seven Black actors Penny had placed in the movie. The young cast shared a natural rapport, injecting verve and unforced humor into an otherwise earnest and dreary labor of blah, overlong by half an hour.

Sara Colleton, a producer on *Renaissance Man*, had sent Penny the movie's script written by her friend, University of Michigan professor Jim Burnstein. "I didn't think *Renaissance Man* was a blockbuster (and I didn't know about the blockbuster part of the business anyway), but I liked its message," Penny said. She pursued Tupac Shakur to play a rapping trooper who gets sent to prison for dealing drugs, but he rebuffed her offer. She narrowed her cast to mostly unknown soldiers (plus Marky Mark) and gave Ann Cusack some lines as an office secretary. She brought on a new camera department, breaking from Tom Priestley and his guys, and retained Greenhut, Abbott, Tim Bourne, and Amy Lemisch as producers.

"I watch my movies and I only see what's wrong with them," she told a journalist in 1992. "If you're lucky enough to have a hit, then you're allowed four failures, they say. But I don't know if that applies to women. And I don't wish to find out."

She began to stop rolling the dice, taking big swings and risks. She began to lose the recipes for the secret sauce that added zing to *Big* and *A League of Their Own*. While Garry stuck to formulas and franchises that rained dollars, Penny was digging herself into a rut. Still, she maintained, "You just have to get out there and function no matter how scary it is. And, of course, you've got to keep your sense of humor. I laugh in the face of failure."

Penny wasn't the only director who shunned *Forrest Gump*. Terry Gilliam (*Brazil*, *The Fisher King*) turned down the job because he "didn't believe in that script." Barry Sonnenfeld had to choose between *Gump* and *Addams Family Values*, his sequel to 1991's *The Addams Family*, which made $192 million globally despite a stressful shoot in which he replaced the cinematographer. (Sonnenfeld went on to helm the *Men in Black* trilogy, a visual feast of slick production design and computer-generated imagery.) Ultimately, Robert Zemeckis accepted *Forrest Gump*, continuing the work that made him a leader in the visual effects space with his *Back to the Future* movies and *Death Becomes Her*. His team CGI-ed Tom into archival footage with JFK, Nixon, and Lennon, and digitally cloned thousands of hippies attending a peace rally at the Lincoln Memorial.

In rejecting *Forrest Gump*, in drawing a line around her interests, was Penny being selfish, or reasonable? By saying no so Zemeckis could say yes, she steered Tom toward a fruitful creative partnership. *Forrest Gump* opened July 4, 1994, raking in an ultimate total of $678 million and making him a very, very rich man. He and Zemeckis later teamed up on the lucrative instant classics *Castaway* and *The Polar Express*.

That June, two summers after *League*'s home run, *Renaissance Man* debuted fourth at the box office, with *The Flintstones*, costarring Rosie O'Donnell and Elizabeth Perkins, atop the list of new releases. The live-action Universal Pictures adaptation of the cartoon overcame negative reviews to pull $131 million domestically. Critics savaged *Renaissance Man* too, but the picture did not turn the jeers into a profit. Instead, it made $24 million on a $40 million budget, and Penny blamed Disney for dropping poor DeVito into the heady stew of Gump, Fred Flintstone, *The Lion King*, and *Speed*. She "had a singular vision and she had drive but she could be wounded," Todd Smith says of his former agency client, who was sensitive about the box office and "quietly competitive with everybody." In September, Cinergi Pictures, which financed *Renaissance Man*, reissued it in seventeen Seattle theaters under a new title: *By the Book*. "If You Loved *Forrest Gump*, Don't Miss This Movie," a promotion urged. The Hail Mary failed to move the needle. *Renaissance Man* died an ignoble death.

In October 1994, Penny organized a star-studded reading of Ganz and Mandel's adaptation of the Stephen Sondheim musical *Into the Woods*, in development at Columbia. Among the readers: DeVito (the Giant); Robin Williams (the Baker); Goldie Hawn (the Baker's Wife); Cher (the Witch); Steve Martin (the Wolf); Moira Kelly (Cinderella), and Roseanne (Jack and the Beanstalk's mother). Penny was attached as a potential director, but nothing came of the script.

A few months later, DeVito invited Penny to play herself (who else?) in the last scene of his gangster comedy, *Get Shorty*. Sonnenfeld was directing, and while they'd sworn never to work together again, he welcomed her onto the set. Penny's uncredited cameo called for her to "say a few lines and then get in an SUV and drive away," she said. "It was the end of a movie—a wrap. As a stickler for detail, though, I explained that I didn't drive. I always had a driver. Everyone knew that about me." Her assistant, Kristin, got behind the wheel.

Penny, still smarting from *Renaissance Man*, hit a wall securing studio interest in *The Boys of Neptune*, a comedy about middle-aged lifeguards that she hoped to make, ideally with De Niro or Bruce Willis. Her proposed $50 million budget would cover actors' salaries, but studios balked at the price tag. In June of 1995, *Variety* revealed that executives "feel a beach pic with no special effects shouldn't cost so much." She had carefully mulled several compelling projects, including *Hot Flashes*, based on Barbara Raskin's 1987 novel about female friends reuniting at a funeral, but that picture cooled as she shifted attention to *Boys of Neptune*. At Columbia, where she had a first-look deal, a sequel to *A League of Their Own* that focused on Jimmy Dugan was in the works. Ganz and Mandel were down to spawn new catchphrases, and if the spin-off was a go, Penny would return to direct. According to Geena, who had wanted to star in a follow-up with her fellow Peaches, "It was about [Jimmy] getting recruited to coach the Negro League," she wrote in her memoir. "So, a sequel to a movie about women, where the only character to reappear would be the male coach. To me it was unimaginable that the idea would even come up. The movie didn't end up getting made; evidently, they were never satisfied with the script."

Tom's participation had been unconfirmed. He had another Best Actor Oscar (*Forrest Gump*), another megahit (*Toy Story*), and the unconditional love of millions. Floating above the clouds, he didn't need to revisit Jimmy, who was probably sitting in a pub somewhere below. He had moved on.

In September of 1995, Penny announced that she was making *The Preacher's Wife* for Touchstone Pictures, a Disney subsidiary targeting adult filmgoers. The plot, a fresh spin on *The Bishop's Wife*, the 1947 holiday romance starring Cary Grant, Loretta Young, and David Niven, involved a ridiculously handsome angel sent to help a New York City pastor save his struggling Baptist church. His noble mission hits a snag when he falls for, you guessed it, the pastor's better half. (Oops.) Penny put together an exciting and prestigious Black cast led by Denzel Washington as the heavenly messenger, Courtney B. Vance as the clergyman, and Whitney Houston as his spouse. On the crew side, she reteamed with former *League*-ers Miroslav Ondricek, Bill Groom, Cynthia Flynt, and Billy Kerwick, and she hired Bonnie Hlinomaz, who once fetched snacks and puzzles for her, as a producer.

When Disney courted Penny for *The Preacher's Wife*, she refused the job at first, believing the story should hinge on Vance's loss of faith—not a flirtation between Whitney and a hot angel. In her gut she thought Denzel should lead the sermons, but he understandably wanted to play the Cary Grant role. She scolded him for missing a rehearsal, and he made sure to show up the next day. Whitney, who brought down the house in magical Gospel numbers, occasionally missed call times and could be heard arguing with husband Bobby Brown on the phone. Penny accommodated Whitney's shifting schedule. "I know years later she told Oprah Winfrey that her drug use was already such a problem that she was getting high every day," Penny said. "She qualified that by explaining that she only did them at night, after work, so that could explain why I didn't see her misbehaving or high. If she had been high, I would have noticed. We talked before, during, and after scenes. We pushed in close often enough that I would have seen a change in her eyes."

Penny, true to form, went long: *The Preacher's Wife* came in at three hours and twenty-four minutes. She edited down the movie while playing herself—again, who else?—in a series of funny Kmart commercials with Rosie, whose talk show had made her a media darling. (*Newsweek* magazine dubbed Rosie the "Queen of Nice.") Penny and Rosie "met up on weekends, got paid a lot of money, and became best of friends," she said. Better yet, "We were allowed to take whatever we wanted from the stores."

*The Preacher's Wife* received warm reviews from the *New York Times* as well as Ebert, who nonetheless felt Penny holding back, playing it safe. He desired extra sizzle between Denzel and Whitney, and more jealousy from Vance. "This movie could have done more," he wrote, "but what it does, it makes you feel good about." In the peanut gallery, *Entertainment Weekly* and the *Miami Herald* criticized the remake as tedious, and they weren't exactly wrong: the slow pace often makes *The Preacher's Wife* feel like a chore, save for the exuberant scenes of Whitney leading the church choir. The soundtrack became the best-selling Gospel album of all time while the film performed below its budget, recovering $48 million of its estimated $75 million production and marketing costs. Disney had angled to attract white audiences who avoided films with Black casts. As one Black producer pointed out to the *LA Times*, the studio's retrograde print ads appeared "painted by a black Norman Rockwell."

Penny grew disillusioned by the industry. She left CAA for International Creative Management and tried to make things happen. On her director's wish list: *Cinderella Man*, a boxing biopic she optioned about Depression-era pugilist James Braddock. She envisioned her friend Mark Wahlberg as Braddock, but Harvey Weinstein, butting in to produce, pushed Ben Affleck for the role. "It was one of the few times people were really shitty to me," she recalled. Ron Howard, who went on to direct Russell Crowe in the movie, gave Penny a producing credit. As the 1990s waned, she produced the little-seen comedies *Getting Away with Murder* and *With Friends Like These*, the latter failing to find a distributor. She guest-starred on *Nash Bridges*. Garry tried to resurrect *Laverne & Shirley* on the big screen, which excited her, though his efforts were for naught. Penny aired her grievances to Hollywood columnists Marilyn Beck and Stacy Jenel Smith in February 1999, saying, "I go to basketball games a lot. It helps with the frustration."

That May, the trades published some promising news: Penny would direct the Columbia Pictures drama *Riding in Cars with Boys*, based on Beverly Donofrio's memoir of the same name. She wasn't gaga over the script but connected to its central character: a teen girl who gets pregnant, marries too young, and tries to rise above the mess. Penny read Kate Hudson, Reese Witherspoon, Anne Hathaway, Angelina Jolie, Hilary Swank, and Marisa Tomei. When Amy Pascal, the studio's president, told her that Jim Brooks, the movie's producer, had given the part to Drew Barrymore, "I was furious," she said. "If that was the case, why not tell me? That's all I ever asked from anyone. Tell me the truth. I wouldn't have wasted so many people's time, including mine."

While Penny prepped *Riding in Cars with Boys*, she replaced David Anspaugh as the director of a Harlem Globetrotters biopic brewing at Columbia. Pascal found the script from Anspaugh's *Hoosiers* partner, Angelo Pizzo, too depressing. Anspaugh disagreed, losing another great gig to Penny. Was history repeating itself? Could she do with the Globetrotters what she did with the All-Americans? Would Anspaugh do her a solid and take the wheel of *Riding in Cars*? (Wishful thinking.)

Cameras rolled in August 2000. Drew, who wrapped *Charlie's Angels* several weeks beforehand, was unhappy on the New Jersey set. She didn't like how Penny's cinematographer, Chris Menges, was lighting her. Brooks, distracted by his divorce and other professional obligations, "made me fire Chris, one of the nicest people in the business, and I had to bring Miroslav out of retirement," Penny said, adding, "This was the first of all the pictures I did where I felt less than fully in control of the challenges, and it was because I didn't have any support."

A colleague who worked with Penny since the 1980s witnessed her change for the worse. Toward the end of *Renaissance Man*, "that sweet part of her vanished," he says. "And she became very ugly and biting and, in some cases, cruel in the way she spoke to people. More so than ever. She always spoke harshly, but it was always with a tinge of healthy sarcasm. But it had turned into more of a not-OK version of that. You know, mix that in with a little bit of substance abuse . . . It got ugly. She became bitter and angry and more alone."

Frank Price liked her a lot, but "she had a problem," he says. "She drank too much. But that didn't interfere with her work."

Anjelica Huston told *New York* magazine that she began to pull away from her friendship with Penny. Their lifestyles were too different. "She stayed up all night smoking cigarettes in subzero temperatures," Huston said in 2019. Penny "followed QVC for beanbag dolls and stuff. She had this collection of sports memorabilia. She had a sort of museum in her basement full of signed baseballs and Lakers shirts. I just couldn't relate. And, also, frankly, she took a lot of coke."

(For the record, Penny's sports collection was tremendous, boasting priceless artifacts of eye-popping value and rarity. Athletes, fans, collectors, and museum curators spoke of it in hushed tones and dreamed of getting a private tour. Penny owned baseballs with Joe DiMaggio's signature and one of the last Bulls jerseys ever worn by Michael Jordan, signed by Jordan. She collected mushroom bats manufactured in the early 1900s. She had a 1930s mutoscope machine with images of New York Giant Bobby Thomson's winning home run against the Brooklyn Dodgers in 1951. She planned to donate some of her keepsakes to the Baseball Hall of Fame, the Naismith Memorial Basketball Hall of Fame, and the Negro Leagues Baseball Museum.)

In Hollywood, it was hard to watch her go down an unhealthy path. Since she no longer made the studios money, the studios were less willing to indulge her.

"*Riding in Cars with Boys* was sort of the nail in the coffin," her longtime colleague says. "Everybody was miserable. Everybody hated everybody. Drew Barrymore hated Penny; Penny hated her."

Nevertheless, the mutual animosity got results. Penny and Drew were doing interesting and personal work. Neither made the striving mother, Bev, into a Horatio Alger cliché: *the plucky and winsome hero who turns the world on with her smile, earning her Master's degree and a book deal by sheer moxie!* Drew, twenty-five years old at the time, aged convincingly from fifteen to thirty-six; her portrait of self-absorbed, spiky Bev, who makes her tormented son feel responsible for her misery, was unvarnished, warts and all—a slice of something like real life. Penny let the movie breathe, and while she gazed at Drew with contempt, her lens exposed darker truths about motherhood and how trauma cycles through generations. She directed Steve Zahn with equal aplomb. As Bev's ex, a decent man hooked on heroin, Zahn offered a compassionate study of addiction. Penny, wrestling with her own vices, had seen drugs kill John Belushi and send Carrie spiraling. After Carrie accidentally overdosed on pain medication and sleeping pills in 1985, she mined the experience in her thinly veiled novel *Postcards from the Edge*, an acclaimed, no-holds-barred cultural document. "Take your broken heart, make it into art," she once told Meryl Streep, who played her in *Postcards* the film.

Most critics were unimpressed with *Riding in Cars with Boys*. Edward Guthmann of the *San Francisco Chronicle* sensed the director and her actress straining too hard to make Bev likable "despite her irritating qualities." Drew, he suggested, belonged to the class of American movie stars "terrified of playing unsympathetic characters, particularly when they've gained the celebrity and box-office appeal that Barrymore has." Rita Kempley of the *Washington Post* found Bev plenty unlikable and Drew lacking in the part. She "comes off as abrasive and neglectful as opposed to headstrong and ambitious, winning no empathy for this sour single mom," Kempley griped.

Ebert hated Bev too. But he praised Drew and gave Penny props for bravery. "A film like this is refreshing and startling in the way it cuts loose from formula and shows us confused lives we recognize," he opined.

> Hollywood tends to reduce stories like this to simplified redemption parables in which the noble woman emerges triumphant after a lifetime of surviving loser men. This movie is closer to the truth: A lot depends on what happens to you, and then a lot depends on how you let it affect you. Life has not been kind to Beverly, and Beverly has not been kind to life. Maybe there'll be another book in a few years where she sees how, in some ways, she can blame herself.

The movie opened a month after the September 11 attacks. It tanked. Penny had wanted to have a premiere in New York, which she felt would be good for the city in the wake of the tragedy. But Brooks, who did not want to fly in from LA, rejected the idea. "I was furious," Penny said. "I took it personally."

The market for movies was changing, and Penny no longer fit into it. She wasn't allowed another failure. She became poisonous. The industry backed away. Penny "brought it on herself," says an old friend. "There's no doubt about that."

In early 1993, Lori Petty was fired three days into filming *Demolition Man*, a sci-fi thriller starring Sylvester Stallone and Wesley Snipes. "It was the most uncool day in Hollywood for me," Lori said later, not wanting to talk about it. At the time, *Entertainment Weekly* reported that Warner Brothers had been unhappy with her dailies and decided "they could do better with someone else." The studio promptly installed Sandra Bullock in Lori's role as a futuristic cop caught in a cat-and-mouse game between LAPD Sergeant Stallone and criminal psychopath Snipes. In his memoir, Nigel Hawthorne, who played an amoral megalomaniac (with a British accent, natch), said Warner had wanted Bullock from the beginning, and as soon as she became available, Lori was paid off and kicked out. Stallone "liked to parade around," he wrote, "with a large cigar jammed between his lips, cheerfully wisecracking, until dragged forcibly away by the ever-indulgent [producer] Joel Silver, who dressed in what [appeared] to be brown silk pyjamas." Lori, conceding their lack of chemistry, remarked, "Sly and I were like oil and water."

Doug Robinson, Lori's then-agent at CAA, admired the twenty-nine-year-old for always staying true to who she was. He'd signed her right after *Point Break*. She was beautiful and tough in a captivating way, and she had momentum, following *A League of Their Own* with an important role in the hit family film *Free Willy*. But *Demolition Man* stalled Lori's rise in Hollywood. The big-league scripts and offers petered out. She kept her hair short, displeasing men who preferred an actress conform to conventional standards of womanly beauty. Women like Penny and Kathryn Bigelow had seen and valued Lori, as had director Rachel Talalay, who captured her irreverence in 1995's *Tank Girl*, an antic, post-apocalyptic romp that pocketed a paltry $4 million in ticket sales but gained a cult following. Lori replaced British actress Emily Lloyd in the lead role; Lloyd apparently refused to shave her head. "Lori just knew that she was Tank Girl," Talalay said, adding that she "did everything, she did half of her own stunts."

Lori thought an arbitrary R-rating sabotaged *Tank Girl* at the multiplex—that, and MGM hadn't really promoted it.

"Well, for no reason whatsoever, the film was rated R," she said. "The only reason being that I'm a female. That was it. There was no violent bloody murder, you know, there was blowing up stuff, but there was no nudity. I'd have been naked the whole damn movie if I knew it was going to be R! We thought it was going to be PG-13, and that's what we made. And they gave us an R because the only reason I could think of is that I was a woman, you know, ruling shit."

After *Tank Girl*, Lori starred opposite Karyn Parsons in the Fox roommate comedy *Lush Life*, which lasted just four episodes and drew parallels to *Laverne & Shirley* and *The Odd Couple*. Parsons (Hilary Banks from *The Fresh Prince of Bel-Air*) played the stuck-up foil to Lori's character, the free-spirited artist Georgette "George" Sanders. The women created the show, with Lori one of the last to hear of its cancellation. "You're gonna have to move your car," a studio security guard told her. "They gave your parking place away to someone else." For the next eighteen years until the Netflix prison series *Orange Is the New Black* put her back on a fancier map, Lori endured as a bit player on TV, nabbing parts in B-movies here and there.

Explaining her roller-coaster trajectory, Lori told the *Daily Beast*: "Well, because I was thirty-something and I hadn't married my agent, married any guy co-stars, or gotten fake titties or Botox. I never wanted to be a bombshell; I wanted to be an actor. I would much prefer to be a woman than a man, but if I was a dude, maybe I'd have Johnny Depp's island because women in this industry after a certain age definitely don't get to do *Pirates of the Caribbean*. Poor Keira [Knightley], they even airbrushed huge tits on her on the poster, and she's flawless! I was trying to play football with a baseball, and you can't really do that."

In 2008 she debuted as a director on the indie drama *The Poker House*, a retelling of her traumatic childhood and teenage sexual assault. Lori and her friend, actor David Alan Grier, cowrote the script, and she cast an unknown Jennifer Lawrence in her first leading role. Lori immediately grasped Lawrence's raw talent. She possessed maturity and intuition, and rang no false notes as smart, athletic Agnes, who takes care of her two younger sisters (Chloe Grace Moretz and Sophi Bairley) because their mother (Selma Blair) is too strung-out to care. Lori had an out-of-body experience while she filmed Agnes's brutal rape inside the house of prostitution where she lives with her dysfunctional family. "I guess it's something I had to do to get rid of it," she said. "I mean, I never consciously thought I was holding on to this and had to get rid of it, but now that it's done and I look at it, I go, 'What in the hell did you do, you crazy person?'"

With a $1 million budget, Lori shot *The Poker House* over twenty days in Illinois. She kept it moving, doing few takes. In her first crew meeting, she advised her team of fifty or so to use inside voices on set. "If you need something, you use your walkie-talkie or have a PA go do it for you," she said. "You don't yell. There's no yelling." Because, she explained, "if you have actors trying to do their work and all of a sudden someone is screaming it just wrecks your life."

*A League of Their Own* remains Lori's most famous movie, and she embraces its outsized part in her acting legacy. When people yell at her from their cars, they'll say, "Lay off the high ones!" A good sport, she'll respond with "I like the high ones!" Cue the delighted screams. She'll always be Kit Keller, and Kit Keller will always be her.

When Geena Davis turned forty in 1996, her star began to fade. Or, as she put it, "I fell off the cliff. I really did."

She had once been optimistic about her future as an actress. The careers of Meryl and Jessica Lange and Sally Field offered hope that she could survive as a leading lady. After Thelma and Dottie, she kept winning big roles in big movies, though none reached the heights of her hot streak in 1991 and 1992. There was *Hero* with Dustin Hoffman, *Speechless* with Michael Keaton, and *Angie*, a drama about a Brooklyn woman's path to self-discovery that she carried on her own. The screenplay was written with Madonna in mind, but Joe Roth offered the part to Geena instead. ("I can understand why you had reservations about my ability," Madonna, two years from headlining *Evita*, penned in a sarcastic note to the producer. "I can see why you would think Geena Davis the better actress for the part. After all she's Italian and she has an edge. How foolish of me to think I had the ability to play a vulnerable character unlike anything I've done to date.") *Angie* sputtered, earning back a third of its $26 million budget. Next, Geena played a pirate in the megaflop *Cutthroat Island*, directed by then-husband Renny Harlin, and an amnesiac schoolteacher in Harlin's modest thriller *The Long*

*Kiss Goodnight*, released four years after *A League of Their Own*. She did not appear onscreen again until the 1999 family film *Stuart Little*, in a charming turn as matriarch Mrs. Little.

"In my entire 40s, I made one movie, *Stuart Little*," Geena told *The Cut* in 2016, adding, "I was getting offers, but for nothing meaty or interesting like in my 30s. I'd been completely ruined and spoiled. I mean, I got to play a pirate captain! I got to do every type of role, even if the movie failed."

*A League of Their Own* taught Geena that "it was okay to take up this much space in the world, and to feel good about my body," she reflected in her autobiography. "And I now knew that I was athletic." She added, "Once again, the demands of the movie and the character spread out in a magical way into my real life. I was using acting to fill out the persona of someone confident in their abilities—someone I was determined to be more like in real life."

She took up archery, practicing the sport six days a week and winning tournaments around the world, nearly qualifying for the 2000 Sydney Olympics. Her interest predated 2012's *The Hunger Games*, in which Jennifer Lawrence, an overnight global action hero, brandished a bow and arrow, popularizing the weapon. Katniss Everdeen was a direct descendant of Dottie Hinson, but she didn't play team sports for fun. The *Hunger Games* franchise was Teen Torture Cinema where athletes murder to survive. While pundits predicted that *A League of Their Own* would spawn more female-driven sports movies, nothing happened of the sort. The year 1992 had also spotlighted a fiercely competitive figure skater in *The Cutting Edge*, as well as a girls' soccer team in *Ladybugs*, although that widely panned, poor-grossing comedy was merely a showcase for star Rodney Dangerfield's shtick. Soon after *League*, boy jocks outnumbered girls in the movies—look no further than *Little Big League*, *Rookie of the Year*, *Angels in the Outfield*, and *The Sandlot*, in which catcher Hamilton "Ham" Porter insults a rival by taunting, "You play ball like a girl!"

At the turn of the millennium, girls were better represented in soccer-themed films. In 2003, the acclaimed British comedy *Bend It Like Beckham*, costarring Keira Knightley and Parminder Nagra as aspiring pros, reached American shores, where it remains the third most successful soccer—er, *football*—movie ever behind *Kicking & Screaming* and *She's the Man*. In *She's the Man*, an enjoyable twist on *Twelfth Night*, Amanda Bynes plays a teenager who impersonates a boy so she can play on the soccer team at an elite boarding school. (Triumphantly, she scores a winning goal.)

Abby Wambach, the Olympic gold medalist and Women's World Cup champion, told me that *A League of Their Own* inspired her to play soccer as a kid and to take pride in her special talent. She was wowed by Geena and the way she was in the movie.

"Two things: one, her presence as a leader," Wambach says. "Two, the fact that she was one of the most talented ones on the team," but also the most conflicted in terms of wielding her superpowers. "It was just in her," the legendary athlete continues. "Sometimes the roles that we are, that we embody in our life, are roles that we wouldn't necessarily want to choose for a lot of reasons—for social pressure, peer pressure, and just wanting to fit in and not have to be the person who steps up and stands up and speaks up and leads." When Dottie agrees to join the league, stepping into her authority, "what she showed me on film was that it was possible to be one of the best players and also be a good leader."

While young Wambach chose soccer, schoolgirls' participation in fast-pitch softball surged significantly the year after the Peaches entered theaters. According to data from the National Federation of State High School Associations, 324,344 girls played high school softball in 1993, up from 268,522 the previous year—that's an increase of 20 percent. That is what I'd call the League of Their Own Effect. At the same time, the needle barely budged for girls in high school baseball, where boys continue to reign. There were 353 girls playing high school baseball during the 1993–1994 school year, compared with 438,846 boys. The girls' numbers took two years to grow, expanding to 1,340 players in 1995 and peaking at 1,924 in 2003. For teenagers who aren't cisgender males, softball has replaced baseball while other school sports like basketball, tennis, and track are played by both girls and boys, though separately, with nearly equivalent rules and parameters. Recently, there have been growing signs of progress as women baseball players and coaches filter into the sport's upper echelons. On July 20, 2020, Alyssa Nakken of the San Francisco Giants became the first woman to coach on the field in a Major League Baseball game. Two years later, the New York Yankees installed Rachel Balkovec as the manager of its Class A minor league team, the Tampa Tarpons, another history-making move. And on Staten Island, home of the FerryHawks,

Kelsie Whitmore, an ex-college softball player with baseball in her soul (and a fearsome tattoo of crocodile teeth near her left wrist), broke ground as the first woman to play for an MLB-affiliated minor league team since 1994, when Julie Croteau and Lee Anne Ketcham joined the Maui Stingrays of the short-lived Hawaii Winter Baseball league. Croteau had done a one-season stint with the Colorado Silver Bullets, the first all-female pro baseball team on US soil in the decades after the AAGPBL. The Silver Bullets barnstormed around the country, battling men's professional and semi-pro teams from 1994 until 1997, until Coors Brewing Company dropped its sponsorship. Following her time as a Stingray, Croteau became the first woman to coach men's NCAA Division I baseball, and later, without fanfare or media attention, she coached the Women's Baseball World Cup in 2004 and 2006, leading the American team to victory twice. Her college baseball glove is on display in Cooperstown.

During *A League of Their Own*'s press tour, Geena had described it to journalists as a "feminist film."

"Can we write that?" they asked, horrified, wanting to protect her from the potential backlash of publicly associating herself with the F-word.

*Yes, you can*, she said.

Penny, however, took pains to emphasize that *League* wasn't a conscious feminist undertaking but rather an act of universal uplift. *Don't be ashamed of your talents*. That message was for everyone, she argued. Women scared men in Hollywood, and men turned their fears into nightmare scenarios like *Fatal Attraction* and *Misery*. If Penny wanted to keep playing with the boys, and holding court on and off her movie sets, then downplaying her film's inherent feminism was obvious self-preservation.

Geena had no use for that. Ever since *Thelma & Louise*, she selected films with female ticket-buyers in mind. She cared what they thought and wanted to keep reaching them. Innumerable women and girls told her that *A League of Their Own* motivated them to take up sports. That was the power of representation, of identification, of feeling seen and heard. Geena cringed at the memory of the descriptive copy on the back of a *League* VHS tape, which made it sound like the movie was all about Jimmy Dugan. She felt a swelling social responsibility: she became a trustee at the Women's Sports Foundation and campaigned for women to know their rights under Title IX. In 2004, she quietly launched the Geena Davis Institute on Gender in Media, collecting hard data to educate industry leaders on their internalized biases. She and her partner, surgeon Reza Jarrahy, had a toddler daughter, Alizeh, with whom Geena watched kiddie programs that included one girl character or none. "What the heck was this?" she wondered. "How haven't we fixed this?"

Over time, Geena began to see the impact of her efforts—in 2017, she reported that 68 percent of the entertainment companies partnered with her namesake nonprofit had changed male characters to female and added more female characters, among other corrections. There was still much work to be done. That year, Fox canceled *Pitch*, a well-received drama series about a woman (Kylie Bunbury) pitching for the San Diego Padres, a scenario simultaneously out of reach and within the realm of possibility, as when Geena portrayed the first female president of the United States in ABC's *Commander in Chief.* Like *Pitch*, that show lasted just one season, yanked before it had a chance to find its footing and build steady viewership.

Geena, by the way, still wants to make a sequel to *A League of Their Own.* This one would be called *A Little League of Their Own*, and her proposed premise induces goosebumps: *Dottie comes out of retirement to challenge a boys' team that won't let girls join.* The *Ted Lasso* writers' room should get on it! And bring back key cast members in cameos—excluding Lovitz. On second thought: Why *not* Lovitz? (Taking notes, Hollywood?)

In 2005, Byron Motley received a handwritten note from Garry Marshall politely rejecting a screenplay on which Motley and writer Jeff Miller collaborated. It was a biopic about Effa Manley, who co-owned the Newark Eagles, a Negro League club, in the 1930s and 1940s. Manley was the first woman to be inducted into the Baseball Hall of Fame.

*I've read your script*, he wrote, *and I really like it, but it's not right for me. My sister, Penny, might be more right for this project.*

Motley, a singer-songwriter whose father was an umpire in the Negro Leagues, thought, *Forget it.* She'd already done a baseball movie. She wasn't going to be interested in Effa.

About a month later, Motley's phone rang. A familiar voice: *Laverne.*

"I read your script," Penny said. "And I like it. Let's talk about it."

Motley and Miller worked with Penny for eight years to punch up the material. In story meetings, she stood up and acted out her verbal notes, encouraging the pair to lighten up their original draft, which skewed toward the serious. She made them laugh. She was a gas. Her wheels were always turning, and she seemed ready to get back to work, but her health delayed progress on *Effa*. "She sometimes was lucid and all right with the world," Motley says. "And then she got sicker and sicker."

Penny was diagnosed with lung cancer and a brain tumor in October 2009. Bonnie Hlinomaz, at the hospital with her for the news, "ran out and threw up in the bushes," Penny recalled. Yet she herself was oddly calm, predisposed to "accepting life for what it is, rather than dwelling on what it isn't." Tracy cared for her as she recovered from successful brain surgery, and radiation and chemotherapy cleared her head and lungs of cancer. She gained sixty pounds and tried to quit smoking. Then she had a cigarette. And another. "I can't have just one of anything," she said. "Lamps. Tomato plants. Hummingbird feeders. Autographed baseballs. And most certainly cigarettes."

Dennis Rodman, the former NBA rebel who infamously dated Madonna, asked Penny, a basketball groupie, to make an honest (and still unfinished) documentary about his life. She interviewed Rodman as well as his family, teammates, and coaches, among other talking heads. "I came to realize," she reflected, "that he had enlisted me to help him figure out his life."

In 2012 she published a best-selling memoir, which Tom blurbed, calling her a "fascinating woman who has lived a life few of us could survive." She looked pulled-together and blasé at the intimate New York book party, held inside Graydon Carter's posh Monkey Bar restaurant. Lorne Michaels, John McEnroe, and Mariah Carey were among the guests who proved that her Rolodex still seeped power and influence. That year, the Library of Congress added *A League of Their Own* to the National Film Registry, citing its "enduring importance to American culture." It was among the films, librarian James Billington said at the time, that "reflect who we are as a people and as a nation."

While Penny kept a lower profile in her sixties and seventies, she cameoed in Garry's romcom *New Year's Eve*, and appeared alongside her brother, sister, and Tracy on the game show *Family Feud*. She guest-starred on *Entourage*, *Mulaney*, and *Portlandia*, and she directed episodes of

*According to Jim* and *United States of Tara*. She liked being a grandma. "They're good kids," she said of her three grandchildren, "and Tracy is a terrific mother—much better than I ever was."

In December 2014, two months after turning seventy, Penny announced that she would direct *Effa*, her first feature film since *Riding in Cars with Boys*. Motley and Miller would produce along with Penny's friend Wendi Laski. Penny, formerly represented by ICM, did not have a powerful agent to go to bat for her. She held a reading at her home that went well. But the group struggled "coming through with the project because she was attached to it," Motley says, adding, "A lot of people turned their backs to Penny and [it] was very unfair for her." She'd been forgotten. Studio people wouldn't take a meeting. The sting of rejection made her wary of reaching out to the high rollers she'd known for years. Motley would ask, *What about Steven Spielberg? What about Tom Hanks?* She had Motley contact Spielberg, who was too busy to join Team Penny, and she sent the script to Tom, envisioning him in the role of Branch Rickey. He responded to the effect of "I love the script, I love the idea, but I've got five other projects I'm doing right now."

That was a common response. One important actor, director, and baseball fanatic wrote a curt note back. He hadn't read the script. Effa's story did not interest him in the slightest.

"How can they dismiss who this woman is, and what her name could give to a project?" Motley asks in hindsight. "It would *explode*."

Without studio resources on the business side, Penny was forced to have a heavier hand in arranging the financing. That wasn't her jam; she was a creative, not a hustling fundraiser. She retreated further into her cocoon. While visiting LA, Paula Herold, the casting director on *Renaissance Man* and *The Preacher's Wife*, called Penny one afternoon, and her assistant said she was sleeping. When Penny finally returned Herold's call, it was 3 a.m. Herold saw Penny in a wheelchair at Garry's memorial in the fall of 2016. He died the previous July after suffering a stroke, and on what would have been his eighty-second birthday, a thousand attendees streamed into Northridge Performing Arts Center. Tom and Julia Roberts made remarks. Bette Midler sang. Even Northwestern's marching band performed.

The next month, Carrie and her mother, Debbie Reynolds, died within days of each other. Carrie went into cardiac arrest during a transatlantic flight. An autopsy revealed later that she had cocaine in her system as well as opiates and MDMA. "My mom battled drug addiction and mental illness her entire life," her daughter, Billie Lourd, said. "She ultimately died of it." Her grandmother, Debbie, succumbed to a stroke brought on, mourners suggested, by a broken heart. Penny attended a starry memorial service at Carrie's home in Beverly Hills. There was fried chicken and cornbread, and an overwhelming feeling of loss.

"I think she just gave up after her brother and Carrie died," Herold says. "And then she was just in her bed."

More than a year later, Abbi Jacobson and Will Graham declared plans to reboot *A League of Their Own* as an Amazon series that delved into the truth of the All-American Girls Professional Baseball League, including the sexual awakenings. The eight episodes dropped in the summer of 2022 and starred Jacobson as a married Peach who carries on a secret affair with a glamorous teammate (D'Arcy Carden). If the show lacked the pizzazz and grandiosity of its original inspiration, it compensated with fuller character development and the wonderful arc of a Black pitcher (Chanté Adams) determined to play professional ball. Rosie returned in the minor but devastating role of the proprietor of a queer speakeasy not unlike the Sho-Bar in 1990s Evansville. In Jacobson's *League*, the stakes were higher, the tone less syrupy and the content more daring. Off network television, a character could freely gripe: "Fucking fuckers!"

The reboot's creators received Penny's blessing over a short phone call of fifteen to twenty minutes. She was very sick.

"We got into the scene with the foul ball and the Black woman who chucks it back," Jacobson told the *Hollywood Reporter*.

> Penny said she felt like she couldn't tell all the stories in the time allotted and she wanted to nod to the other parts that were important, such as that throw. We have more real estate to do that. No one is queer in the movie, and yet it's an iconic queer film. It's just in the air, and I don't think that was necessarily intentional. That's the vibe and the way you feel watching the film if you happen to feel and look like a little bit of an outsider. And a lot of queer people feel that way. We talked about the queerness. Penny was telling this story in 1992, and that was a very different time [in terms of] what stories were accepted for a huge studio movie. If it's tricky for us to do it now, it was for her then.

Penny died at home on December 17, 2018, from complications related to diabetes. She was seventy-five years old, but a kid at heart. Tom memorialized her on Twitter: "Goodbye, Penny. Man, did we laugh a lot! Wish we still could. Love you." He said later that *A League of Their Own* was the most fun he ever had working on a movie.

"The players are truly grateful for her and this film," the AAGPBL Association stated. "Without it, the AAGPBL would still be the 'best kept secret in baseball.' Thank you & we love you." The following September, the city of Rockford held a Penny Marshall Celebration Weekend, inviting Tracy to be the guest of honor. Fans dressed up like Peaches. They were excited to meet Betty Spaghetti.

At a golf event in the mid-2000s, Jessica Mendoza asked Geena Davis to sign a baseball. Both were giving speeches, and Geena was the top-billed speaker.

"You changed me, like, totally," Mendoza gushed of Dottie Hinson's effect on her younger self. "Your character helped me get to where I'm at right now." Dottie brought out what had always been inside of the budding softball champion: the skill and will to compete, and when things got difficult, to outlast athletes who were better than her.

Geena signed her ball: *Geena Davis, Rockford Peach #8.*

Mendoza cried. *This is the coolest*, she thought. The treasure topped her collection of signed balls, which include Hank Aaron's autograph. All told, Mendoza accumulated plenty of reasons for Geena to fangirl over *her*. The outfielder crushed her four years at Stanford, breaking records for batting average, home runs, doubles, triples, and stolen bases. She won Olympic gold with the US women's national softball team. She would go on to win the silver medal and play for the National Pro Fastpitch, an obsolete professional women's softball league. She would join ESPN as a full-time baseball analyst. In Major League Baseball, the Dottie Hinsons remained outside the foul lines as the men took the field.

When Mendoza's five-year-old son played his very first Little League game, he had performance anxiety beforehand.

"Mom, I have ticklies in my belly," he said.

She laughed. "Ticklies are a good thing, bud," she reassured. "The biggest things you're gonna do in life, you're gonna have ticklies in your belly."

He kind of looked at her like she was crazy.

The nerves, the butterflies, "That's what we live for," Mendoza said, in that moment invoking Jimmy Dugan as he tried to fire up a doubting Dottie with a pep talk. Jimmy's words, first spoken by Ganz and Mandel, also applied to making movies way back when.

It was supposed to be hard. If it wasn't hard, everyone would've done it. The hard was what made it great.

# ACKNOWLEDGMENTS

THANK YOU TO THE WARM, FUNNY ROCKFORD PEACHES FOR SHARING THEIR experiences with me. I'm forever indebted to Geena Davis, Lori Petty, Rosie O'Donnell, Megan Cavanagh, Tracy Reiner, Bitty Schram, Patti Pelton, Renée Coleman, Freddie Simpson, Anne Ramsay, Ann Cusack, Robin Knight, Kelli Simpkins, Kathleen Marshall, Neezer Tarleton, and Sharon Szmidt. Special shout-outs to Patti for connecting me with her teammates, and DeLisa Chinn-Tyler, an honorary Peach. You are all legends from the greatest baseball movie ever made.

Thanks for your time and memories, Julie Croteau (a hero), Shelly Adlard, Lita Schmitt, Mary Moore, Jon Lovitz, David Strathairn, Justin Scheller, Tony Savino, Mark Holton, Alan Wilder, Douglas Blakeslee, Joey Slotnick, Ryan Olsen, Lowell Ganz, Babaloo Mandel, Kelly Candaele, Kim Southerland, Robert Greenhut, Elliot Abbott, Amy Lemisch, Tim Bourne, Joseph Hartwick, Bill Pace, Ellen Lewis, Mary Bailey, Bill Groom, Tim Galvin, George DeTitta Jr., Cynthia Flynt, Bernadette Mazur, Francesca Paris, Paul Gebbia, Linda Boykin-Williams, Michele Paris, Sam Hoffman, Tom Priestley, Gary Muller, Craig DiBona, Ondrej Kubicek, Lew Baldwin, Mollie Mallinger, Billy Kerwick, Bonnie Hlinomaz, Alexis Alexanian, Dennis Benatar, Rebecca Saoinz, Fredda Slavin, Dennis Drummond, Matt Salvato, Bo Hughes, Abe Flores, Gloria Mallah, Lou Conte, Jim Kleverweis, Patty Willett, Anitra Larae Donahue, Alina Martinet, Christie Wenger, Tom Morales, Doron Shauly, Christopher Capp, Suzanne McCabe, David Dumais, Erica Arvold, David

Obermeyer, Dana Dru Evenson, Amy Pascal, Michael Nathanson, Frank Price, Mark Canton, Sid Ganis, Susan Cartsonis, David Anspaugh, Cindy Williams, Todd Smith, Charlie Wessler, Susan Seidelman, Elizabeth Perkins, David Moscow, Matt Leonetti, Byron Motley, Jeff Miller, Laurie Perlman, Jim Belushi, Lindsay Frost, Brenda Feigen, Connie Nass, Dale Payne, Mike Duckworth, Patrick Higgs, J. Patrick Redmond, Jeff Lyons, Beth and Dan Katz, Brian Jackson, Barry Witherspoon, Gordon Engelhardt, Jessica Mendoza, Abby Wambach, Amy Guittierez, and Justine Siegal. John Rusk: you were a tremendous resource for helping me piece together the production's timeline. (I can see why you are very good at your job!) To those with whom I spoke on background: I appreciate you.

Thank you to the generous Bill Bussing and Shannon Fuhs for taking me through Bosse Field and League Stadium on separate tours. *A League of Their Own* fans: you must make a special trip to witness film history in person. (Go Evansville Otters!)

Thank you to Jennifer Armstrong, Kirthana Ramisetti, Saul Austerlitz, Thea Glassman, Gavin Edwards, and Tim Grierson for your sage advice and countless pep talks.

It takes a village to raise a book—or, in this case, an especially fantastic team. Thank you to my agent, Monika Verma, and my editor, Brant Rumble, for coaching me through this project. You are forces of competence and calm. Another round of thanks to Hachette's Michael Barrs, Mollie Weisenfeld, Cisca Schreefel, and Duncan McHenry, not to mention my clever research assistant, Caroline Jorgensen, and the patient Genevieve Maxwell at the Margaret Herrick Library. You are truly in a league of your own.

Finally, thank you to my amazing husband, daughter, parents, and in-laws. This book would not exist without your unwavering support. I love you.

# SOURCE NOTES

## Introduction: Dirt in the Skirt

**her first at bat:** Elias Stimac, "The Girls of Summer Discover 'A League of Their Own,'" *Drama-Logue*, July 2–8, 1992.

**"Omigod, hit the ball":** Ibid.

**more than $100 million at the box office:** Penny Marshall, *My Mother Was Nuts* (New York: Houghton Mifflin Harcourt, 2012), 230.

**eighty-eight-day shoot:** Peggy Orenstein, "Making it in the Majors," *New York Times Magazine*, May 24, 1992.

## First Inning: An Underdog and Insider

**Charlie Wessler trembled:** Charles Wessler, "How Penny Marshall Saved My Life," vanityfair.com, December 21, 2018.

**The suits in charge:** Mary Murphy, "The 'Laverne & Shirley' Feud: 'It Was War,'" *TV Guide*, August 28, 1982.

**even in Paris:** https://www.youtube.com/watch?v=LF4dVas6FDc.

**"no one's gonna hire you as an actress":** Charlie Wessler to the author.

**"I think you should be a director":** Ibid.

**Xerox machines:** Charles Wessler, "How Penny Marshall Saved My Life," vanityfair.com, December 21, 2018.

**her physical appearance mattered less:** Mary Murphy, "The 'Laverne & Shirley' Feud: 'It Was War,'" *TV Guide*, August 28, 1982.

**her nose, her teeth:** Tom Cunneff, "Penny Marshall Finally Leaves *Laverne* Behind and Scores *Big* as a Director—So Why the Long Face?," *People*, August 15, 1988.

**"I'm insecure mostly because of my looks":** Burt Prelutsky, "It May Be Called 'Laverne & Shirley' . . . but for Penny Marshall, It's All in the Family," *TV Guide*, May 22, 1976.

**a girl of thirteen:** Rachel Abramowitz, *Is That a Gun in Your Pocket?: Women's Experience of Power in Hollywood* (New York: Random House, 2000), 289.

**"I hit Ronnie and ran":** Jane Ardmore, *Sunday Woman*, January 28, 1979.

**"relished her victory":** Ibid.

**"I wasn't pretty so I played ball with them":** Abramowitz, *Is That a Gun in Your Pocket?: Women's Experience of Power in Hollywood*, 289.
**box-baseball or stoopball:** Harvey Steinberg, "Sidewalks Are For Playing," *New York Times*, July 18, 1976.
**She and her friends cut class:** https://www.youtube.com/watch?v=6yrLFGWr-Kg.
**bask in their glory:** Abramowitz, *Is That a Gun in Your Pocket?: Women's Experience of Power in Hollywood*, 290.
**She dreamed of becoming an Olympic runner:** https://www.youtube.com/watch?v=86Kp_icv4ng&t=4299s.
**discouraged a future in sports:** https://www.youtube.com/watch?v=6yrLFGWr-Kg.
**climbed into the gutter:** Joe Morgenstern, *Playboy*, January 1991.
**more time outside:** Marshall, *My Mother Was Nuts*, 2.
**"the bad seed":** Lorenzo Benet and George Kalogerakis, "Penny Marshall: *The Preacher's Wife* Director Finds Peace in a Riot of Work," December 23, 1996.
**"had the personality of a lamppost":** Abramowitz, *Is That a Gun in Your Pocket?: Women's Experience of Power in Hollywood*, 289.
**St. Vincent's Hospital:** Marshall, *My Mother Was Nuts*, 9.
**Marjorie's favorite actress:** Marshall, *My Mother Was Nuts*, 10.
**"Listen, we're not getting much help here":** https://www.youtube.com/watch?v=86Kp_icv4ng&t=4299s.
**when Penny was eight years old:** Ibid.
**"There was always some lady hanging out the window":** Ibid.
**the Magnets:** Benet and Kalogerakis, "Penny Marshall: *The Preacher's Wife* Director Finds Peace in a Riot of Work," December 23, 1996.
**she planned to divorce Tony:** Marshall, *My Mother Was Nuts*, 47.
**"You were a miscarriage":** Marshall, *My Mother Was Nuts*, 7.
**suicide jar:** Morgenstern, *Playboy*, January 1991.
**Those buck teeth:** Marshall, *My Mother Was Nuts*, 23.
**on Johnny Carson:** Abramowitz, *Is That a Gun in Your Pocket?: Women's Experience of Power in Hollywood*, 289.
**"Oh, you're going to wear that":** Ibid.
**She wore pants:** Morgenstern, *Playboy*, January 1991.
**If Penny didn't dance:** Prelutsky, "It May Be Called 'Laverne & Shirley' . . . but for Penny Marshall, It's All in the Family," *TV Guide*, May 22, 1976.
**Penny unzipped:** Benet and Kalogerakis, "Penny Marshall: *The Preacher's Wife* Director Finds Peace in a Riot of Work," December 23, 1996.
**"This was her life's work":** Marshall, *My Mother Was Nuts*, 26.
**the wrong color for the broadcast:** Ibid., 28.
**"Do you want her to be in the show instead of you?":** Ibid., 28.
**"Keep close":** Ibid., 30.
**majoring in recreation:** Ibid., 54.
**typing course to prepare herself:** Ibid., 50.
**tall and Waspy:** Lois Armstrong, "Penny Marshall & Rob Reiner: Laverne and the Meathead Keep Their Hits All in the Family," *People*, March 22, 1976.
**"I was in heaven":** Prelutsky, "It May Be Called 'Laverne & Shirley' . . . but for Penny Marshall, It's All in the Family," *TV Guide*, May 22, 1976.
**"I got nailed":** Abramowitz, *Is That a Gun in Your Pocket?: Women's Experience of Power in Hollywood*, 290.

**played football on scholarship:** Orenstein, "Making it in the Majors," *New York Times Magazine*, May 24, 1992.
**She got a job at the area's best dance school:** Marshall, *My Mother Was Nuts*, 68.
**seventy words per minute:** Morgenstern, *Playboy*, January 1991.
**gotten married too young:** Benet and Kalogerakis, "Penny Marshall: *The Preacher's Wife* Director Finds Peace in a Riot of Work," December 23, 1996.
**playing Ado Annie:** Marshall, *My Mother Was Nuts*, 73.
**They tried to hide Tracy:** Ibid.
**I'm no good:** Abramowitz, *Is That a Gun in Your Pocket?: Women's Experience of Power in Hollywood*, 290.
**Dating was impossible:** Prelutsky, "It May Be Called 'Laverne & Shirley' . . . but for Penny Marshall, It's All in the Family," *TV Guide*, May 22, 1976.
**The call from his baby sister:** Ibid.
**"What do you have in mind?":** Ibid.
**"Well, we could have dinner and we could talk":** Morgenstern, *Playboy*, January 1991.
**He watched her frowning face:** Prelutsky, "It May Be Called 'Laverne & Shirley' . . . but for Penny Marshall, It's All in the Family," *TV Guide*, May 22, 1976.
**"But you don't sing so good":** Morgenstern, *Playboy*, January 1991.
**he understood exactly who she was:** Ibid.
**Penny had trouble landing auditions:** Ibid.
**Penny witnessed a humiliating sight:** Abramowitz, *Is That a Gun in Your Pocket?: Women's Experience of Power in Hollywood*, 291.
**thought about quitting:** Marshall, *My Mother Was Nuts*, 84.
**LA overflowed with fellow neurotics:** Armstrong, "Penny Marshall & Rob Reiner: Laverne and the Meathead Keep Their Hits All in the Family," *People*, March 22, 1976.
**Garry asked Penny to ask Klugman:** Marshall, *My Mother Was Nuts*, 86.
**Klugman had to carry her to her mark:** Prelutsky, "It May Be Called 'Laverne & Shirley' . . . but for Penny Marshall, It's All in the Family," *TV Guide*, May 22, 1976.
**earned raises of $100 per week:** Morgenstern, *Playboy*, January 1991.
**She married the actor:** Armstrong, "Penny Marshall & Rob Reiner: Laverne and the Meathead Keep Their Hits All in the Family," *People*, March 22, 1976.
**he had lived across the street:** Ibid.
**wore lots of sweaters:** Tracy Reiner to the author.
**Sometimes women came over:** Abramowitz, *Is That a Gun in Your Pocket?: Women's Experience of Power in Hollywood*, 292.
**Carl raised an eyebrow:** Prelutsky, "It May Be Called 'Laverne & Shirley' . . . but for Penny Marshall, It's All in the Family," *TV Guide*, May 22, 1976.
**Penny sank deeper into a funk:** Ibid.
**She would often lie in bed:** Abramowitz, *Is That a Gun in Your Pocket: Women's Experience of Power in Hollywood*, 292.
**Penny joined a hip collective:** Cindy Williams, *Shirley, I Jest!: A Storied Life* (Guilford, Connecticut: Lyons Press, 2015), 87.
**"We had the exact same sense of humor":** Cindy Williams to the author.
**"The Salem Witch Trials":** Williams, *Shirley, I Jest!: A Storied Life*, 89.
**"Hookers":** Cindy Williams to the author.
**Penny's vintage record collection:** Williams, *Shirley, I Jest!: A Storied Life*, 97.

**dressed Audrey Hepburn in her heyday:** Cindy Williams to the author.

**Garry purposely staged his family-friendly sitcoms in the '50s:** https://www.youtube.com/watch?v=X6qOzGatGww.

**soundstage 20:** Williams, *Shirley, I Jest!: A Storied Life*, 95.

**"We wanted it better":** https://www.youtube.com/watch?v=X6qOzGatGww.

**"It was an asylum":** Ibid.

**Laverne and company stayed late:** Ibid.

**Penny put her foot down:** Marshall, *My Mother Was Nuts*, 130.

**Garry had hired Tony Marshall:** Pamela G. Hollie, "Marshalls Stage a TV Success," *New York Times*, October 2, 1980.

**"Pop, she's a star":** Ibid.

**"We were like sisters":** Cindy Williams to the author.

**"Are you gonna get that time step?":** Ibid.

**"That's the best it's gonna be":** Ibid.

**"That's not funny":** Ibid.

**the badgering pushed Cindy:** Ibid.

**Penny considered Cindy the better actress:** Marshall, *My Mother Was Nuts*, 129.

**Cindy deemed Penny brilliant:** Cindy Williams to the author.

**"I simply tried to make the bed":** Marshall, *My Mother Was Nuts*, 127.

**"Not one award":** Cindy Williams to the author.

**The critical gatekeepers' hauteur rankled them:** William Hickey, "Laverne and Shirley funnier off-camera," *Plain Dealer*, January 19, 1978.

**made double their salaries:** Cindy Williams to the author.

**"Yeah, but they're men":** Ibid.

**"We actually believed that":** Ibid.

**"That's where she would not have confidence in the show":** Ibid.

**could disrupt her marriage:** Abramowitz, *Is That a Gun in Your Pocket?: Women's Experience of Power in Hollywood*, 293.

**played first base on the Happy Days softball team:** https://www.youtube.com/watch?v=PoAP-YazsZw.

**which counted Tom Hanks:** Susan Orlean, "Tom Hanks's Common Touch," *Rolling Stone*, September 25, 1986.

**loved having TV money:** Bruce Buschel, "Tom Hanks, Unpeeled," *GQ*, January 1988.

**"I was an asshole for six months":** Ibid.

**he wanted off the show:** https://www.youtube.com/watch?v=a1oVzeMuJi4.

## Second Inning: First Strike

**Penny found herself alone:** Lois Armstrong, "It's Thumbs Up—Sort Of—As Penny Marshall Copes With Life Without Meathead," *People*, April 28, 1980.

**"Why exchange an imperfect husband":** Ibid.

**"What, are you crazy?":** Abramowitz, *Is That a Gun in Your Pocket?: Women's Experience of Power in Hollywood*, 293.

**He should have known:** Ibid.

**The headache of renovating:** Armstrong, "It's Thumbs Up—Sort Of—As Penny Marshall Copes With Life Without Meathead," *People*, April 28, 1980.

**Twilight was the loneliest time:** Ibid.

**she leased the guesthouse to Richard Dreyfuss:** Ibid.

**a mid-century estate:** https://www.architecturaldigest.com/story/penny-marshalls-longtime-hollywood-hills-home-sells.

**She made her houseguests pay their own phone bills:** Morgenstern, *Playboy*, January 1991.
**she liked to hunker down in bed:** Ibid.
**dating actor David Dukes and musician Art Garfunkel:** Armstrong, "It's Thumbs Up—Sort Of—As Penny Marshall Copes With Life Without Meathead," *People*, April 28, 1980.
**"I tried to get a Quaalude in him":** Marshall, *My Mother Was Nuts*, 149.
**"My neck and chest froze":** Ibid., 158.
**The women rode up and down the elevator:** Ibid.
**"Well, I think you just need to get through it":** Ibid., 159.
**she began thinking about directing as a safety net:** Armstrong, "It's Thumbs Up—Sort Of—As Penny Marshall Copes With Life Without Meathead," *People*, April 28, 1980.
**"Directing is babysitting":** Abramowitz, *Is That a Gun in Your Pocket?: Women's Experience of Power in Hollywood*, 295.
**"She used to cut film in her head while she was acting":** Ibid.
**"This [show] isn't worth me doing":** Todd Smith to the author.
**Would Marty Scorsese do this film?:** Murphy, "The 'Laverne & Shirley' Feud: 'It Was War,'" *TV Guide*, August 28, 1982.
**He thought Laverne & Shirley was garbage:** Abramowitz, *Is That a Gun in Your Pocket?: Women's Experience of Power in Hollywood*, 293.
**he undermined women performers and writers:** Yael Kohen, *We Killed: The Rise of Women in American Comedy* (New York: Farrar, Straus and Giroux, 2012), 103.
**"Women are just fundamentally not funny":** Sarah Frank, "Jane Curtin Says John Belushi Was a Total Sexist," vulture.com, April 12, 2011.
**hosted a reading at her home:** Abramowitz, *Is That a Gun in Your Pocket?: Women's Experience of Power in Hollywood*, 295.
**The night before John was to meet with the studio:** Ibid., 296.
**she had flushed John's heroin down the toilet:** Marshall, *My Mother Was Nuts*, 179.
**died after battling Alzheimer's:** Benet and Kalogerakis, "Penny Marshall: *The Preacher's Wife* Director Finds Peace in a Riot of Work," December 23, 1996.
**"Maybe it's good":** Ibid.
**their $1 million gift to her:** https://www.northwestern.edu/magazine/fall2012/feature/whats-in-a-name-sidebar/lizabet-ward-marshall-dance-center.html.
**she sprinkled her ashes:** Marshall, *My Mother Was Nuts*, 192.
**She took exciting trips abroad:** Ibid., 194–195.
**The actresses famously clashed during the filming:** J. D. Heyman and Alexia Fernández, "No 'Terms of Endearment': The Story Behind Debra Winger and Shirley MacLaine's Hollywood Feud," People.com, October 31, 2018.
**"I deserve this":** http://aaspeechesdb.oscars.org/link/056-3/.
**"must have felt like shit":** Marshall, *My Mother Was Nuts*, 196.
**"Why don't you direct?":** Ibid.
**after a conflict with Debra:** Unbylined, "Marshall, Winger Pull Out of 'Peggy,'" *Variety*, October 31, 1984.
**Debra encouraged producer Ray Stark to hire her:** Marshall, *My Mother Was Nuts*, 196.
**launched into casting mode:** Ibid., 197.
**Stark thought Peggy Sue was too big:** Anne Thompson, "Laverne Goes to Hollywood," *LA Weekly*, December 20, 1985.

**In a rare gesture:** Ibid.

**that Penny and Debra wanted to make:** "Marshall, Winger Pull Out of 'Peggy,'" *Variety*, October 31, 1984.

**she set up a development deal at Warner Brothers:** Ibid.

**Penny understood well that unlike Hawn:** Todd Smith to the author.

**the fitness craze that swept the nation:** Susan K. Cahn, *Coming on Strong: Gender and Sexuality in Twentieth-Century Women's Sport* (Cambridge, Massachusetts: Harvard University Press, 1994), 273–275.

**"I wasn't anxious to work":** Mary Murphy, "Schlemiel, Schlimazel, Hasenpfeffer Incorporated!," *TV Guide*, May 4, 2002.

**she got complacent:** Nancy Mills, "Penny Marshall: Director in a 'Flash,'" *Los Angeles Times*, October 28, 1986.

**decided to buy an apartment in New York:** *My Mother Was Nuts*, 203.

**she bumped into Debra:** Ibid.

**"I had concluded that Debra has a problem when there's another attractive woman":** Frank Price to the author.

**"The movie did fine":** James Andrew Miller, *Power House CAA: The Untold Story of Hollywood's Creative Artists Agency* (New York: Custom House, 2016), 199–200.

**went out to dinner with Whoopi Goldberg:** Marshall, *My Mother Was Nuts*, 203.

**soon phoned Penny with an urgent request:** Ibid., 204.

**"Can I read the script?":** Ibid., 204.

**The script was such a mess:** Morgenstern, *Playboy*, January 1991.

**Nancy Meyers and David Mamet:** *My Mother Was Nuts*, 204.

**"It's like picking up somebody else's trash":** Charlie Wessler to the author.

**"You're going to learn":** Ibid.

**"Just don't fall down":** Marshall, *My Mother Was Nuts*, 204.

**Spielberg reminded her:** Ibid.

**replacing Jan de Bont:** Thompson, "Laverne Goes to Hollywood," *LA Weekly*, December 20, 1985.

**"I ask only one thing":** Marshall, *My Mother Was Nuts*, 205.

**She lacked know-how about lenses and lighting:** Jami Bernard, "Penny Marshall: Bobby De Niro's Favorite Director," *Tower Video Collector*, August/September 1991.

**Sometimes she had him act out a scene:** Matt Leonetti to the author.

**"That wasn't too pleasant":** Mills, "Penny Marshall: Director in a 'Flash,'" *Los Angeles Times*, October 28, 1986.

**Kill me now:** Marshall, *My Mother Was Nuts*, 205.

**Whoopi invited Penny into her makeup trailer:** Ibid., 206.

**"What are you doing?":** Abramowitz, *Is That a Gun in Your Pocket?: Women's Experience of Power in Hollywood*, 295.

**she connected with Whoopi's character:** Marshall, *My Mother Was Nuts*, 204.

**"She is a television actress":** Abramowitz, *Is That a Gun in Your Pocket: Women's Experience of Power in Hollywood*, 295.

**Whoopi hesitated to go off-script:** Bob Strauss, "A Penny for Your Thoughts," *Movieline*, October 24, 1987.

**"Do you know what it's like doing something stupid over and over again?":** Marshall, *My Mother Was Nuts*, 207.

**"I don't feel so good":** Abramowitz, *Is That a Gun in Your Pocket?: Women's Experience of Power in Hollywood*, 298.

**Whoopi was loath to leave the comfort of her trailer:** Miller, *Power House CAA: The Untold Story of Hollywood's Creative Artists Agency*, 172–173.
**"all they could really see is what I look like":** Ibid., 172.
**"Everybody gets crazy":** Abramowitz, *Is That a Gun in Your Pocket?: Women's Experience of Power in Hollywood*, 297.
**She solicited the crew's opinion:** Ibid.
**Leonetti sought to break up the tension:** Matt Leonetti to the author.
**Wessler noticed the DP placing his hand on Penny's shoulder:** Charlie Wessler to the author.

## Third Inning: Another Swing at Bat

**Harrison Ford threw a script:** Wessler, "How Penny Marshall Saved My Life," vanityfair.com, December 21, 2018.
**six or seven potential directors:** Ibid.
**a Spielberg-Ford collaboration:** Bernard, "Penny Marshall: Bobby De Niro's Favorite Director," *Tower Video Collector*, August/September 1991.
**"He's too cool for that shit":** Wessler to the author.
**"I just don't see how this is you":** Ibid.
**As soon as possible:** Ibid.
**"you need to call Jim Brooks":** Ibid.
**Penny got her agents to send her the script:** Ibid.
**Brooks popping into Penny's office:** Marshall, *My Mother Was Nuts*, 214.
**"This is your next movie":** Morgenstern, *Playboy*, January 1991.
**What Brooks failed to mention:** Marshall, *My Mother Was Nuts*, 214.
**Reitman:** https://www.imdb.com/title/tt0094737/trivia/.
**John Hughes:** https://www.imdb.com/title/tt0094737/trivia/.
**A perfectionist, Brooks spent a year retooling the script:** Aljean Harmetz, "Tom Hanks: From Leading Man to Movie Star," *New York Times*, July 6, 1988.
**nearly $30 million:** https://www.boxofficemojo.com/release/rl2573043201/weekend/.
**"Miss Marshall directs Jumpin' Jack Flash":** Vincent Canby, "Screen: Whoopi Goldberg in 'Jumpin' Jack Flash,'" *New York Times*, October 10, 1986.
**"Hey, hey, lay back!":** Todd Gold, "Rappin' With Penny and Carrie," *People*, Spring 1991.
**"It took literally like a month of beating the crap out of Fox":** Wessler interview with the author.
**"No one's gonna give you money to make a movie with Bob De Niro":** Ibid.
**"Bobby D.":** Marshall, *My Mother Was Nuts*, 216.
**was unavailable:** Jason S. Stewart, "A thought for Penny," UCLA *Daily Bruin*, January 11, 1991.
**"Let me take it a different way":** Ibid.
**Penny held a casting call:** David Moscow to the author.
**"Where are you from?":** Ibid.
**Debra thought Big should flip genders:** Elizabeth Perkins interview with the author.
**Debra . . . recommended Elizabeth Perkins:** Ibid.
**he also suggested her to Penny:** Ibid.
**"He was more moody":** https://www.indiewire.com/2021/04/elizabeth-perkins-big-horror-movie-robert-de-niro-casting-1234628860/.
**"Penny really knows what she wants":** Wessler to the author.

**"I asked if he would listen to me if I directed him":** Marshall, *My Mother Was Nuts*, 217.

**Penny told De Niro the truth:** Ibid.

**$3 million:** Unbylined news item, *Hollywood Reporter*, July 27, 1988.

**Penny offered her salary to Bobby:** Marshall, *My Mother Was Nuts*, 218.

**De Niro's fleeting attachment sparked renewed interest:** Ibid., 216–217.

**followed her instincts:** Ibid., 220.

**"Do you want The Nutty Professor or Being There?":** Ibid.

**Tom feared that he would never work again:** Bill Zehme, "Mr. Big," *Rolling Stone*, June 30, 1988.

**What if they caught on and shelved the imposter?:** David Sheff, "Playboy Interview: Tom Hanks," *Playboy*, March 1989.

**in March 1987:** https://prod-www.tcm.com/tcmdb/title/18502/punchline#notes.

**hitting comedy clubs:** Harmetz, "Tom Hanks: From Leading Man to Movie Star," *New York Times*, July 6, 1988.

**"I was really terrible the first 15 times":** Ibid.

**"That kind of power corrupts":** Ibid.

**He invented a backstory for Steven:** David Ansen, "A Stand-Up Guy," *Newsweek*, September 26, 1988.

**"I felt sorry for the guy":** Ibid.

**"probably has the worst aspects of my worst aspects":** Sheff, "Playboy Interview: Tom Hanks," *Playboy*, March 1989.

**"I'm constantly reminded of how unfair the world in general is":** Harmetz, "Tom Hanks: From Leading Man to Movie Star," *New York Times*, July 6, 1988.

**When Tom was five years old:** Ibid.

**nicknamed Bud:** Gavin Edwards, *The World According to Tom Hanks: The Life, The Obsessions, The Good Deeds of America's Most Decent Guy* (New York: Grand Central Publishing, 2018), 2.

**went on to marry three times:** Zehme, "Mr. Big," *Rolling Stone*, June 30, 1988.

**"I just felt lonely":** Edwards, *The World According to Tom Hanks: The Life, The Obsessions, The Good Deeds of America's Most Decent Guy*, 3.

**Frances Wong:** Ibid., 7.

**"I read all the time 'Tom Hanks is the product of a broken, tragic childhood'":** Buschel, "Tom Hanks, Unpeeled," *GQ*, January 1988.

**Tom grew up funny and shy:** Zehme, "Mr. Big," *Rolling Stone*, June 30, 1988.

**a sport that obsessed him:** Edwards, *The World According to Tom Hanks: The Life, The Obsessions, The Good Deeds of America's Most Decent Guy*, 6.

**in Little League:** Ibid., 5.

**spent much of his time indoors watching TV:** Ibid., 6.

**His favorite show:** Ibid.

**Several other experiences:** Sheff, "Playboy Interview: Tom Hanks," *Playboy*, March 1989.

**A photograph of Nazis:** Edwards, *The World According to Tom Hanks: The Life, The Obsessions, The Good Deeds of America's Most Decent Guy*, 9.

**At Skyline High School he found his tribe:** Erin Carlson, *I'll Have What She's Having: How Nora Ephron's Three Iconic Films Saved the Romantic Comedy* (New York: Hachette Books, 2017), 40. (Yes, I cited myself!)

**"Mr. Hill":** Edwards, *The World According to Tom Hanks: The Life, The Obsessions, The Good Deeds of America's Most Decent Guy*, 14.

**studying theater production:** Ibid., 17.
**three summers onstage:** Buschel, "Tom Hanks, Unpeeled," GQ, January 1988.
**he sat in the right field section:** Stu Schreiberg, "the 'Big' leagues . . . ," *USA Weekend*, June 3–5, 1988.
**The 1980 season:** Buschel, "Tom Hanks, Unpeeled," GQ, January 1988.
**captivating the city:** Steve Wulf, "Super Joe: Legend in His Own Time," *Sports Illustrated*, September 8, 1980.
**dyed hair:** https://www.sportscasting.com/wheres-joe-charboneau-the-cleveland-indians-quirky-one-hit-wonder-who-once-ate-six-lit-cigarettes/.
**drinking beer through his nose:** Ibid.
**injured his back:** Ibid.
**"Baseball is the perfect metaphor for life":** Buschel, "Tom Hanks, Unpeeled," GQ, January 1988.
**If only Tom could hit a curveball:** Ibid.
**He resented the pressure:** David Blum, "Tom Hanks's Real Splash," *New York*, July 28, 1986.
**landing a minor role in a low-budget slasher movie:** Carlson, *I'll Have What She's Having: How Nora Ephron's Three Iconic Films Saved the Romantic Comedy*, 40.
**his Bosom Buddies break:** Ibid., 41.
**which delighted Garry:** Blum, "Tom Hanks's Real Splash," *New York*, July 28, 1986.
**"The film tries to show that life is funny and life is sad":** Unbylined, "Tom Hanks," *Cable Guide*, August 1986.
**Susan mostly cared for Colin:** https://uproxx.com/tv/colin-hanks-growing-up-tom-hanks/.
**"I guess I've been like a classic absentee father":** Mary Murphy, "Tom Hanks: One Hunk Who Refuses to Go Hollywood," *Cosmopolitan*, March 1987.
**"He's one of the few young actors":** Ibid.
**"But what if people don't care about this movie?":** Patrick Goldstein, "Tom Hanks, New King of Cutups," *Los Angeles Times*, August 1, 1986.
**nerdy male screenwriters:** Blum, "Tom Hanks's Real Splash," *New York*, July 28, 1986.
**He romanticized the game:** Robert Goldberg, "Hollywood's Hottest Comic Actor is Branching Out," *Connoisseur*, September 1986.
**He wanted to sit in the stands:** Murphy, "Tom Hanks: One Hunk Who Refuses to Go Hollywood," *Cosmopolitan*, March 1987.
**"When I go to sleep":** Lisa Birnbach, "Tom Hanks' Fantasy: If Only I Were a Cleveland Indian," *Parade*, November 8, 1987.
**On the night of August 9, 1987:** https://www.tcm.com/tcmdb/title/68599/big/#notes.
**was to begin filming at Rye Playland:** Barry Sonnenfeld, *Barry Sonnenfeld, Call Your Mother* (New York: Hachette Books, 2020), 213.
**"Oh, shit":** Elizabeth Perkins to the author.
**on Fifty-Seventh Street:** Tim Bourne to the author.
**Greenhut nixed that idea:** Robert Greenhut to the author.
**He connected the dots ahead of time:** Sonnenfeld, *Barry Sonnenfeld, Call Your Mother*, 213.
**"Penny didn't like to make decisions":** Ibid.
**"Barry didn't do a good job shooting the tests":** Ibid., 214.

**"So, the first night of *Big*":** Ibid.

**"I had to make it look nice":** Abramowitz, *Is That a Gun in Your Pocket?: Women's Experience of Power in Hollywood*, 302.

**This is really smart:** Susan Cartsonis to the author.

**studio heads phoned Barry:** Abramowitz, *Is That a Gun in Your Pocket?: Women's Experience of Power in Hollywood*, 302.

**"I'm not a film expert":** Patrick Goldstein, "Penny Marshall Makes 'Big' Impact," *Los Angeles Times*, June 8, 1988.

**having no depth:** Elaine Wohl, "TV's Laverne Makes Her Speaking Debut," UCLA *Daily Bruin*, January 7, 1980.

**"I think my problem":** Goldstein, "Penny Marshall Makes 'Big' Impact," *Los Angeles Times*, June 8, 1988.

**I'm gonna get fired:** David Moscow to the author.

**"I did forty takes yesterday":** Ibid.

**"probably saved my career":** Ibid.

**"insh":** Marshall, *My Mother Was Nuts*, 221.

**"I knew that took away":** Goldstein, "Penny Marshall Makes 'Big' Impact," *Los Angeles Times*, June 8, 1988.

**mined memories of his own preadolescence:** Sheff, "Playboy Interview: Tom Hanks," *Playboy*, March 1989.

**They worked hard to improve the sequence:** Marshall, *My Mother Was Nuts*, 222.

**Tom showed up at a Midtown screening room:** Hanks recalled his lecture from Penny in the March 10, 2022, episode of the *Dead Eyes* podcast.

**"Popo the Mute Boy":** Marshall, *My Mother Was Nuts*, 222.

**"There was no, 'Oh, let's cut and discuss the eating of the corn'":** Perkins to the author.

**he flinched:** Marshall, *My Mother Was Nuts*, 223.

**"Well, let's fire him":** Wessler to the author.

**"We'll make it work":** Ibid.

**Greenhut blocked Barry from getting the ax:** Greenhut to the author.

**"They don't like me":** Morgenstern, *Playboy*, January 1991.

**"You're right":** Ibid.

**"I think he just didn't like her":** Wessler to the author.

**The second week of filming:** Sonnenfeld, *Barry Sonnenfeld, Call Your Mother*, 217.

**"I tried to fi-a you this weekend":** Ibid.

**yelled "CUT":** Ibid., 218.

**"Sometimes, you'd still be rolling":** Perkins to the author.

**"self-confidence to keep shooting":** Abramowitz, *Is That a Gun in Your Pocket?: Women's Experience of Power in Hollywood*, 302.

**Penny suggested that Elizabeth dab Tom's wounds with alcohol:** Perkins to the author.

**to drive her to the gynecologist:** Marshall, *My Mother Was Nuts*, 223.

**"I had no idea that I was pregnant":** Ibid., 223–224.

**But Penny kept it relatively PG-rated:** Bernard, "Penny Marshall: Bobby De Niro's Favorite Director," *Tower Video Collector*, August/September 1991.

**"In defense of the movie":** Perkins to the author.

**that showed the couple at play:** Marshall, *My Mother Was Nuts*, 226.

**"I know what we're gonna do":** Perkins to the author.

**would cost too much:** Marshall, *My Mother Was Nuts*, 226.

**"ridiculed Penny like crazy":** Abramowitz, *Is That a Gun in Your Pocket?: Women's Experience of Power in Hollywood*, 302.
**circumvented a sleeping Greenhut:** Marshall, *My Mother Was Nuts*, 226.
**"You know what?":** Perkins to the author.
**Penny used a walkie-talkie:** Ibid.
**Elizabeth secretly crushed on Tom:** https://people.com/movies/elizabeth-perkins-opens-up-about-kissing-her-then-crush-tom-hanks/.
**He kissed her:** Schreiberg, "the 'Big' leagues . . . ," *USA Weekend*, June 3–5, 1988.
**Penny among the witnesses:** Ibid.
**"Tom and I used to joke":** Perkins to the author.
**Tom and Rita showed up fifteen minutes late:** Zehme, "Mr. Big," *Rolling Stone*, June 30, 1988.
**The Hanks progeny::** https://uproxx.com/tv/colin-hanks-growing-up-tom-hanks/.
**visited their father often and on schedule:** Zehme, "Mr. Big," *Rolling Stone*, June 30, 1988.
**Elizabeth cried:** Perkins to the author.
**"It was so sad":** Zehme, "Mr. Big," *Rolling Stone*, June 30, 1988.
**"I went into a depression":** Abramowitz, *Is That a Gun in Your Pocket?: Women's Experience of Power in Hollywood*, 302.
**"I know you guys didn't think I knew what I was doing":** David Obermeyer to the author.
**"Everybody was like, Wow":** Tim Bourne to the author.
**"And here's Penny!":** Zehme, "Mr. Big," *Rolling Stone*, June 30, 1988.
**a "very cute guy":** Cunneff, "Penny Marshall Finally Leaves *Laverne* Behind and Scores *Big* as a Director—So Why the Long Face?," *People*, August 15, 1988.
**she encountered a child:** Marshall, *My Mother Was Nuts*, 229.
**she loved that it made audiences happy:** Ibid.

## Fourth Inning: The Hall of Famers

**She raised five boys under one roof:** Andrea Moret, "Back at the Plate Again," *Los Angeles Times*, June 28, 1992.
**She played catch with her sons:** Christina De Nicola, "The real women who inspired 'A League of Their Own,'" mlb.com, July 1, 2022.
**"the feminine Ted Williams":** Ibid.
**Kelly beamed with pride:** Kelly Candaele, "Mom Was in a League of Her Own," *Los Angeles Times*, June 7, 1992.
**"Where did your mom learn to play?":** Ibid.
**Why didn't I get her swing?:** Ibid.
**"It's the kind of swing you associate with Ted Williams":** Ibid.
**snapped the image in 1945:** Ibid.
**she batted .299:** Jim Sargent, "Marge and Helen Callaghan: The Inspiration for the Movie 'A League of Their Own,'" aagpbl.org, 2013.
**a thirty-six-ounce Louisville Slugger:** Moret, "Back at the Plate Again," *Los Angeles Times*, June 28, 1992.
**ranking first in the league:** Ibid.
**averaged a moderate .196:** Sargent, "Marge and Helen Callaghan: The Inspiration for the Movie 'A League of Their Own,'" aagpbl.org, 2013.
**a combination of baseball and softball:** Lois Browne, *Girls of Summer* (Toronto: HarperCollins, 1992), 26.

**longer geometry, overhand pitching, and smaller ball size:** Ibid., 138–139.

**Joe DiMaggio became a sergeant:** https://www.joedimaggio.com/the-man/armed-forces/.

**and Ted Williams a second lieutenant:** Justin Leger, "A look back at Ted Williams' service in the U.S. military," nbcsports.com, May 13, 2021.

**The Office of War Information issued a stark warning:** Moret, "Back at the Plate Again," *Los Angeles Times*, June 28, 1992.

**Branch Rickey:** Candaele, "Mom Was in a League of Her Own," *Los Angeles Times*, June 7, 1992.

**The sisters Callaghan:** Sargent, "Marge and Helen Callaghan: The Inspiration for the Movie 'A League of Their Own,'" aagpbl.org, 2013.

**Helen ran track and joined Marge on the Young Liberals:** Tom Hawthorn, "Home Runs and Charm School: Baseball's Girls of Summer," *The Tyee*, June 12, 2018.

**when Helen was eight and Marge was nine:** Ibid.

**a truck driver and machine operator:** Ibid.

**"we could make $60 a week":** Moret, "Back at the Plate Again," *Los Angeles Times*, June 28, 1992.

**the Vancouverite craved the experience:** She explained her decision to join the league in an interview in Kelly Candaele's PBS documentary about the All-American Girls Professional Baseball League, which aired nationally in 1987.

**Alongside a third sister:** Hawthorn, "Home Runs and Charm School: Baseball's Girls of Summer," *The Tyee*, June 12, 2018.

**branded identification numbers onto bomber equipment:** Ibid.

**"Helen was more forward than I was":** Sargent, "Marge and Helen Callaghan: The Inspiration for the Movie 'A League of Their Own,'" aagpbl.org, 2013.

**Playing ball was a lot better than working inside all day:** Marge Callaghan interview in Kelly Candaele's PBS documentary.

**that quickly folded:** Browne, *Girls of Summer*, 56–57.

**The league shipped:** Ibid.

**Standing five feet, three inches tall:** Sargent, "Marge and Helen Callaghan: The Inspiration for the Movie 'A League of Their Own,'" aagpbl.org, 2013.

**105 pounds:** Scott Ostler, "A Hard-Nosed Kid Learned How From His Dear Old Mom," *Los Angeles Times*, March 10, 1987.

**self-professed tomboy:** Kelly Candaele to the author.

**"My reflexes were faster":** Sargent, "Marge and Helen Callaghan: The Inspiration for the Movie 'A League of Their Own,'" aagpbl.org, 2013.

**fear of lesbianism:** Browne, *Girls of Summer*, 26.

**babes who played like men:** Ibid., 27.

**Helena Rubinstein's charm school:** Ibid., 43.

**No shorts or slacks in public:** Moret, "Back at the Plate Again," *Los Angeles Times*, June 28, 1992.

**No drinking:** Ibid.

**The Look even required lipstick:** Information displayed in an exhibit on the All-American Girls Professional Baseball League at the History Museum in South Bend, Indiana.

**parading the short-skirted, one-piece uniforms:** Ibid.

**Otis Shepard, and Wrigley's wife:** Joanna Rachel Turner, "AAGPBL History: Diamonds Are a Girl's Best Friend," aagpbl.org, undated.

**cutesy headlines:** Hawthorn, "Home Runs and Charm School: Baseball's Girls of Summer," *The Tyee*, June 12, 2018.

**"To me, it was just funny":** Moret, "Back at the Plate Again," *Los Angeles Times*, June 28, 1992.

**When Josephine "JoJo" D'Angelo:** Cahn, *Coming on Strong: Gender and Sexuality in Twentieth-Century Women's Sport*, 186–187.

**a rare chance to form intimate bonds:** Ibid., 187.

**As homophobia rose within the culture:** https://press.uchicago.edu/Misc/Chicago/404811in.html.

**play it, don't say it:** Cahn, *Coming on Strong: Gender and Sexuality in Twentieth-Century Women's Sport*, 187.

**amateur hockey player Bob Candaele:** Moret, "Back at the Plate Again," *Los Angeles Times*, June 28, 1992.

**sat out the season:** Hawthorn, "Home Runs and Charm School: Baseball's Girls of Summer," *The Tyee*, June 12, 2018.

**"My husband became the woman of the house":** Nancy Dworsky, "At Bat: Helen Callaghan and women's professional baseball," *LA Weekly*, July 12, 1991.

**Helen caused trouble from time to time:** Sargent, "Marge and Helen Callaghan: The Inspiration for the Movie 'A League of Their Own,'" aagpbl.org, 2013.

**"We did a lot of short-sheeting":** Hawthorn, "Home Runs and Charm School: Baseball's Girls of Summer," *The Tyee*, June 12, 2018.

**soldiered through eight games a week:** Dworsky, "At Bat: Helen Callaghan and women's professional baseball," *LA Weekly*, July 12, 1991.

**four-month season:** Sargent, "Marge and Helen Callaghan: The Inspiration for the Movie 'A League of Their Own,'" aagpbl.org, 2013.

**110-degree heat:** Ibid.

**ten hours by bus:** Dworsky, "At Bat: Helen Callaghan and women's professional baseball," *LA Weekly*, July 12, 1991.

**millions of fans:** Candaele, "Mom Was in a League of Her Own," *Los Angeles Times*, June 7, 1992.

**"I think men liked the way we wore short skirts":** Dworsky, "At Bat: Helen Callaghan and women's professional baseball," *LA Weekly*, July 12, 1991.

**In her words:** Moret, "Back at the Plate Again," *Los Angeles Times*, June 28, 1992.

**was earning $125 per week:** Dworsky, "At Bat: Helen Callaghan and women's professional baseball," *LA Weekly*, July 12, 1991.

**What did I need with a fur coat?:** Ibid.

**"Why are you leaving all this money?":** Ibid.

**the Canadian had not been exposed to Black people or racial segregation:** Ibid.

**a freeze-out that shunned talents such as Mamie "Peanut" Johnson:** https://www.youtube.com/watch?v=iw-ACi9TPBc&t=294s.

**vivacious and talkative:** Hawthorn, "Home Runs and Charm School: Baseball's Girls of Summer," *The Tyee*, June 12, 2018.

**She liked bunting:** Sargent, "Marge and Helen Callaghan: The Inspiration for the Movie 'A League of Their Own,'" aagpbl.org, 2013.

**When Helen fell ill in 1948:** Ibid.

**Marge gave her blessing:** Hawthorn, "Home Runs and Charm School: Baseball's Girls of Summer," *The Tyee*, June 12, 2018.

**Scandal swirled around her:** Browne, *Girls of Summer*, 168.

**"She says they never dated":** Ibid.
**Helen returned to form:** Sargent, "Marge and Helen Callaghan: The Inspiration for the Movie 'A League of Their Own,'" aagpbl.org, 2013.
**ran a taxi business:** Ibid.
**Helen had no regrets:** Moret, "Back at the Plate Again," *Los Angeles Times*, June 28, 1992.
**she broke her ankle and her average slipped to .157:** Sargent, "Marge and Helen Callaghan: The Inspiration for the Movie 'A League of Their Own,'" aagpbl.org, 2013.
**engaged in a shouting match:** Ibid.
**The ex–major leaguer:** https://www.aagpbl.org/profiles/john-rawlings-johnny/769.
**"I was always taught if I couldn't get two outs":** Sargent, "Marge and Helen Callaghan: The Inspiration for the Movie 'A League of Their Own,'" aagpbl.org, 2013.
**Marge, incredulous, sat down on the bench:** Ibid.
**Within three weeks, she was traded:** Ibid.
**decided that 1951 would be her last year:** Ibid.
**She went out with a bang:** Ibid.
**That ball soared over a rival's head:** Ibid.
**After eight seasons and more than seven hundred games:** Hawthorn, "Home Runs and Charm School: Baseball's Girls of Summer," *The Tyee*, June 12, 2018.
**She looked back fondly:** Sargent, "Marge and Helen Callaghan: The Inspiration for the Movie 'A League of Their Own,'" aagpbl.org, 2013.
**affecting the All-Americans' bleacher turnout:** The South Bend–based History Museum cites television as a factor in the league's demise.
**faced difficulties managing embittered team owners:** Browne, *Girls of Summer*, 173.
**the clubs slashed the budgets:** Ibid.
**received her pay in single dollar bills:** Ibid., 189.
**"indecorous femininity":** Ibid., 186.
**"Avoid noisy, rough, and raucous talk":** Ibid., 45.
**"At the start, the league resembled softball":** Sargent, "Marge and Helen Callaghan: The Inspiration for the Movie 'A League of Their Own,'" aagpbl.org, 2013.
**ownership leaned too heavily upon veteran athletes:** Browne, *Girls of Summer*, 171–172.
**reteamed on fastpitch squads:** Sargent, "Marge and Helen Callaghan: The Inspiration for the Movie 'A League of Their Own,'" aagpbl.org, 2013.
**in 1973:** Moret, "Back at the Plate Again," *Los Angeles Times*, June 28, 1992.
**Helen's righteous competitive spirit resurfaced:** Candaele, "Mom Was in a League of Her Own," *Los Angeles Times*, June 7, 1992.
**"It's not that she was insensitive":** Ostler, "A Hard-Nosed Kid Learned How From His Dear Old Mom," *Los Angeles Times*, March 10, 1987.
**"Mighty Mite":** "Casey Candaele Stats," baseball-almanac.com.
**"Casey didn't get my mom's swing either":** Candaele, "Mom Was in a League of Her Own," *Los Angeles Times*, June 7, 1992.
**"Did he do good?":** Hawthorn, "Home Runs and Charm School: Baseball's Girls of Summer," *The Tyee*, June 12, 2018.
**"It meant she was out there playing with me":** Ibid.
**His teammates poked fun:** Moret, "Back at the Plate Again," *Los Angeles Times*, June 28, 1992.
**when the sports journalist:** Michael Clair, "Former pro's mom was in a league of her own," mlb.com, December 19, 2021.

**went out to lunch with a reporter from Channel 4:** Kelly Candaele to the author.
**"What?":** Ibid.
**"I want to do a story on this":** Ibid.
**Wallace produced a three-part series:** Ibid.
**brought the footage to LA's public television station, KCET:** Ibid.
**"This league existed":** Ibid.
**The two met in 1984:** Kim Southerland to the author.
**"He didn't even own a television set":** Ibid.
**was working as an executive assistant to Eileen Berg:** Ibid.
**Kim loved Helen:** Ibid.
**They combed through vintage reels:** Merrie A. Fidler, *The Origins and History of the All-American Girls Professional Baseball League* (Jefferson, North Carolina: McFarland & Company, 2006), Location 5419 on Kindle's iPhone app.
**"I was completely obsessed with it":** Ibid.
**"We had no money":** Ibid.
**The enterprise gained momentum:** Fidler, *The Origins and History of the All-American Girls Professional Baseball League*, Location 5387 and 5396 on Kindle.
**in September 1986:** Ibid., Location 5396.
**"The highlight of the reunion":** Candaele, "Mom Was in a League of Her Own," *Los Angeles Times*, June 7, 1992.
**"It's the second-dearest memory in my heart":** Pepper Paire Davis to the documentarians of PBS' *A League of Their Own* (1987).
**Taylor heard about the reunion through Katie Horstman:** Fidler, *The Origins and History of the All-American Girls Professional Baseball League*, Location 5396 on Kindle.
**when the All-Americans reconnected through a monthly newsletter:** Ibid., Location 5372.
**began printing articles and player profiles:** Ibid., Locations 5372–5380.
**premiere at Northwestern in May 1987:** Ibid., Location 5396.
**on KCET that March:** Ostler, "A Hard-Nosed Kid Learned How From His Dear Old Mom," *Los Angeles Times*, March 10, 1987.
**nationwide on PBS in September:** Fidler, *The Origins and History of the All-American Girls Professional Baseball League*, Location 5425 on Kindle.
**Kelly took her to the Elizabeth Arden Red Door Salon:** Candaele to the author.
**"She was not saying, 'What show can I go on next?'":** Ibid.
**won awards on the festival circuit:** Moret, "Back at the Plate Again," *Los Angeles Times*, June 28, 1992.
**"Don't be ridiculous":** Southerland to the author.
**"He thought it was silly, you know?":** Ibid.
**prepared a script treatment:** Josef Woodard, "Playing Ball in Hollywood," *Santa Barbara Independent*, July 9, 1992.
**they heard from Charlie Wessler:** Wessler, "How Penny Marshall Saved My Life," vanityfair.com, December 21, 2018.
**Lissa August:** Ibid.
**sent Wessler a copy on VHS:** Ibid.
**"Oh my god, this is fantastic":** Wessler to the author.
**She loved the show:** Candaele to the author.
**Kelly wasn't familiar with her at all:** Ibid.

**Penny opened the door wearing her bathrobe:** Southerland to the author.
**"Oh, hello":** Ibid.
**"Go sit out at the pool":** Ibid.
**"You know, she's kind of eccentric":** Ibid.
**she listened with interest as they shared their vision:** Ibid.
**She immediately grasped the league's importance:** Candaele, "Mom Was in a League of Her Own," *Los Angeles Times*, June 7, 1992.
**"It was like Zen archery":** Moret, "Back at the Plate Again," *Los Angeles Times*, June 28, 1992.
**Penny invited them to her birthday party:** Candaele to the author.
**he and his wife would hide behind a bush:** Babaloo Mandel to the author.
**Fox offered Penny a permanent office:** Marshall, *My Mother Was Nuts*, 232.
**"My first instinct was to find a woman to write it":** Ibid.
**"I sat on the couch between Ganz and Mandel":** Candaele, "Mom Was in a League of Her Own," *Los Angeles Times*, June 7, 1992.
**The pair tinkered with a plot:** Ibid.
**It involved a climactic championship game:** Candaele to the author.
**Kelly drafted a character outline:** Candaele shared a copy of the outline with the author.
**November 5, 1988:** https://baseballhall.org/discover/women-in-baseball-exhibit-made-history-in-cooperstown.
**eight feet by eight feet:** Ibid.
**He had a personal connection to the league:** Ibid.
**Penny lurked in the background:** Carolyn M. Trombe, *Dottie Wiltse Collins: Strikeout Queen of the All-American Girls Professional Baseball League* (Jefferson, North Carolina: McFarland & Company, 2005), Location 2548 on Kindle's iPhone app.
**"was asking a lot of questions":** Ibid., Location 2543.
**Spencer spotted Penny chain-smoking:** Ibid., Location 2549.
**Collins took it away from her:** Ibid., Location 2537.
**"why Penny Marshall should be at the dinner and not Harvey":** Ibid., Locations 2537 and 2543.
**Pepper simmered with anger:** Pepper Paire Davis, *Dirt in the Skirt* (Bloomington, Indiana: AuthorHouse, 2009), 432–433.
**with two requests:** Ibid., 430.
**Pepper managed to corral her close friend:** Ibid., 432–433.
**"We didn't say a word":** Elliot Abbott to the author.
**"Do you have what you need?":** Ibid.
**"The reason they gave":** Paire Davis, *Dirt in the Skirt*, 432.
**After reading an article about the league in the Boston Globe Magazine:** Bill Pace to the author.
**"We were not Hollywood types":** Ibid.
**slicker opportunists had courted them:** Ibid.
**Bill and Ronnie secured the board's trust:** Ibid.
**Penny phoned Bill and Ronnie:** Martin A. Grove, *Hollywood Reporter*, August 21, 1992.
**He'd once rooted for the Daisies in Fort Wayne:** David Anspaugh to the author.
**Feigen collected a bunch of material on the AAGPBL:** Brenda Feigen, *Not One of the Boys: Living Life as a Feminist* (New York: Alfred A. Knopf, 2000), 210.

**Feigen hated cigarette smoke:** Feigen to the author.

**What the hell?:** Ibid.

**"At her urging":** Feigen, *Not One of the Boys: Living Life as a Feminist* (New York: Alfred A. Knopf, 2000), 210.

**Pascal called Feigen:** Ibid., 211.

**She hired an attorney:** Feigen to the author.

**"I settled for $50,000":** Ibid.

**Ganz and Mandel were taking their time:** Marshall, *My Mother Was Nuts*, 233.

**seven-hundred-page master's thesis:** Lowell Ganz to the author.

**She didn't want anyone to look at the movie and go, Oh, that's a pile of crap:** Ibid.

**"This will sound weird":** Ibid.

**Both were the Dotties of their families:** Babaloo Mandel to the author.

**a heavy drinker who fell on hard times:** https://sabr.org/journal/article/the-real-jimmie-foxx/.

**drank himself out of the Majors:** Ira Berkow, "Hack Wilson's Lesson Still Valid," *New York Times*, September 5, 1998.

**Ganz and Mandel shared a desk:** Ganz to the author.

**weeping during a story meeting:** David Scheiderer, "Another Secret Chapter in Film History," *Los Angeles Times*, July 19, 1992.

**"What is this crying?":** Ibid.

**"Crying? There's crying?":** An excerpt from Ganz and Mandel's handwritten script, via ESPN.com's oral history of *A League of Their Own*, published June 29, 2017.

**she wasn't interested in the high-concept elevator pitches:** Morgenstern, *Playboy*, January 1991.

**a promising script appeared on her desk:** Ibid.

**She felt guilty for complaining as much as she did:** Sean Mitchell, "Backpedaling to Fame," *Los Angeles Times*, December 16, 1990.

**She thought of her mother:** Marshall, *My Mother Was Nuts*, 233.

**She appreciated the way screenwriter Steven Zaillian handled:** Ibid.

**released Penny from the intense pressure:** Stewart, "A thought for Penny," UCLA *Daily Bruin*, January 11, 1991.

**"What do I know about any of this?":** Elliot Abbott to the author.

**"She's extremely bright":** Morgenstern, *Playboy*, January 1991.

**called Robin Williams and Robert De Niro directly:** Abbott to the author.

**he gave Penny permission:** Marshall, *My Mother Was Nuts*, 236.

**"Don't trust any of these guys":** Ibid.

**Diller dialed Penny at Santa Monica's Pritikin Longevity Center:** Marshall, *My Mother Was Nuts*, 234.

**What makes a woman unforgettable?:** Ibid., 235.

**a sheepish Penny shrouded her eyes:** Ibid., 236.

**"It's gonna be hard to live this year down, isn't it?":** Joe Rhodes, "Back From the Bonfire," *Los Angeles Times*, July 5, 1992.

**Penny never told them out-and-out that she loved the result:** Ganz to the author.

**she got angry:** Ibid.

**"You had to make it so good":** Ibid.

**Penny preferred to direct men over women:** Stewart, "A thought for Penny," UCLA *Daily Bruin*, January 11, 1991.

**"I get a better reaction":** Ibid.

## Fifth Inning: The Tryouts

**February 1990:** Megan Cavanagh to the author.
**showed up in ballet slippers:** https://www.youtube.com/watch?v=ZMpETGQ6Tjs.
**antique Yankees uniform:** Anspaugh to the author.
**full-glam makeup:** Shannon Carlin, "Lori Petty Answers Every Question We Have About *A League of Their Own*," vulture.com, August 20, 2021.
**"She wasn't bad":** https://www.youtube.com/watch?v=ZMpETGQ6Tjs.
**send only their best:** Anspaugh to the author.
**"You could bring me the greatest actress in the world":** Ganz to the author.
**Athletes, Trainable, and Hopeless:** Ibid.
**"Is she trainable?":** Abbott to the author.
**Among the auditioners:** Anspaugh to the author.
**"You throw like a girl":** Perkins to the author.
**Daryl Hannah requested a private audition:** Anspaugh to the author. Via the Margaret Herrick library archives, a memo dated January 25, 1990, from casting agent Amanda Mackey to Anspaugh, listed other actresses requesting private auditions.
**the first contender to practice with Dedeaux and Hughes:** Bo Hughes to the author.
**"I had run into [Demi] prior to Awakenings":** Marshall, *My Mother Was Nuts*, 249.
**Tracy Reiner entered the competition:** Reiner to the author.
**"afraid to be around two thousand actresses":** Ibid.
**"I wasn't supposed to be there":** Ibid.
**"Damn, that girl's got an arm":** Ibid.
**"I took a whole bunch of aspirin":** Ibid.
**She got excited:** Ibid.
**"You gotta do this":** Ibid.
**"I don't want you to think just 'cause she's my daughter":** Anspaugh to the author.
**"I know, Penny":** Ibid.
**If I don't get this part:** Marjorie Rosen, "On Base With a Hit," *People*, July 20, 1992.
**A League of Their Own was said to have interested Meryl:** Jane Burns, "Former Lincoln softball player impressed Penny Marshall, earned role in 'A League of Their Own,'" *Des Moines Register*, July 1992.
**Little League remained off-limits to her:** Rosie O'Donnell to the author.
**She'd sit on the margins at her brothers' games:** Ibid.
**"I went to LA to the batting cages":** Ibid.
**The night before her tryout:** Freddie Simpson to the author.
**pretty girls who could play baseball and act:** Ibid.
**"I would say baseball was my best sport":** Ibid.
**Scouts from John Casablancas:** Ibid.
**"I don't think I ever even wore a dress":** Ibid.
**She moved to LA:** Ibid.
**"It was one of those magical days":** Ibid.
**"I killed it":** Neezer Tarleton to the author.
**Neezer recognized Hunt:** Ibid.
**"Don't worry about her":** Ibid.
**most inspired baseball audition of her life:** Megan Cavanagh to the author.
**crashed the tryouts:** Ibid.
**She had read the script:** Daniel Brown, "'A League of Their Own' Turns 30: Catching up with mighty Marla Hooch," *The Athletic*, June 30, 2022.

**paying the bills:** Cavanagh to the author.
**You can call me Glad:** Ibid.
**loved the Cubs:** Ibid.
**covered second base:** Ibid.
**"I got into my game face":** Ibid.
**You know we're playing baseball, right?:** Carlin, "Lori Petty Answers Every Question We Have About *A League of Their Own*," vulture.com, August 20, 2021.
**She was born in Chattanooga, Tennessee:** Susan King, "Lori Petty Hails From Green Acres, Finds Greener Pastures in 'Point,'" *Los Angeles Times*, July 13, 1991.
**always wanted a son:** https://www.youtube.com/watch?v=PoAP-YAzsZw.
**"So ever since I picked up a ball":** Ibid.
**Lori's mother left an abusive marriage:** Lisa Rosen, "Lori Petty's Hard Look," *New York Times*, June 19, 2008.
**moved to New York at age eighteen and waited tables between auditions:** Ibid.
**"I was like, 'Nobody's better than me at baseball'":** Lori Petty to the author.
**graduated from Indiana University and traveled westward:** https://www.imdb.com/name/nm0000770/bio.
**scouted Indiana locations:** Anspaugh to the author.
**took Elliot Abbott to a high school basketball game:** Abbott to the author.
**narrowed down the search:** Dennis Benatar to the author.
**The green-light process terrified the suits:** Susan Cartsonis to the author.
**Raved Roger Ebert:** https://www.rogerebert.com/reviews/field-of-dreams-1989.
**The first major actors cast:** Unbylined, "Indiana site of Belushi baseball film," Associated Press, April 27, 1990.
**"I mean, he was that character":** Anspaugh to the author.
**Gina Gershon and Joan Jett:** From the Ellen Lewis casting notebooks at the Margaret Herrick Library in Los Angeles.
**"Well, you work at a garage or something":** Anspaugh to the author.
**"No, I'm a welder":** Ibid.
**Anspaugh added Leoni to his team:** Ibid.
**"You are a beautiful, talented actress":** Simpson to the author.
**from April to July:** Unbylined, *Screen International*, April 5, 1991.
**"so good":** Anspaugh to the author.
**"pretty good":** Ibid.
**"His movie was great":** Mandel to the author.
**"Look, we're begging you":** Abbott to the author.
**with Hannah and Dern:** *Screen International*, June 2, 1990.
**a head-spinning update:** https://catalog.afi.com/Catalog/moviedetails/59298.
**She withdrew:** Unbylined, "How Budgets Swell," *Variety*, September 30, 1992.
**"Actors don't want to embarrass themselves":** Bill Pace to the author.
**You gotta be kidding me:** Anspaugh to the author.
**"You work with Lowell and Babaloo":** Ibid.
**"I loved the material":** Elaine Dutka, "Batter Up: Yes, Sports Fans, It's 'Truth or Dare' in the Bullpen," *Los Angeles Times*, June 9, 1991.
**around $18 million:** Unbylined, "How Budgets Swell," *Variety*, September 30, 1992.
**Roth put A League of Their Own into turnaround:** Dutka, "Batter Up: Yes, Sports Fans, It's 'Truth or Dare' in the Bullpen," *Los Angeles Times*, June 9, 1991.
**"If you come with us":** Marshall, *My Mother Was Nuts*, 248.
**$3.4 billion:** https://www.latimes.com/archives/la-xpm-1991-08-08-fi-464-story.html.

**$29 million:** Mitchell, "Backpedaling to Fame," *Los Angeles Times*, December 16, 1990.
**never yelled at Penny:** Ibid.
**"You can't make Penny":** Michael Nathanson to the author.
**They'd call down to Nathanson:** Ibid.
**"Nobody wants to do a baseball movie":** https://www.youtube.com/watch?v=PoAPYAzsZw.
**Diller did not match Sony's offer:** Marshall, *My Mother Was Nuts*, 248.
**"I remember telling Frank":** Nathanson to the author.
**$7 million:** https://www.youtube.com/watch?v=86Kp_icv4ng&t=4299s.
**"Don't you wish we had a comedy?":** Abbott to the author.
**Abbott heard people crying:** Ibid.
**Give the audience time to gather itself:** Ibid.
**"they were just destroyed":** Ibid.
**trimmed from six long hours:** Ibid.
**twelve theaters:** https://www.boxofficemojo.com/release/rl558204417/weekend/.
**Janet Maslin hated the movie:** Janet Maslin, "From a Living Death To Life in 'Awakenings,'" *New York Times*, December 20, 1990.
**"masterfully plays our strings":** Rita Kempley, "Awakenings," *Washington Post*, January 11, 1991.
**During an interview with Us magazine:** Patrick Goldstein, "Marshall's Law," *Us*, December 24, 1990.
**Kingsboro Psychiatric Center:** https://www.tcm.com/tcmdb/title/67829/awakenings#film-details.
**"I have these strange diseases":** Goldstein, "Marshall's Law," *Us*, December 24, 1990.
**"I stopped smoking for three weeks":** Mitchell, "Backpedaling to Fame," *Los Angeles Times*, December 16, 1990.
**Tracy brought her a Diet Pepsi:** Ibid.
**"People said it was so brave":** Ibid.
**Penny picked up the phone and called Rob:** Ibid.
**$61 million:** https://www.boxofficemojo.com/release/rl3781330433/weekend/.
**Penny was amused:** https://www.youtube.com/watch?v=86Kp_icv4ng&t=4299s.
**mistakenly seated them together:** Unbylined, "Musical chairs," *People*, June 4, 1990.
**blamed the sexism:** https://www.youtube.com/watch?v=86Kp_icv4ng&t=4299s.
**"The Academy screwed Penny":** Todd Smith to the author.
**non-nominees party:** Marshall, *My Mother Was Nuts*, 246.
**"Look, first of all, you're Italian":** https://www.youtube.com/watch?v=86Kp_icv4ng&t=4299s.
**Barbra Streisand presented:** https://www.youtube.com/watch?v=_Fl7vDRKUho.
**captured seven nominations:** https://www.youtube.com/watch?v=UCAi1744Sao&t=491s.
**"I loved seeing her walk through the door":** Marshall, *My Mother Was Nuts*, 246.
**"Let's do the baseball picture":** Ibid., 248.
**earning a salary of $3.75 million:** John Rusk to the author.
**"She literally got fucked out of the part":** Marshall, *My Mother Was Nuts*, 249.
**the footage left Penny unimpressed:** Ibid., 250.
**aged out of the part:** Ibid.
**Other Dotties considered:** From the Ellen Lewis casting notebooks at the Margaret Herrick Library in Los Angeles.
**In March 1991:** Unbylined, "Debra Winger: Batter Up!," *People*, April 15, 1991.

**She liked the idea of Moira Kelly:** Marshall, *My Mother Was Nuts*, 250.

**The daughter of Irish immigrants:** Jeff Giles, "Playing Two Roles in 'Chaplin' While Dreaming of Joan of Arc," *New York Times*, January 3, 1993.

**Kelly broke her leg:** Hillary Busis, "'Cutting Edge' star D.B. Sweeney on making a toe-picking classic," ew.com, February 7, 2014.

**She scouted other would-be, could-be Kits:** Names and notes from casting agent Ellen Lewis's notebooks archived at the Margaret Herrick Library.

**"They flew me to New York to audition":** Lori Petty to the author.

**"Scrappy, athletic, confident":** Marshall, *My Mother Was Nuts*, 250.

**"I was young, I was grateful":** https://www.youtube.com/watch?v=ZMpETGQ6Tjs.

**"Can I have it?":** Marshall, *My Mother Was Nuts*, 250.

**had championed off-brand Hanksian decency:** Julie Salamon, *The Devil's Candy: The Anatomy of a Hollywood Fiasco* (Cambridge, Massachussetts: Da Capo Press, 1991), 9–10.

**"You look at this arrogant rich guy":** Ibid., 10.

**It amazed Tom that Guber wanted him:** Ibid., 10–11.

**"Maybe I'm perfect":** Ibid., 11.

**made for $47 million:** https://www.boxofficemojo.com/title/tt0099165/.

**still kissed his ass:** David Wild, "Big Again," *Vogue*, July 1993.

**"didn't jump up and down":** Ganz to the author.

**"Penny, surprisingly, had a little bit of a wrestling match":** Ibid.

**Michael Douglas and even Paul Newman:** Ganz and Mandel to the author.

**William Morris agent Frank Frattaroli:** Names from casting agent Ellen Lewis's notebooks archived at the Margaret Herrick Library.

**"She dragged [Riley] in":** Greenhut to the author.

**"basically went through the entire script":** Ibid.

**Lewis sent a memo to Amy Pascal:** Names and notes from Lewis's notebooks at the Margaret Herrick Library.

**Jim still got paid:** https://www.youtube.com/watch?v=PoAP-YAzsZw.

**"They didn't want Tom either":** Ibid.

**His salary had climbed to $5 million:** Salamon, *The Devil's Candy: The Anatomy of a Hollywood Fiasco*, 10.

**"I thought he was wrong for the part":** Marshall, *My Mother Was Nuts*, 250–251.

**"I had the role on Saturday":** Jim Belushi to the author.

**Columbia announced Tom's casting:** *Screen International*, June 14, 1991.

**the gear sat in a corner, unclaimed:** David Dumais to the author.

**"Tom wanted to hide in the movie, not star in it":** Mandel to the author.

**"He was built like a Greek God":** https://sabr.org/journal/article/the-real-jimmie-foxx/.

**He suffered chronic pain:** Ibid.

**he turned to the bottle:** Ibid.

**While facing the Pittsburgh Pirates:** Ibid.

**He dozes in the dugout:** Paire Davis, *Dirt in the Skirt*, 335–336.

**sporting goods in a Cleveland department store:** Vince Guerrieri, "Foxx's Hard Life After Baseball Included Stop in Cleveland," didthetribewinlastnight.com, May 10, 2017.

**car salesman and a coal truck driver:** https://sabr.org/bioproj/person/Jimmie-Foxx/.

**collapses during dinner:** Ibid.

**"Jimmie was a great guy":** Paire Davis, *Dirt in the Skirt*, 336.

**"I just think he's a guy":** https://www.youtube.com/watch?v=XQTFUe7uwaU.
**He also liked that Jimmy was not the main story:** Wild, "Big Again," *Vogue*, July 1993.
**questioned his judgment:** Rhodes, "Back From the Bonfire," *Los Angeles Times*, July 5, 1992.
**He left William Morris:** Claudia Eller, "Starr Exits Morris to Go Indie Route," *Variety*, April 10, 1991.
**He bought a beachside home:** Ruth Ryon, "New Mr. 'Big' in Malibu Colony," *Los Angeles Times*, May 5, 1991.
**He dabbled in screenwriting:** Unbylined, *Variety*, April 12, 1991.
**jointly lobbied to remove Pakula:** Unbylined, "Stars Talk, Pakula Walks," *People*, March 18, 1991.
**"She wanted to bring in some New York buddies":** Mandel to the author.
**seemed to have fun diving into baseball training with Lori:** John Rusk to the author.
**"She started to practice":** Marshall, *My Mother Was Nuts*, 248.
**read for Marla Hooch:** "Special Features" commentary for *A League of Their Own* DVD released in 2004.
**Penny didn't see Rosie as Marla:** Ibid.
**"I told her not to eat":** Marshall, *My Mother Was Nuts*, 251.
**followed her out of the building:** Cavanagh to the author.
**Deflated, she phoned her friend Amy:** Ibid.
**Lori walked into the diner with an entourage:** Ibid.
**"Megan?":** Ibid.
**managed to audition for Ellen Lewis in New York:** Bitty Schram to the author.
**Parker Posey:** Name mentioned in Lewis's casting papers.
**I am not right for this role:** Schram to the author.
**"That was up my alley":** Ibid.
**"Oh no, I'm gonna get this role":** Ibid.
**Penny asked Diller to adjust the taping schedule:** Katie Baker, "'A League of Their Own' Is an All-Time Great Sports Film," theringer.com, June 30, 2017.
**Penny lost Lindsay Frost:** Marshall, *My Mother Was Nuts*, 251.
**She had read a magazine article:** Ibid.
**She wanted that for herself:** J. Randy Taraborrelli, *Madonna: An Intimate Biography* (New York: Simon & Schuster, 2001), 33.
**persuaded Madonna to work for scale:** Lynn Hirschberg, "The Misfit," *Vanity Fair*, April 1991.
**She brought rival pop phenomenon Michael Jackson as her platonic date:** Elaine Dutka, "Well, They Both Wore Gloves," *Los Angeles Times*, March 31, 1991.
**"Do you want to see me pitch?"** https://www.youtube.com/watch?v=POAP-YAzsZw.
**"I don't think you need to carry a movie right now":** Ibid.
**three-hour session:** Marshall, *My Mother Was Nuts*, 251.
**"Take your stance":** https://vault.si.com/vault/1991/06/10/scorecard.
**"What's a stance?":** Ibid.
**"A very strong and compact girl":** Ibid.
**At a seaside dinner party:** Unbylined, "Tongue Is On Madonna's Menu In Cannes," *New York*, May 27, 1991.
**"I was like, holy shit":** Rosie O'Donnell to the author.
**"tomorrow Madonna's coming in here":** Ibid.
**Rosie wondered how:** Ibid.

**In the exhibitionist she recognized a common origin story:** Ibid.
**"Hey, I saw your movie last night":** Ibid.
**"You did?":** Ibid.
**"Yeah":** Ibid.
**"Ro and Mo":** Marshall, *My Mother Was Nuts*, 251.
**"You're going to be best friends":** Ibid.
**Mae became brassier:** Ibid.
**Columbia pictures hoped Madonna would play Kit:** Dutka, "Batter Up: Yes, Sports Fans, It's 'Truth or Dare' in the Bullpen," *Los Angeles Times*, June 9, 1991.
**She threatened Penny:** Frank Price to the author.
**"You're making an Elvis movie!":** Marshall, *My Mother Was Nuts*, 251.
**she hadn't asked for cast approval:** Army Archerd, *Variety*, June 11, 1991.
**to protest how it stuffed Legal Eagles:** Paul Rosenfield, "Hollywood and the Exercise of Power: The Movie Star," *Los Angeles Times*, August 28, 1988.
**"Debra Winger was so wrong":** https://www.advocate.com/news/2007/07/23/madonna-x-rated-interview.
**"No one tells me how to cast my movies":** Elliot Abbott to the author.
**Price notified Debra's agent:** Frank Price to the author.
**"Debra, I've heard you for an hour":** Ibid.
**about $3 million to go away:** Michael Nathanson to the author.
**"Are you crazy?":** Ibid.
**"Well, contractually, that's what we had to do":** Ibid.
**"It was the only time I ever collected a pay-or-play on my contract":** https://www.yahoo.com/entertainment/debra-winger-ways-metoo-gone-170155188.html.
**Geena Davis phoned Ganz and Mandel:** Ganz to the author.
**"I read that movie":** Ibid.
**Penny had already cast the only part that interested her:** Ibid.
**"Don't go anywhere":** Ibid.
**They phoned Penny and Elliot Abbott:** Ibid.
**Geena had played catch in New York:** Geena Davis, *Dying of Politeness* (San Francisco: HarperOne, 2022), 171.
**"I was sure that with training":** Ibid.
**Penny summoned Geena to her house on La Presa Drive:** Ibid., 172.
**"This meeting is simply about your ability to play the role":** Ibid.
**"less just see you trow da bawl":** Ibid.
**"Come on, just for one second":** Ibid.
**"Fully five minutes went by":** Ibid.
**"Her agent said not to play ball with her":** Marshall, *My Mother Was Nuts*, 252.
**Weeping, Debra told the Peaches:** "'A League of Their Own' Turns 30: Catching up with mighty Marla Hooch," *The Athletic*, June 30, 2022.

## Sixth Inning: Chicago

**Well, then, fuck:** Lori Petty to the author.
**Then Penny Marshall called:** Ibid.
**"I'm like, 'Yeah! I'll have dinner with Geena Davis!'":** Ibid.
**"Maybe Geena got to see if she liked me or if I was an asshole or what?":** Ibid.
**"Does that mean I'm still in the movie?":** Ibid.
**"Of course, you're still in the movie":** Ibid.
**The shoot was scheduled to commence July 10:** John Rusk to the author.

**Coach Hughes wanted the women's movements to appear clean and fluid on camera:** Bo Hughes to the author.
**"I crouched down into position and tried to catch the ball":** Geena Davis to the author.
**once told Tom Hanks:** Hanks interviewed Davis in a feature in *Interview* magazine, March 1992.
**filed to end their three-year marriage:** Jim Jerome, "Riding Shotgun," *People*, June 24, 1991.
**"Ultimately it had been my decision to end it":** Davis, *Dying of Politeness*, 166.
**Susan Sarandon had shown her how to be assertive:** Becky Aikman, *Off the Cliff* (New York: Penguin Press, 2017), 117.
**"On page one, I don't think I would do that":** Ibid.
**People can be like her?:** Ibid.
**Geena asked Ganz and Mandel to make Dottie funnier:** Davis, *Dying of Politeness*, 174.
**"They happily agreed to punch it up":** Ibid., 175.
**"It can't be that hard, guys":** Ibid.
**"No, it is hard":** Ibid.
**"Why not imagine I'm Billy Crystal":** Ibid.
**"I'd decided I was going to become Gary Cooper":** Ibid.
**"The funny thing is":** Davis to the author.
**the tallest kid in her class:** Aikman, *Off the Cliff*, 110.
**on the track team:** From Tom Hanks's interview with Davis for a feature in *Interview* magazine, March 1992.
**She was also an honor student and fluent musician:** Aikman, *Off the Cliff*, 110.
**She grew up middle-class in Wareham, Massachusetts:** Ibid.
**pretended to be the rugged ranchers in The Rifleman:** Ibid.
**"It never occurred to us that there were no female characters we wanted to perform":** Ibid.
**posing as a mannequin in the store window:** Kevin Sessums, "Geena's Sheen," *Vanity Fair*, September 1992.
**Henri Bendel hired her:** Aikman, *Off the Cliff*, 111.
**fastest route to Hollywood:** https://www.youtube.com/watch?v=PA_2ollrNcA.
**sent her to audition for director Sydney Pollack:** Judith Michaelson, "Downright Serious," *Los Angeles Times*, May 12, 1991.
**needed a real model:** https://www.youtube.com/watch?v=PA_2ollrNcA.
**a life-size cow sculpture:** Roy Sekoff, "A Love of the Ludicrous," *Elle*, January 1989.
**Geena bristled at the word:** Sessums, "Geena's Sheen," *Vanity Fair*, September 1992.
**"I was the center of the storm in that movie":** Ibid.
**"She was a love":** Renée Coleman to the author.
**"this funny, self-deprecating, adorable nut":** Ibid.
**"Like, Geena is severely laid-back":** Lori Petty to the author.
**in the vicinity of $2 million:** John Rusk to the author.
**about $175,000, equal to Jon Lovitz:** Ibid.
**"it was very, very easy to feel like the lesser-than":** Lori Petty to the author.
**Freddie Simpson didn't recognize her at first:** Freddie Simpson to the author.
**Ramsay had not made David Anspaugh's cut:** Anne Ramsay to the author.
**You're on the intelligent side:** Ibid.
**"It was the beginning of my career and I was scared shitless":** Ibid.

**she had to decide whether to come out on set:** Ibid.
**"Carol, here's Madonna":** Ibid.
**"Roommate, huh?":** Ibid.
**"She can see that we both have rings on":** Ibid.
**She rose at 4 a.m.:** https://www.youtube.com/watch?v=PoAP-YAzsZw.
**"If anybody stays and plays until we can't see the ball anymore, then I'll take you to dinner":** Megan Cavanagh to the author.
**did not know how to act around Madonna:** Ibid.
**"What are we supposed to call you?":** Lori Petty to the author.
**"Any of you girls break it, you're buying a new one!":** "Special Features" commentary for *A League of Their Own* DVD released in 2004.
**"You're richer than most third-world nations":** Ibid.
**While Penny wasn't watching:** Ibid.
**"Penny was always screaming at me that I was playing baseball like a dancer":** Ibid.
**As Tom Hanks observed:** Ibid.
**Coach Hughes mentally moved the human chess pieces:** Hughes to the author.
**could neither hit nor throw:** Robert Greenhut to the author.
**Hughes put her on center field:** Hughes to the author.
**Ramsay broke her nose:** Anne Ramsay to the author.
**"Hey, Anne, don't worry if it's not healed by the time we start filming":** Ibid.
**Coach Hughes asked a production assistant to procure a Slip 'N Slide:** Hughes to the author.
**"I'm first!":** Megan Cavanagh to the author.
**She ran, slipped, and whacked her head on the ground:** Ibid.
**Then Tracy and Bitty banged their heads:** Ibid.
**"I had five saline bags before I peed":** Ibid.
**these girls did not care about the risks of getting hurt:** Bo Hughes to the author.
**taught Rosie how to throw two balls at once:** "Special Features" commentary for *A League of Their Own* DVD released in 2004.
**"You need to bend your knees":** Renée Coleman to the author.
**"She was so open and smiley":** Cavanagh to the author.
**The meet-and-greet served a dual purpose:** Mary Moore to the author.
**redlining and housing discrimination marginalized Black residents:** Ta-Nehisi Coates, "The Case for Reparations," *The Atlantic*, June 2014.
**requested Jordan's jersey number:** John Rusk to the author.
**In a handwritten letter to fashion photographer Steven Meisel:** https://www.tapatalk.com/groups/jjb/madonna-s-1991-letter-to-steven-meisel-hates-chica-t642921.html.
**He doesn't know how to partner:** Lou Conte to the author.
**"Geena Davis is the most uncoordinated person I've seen in my life":** Ibid.
**At five feet, three inches tall:** https://www.imdb.com/name/nm0577284/.
**She much preferred the gifted Tony Savino:** Lou Conte to the author.
**When the principal cast arrived without advance warning:** Tony Savino to the author.
**She disappeared behind a column:** Ibid.
**"He is":** Ibid.
**he stepped over her legs and spun her around:** Ibid.
**"You're very brave":** Ibid.

**wasn't crazy about what they were doing:** Lou Conte to the author.
**"No. Eddie has a little part called Guy in Bar":** Ibid.
**Conte forged a compromise:** Ibid.
**Madonna and Savino started hanging out:** Tony Savino to the author, telling stories about Melissa Crow's birthday dinner at the Rosebud and their next destination at the Baton.
**whom she teased for being "boring":** Bo Hughes to the author.
**As they took their seats on the upper level:** Tony Savino to the author.
**Hughes advised the real Madonna to tip her:** Hughes to the author.
**"Do you have dollars I can tip?"** Savino to the author.
**Are you kidding me?:** Ibid.
**"I'll pay you back":** Ibid.
**What is my life at this second?:** Ibid.
**brought her famous younger brother, actor John Cusack:** Hughes to the author.
**"He showed up and he was, like, sitting with Madonna and hitting on her":** Savino to the author.
**on July 7:** Tracy Reiner's birthday.
**She asked Savino to pick her up at the Zebra Lounge:** Savino to the author.
**Savino went inside and extracted Madonna and a sexy companion:** Ibid.
**called it quits:** Item in *People* magazine, April 15, 1991.
**"He was stunning":** Savino to the author.
**The three piled into Savino's Toyota Tercel:** Ibid.
**"You need to get a car with stronger air-conditioning":** Ibid.
**He drove them to a Black gay bar on Halsted:** Ibid.
**"Edna Poopaleedoop":** Jon Lovitz to the author.
**"Louise Oriole":** Lou Conte to the author.
**Mo . . . wanted a frozen yogurt:** Savino to the author.
**One night late in pre-production:** Gary Muller to the author.
**eighty-five pounds of gear attached to his body:** Craig DiBona to the author.
**"It's like an American picnic":** https://www.youtube.com/watch?v=PoAP-YAzsZw.
**bruising crew members:** John Rusk to the author.
**When he was happy, he tapped his cane:** Dennis Benatar to the author.
**"I could look in his eyes and know exactly what he thought":** Marshall, *My Mother Was Nuts*, 238.
**He showed Muller a photograph:** Gary Muller to the author.
**"Mirek":** Ibid.
**"Oh, you go back to New York":** Ibid.
**Ondricek directed Muller to relay the message:** Ibid.
**"I gotta talk to you guys":** Ibid.
**What's the matter?:** Ibid.
**He showed Ondricek's baseball book to Greenhut:** Ibid.
**"What, are you nuts?":** Ibid.
**"You go back to New York, and you get what he wants":** Ibid.
**added a least a million dollars to the budget:** Ibid.
**They shot the girls catching fly balls:** John Rusk to the author.
**"All these people are my bridesmaids?":** Megan Cavanagh to the author.
**She flew to Chicago anyway and talked her way onto the team:** Marshall, *My Mother Was Nuts*, 252.
**"How do you say no to that kind of effort?":** Ibid.

**"Could we get some more stuffing for Robin?":** Robin Knight to the author.
**Tom walked toward the altar and genuflected:** Francesca Paris and Paul Gebbia to the author.
**"Please forgive me for Joe Versus the Volcano":** Paul Gebbia to the author.
**"Please, god, make this movie a hit":** Francesca Paris to the author.
**could hardly keep a straight face:** "Special Features" commentary for *A League of Their Own* DVD released in 2004.
**"You know, you really are a good-lookin' girl":** Ibid.
**"Jon, I don't care":** Ibid.
**Megan would put spit in her hair:** https://www.youtube.com/watch?v=PoAP-YAzsZw.
**"I don't call 'cut' because you never know what's gonna happen":** "Special Features" commentary for *A League of Their Own* DVD (2004).
**Bitty wanted to have a black tooth:** Freddie Simpson to the author.
**However, Madonna copied Bitty, stealing her bit:** Ibid.
**the prop man told her that Madonna took them:** Ibid.
**"What? And you let her?":** Ibid.
**"We had a shoot, and I got a lot of attention":** Ibid.
**"dressed like white trash":** Ibid.
**As Mollie crawled on the filthy floor:** Mollie Mallinger to the author.
**"Excuse me":** Ibid.
**Madonna slammed her foot down on the mark:** Ibid.
**afterward, they played Truth or Dare:** *League of Their Own* DVD commentary.
**he was too pricey:** Baker, "'A League of Their Own' Is an All-Time Great Sports Film," theringer.com, June 30, 2017.
**Penny had a crush on Strathairn:** Anitra Larae Donahue to the author.
**He went to jazz clubs:** Tracy Reiner to the author.
**One day, he approached her to compliment her great attitude on set:** Ibid.
**"You don't know Penny's my mom":** Ibid.
**"Tracy got involved with his personal trainer":** Marshall, *My Mother Was Nuts*, 253.
**Penny's masseuse and part-time driver:** *League of Their Own* DVD commentary.
**Lovitz's asthma ignited as the train suddenly caught fire:** Jon Lovitz to the author.
**Penny handed Megan ammonia tablets:** Megan Cavanagh to the author.
**"She was an actor's director":** Ibid.
**The grid seemed to cover the entire space:** Lew Baldwin to the author.
**At 9:05 p.m., the wood made a loud cracking sound:** John Rusk to the author.
**striking Greenhut in the head:** Baldwin to the author.
**Ondricek in the ribs:** Ondrej Kubicek to the author.
**At least fifteen ambulances showed up:** Baldwin to the author.
**Greenhut and a gaffer:** Rusk to the author.
**Greenhut wore a neck brace:** Baldwin to the author.
**An on-site first-aid nurse treated Ondricek, Tim Bourne, and camera assistant Eddie Effrein:** Rusk to the author.
**"That was the ugliest, ugliest accident":** Billy Kerwick to the author.
**The sconces that lined the walls:** Rusk to the author.
**"I'm surprised they let us back into the place":** Kerwick to the author.
**Penny jumped right into the shipwreck:** Ibid.
**"She didn't run":** Ibid.
**Garry ate a sandwich:** Rusk to the author.
**He flew in museum-caliber art restorers from New York:** Bill Groom to the author.

**spotted a former high school classmate named Barb:** Megan Cavanagh to the author.
**"I am 'hometown girl does good'":** Ibid.
**the crew turned off the air-conditioning:** Ibid.
**her masseuse worked her neck and shoulders:** Tony Savino to the author.
**"First of all, I'm jealous":** Ibid.
**"it's kind of excessive":** Ibid.
**Originally, Geena was supposed to participate in the swing dancing:** Lou Conte to the author.
**She took Oreos from the craft services table and replaced the cookies' frosting with mayonnaise:** Doug Blakeslee to the author.
**"So Madonna really wants to do great":** Lori Petty to the author.
**"We're shooting into it":** Conte to the author.
**"Penny was holding on to the cameraman":** Ibid.
**"Tell her to keep her legs together":** Ibid.
**"Story of my life":** Ibid.
**Team Penny shot a series of scenes that she never used:** Via my copy of Ganz and Mandel's original shooting script as well as the deleted scenes included in the 2004 *League* DVD's Special Features.
**Megan had spoken highly of Alan to Ellen Lewis:** Cavanagh to the author.
**"He maybe thought of himself as not that attractive":** Alan Wilder to the author.
**"She saw his sweetness":** Cavanagh to the author.
**She hunched her shoulders:** https://www.youtube.com/watch?v=PoAP-YAzsZw.
**wore a little microphone in her ear so she could hear the music:** Cavanagh to the author.
**a background saxophonist was flirting with Lori:** Lori Petty to the author.
**"You wanna go to a gig with me?":** Ibid.
**The saxophonist took her to an office building that had a stage area:** Ibid.
**They sat with Aretha and the rest of her band:** Ibid.
**"You ready, Ms. Franklin?":** Ibid.
**"Where's my money?":** Ibid.
**The man was flummoxed:** Ibid.
**"Well, that's not my problem now":** Ibid.
**They waited until the wee hours of the morning:** Ibid.
**Afterward, Lori hopped in a taxi:** Ibid.
**hurling seventeen bats onto the field:** https://www.youtube.com/watch?v=oAKkHxkkCyA.
**worked overnight to cover Wrigley's skyboxes with canvas:** Bill Groom to the author.
**"They hated the fact that we were on the grass":** Abbott to the author.
**The franchise set strict ground rules:** Craig DiBona to the author.
**"I mean, you got a major league team":** Ibid.
**"When we say to him, 'Go to first base,' he doesn't know what base that means":** Michael Nathanson to the author.
**Nathanson called in reinforcements:** Ibid.
**each of whom Penny picked because they were tall:** A decision acknowledged by Kelli Simpkins, Sharon Szmidt, and Connie Pounds-Taylor.
**In Chicago, Penny sized up the lanky twenty-seven-year-old nonprofit worker:** Melody Ann Wallace, "In a League of Her Own," *Owensboro Living*, March 6, 2020.

**"I had a baseball mentality":** Ibid.

**"For young boys it is culturally acceptable":** James Fallows, "Throwing Like a Girl," *The Atlantic*, August 1996.

**When she was seventeen, Croteau and her parents filed a sex discrimination lawsuit:** Alice Digilio, "Girl Sues to Play Ball," *Washington Post*, March 17, 1988.

**"Softball is an entirely different game":** Ibid.

**Croteau lost her case:** Brad Parks, "Croteau's Love of Baseball Exceeds Pain of Past Slights," *Washington Post*, June 21, 1997.

**batted .222 her first season:** Paula Edelson, *A to Z of American Women in Sports* (Infobase Publishing, 2014), 51–52.

**hit .171 in seventy-six at bats:** Unbylined, "'Boys Will Be Boys' Sad Excuse For Fouling Her Out, She Says," *Washington Post*, June 25, 1991.

**In June 1991, she publicly detailed a toxic environment:** Ibid.

**Baseball had stopped being fun for her:** Ibid.

**sent an audition tape to Columbia Pictures:** Ibid.

**contacted her out of the blue:** Julie Croteau to the author.

**Would she send over pictures of her legs?:** Ibid.

**She also observed improper slides and other wrong moves:** Ibid.

**This is gonna take us backward:** Ibid.

**The spectacle recalled the late nineteenth century:** Debra Shattuck, *Bloomer Girls: Women Baseball Pioneers* (Urbana, Chicago, and Springfield: University of Illinois Press, 2017), location 1690 on Kindle.

**"They put on a show for fans":** Ibid.

**The traveling performances offended polite society:** Ibid., Location 1705 on Kindle.

**an English bat-and-ball game:** https://web.archive.org/web/20071112065508/http://www.nra-rounders.co.uk/dyncat.cfm?catid=17177.

**Jane Austen referenced the game:** Jennifer Ring, *Stolen Bases: Why American Girls Don't Play Baseball* (Urbana, Chicago, and Springfield: University of Illinois Press, 2013), 33.

**launched intramural baseball at single-sex colleges such as Vassar and Wellesley:** Ibid., 34–35.

**played the sport professionally on teams that were women-only or blended women and men:** Ibid., 17.

**founded the Dolly Vardens:** Mary Craig, "The Dolly Vardens, Philadelphia's 19th-century all-Black women baseball teams," beyondtheboxscore.com, October 12, 2017.

**"the first professional women's baseball team in the United States":** Ring, *Stolen Bases: Why American Girls Don't Play Baseball*, 17.

**growing appetite for "novelty" games:** https://ourgame.mlblogs.com/strangest-of-all-baseball-attractions-f60724613898.

**his stunt lasted only one season:** Craig, "The Dolly Vardens, Philadelphia's 19th-century all-Black women baseball teams," beyondtheboxscore.com, October 12, 2017.

**Maud Nelson:** https://collection.baseballhall.org/people/19451/nelson-maud-18811944.

**Chicago Stars:** Mary Craig, "Maud Nelson and the Chicago Stars," wrigleyville.locals.baseballprospectus.com, July 23, 2018.

**Lizzie Arlington:** Shattuck, *Bloomer Girls: Women Baseball Pioneers*, Locations 3319, 3382, and 3722 on Kindle.

**Arlington's successors:** Ibid., Location 5453 on Kindle.

**Famously, Mitchell:** Brian Cronin, "Sports Legend Revealed: Did a female pitcher strike out Babe Ruth and Lou Gehrig?," *Los Angeles Times*, February 23, 2011.

**Commissioner of Baseball Kenesaw Mountain Landis voided her contract:** Browne, *Girls of Summer*, 17.

**"Mitchell continued to play baseball as a barnstormer":** Cronin, "Sports Legend Revealed: Did a female pitcher strike out Babe Ruth and Lou Gehrig?," *Los Angeles Times*, February 23, 2011.

**Schmitt had auditioned at Evansville's Harrison Baseball Field:** Lita Schmitt to the author.

**the first women's basketball player inducted into the University of Evansville's Athletic Hall of Fame:** https://hoopshall.com/inductees/shelly-brand-adlard/.

**The actresses adored Brenda:** Schmitt to the author.

**"I don't want to be Madonna's double":** Ibid.

**"I think she was religious":** Ibid.

**DeLisa Chinn-Tyler and another Black woman were the only players of color to try out:** DeLisa Chinn-Tyler to the author.

**had once been a star center fielder on the Evansville Express:** Gordon Engelhardt, *Evansville Courier & Press*, June 18, 2021.

**Penny, standing by the fence with a clipboard:** Chinn-Tyler to the author.

**"Yes, I know":** Ibid.

**They both laughed:** Ibid.

**Penny told her that she conferred with Lisa Beasley:** Ibid.

**Lori Petty had urged Penny to acknowledge the league's racist history:** Lori Petty to the author.

**"Suddenly I feel uncomfortable about this":** Ibid.

**"You're right":** Ibid.

**She scribbled copious notes in the margins of her script, and yet she was loose on set:** Hanks interviewed Davis in a feature in *Interview* magazine, March 1992.

**Geena caught a ball made of foam material:** Lita Schmitt to the author.

**the crew repeatedly threw it at her:** Ibid.

**subbed in for Geena in the catcher's position:** Sam Hoffman to the author.

**"Let me try":** Ibid.

**"Go put the wig on":** Ibid.

**"I used to be a star":** *League of Their Own* DVD commentary.

**she demanded Evian over ordinary water and took her time:** Lew Baldwin to the author.

**"What are you doing here?":** Elliot Abbott to the author.

**"What? Are you kidding?":** Ibid.

**sensed Lori's struggle to find her footing:** Baldwin to the author.

**she ran around like a little puppy:** Lori Petty to the author.

**Tom and Lori played catch during one of her breaks:** Ibid.

**"Petty":** Ibid.

**"What?":** Ibid.

**"You know when people say, 'Remember when? Wasn't it cool when . . . ?'":** Ibid.

**"Yeah":** Ibid.

**"This is that day. Right now. It's not always going to be like this. This isn't always how it is. You're gonna remember this":** Ibid.

**She brought her father to the set:** Megan Cavanagh to the author.
**"None of my sons made it into the major leagues, but my daughter did":** Ibid.
**The teams complained:** Billy Kerwick and David Dumais to the author.

## Seventh Inning: Indiana

**Gloria Mallah pulled up:** Gloria Mallah to the author.
**thermometers ticking toward ninety-five degrees:** https://www.wunderground.com/history/monthly/us/in/evansville/KEVV/date/1991-8.
**"Welcome to hell":** Mallah to the author.
**needed a break from working seven days a week:** Bonnie Hlinomaz to the author.
**Her friend in Indiana's film office:** Mallah to the author.
**"This is where we keep her sake":** Ibid.
**might wind up in her cup:** Abe Flores to the author.
**open a bottle of Santa Margherita white wine:** Patty Willett to the author.
**Greenhut preferred Dewar's:** Lew Baldwin to the author.
**"lost her Penny accent":** Bill Groom to the author.
**sometimes napped during pre-production:** Willett to the author.
**good about getting Penny up and going:** Alina Martinet to the author.
**Penny loved doing jigsaw puzzles in her trailer:** Hlinomaz to the author.
**"Bobby":** Ibid.
**"Penny, what do you want?":** Tim Bourne to the author.
**"I'll have a coffee":** Ibid.
**"This was her favorite movie":** Bernadette Mazur to the author.
**a different pair of sneakers every day:** Willett to the author.
**She'd run around in a terry cloth tube top:** Mazur to the author.
**"You couldn't even believe that she could eat that much bacon":** Sam Hoffman to the author.
**she refused to eat anything that "takes a shit":** Tom Morales to the author.
**Penny would grab it and eat the skin:** Bourne to the author.
**She buckled a fanny pack on her waist:** Hlinomaz to the author.
**she stuck around after touring Penny's trailer:** Mallah to the author.
**Lori was faster than Geena:** Marshall, *My Mother Was Nuts*, 253.
**"If you watch the scene":** Ibid.
**the cameramen thought she ran like a duck:** Tom Priestley to the author.
**showed them how:** Mike Haley to the author.
**began giving birth:** Marshall, *My Mother Was Nuts*, 254.
**"Cut!":** Ibid.
**"What?":** Ibid.
**"Didn't you notice the cow behind you just fell over?":** Ibid.
**"Oh":** Ibid.
**"Have you ever seen a placenta come out of a cow?":** Hoffman to the author.
**its owners named it Penny:** Eileen Dempsey, "A Movie of Our Own," *Evansville Courier*, June 21, 1992.
**As rain began to fall:** Shelly Adlard to the author.
**Penny picked up her namesake and grinned:** Dempsey, "A Movie of Our Own," *Evansville Courier*, June 21, 1992.
**making a sound ten times louder than any plane flying overhead:** https://www.youtube.com/watch?v=gpOB7PnZk_A.
**"Why are you stopping?":** Lovitz to the author.

**"Because the cow":** Ibid.
**"Well, then tell it to shut up":** Ibid.
**Lovitz remained in full costume inside his individual trailer:** Hoffman to the author.
**"much harder to get Lovitz out of hair and makeup than any of the ladies":** Ibid.
**He teased the comedian:** Ibid.
**"Shut up, shut up!":** Ibid.
**some twenty-five crew members:** Mary Bailey to the author.
**ate good food and drank wine:** Mazur to the author.
**logged ninety to one hundred hours each week:** Doron Shauly to the author.
**Bowers always in a good mood:** Ibid.
**helped lift Bowers up the ladder:** Mike Barnes, "George Bowers, Film Editor for Penny Marshall, Dies at 68," *Hollywood Reporter*, September 13, 2012.
**"He was so patient":** Bourne to the author.
**died in 2012 of complications related to heart surgery:** Barnes, "George Bowers, Film Editor for Penny Marshall, Dies at 68," *Hollywood Reporter*, September 13, 2012.
**cried during the heart-wrenching takes:** Kathleen Marshall to the author.
**"You fake going to the bathroom":** Gary Muller to the author.
**How many times:** Ibid.
**On occasion, Penny got tired:** Shauly to the author.
**Gloria, whom she called "Glor," would show up in a Volvo 740:** Mallah to the author.
**owning hundreds of them:** Hlinomaz to the author.
**rough-hewn tables:** Dennis Benatar to the author.
**duck decoys:** Marshall, *My Mother Was Nuts*, 255.
**Once she bought a rug:** Hlinomaz to the author.
**"The Mall":** Ibid.
**Penny's antique-hunting fervor rubbed off on:** Hlinomaz and Amy Pascal to the author.
**"I got something really special I can show you":** Benatar to the author.
**"He goes behind the counter, and he pulls out two Nazi flags in pristine condition, in plastic bags":** Ibid.
**"Bill, I think it's time to go now":** Ibid.
**Gloria, packing drawers in her boss's bedroom, stumbled upon large photographs:** Mallah to the author.
**She kept her sleeping quarters dark and goosebump-cold:** Ibid.
**"Looking through these black-and-white photos of things in the freezer":** Ibid.
**"What is this place?":** Kelli Simpkins to the author.
**"Even though it's the third-largest city in Indiana":** Ibid.
**a rich manufacturing hub for automobiles, appliances, and construction equipment:** Darrel E. Bigham, *We Ask Only a Fair Trial: A History of the Black Community of Evansville, Indiana* (Bloomington & Indianapolis: Indiana University Press, 1987), 152.
**more than six thousand P-47 Thunderbolt fighter planes:** Brook Endale, "Proposed bill would make Evansville's P-47 Thunderbolt official state aircraft," *Evansville Courier & Press*, January 12, 2021.
**"bullets by the billions":** https://www.youtube.com/watch?v=XdagRWxy9PI.
**made up a sixth of the labor force:** Dawn Mitchell, "War on the Homefront: Indiana's Rosie the Riveters," indystar.com, March 28, 2019.

**Indiana used government funds to set up daycare centers:** Ibid.
**126,272:** 1990 U.S. census data.
**"You had the east side, which was kind of bougie, upper middle class":** Anitra Larae Donahue to the author.
**the third-oldest American ballpark still in regular use for professional baseball:** Gordon Engelhardt, "Bosse Field a comfortable Evansville fixture for 100 years," *Evansville Courier & Press*, June 17, 2015.
**"people like the old way of doing things, and so the ballpark prevailed":** Jeff Lyons to the author.
**"Everywhere we looked":** Paul Gebbia to the author.
**Gebbia and his coworkers in hair and makeup:** Ibid.
**"We were like, 'Corn dogs: What the hell is that?'":** Ibid.
**He devoured Dairy Queen:** https://www.youtube.com/watch?v=peX8J6Bs6ls&t=218s.
**Tom and Rita's rental:** Mike Duckworth to the author.
**"Come here!":** Ibid.
**"You'd think that I had given the guy a million dollars":** Ibid.
**"What do I do?":** Ibid.
**even declining to share her address:** John Rusk to the author.
**swimming pool built specifically for her:** Dempsey, "A Movie of Our Own," *Evansville Courier*, June 21, 1992.
**"I think it's my height":** Renée Coleman to the author.
**white-picket-fenced refuge in McCutchanville:** Dempsey, "A Movie of Our Own," *Evansville Courier*, June 21, 1992.
**she made Rice Krispies treats:** Unbylined, "'A League of Their Own' Stands the Test of Time," espn.com, June 29, 2017.
**"We had fun everywhere we went, and we would go just the two of us":** Eric Alter, "Vanilla Ice remembers making 'Cool as Ice' and watching the movie with Madonna," yahoo.com, October 29, 2021.
**"Spit the food out":** Ibid.
**"You need to get her paper":** Mike Duckworth to the author.
**"I'm not her paperboy":** Ibid.
**As she opened the door:** Ibid.
**De Becker thought she needed a decoy:** John Rusk to the author.
**police caught a deranged man:** Dale Payne to the author.
**"What they ended up doing":** Ibid.
**On the call sheet:** Rusk to the author.
**One guy made an unexpected visit:** Rhodes, "Back From the Bonfire," *Los Angeles Times*, July 5, 1992.
**"Every now and then":** Ibid.
**Tracy and Lori opted for a house with a pool:** Carlin, "Lori Petty Answers Every Question We Have About *A League of Their Own*," vulture.com, August 20, 2021.
**she found $20,000 in tiny yellow envelopes:** Petty to the author.
**Megan Cavanagh and her then-husband:** Cavanagh to the author.
**On August 17:** Ibid.
**two failed utopian communities in the 1800s:** https://www.indianamuseum.org/historic-sites/new-harmony/.
**dating from 1924:** https://www.indianalandmarks.org/2021/03/historic-indiana-gyms-on-the-rebound/.
**"All right, bring out [her] double":** https://www.youtube.com/watch?v=PoAP-YAzsZw.

**referencing stand-in Shelly Niemeyer:** Lita Schmitt to the author.
**"Wait, wait, wait, wait":** https://www.youtube.com/watch?v=PoAP-YAzsZw.
**As Coach Hughes pitched to Megan:** Bo Hughes to the author.
**Please, god, please let me get through this:** https://www.youtube.com/watch?v=PoAP-YAzsZw.
**"We're not gonna use any of your double's footage":** Ibid.
**awarded a batting champion trophy:** Cavanagh to the author.
**hurling a ball through six different windows:** Hughes to the author.
**a population of 5,242 residents, 99 percent of whom were white:** 1990 U.S. census data.
**She crashed a meeting between Evansville officials and the Indiana Film Commission:** Connie Nass to the author.
**she met Penny and Bill Groom underneath Huntingburg's rickety grandstand:** Ibid.
**built in 1894:** "League Stadium," www.huntingburg-in.gov.
**In May 1991, she struck a deal:** Dale Payne to the author.
**Collins's workers hustled twelve hours a day:** Ibid.
**The makeover cost about $800,000:** Connie Nass to the author.
**Groom installed old-fashioned subway turnstiles from New York:** Bill Groom to the author.
**"They had period garbage":** Ann Cusack to the author.
**The Peaches arrived the week of August 18:** Dale Payne to the author.
**"It's just too many people":** https://www.youtube.com/watch?v=gpOB7PnZk_A.
**"I was there to do a job and be ready for it":** Anne Ramsay to the author.
**Megan spent eight hours idle:** Cavanagh to the author.
**jog with her trainer on country roads:** Payne to the author.
**"We need to go work out":** Hughes to the author.
**"I want to eat":** Ibid.
**Geena would find a shady spot:** Payne to the author.
**sought out Robin Knight to play catch and goof off:** Robin Knight to the author.
**"He doesn't come to get me!":** Ibid.
**"stupid little games":** Ibid.
**workday dragged on for eighteen hours:** Renée Coleman to the author.
**about $140,000:** Dave Weatherwax, "Memories always in 'League of Their Own,'" *Dubois County Herald*, June 14, 2017.
**"too big for the people involved to know what was going on":** Coleman to the author.
**"Is this going straight to video?":** Cavanagh to the author.
**"Why am I doing this movie?":** Ibid.
**"The ballplayers can't act":** Alan Wilder to the author.
**"My next film is going to be two men in a room":** Kathleen Marshall to the author.
**"thought that she was gonna go off to Indiana":** https://www.youtube.com/watch?v=a1oVZeMuJi4.
**One elderly couple suffered double heart attacks:** John Rusk to the author.
**Others accidentally swallowed bees that fell into their sodas:** Suzanne McCabe to the author.
**"They thought, Oh, this is a small thing, really":** Tim Galvin to the author.
**How could this cost so much?:** Ibid.
**Geena and Tom and Madonna and Lori:** Rusk to the author.

**"I got everybody else's period":** Tracy Reiner to the author.
**mostly avoided the stylized '40s-style pompadours that aged certain actresses:** Francesca Paris to the author.
**Francesca thought Bitty Schram:** Ibid.
**inspired by Hedy Lamarr:** Ibid.
**stylists dyed Lori's black hair red:** Ibid.
**When she wasn't in costume head-to-toe:** Patty Willett to the author.
**"I'm a hairstylist, not a fucking chemist!":** Sam Hoffman to the author.
**As she got a rinsing:** Rusk to the author.
**low-key, just like her:** Paul Gebbia to the author.
**"was on a different plane than everybody else":** Ibid.
**"You're going to share a makeup trailer with [Mo]":** Carlin, "Lori Petty Answers Every Question We Have About *A League of Their Own*," vulture.com, August 20, 2021.
**"Why?":** Ibid.
**"'Cause you can handle her":** Ibid.
**During lunch breaks, Lori and Madonna were "joined at the hip":** Tom Morales to the author.
**"She was pantomiming giving a blow job":** Ibid.
**"Well, I sucked James Woods's cock in the elevator":** Ibid.
**"Well, I thought you didn't eat anything that took a shit":** Ibid.
**"Sam! Don't you understand I have an empire to run?":** Sam Hoffman to the author.
**"In your mouth":** Ibid.
**"So, you gave Geena your script to read?":** Ibid.
**When he asked her to sign a photo of her:** Ibid.
**"All right, girls, roll in the dirt":** Rusk to the author.
**made Irene Ferrari, the wardrobe supervisor, want to quit:** Suzanne McCabe to the author.
**"Just play":** Megan Cavanagh to the author.
**"They had a giant slingshot":** Geena Davis to the author.
**Madonna hit a pitch and froze in disbelief:** Ondrej Kubicek to the author.
**"Put the flags out!":** Ibid.
**"The wig, the hat, the wool socks, and the creepy spiked shoes":** Carlin, "Lori Petty Answers Every Question We Have About *A League of Their Own*," vulture.com, August 20, 2021.
**Renée badly injured her thigh:** Renée Coleman to the author.
**Her double, Vickie Buse, was MIA:** Lita Schmitt to the author.
**"I did it not knowing what I was signing up for":** Coleman to the author.
**She got bruised on the first attempt:** Ibid.
**The bump grew larger and more gruesome over five takes:** Ibid.
**Like a good soldier, Renée continued filming:** Ibid.
**"They had to put makeup on it to tone it down":** Ibid.
**It took her fifteen years to regain the feeling in her leg:** Ibid.
**"She also got fish tattooed on her stomach":** *League of Their Own* DVD commentary, 2004.
**Greenhut worried about the women throwing their arms out:** Dennis Benatar to the author.
**Ondricek just wanted to keep shooting:** Ibid.
**"He was very slow":** Greenhut to the author.

**"Mirek is waiting for some clouds":** Ibid.
**"Clouds? It's a baseball movie. I mean, shoot it in the sun":** Ibid.
**"I just went crazy":** Ibid.
**"Hey, you gotta stop this shit":** Ibid.
**received an apology written on two white cards:** Letter from Madonna to Greenhut, shown to the author at Greenhut's home in Los Angeles in February 2022.
**Madonna was in negotiations with Time Warner:** Ron Givens, "Madonna's mega-deal," *Entertainment Weekly*, December 6, 1991.
**on the verge of losing:** Unbylined, "Cat Tale," *Long Beach Press-Telegram*, September 18, 1991.
**"Hide me, Penny's coming":** Patti Pelton to the author.
**In Huntingburg, Madonna wrapped herself one day:** Mollie Mallinger to the author.
**"Where's Mo?":** Ibid.
**"That's it":** Ibid.
**As Gloria chauffeured her home:** Gloria Mallah to the author.
**"I'll have her fucking written out of the script":** Ibid.
**She left a mea culpa on Penny's answering machine:** Ibid.
**"They were like, 'OK, shoot this scene now'":** Bitty Schram to the author.
**"I took all my fears and just put it in the scene":** Ibid.
**As Tom gave her a mouthful:** Ibid.
**"not to blow my wad":** Ibid.
**Bitty felt like she was in trouble:** Ibid.
**managed to persuade Penny to cast him:** John Rusk to the author.
**sticking his bare butt through the scoreboard:** Ibid.
**he took an electric trimmer:** Ibid.
**OK, you're in:** Ibid.
**I hope we did a good job:** Schram to the author.
**"You leave it up to the gods":** Ibid.
**ordering T-shirts:** Michael Nathanson to the author.
**"by no means did I think that scene":** Schram to the author.
**"If a ball came on the inside":** Coleman to the author.
**Her self-aware intelligence earned Coach Hughes's respect:** Hughes to the author.
**male gymnast from the University of Evansville:** Lita Schmitt to the author.
**had "untapped athletic ability":** Davis, *Dying of Politeness*, 176.
**"They planned to have the stunt double do it":** Davis to the author.
**"There were little cliques that formed":** https://www.youtube.com/watch?v=ceDvg-Drepo&t=113s.
**"this running battle for a while":** Benatar to the author.
**listened to Garth Brooks:** Robin Knight to the author.
**In early June, the twenty-five-year-old had married Neil Tardio:** https://www.nytimes.com/1991/06/09/style/miss-pantaleoni-actress-marries.html.
**"I thought Janet Jones":** Schmitt to the author.
**a grand ceremony:** https://www.cbc.ca/archives/from-1988-wayne-gretzky-marries-janet-jones-in-edmonton-1.4745578.
**autographed a hockey stick for Ondricek:** Ondrej Kubicek to the author.
**"Don't you want to be in the movie?":** Liz Shannon Miller, "A League of Their Own: DeLisa Chinn-Tyler, the Woman Who Threw the Baseball Back, Speaks," consequence.net, July 6, 2022.

**"Yes, I want to be in the movie":** Ibid.
**"Well, you need to get out there":** Ibid.
**Penny told her she couldn't be seen in the crowd scenes:** Ibid.
**She wasn't much of a hat person:** Ibid.
**"very, very tiny":** Ibid.
**The set got quiet:** Coleman to the author.
**"They told me to throw the ball":** DeLisa Chinn-Tyler to the author.
**DeLisa laughs as she remembers:** Ibid.
**the heel of her shoe broke:** Shannon Miller, "A League of Their Own: DeLisa Chinn-Tyler, the Woman Who Threw the Baseball Back, Speaks," consequence.net, July 6, 2022.
**Celebrities paid their respects:** Ibid.
**succeeding Hank Aaron on second base:** https://www.si.com/mlb/2020/02/28/black-history-month-toni-stone.
**batted .243 and hit one of Satchel Paige's fastballs:** Ibid.
**endured hostility from some of the Clowns:** https://www.npr.org/templates/story/story.php?storyId=130401393.
**was barred from changing in the locker room:** https://www.si.com/mlb/2020/02/28/black-history-month-toni-stone.
**"would throw the ball to her":** https://www.npr.org/templates/story/story.php?storyId=130401393.
**Stone flaunted her spike-induced wounds:** https://www.si.com/mlb/2020/02/28/black-history-month-toni-stone.
**earning their respect:** Ring, *Stolen Bases: Why American Girls Don't Play Baseball*, 19.
**"She maybe weighed ninety-eight pounds wet":** Brigit Katz, "Remembering Mamie 'Peanut' Johnson, the First Woman to Take the Mound as a Major-League Pitcher," *Smithsonian*, December 26, 2017.
**When Peanut was seventeen:** Ibid.
**"They just looked at us, as if to say, 'What do you want?'":** https://www.youtube.com/watch?v=iw-ACi9TPBc&t=294s.
**"No Blacks Allowed" policy:** A.J. Richard, "Playing With the Boys: Gender, Race, and Baseball in Post-War America," *Baseball Research Journal*, Spring 2019.
**While traveling with twenty-eight men:** https://www.npr.org/templates/story/story.php?storyId=130401393.
**"directed her to the nearest brothel":** Ibid.
**Stone thus began a habit of lodging at brothels:** Ibid.
***Laverne & Shirley* had been one of her favorite shows:** DeLisa Chinn-Tyler to the author.
**She used to dream of Olympic greatness:** Ibid.
**"kind of a tomboy":** Ibid.
**"I would just take the ball":** Ibid.
**At eleven years old:** Ibid.
**"I wasn't much of a talker":** Ibid.
**"would say, 'look at those little girls'":** Engelhardt, *Evansville Courier & Press*, June 18, 2021.
**In the 1979 season:** https://usiscreamingeagles.com/sports/2009/6/1/softballrecords.aspx?id=79.
**"My arm was so strong":** Chinn-Tyler to the author.
**"Lisa used to take balls away from me":** Ibid.

**"Well, you wouldn't go out far enough to get 'em":** Ibid.
**she brought white players to the team:** Ibid.
**"Girl, nobody's gonna bother you":** Ibid.
**"We accepted white people in our area":** Ibid.
**DeLisa was called the N-word:** Ibid.
**"I just want to be able to get back to Evansville safely":** Ibid.
**Black people accounted for 9.5 percent of Evansville's residents:** 1990 U.S. census data.
**Black migrants:** Bigham, *We Ask Only a Fair Trial: A History of the Black Community of Evansville, Indiana*, 24.
**settled downtown and along the riverfront after the Civil War:** https://www.evansvillegov.org/egov/documents/1600358619_81965.pdf.
**The community created a vibrant residential and business district:** Ibid.
**"Racial hostility kept the Black population of Indiana small":** Heather Cox Richardson, "Replacement Theory: The Violent Fragility of White Men Who Fear Their Power Will Be Taken By People of Color," *Milwaukee Independent*, May 16, 2022.
**Indiana's Klan established its first branch in Evansville:** https://www.youtube.com/watch?v=nHpaXoIWHMw.
**half a million Hoosiers:** Karen Abbott, "Murder Wasn't Very Pretty: The Rise and Fall of D.C. Stephenson," *Smithsonian*, August 30, 2012.
**By 1928, just four thousand members remained:** Ibid.
**"Absolutely there are members of the Klan":** J. Patrick Redmond to the author.
**the Southern Poverty Law Center tracked active Klan branches:** https://www.splcenter.org/hate-map?state=IN.
**saw the Klan gathered in a park:** Melissa Crow to the author.
**Lori Petty saw a Klan supporter collecting donations:** Petty to the author.
**"They had to sit on me to keep me from murdering that person":** Ibid.
**"We had fifty extras quit because we had a Black PA":** Ibid.
**"Look, this is not an indictment of Evansville":** Ibid.
**it was run by a former madam:** Patrick Higgs to the author.
**"ripped out of Dairy Queen":** J. Patrick Redmond to the author.
**The writer grew up in Vincennes:** Ibid.
**"Not thinking at the time":** Ibid.
**he lingered in the parking lot:** J. Patrick Redmond, "My First Gay Bar," huffpost.com, May 27, 2013.
**danced to a remix of Whitney Houston's "I Will Always Love You":** Ibid.
**"That shows that they are allies within the gay community of middle America":** Redmond to the author.
**once cued up Prince's "Gett Off" for Lori:** Patrick Higgs to the author.
**"she was all over the floor":** Ibid.
**Penny rented out the venue for the occasion:** Ibid.
**"She passed out in my DJ booth a couple times":** Ibid.
**One night, Penny "drank too much":** Mollie Mallinger to the author.
**"took her home":** Ibid.
**"She vomited all over Tom's car":** Ibid.
**"I got totally smashed":** Greenhut to the author.
**Gloria Mallah doesn't remember:** Mallah to the author.
**The publicity lured "straight college kids":** Higgs to the author.

**"got into words with Madonna while they were both in the makeup chairs":** Paul Gebbia to the author.
**"I can't believe that you did that":** Ibid.
**"brief hetero period":** https://www.youtube.com/watch?v=luYGglLlPAA&t=1s.
**the magazine would not print her disclosure:** Cavan Sieczkowski, "Rosie O'Donnell Reveals Cosmopolitan Stopped Her From Coming Out As Gay in 1992 Article," huffpost.com, February 15, 2014.
**Rosie surmised:** Ibid.
**"I think Madonna was looking at Rosie as like a mother figure":** Gebbia to the author.
**Madonna stood and stared at her reflection:** Ibid.
**"I miss my Mommy":** Ibid.

## The Bottom of the Seventh: Rockford Versus Racine

**"Do you know how much they're paying me":** Sam Hoffman to the author.
**Madonna teased him:** Suzanne McCabe to the author.
**"There was a gossip sheet":** Hoffman to the author.
**"Nobody knew he was doing it anonymously":** Ibid.
**Hungover Racine Belles dropped like flies:** Lori Petty to the author.
**as she and the girls played Truth or Dare at a Bonanza restaurant:** Paire Davis, *Dirt in the Skirt*, 473.
**That is, like, the hottest man ever:** Patty Willett to the author.
**"It said 'Material Girl with material curls'":** Linda Boykin-Williams to the author.
**like serving watermelon and cappuccinos to the cast:** Patti Pelton and Kelli Simpkins to the author.
**he made Colin earn the coveted sneakers:** Robin Knight and Lita Schmitt to the author.
**Mo brought up the story to Tom:** Alan Wilder to the author.
**"She had a distinct personality":** Joe Bergren, "Tom Hanks on *A League of Their Own*'s Madonna Casting and Why People Love Baseball (Flashback)," etonline.com, July 1, 2022.
**"The tabloids came around":** Tom Morales to the author.
**"Man, I can make $150,000 if I sell this picture":** Ibid.
**"No, you won't":** Ibid.
**"awakening experience":** Hoffman to the author.
**"So suddenly, you take all these girls":** Jim Kleverweis to the author.
**"It wasn't until I got on that set":** Kelli Simpkins to the author.
**Madonna's "super queer":** Ibid.
**"There were people who would come up to me":** Ibid.
**"I don't remember any stories where it was not a positive thing":** Julie Croteau to the author.
**I wanna do a different take:** Simpkins to the author.
**"She was a real leader on that film":** Ibid.
**"Geena's Mensa":** Bernadette Mazur to the author.
**constructed a baseball stadium out of paper:** Ibid.
**"I just started going nuts":** *Interview*'s Hanks-Davis Q&A, March 1992.
**Tom performed the role of Caiaphas:** Ibid.
**"I had a very small but passionate part":** Geena Davis to the author.
**"We cast Madonna as Judas":** *Interview*'s Hanks-Davis Q&A, March 1992.

**"gave me some lines and said, 'Welcome to SAG'":** Patti Pelton to the author.
**a guy in the camera department warned Mollie Mallinger about Penny:** Mallinger to the author.
**She didn't feel that Penny hated women at all:** Ibid.
**"actually cared about everybody":** Ibid.
**"I thought she could be really mean-spirited":** Abe Flores to the author.
**"Hurry up":** Bernadette Mazur to the author.
**Penny grabbed her by the seat of her pants:** Francesca Paris to the author.
**"you're not gonna like it":** Ibid.
**T-shirts were made that had bullseyes on the back:** Paul Gebbia to the author.
**"Yeah, well, something had to happen":** *League of Their Own* DVD commentary, 2004.
**While Brailsford sat in his chair:** Gebbia to the author.
**"No, no, no, no":** Ibid.
**She flung the contents in his face:** Ibid.
**"That's the look I want":** Ibid.
**"I wasn't offended at all":** Gebbia to the author.
**she put him in charge of directing the third camera:** John Rusk to the author.
**shot scoreboard activity:** *League* DVD commentary.
**"She can drive me crazy":** Orenstein, "Making it in the Majors," *New York Times Magazine*, May 24, 1992.
**Then Penny began to yell:** Freddie Simpson to the author.
**"Are you gonna yell at us this entire movie?":** Ibid.
**Freddie, to his amazement, dipped Skoal:** Rhodes, "Back From the Bonfire," *Los Angeles Times*, July 5, 1992.
**substituted Tootsie rolls, Raisinets, and energy bars:** Alina Martinet and Robin Knight to the author.
**spat the crushed-up food upon David Strathairn's shoe:** *League of Their Own* DVD commentary, 2004.
**"I just had to be there and hold my ground":** David Strathairn to the author.
**totally over the top, Penny thought:** *League* DVD commentary.
**"I ain't doing that scene":** Ibid.
**Rosie expressed genuine anger:** Jon Lovitz to the author.
**Penny had the girls improvise reactions:** DVD commentary.
**"Geena the Macheena":** Davis, *Dying of Politeness*, 175.
**an awkward chemistry that bugged Penny:** Gary Muller to the author.
**joke that she weighed only eighty pounds:** DVD commentary.
**Lori was tired:** Lori Petty to the author.
**"Will you go get me some water?":** Mollie Mallinger to the author.
**She could require a bit more time:** John Rusk to the author.
**"she wanted those scenes to be right":** Ibid.
**"She was like that":** Ibid.
**"You don't try to milk an emotion":** Petty to the author.
**nine thousand extras lined up:** Rusk to the author.
**The production needed about five thousand faces:** Eileen Dempsey, "Baseball movie crew details extras' attire," *Evansville Courier*, August 4, 1991.
**Actors sat on the field under umbrellas:** Shannon Fuhs to the author.
**dangling raffle prizes:** Dempsey, "Baseball movie crew details extras' attire," *Evansville Courier*, August 4, 1991.

**Tom danced to "Tequila":** "Gallery: 'A League of Their Own' in Evansville, Henderson," *Evansville Courier & Press*, August 13, 2022.
**performed "Bohemian Rhapsody":** Sam Hoffman to the author.
**Rosie belted out "Like a Virgin":** Rosen, "On Base With a Hit," *People*, July 20, 1992.
**she threw signed baseballs:** Tim Galvin to the author.
**she fawned over the tiniest extra:** Roger McBain, "Memories . . . of the way things were," *Evansville Courier*, June 21, 1992.
**"Now you're no longer loveless":** Ibid.
**Intrepid reporters hid in cornfields:** Jeff Lyons to the author.
**"Searching for Madonna":** Dan Katz to the author.
**Usually, Fink gave off condescending airs:** Lyons to the author.
**"the people around here could see through it":** Ibid.
**"You look just like Pee-Wee Herman":** https://www.14news.com/video/2019/10/25/madonna-rosie-odonnell/.
**arrested in Florida:** Mark Harris and Ty Burr, "The Pee-Wee Herman scandal," *Entertainment Weekly*, August 16, 1991.
**the couple watched an airborne glove topple Justin Scheller:** Katz to the author.
**beat out four hundred other kids:** Justin Scheller to the author.
**"Tom Hanks didn't want to hit me hard":** Ibid.
**People were getting frustrated:** Ibid.
**Everybody went crazy:** Ibid.
**"Nobody likes to get hit in the face":** Ibid.
**His mother, Golda:** Eileen Dempsey, "Right Stuff Put Simple Folk in 'A League of Their Own,'" *Evansville Courier*, June 21, 1992.
**Penny picked "the chunky little kid instead of the skinny brat":** Scheller to the author.
**Bitty was maternal toward Scheller:** Ibid.
**"competitive motherfucker":** Lori Petty to the author.
**"I really like them high and outside":** Carlin, "Lori Petty Answers Every Question We Have About *A League of Their Own*," vulture.com, August 20, 2021.
**Lori puked everywhere:** Petty to the author.
**"Because you drank and smoked":** Behind-the-scenes *League* DVD commentary.
**"Do it again":** Carlin, "Lori Petty Answers Every Question We Have About *A League of Their Own*," vulture.com, August 20, 2021.
**sliding into Geena's stuntwoman:** Shelly Adlard to the author.
**Lori wanted to do the unadulterated stunt:** Adlard to the author.
**"You can see my Marky Mark underwear":** Petty to the author.
**When they met for the first time:** Adlard to the author.
**apologizing for Lori's apparent animus:** Ibid.
**think Dottie dropped the ball intentionally:** Bitty Schram and Kathleen Marshall to the author.
**"Everybody has so much fun arguing about it":** Geena Davis to the author.
**"Everybody has different life experiences":** Petty to the author.
**"why would you ever drop the ball":** Ibid.
**"The biblical scholar John Dominic Crossan":** Kelly Candaele, "There's No Dropping the Ball (On Purpose) in Baseball," *NINE: A Journal of Baseball History and Culture*, Fall 2021/Spring 2022.
**"I don't know if my mom ever thought about the ways":** Ibid.
**Miroslav Ondricek was exhausted:** Ondrej Kubicek to the author.

**Yet that connection fizzled:** Ibid.
**Priestley began his new post:** Tom Priestley to the author.
**Penny sat on the bed in Dottie's bedroom:** Erica Arvold to the author.
**"She was rough-housing in the bedroom":** Ibid.
**"Not because she was obnoxious":** Ibid.
**Ondricek's work was "brilliant":** Priestley to the author.
**"European cinematographers would basically just light":** Ibid.
**Justin Scheller felt uncomfortable hitting the women:** Megan Cavanagh to the author.
**Geena had T-shirts made:** Davis, *Dying of Politeness*, 178.
**"was not very nice":** Freddie Simpson to the author.
**"Watch out!":** Ibid.
**he screamed at her:** Ibid.
**"You are not ever allowed":** Ibid.
**Several Peaches stood:** Ibid.
**He ran off the bus:** Ibid.
**"Penny tried to talk to me":** Ibid.
**Penny shut down the shoot:** Ibid.
**"Are you OK?":** Ibid.
**"Yeah":** Ibid.
**"Yeah, OK, it happens to everybody":** Ibid.
**From that point onward:** Ibid.
**an Eastman Kodak van showed up:** Renée Coleman to the author.
**she shot up to twelve thousand feet each day:** Gary Muller to the author.
**would eclipse two million feet:** Ibid.
**wrap around Manhattan "like three or four times":** Dennis Drummond to the author.
**Kodak pulled out all the stops:** Billy Kerwick and Elliot Abbott to the author.
**Garry hired a plane:** Craig DiBona to the author.
**inside an Evansville airplane hangar:** Matt Salvato to the author.
**on the bathroom floor of a Radisson Hotel lobby:** Kerwick to the author.
**controlling Tom's "urine" flow:** Behind-the-scenes *League* DVD commentary.
**"OK, girls!":** Coleman to the author.
**"You need to tell Laverne":** Jim Kleverweis to the author.
**streaked the set:** David Obermeyer to the author.
**Rosie read a queer subtext between the lines:** Rosie O'Donnell to the author.
**"Rosie, this is not a gay thing":** Ibid.
**"Well, all I'm doing is reciting the lines":** Ibid.
**"No, but don't do it like that":** Ibid.
**"So I did it again":** Ibid.
**"made a choice not to deal with the women's sexuality":** Ibid.
**"[She] was playing in a boy's club":** Cavanagh to the author.
**Nor was she "making a film about gay women":** Coleman to the author.
**Robin Knight cried her eyes out:** Knight to the author.
**Madonna wiped Patti Pelton's tears:** Pelton to the author.
**"I loved my li'l sis":** Davis, *Dying of Politeness*, 183.
**"When it ended, everybody was just convulsively sobbing":** Hoffman to the author.
**October 19:** Alina Martinet to the author.

**George Bowers danced to Santana:** Anitra Larae Donahue to the author.
**when a DJ spun:** Ibid.
**As parting gifts:** Petty and Cavanagh to the author.
**"Don't take any shit":** Cavanagh to the author.
**Ro and Mo got into separate cars:** *League* DVD featurette interviews, 2004.
**"Bye, Ro":** Ibid.

## Eighth Inning: Cooperstown

**A helicopter landed in the middle of Doubleday Field:** Mary Moore to the author.
**"insignificant":** Marshall, *My Mother Was Nuts*, 256.
**"But it is a display":** Moore to the author.
**"When it came to thinking in cinematic terms":** Marshall, *My Mother Was Nuts*, 256.
**Greenhut overrode their youthful enthusiasm:** Greenhut to the author.
**"It could fail":** Ellen Lewis to the author.
**"Do we really even have to go to Cooperstown?":** John Rusk to the author.
**Greenhut volunteered to play Man in Bleachers:** Greenhut to the author.
**"We didn't know she was filming":** Moore to the author.
**"We got any sliders?":** Ibid.
**She invited Mark Holton (Older Stilwell) to watch a baseball documentary:** Mark Holton to the author.
**Holton heard she liked sake:** Ibid.
**not "a dry eye on the set":** Marshall, *My Mother Was Nuts*, 256.
**In one take, his jaw quivered with feeling:** Holton to the author.
**"Where was the quivering thing with the jaw?":** Ibid.
**That would've looked phony, he thought:** Ibid.
**"I had a contingent of AAGPBL ladies":** Marshall, *My Mother Was Nuts*, 257.
**The "Victory Song" burned a hole in Tim Bourne's ear:** Bourne to the author.
**whom Penny handpicked last-minute over Madonna:** Freddie Simpson to the author.
**"She didn't want to say goodbye":** Bourne to the author.
**Jim Kleverweis fell asleep at the wheel:** Kleverweis to the author.
**John Rusk's wife prepared:** Rusk to the author.
**She put four teams of editors to work:** Marshall, *My Mother Was Nuts*, 257.
**though feathers ruffled:** Dennis Drummond to the author.
**In editing mode:** Drummond and Christopher Capp to the author.
**"Do you know you guys are the only ones here in the building?":** Drummond to the author.
**acquitted four LAPD officers:** Anjuli Sastry Krbechek and Karen Grigsby Bates, "When LA Erupted in Anger: A Look Back at the Rodney King Riots," NPR, April 26, 2017.
**The verdict sparked six days of riots:** Carolina A. Miranda, "Of the 63 people killed during the '92 riots, 23 deaths remain unsolved—artist Jeff Beall is mapping where they fell," *Los Angeles Times*, April 28, 2017.
**Penny called Gary Muller and Mollie Mallinger from her cell phone:** Mallinger to the author.
**"I'm in the crew van":** Ibid.
**"Penny":** Ibid.
**"what really made people positive that it was me":** Geena Davis to the author.
**"Penny, where's my limp?"** Drummond to the author.

**"They'd put me in a really boxy suit":** Rhodes, "Back From the Bonfire," *Los Angeles Times*, July 5, 1992.

**shadowed Penny in the edit chambers:** Lori Petty to the author.

**"You guys gotta come in here":** Ibid.

**"Look at this fucking kid":** Ibid.

**"She was just a badass little baseball player":** Drummond to the author.

**Peggy Orenstein grilled Penny in her production office:** Orenstein, "Making it in the Majors," *New York Times Magazine*, May 24, 1992.

**"I'm a director":** Ibid.

**"You hold it too long":** Ibid.

**"Nahhhhh":** Ibid.

**She screened her first cut:** *My Mother Was Nuts* (257), and the author's interview with Joe Hartwick.

**"Is it too schmaltzy?":** Hartwick to the author.

**"Not for me, love":** Ibid.

**"didn't know shit about baseball":** *My Mother Was Nuts*, 257.

**he wore a trench coat:** Christopher Capp to the author.

**One day, Penny and her editors listened:** Ibid.

**Madonna took a two-day break:** "Madonna's 50 Greatest Songs," *Rolling Stone*, July 27, 2016.

**"morose torch ballad":** Tom Breihan, "The Number Ones: Madonna's 'This Used To Be My Playground,'" stereogum.com, January 21, 2022.

**"Goddamn it":** Capp to the author.

**Amy Pascal phoned Penny:** Ibid.

**"Penny had a fight with the studio":** Ibid.

**Penny and Elliot Abbott argued:** Abbott to the author.

**When she informed King of the situation:** King described her conversation with Penny during King's taped 2005 concert special, *Welcome to my Living Room*.

**"did not believe that the sisters would be estranged":** Rusk to the author.

**"Why not end on Geena, Tom, and Lori?":** *My Mother Was Nuts*, 257.

**"Because that ain't the end of the movie":** Ibid.

**"Well, I don't know":** Ibid.

**In October 1991, the forty-two-year-old Canton replaced:** Bernard Weinraub, "From Errand Boy to Studio Chief," *New York Times*, October 4, 1991.

**praised as the best movie he'd ever seen:** Kim Masters and Nancy Griffin, *Hit & Run: How Jon Peters and Peter Guber took Sony for a Ride in Hollywood* (New York: Simon & Schuster, 1996), 367.

**"I'm not slow-moving":** Weinraub, "From Errand Boy to Studio Chief," *New York Times*, October 4, 1991.

**Cooperstown "was hallowed ground":** Mark Canton to the author.

**That doesn't happen when your husband's at war:** Megan Cavanagh to the author.

**We can't keep the kiss:** Abbott to the author.

**"Well, Canton was batshit":** Ibid.

**When they collected the scores:** Ibid.

**"I didn't know that I wielded such power":** *My Mother Was Nuts*, 257.

**Pascal supported Penny's sentimental bookends:** Amy Pascal to the author.

**$45 million to $50 million:** Bernard Weinraub, "Budgets Bloat; Studios Worry," *New York Times*, June 25, 1992.

**"much closer to $60 [million] or $70 million":** Michael Nathanson to the author.

**to the tune of $80 million:** https://catalog.afi.com/Catalog/moviedetails/59187.

**as a potential cautionary tale:** Weinraub, "Budgets Bloat; Studios Worry," *New York Times*, June 25, 1992.

**"It's Penny's third feather":** Ibid.

**At first, Columbia underestimated:** Martin Grove, "'League'-leader Col sporting all-star lineup," *Hollywood Reporter*, July 6, 1992.

**When Abbott showed the movie to his two daughters:** Abbott to the author.

**"Penny, that's the review":** Ibid.

**"Are you serious?":** Ibid.

**"They loved it":** Ibid.

**"Do you think there's a big audience out there for girls?":** Ibid.

**"I think there's a huge audience":** Ibid.

**"Shit":** Ibid.

**The insight spurred the studio to tweak its promotional campaign:** Ibid.

**"Who says girls can't play baseball?":** Martin Grove, "SPE's summer slate: In 'League' of its own?," *Hollywood Reporter*, June 4, 1992.

**The Babes:** Unbylined, *Village Voice*, June 2, 1992.

**"The legs seemed like an attractive way to go":** Andy Marx, "Boys Will Be Boys Will Be . . . Movie Marketeers (No Matter What Language)," *Los Angeles Times*, July 19, 1992.

**forty-two million viewers:** Robert Epstein, "Two Tales of Targeting for Different Audiences," *Los Angeles Times*, June 26, 1992.

**Penny corralled Tom and Lovitz:** Elizabeth Sporkin, "Diamond Duds: A Grand Slam," *People*, August 10, 1992.

**At least two Peaches snuck into focus-group screenings:** Anne Ramsay and Megan Cavanagh to the author.

**thought Penny dropped the ball:** David Denby, "Bad-News Girls," *New York*, July 20, 1992.

**"None of these players is as embarrassingly lumpish":** Lawrence Toppman, "Plenty of hits . . . and a lot of errors," *Press-Telegram*, July 1, 1992.

**"may do better with male leads":** Deborah J. Kunk, "Strictly Minor League," *Saint Paul Pioneer Press*, July 2, 1992.

**"The director has bent over backward":** Michael Sragow, "Three Strikes," *New Yorker*, July 13, 1992.

**"Rarely are feminist attitudes handled as breezily":** Janet Maslin, "A 'League' Where Eddie Can't Play," *New York Times*, July 12, 1992.

**"The ambiguity about a woman's role":** https://www.rogerebert.com/reviews/a-league-of-their-own-1992.

**"afraid of life":** *League* DVD commentary.

**One night she phoned Abbott around 11 p.m.:** Abbott to the author.

**"We never should have done this baseball movie":** Ibid.

**"You're nuts":** Ibid.

**She thought the Academy theater:** *My Mother Was Nuts*, 258.

**"notoriously nervous for her premieres":** Bill Higgins, "One Major League Party," *Los Angeles Times*, June 24, 1992.

**served popcorn, peanuts, and meat rockets:** Nikki Finke, "Let's Do Screwballs," *Los Angeles*, August 1992.

**"Oh, please, please, please":** Ibid.

**"And they make much better sisters":** Ibid.

**there with beau Gavin de Becker:** George Christy, "The Great Life," *Hollywood Reporter*, June 30, 1992.
**She bought the Nicole Miller design in a store:** Geena Davis to the author.
**"I wish I still had it":** Ibid.
**watched the cast step out of their limos:** Shannon Fuhs to the author.
**"Oh my gosh, you're from Huntingburg":** Ibid.
**Special guests Pepper Paire Davis and her son:** Paire Davis, *Dirt in the Skirt*, 494.
**As Penny's limo backed out of her driveway:** Ibid.
**Geena wrangled tickets and sent a limo:** Neezer Tarleton to the author.
**"Are you OK with how much you were in the movie?":** Freddie Simpson to the author.
**"Yeah":** Ibid.
**Before the lights went down:** Babaloo Mandel to the author.
**"This is what they say":** Ibid.
**"You could hear Tracy and Lori":** Paire Davis, *Dirt in the Skirt*, 487.
**"she did a genius job editing that movie":** Geena Davis to the author.
**Tom appreciated:** Elias Stimac, "The Girls of Summer Discover 'A League of Their Own,'" *Drama-Logue*, July 2–8, 1992.
**"We all hated it":** Renée Coleman to the author.
**"I may as well have been in Prague":** Kurt Loder, "Madonna On TV," *TV Guide*, November 23–29, 1991.
**"Prior to her presence in Evansville, I would say they would've built a temple":** Brian Jackson to the author.
**"Nobody's that cool":** Ibid.
**Listeners asked the station:** Ibid.
**"Maybe she's a rat's rear end":** Ibid.
**The station's program director:** Barry Witherspoon to the author.
**Witherspoon saw an opening to capitalize on her candor:** Ibid.
**"Get a life, Madonna!":** https://www.youtube.com/watch?v=s54bSVr2roU.
**On Entertainment Tonight:** I watched this clip on TikTok, of all places! (TikTok is the new YouTube, I'm told.)
**Madonna mulled:** Liz Smith, *Los Angeles Times*, June 10, 1992.
**The two bantered off-the-cuff:** https://www.youtube.com/watch?v=JuZpHDRiSm8.
**"Oh, I think it's cute":** Gavin Martin, "Madonna: I don't see anything pornographic about beautiful pictures of naked women," *The Guardian*, September 1992.
**Bitty Schram closed her eyes:** Schram to the author.
**cried during the credits:** Jon Lovitz to the author.
**"Jon, you're a big star now":** Ibid.
**Justin Scheller rolled up:** Gail King, "Hoosiers' Hollywood Fling," *Wall Street Journal*, July 8, 1992.
**"Anybody who was anybody went to that premiere":** Ibid.
**Afterward he signed autographs:** Ibid.
**DeLisa Chinn-Tyler lingered in her theater seat:** Chinn-Tyler to the author.
**celebrated with one hundred friends and family members:** Megan Cavanagh to the author.
**Kelly Candaele hosted a packed watch party:** Candaele to the author.
**An estimated sixteen million women:** "A true league of their own," *Los Angeles Times*, June 30, 1992.

**The sixty-nine-year-old cancer patient took her last breath:** Obituary in *Variety*, December 21, 1991.
**collected anonymous predictions:** "Handicapping 'League,'" *Variety*, June 29, 1992.
**claiming the number-two spot:** "July 3–5, 1992," boxofficemojo.com.
**"We went to about three or four different theaters":** Abbott to the author.
**League had raked in $23 million:** Joseph McBride, "'League' B.O. scoring big," *Variety*, July 9, 1992.
**$100 million:** "Numbers," *Variety*, September 8, 1992.
**"WE'VE GOT LEGS!!":** *Variety*, September 8, 1992.
**Penny and Tom heard the news:** *My Mother Was Nuts*, 258.
**asked her permission to use the concept in Schindler's List:** Ibid.
**topped the Billboard Hot 100 chart:** Breihan, "The Number Ones: Madonna's 'This Used To Be My Playground,'" stereogum.com, January 21, 2022.
**Julie Croteau and Kelli Simpkins:** Croteau to the author.
**She cried when Doris discussed feeling different:** Ibid.
**their standing ovation surprising her:** Freddie Simpson to the author.
**eight little Rockford Peaches:** Renée Coleman to the author.
**hundreds of times:** Jessica Mendoza to the author.
**"she'd go and do something":** "A League of Their Own—Jessica Mendoza," *This Movie Changed Me* on Apple Podcasts.
**Jimmy Dugan reminded Jessica of her father:** Ibid.
**a football and baseball coach who mentored her and her younger sister, Alana:** Sam Scott, "Sure to Be a Hit," *Stanford*, July/August 2016.
**He hung a sixty-pound punching bag:** Ibid.
**Alana was shorter and feistier:** Mendoza to the author.
**"Stop swinging at the rise ball!":** *This Movie Changed Me* podcast.
**"I like the rise ball!":** Ibid.
**the movie had a fatal flaw:** Mendoza to the author.
**"You're out":** *This Movie Changed Me* podcast.

## Ninth Inning: Beyond the Outfield

**In the summer of 1992:** Gloria Mallah to the author.
**Penny and Gloria bickered like family:** Ibid.
**invited Tom to helm another:** Unbylined, "Tom Hanks Takes the Direct Approach," *People*, April 19, 1993.
**"Will you do it?":** Ibid.
**"For the first time since *Laverne & Shirley*":** Harry F. Waters and Charles Fleming, "TV Sheds Its Stigma," *Newsweek*, April 26, 1993.
**"to keep everybody working":** Mallinger to the author.
**she was wary of working with men:** Cavanagh to the author.
**During a trip to Hawaii:** Ibid.
**$2.6 million:** https://www.boxofficemojo.com/release/rl910722561/weekend/.
**the deaf community protested the choice:** Jay Mathews, "Deaf Activists to Protest Exclusion From New Film," *Washington Post*, August 26, 1993.
**"We were offered the Forrest Gump project":** Greenhut to the author.
**How am I gonna do:** Ibid.
**Let the second unit directors:** Ibid.
**Both Greenhut and Abbott tried:** Ibid.
**Offering an explanation:** https://www.youtube.com/watch?v=6yrLFGWr-Kg.

**delivered her eleven-pound son, Spencer:** *My Mother Was Nuts*, 260–261.
**toasted her fiftieth birthday:** Ibid., 261–262.
**rushed to a hospital:** "Marshall Taken Ill," *Los Angeles Times*, May 31, 1994.
**sent Penny the movie's script:** *My Mother Was Nuts*, 263.
**"I didn't think Renaissance Man":** Ibid.
**She pursued Tupac Shakur:** Ibid., 265.
**"I watch my movies":** Unbylined, "Penny Marshall," *Hollywood Reporter*, December 8, 1992.
**"You just have to get out there":** Ibid.
**"that script":** http://asitecalledfred.com/2013/06/29/terry-gilliam-ken-plume-interview/12/.
**Barry Sonnenfeld had to choose:** Adam Holmes, "The Crucial Forrest Gump Change Barry Sonnenfeld Suggested to Tom Hanks Before Filming," cinemablend.com, April 17, 2020.
**$192 million globally:** https://www.boxofficemojo.com/title/tt0101272/.
**a stressful shoot:** Simon Brew, "How 1991's The Addams Family Nearly Got Derailed," denofgeek.com, November 22, 2019.
**$678 million:** https://www.boxofficemojo.com/title/tt0109830/.
**fourth at the box office:** https://pro.imdb.com/title/tt0110971/boxoffice.
**$131 million:** https://www.boxofficemojo.com/title/tt0109813/.
**$24 million on a $40 million budget:** https://pro.imdb.com/title/tt0110971/boxoffice.
**Penny blamed Disney:** *My Mother Was Nuts*, 267.
**She "had a singular vision":** Todd Smith to the author.
**reissued it in seventeen Seattle theaters:** Michael Fleming, "'Man' Trouble," *Variety*, September 20, 1994.
**Penny organized a star-studded reading:** Michael Fleming, "All-star reading in the 'Woods,'" *Variety*, October 18, 1994.
**DeVito invited Penny to play herself:** *My Mother Was Nuts*, 266–267.
**hit a wall securing studio interest:** Michael Fleming, "Studios balk at spending a pretty Penny on 'Boys,'" *Variety*, June 5, 1995.
**Hot Flashes:** Unbylined, *Publishers Weekly*, May 10, 1993.
**a sequel to A League of Their Own:** Unbylined, "Penny Leaves Man on Base at Columbia," *Variety*, February 5, 1996.
**According to Geena:** *Dying of Politeness*, 183.
**Penny announced:** Adam Sandler, "Marshall Plan," *Variety*, September 29, 1995.
**she refused the job at first:** *My Mother Was Nuts*, 273.
**She scolded him:** Ibid., 275.
**occasionally missed call times:** Ibid., 277.
**"I know years later she told Oprah Winfrey":** Ibid., 277–278.
**three hours and twenty-four minutes:** Marilyn Beck and Stacy Jenel Smith, "Attention: Kmart shoppers: 'Preacher's' on hold," *Los Angeles Daily News*, July 19, 1996.
**"met up on weekends":** *My Mother Was Nuts*, 273.
**"This movie could have done more":** https://www.rogerebert.com/reviews/the-preachers-wife-1996.
**criticized the remake as tedious:** https://ew.com/article/1997/04/25/preachers-wife/; Jackie Potts, "'The Preacher's Wife' Could Use A Prayer," *Miami Herald*, December 13, 1996.
**best-selling Gospel album of all time:** "'The Preacher's Wife' Soundtrack Released This Day in 1996," whitneyhouston.com, November 26, 2019.

**$48 million:** https://www.boxofficemojo.com/release/rl2859173377/weekend/.

**estimated $75 million production and marketing costs:** Patrick Goldstein, "Praying for Crossover Appeal," *Los Angeles Times*, December 11, 1996.

**Disney had angled:** Ibid.

**She left CAA for International Creative Management:** Anita M. Busch, "Marshall Inks at ICM," *Variety*, February 24, 1997.

**On her director's wish list:** Marilyn Beck and Stacy Jenel Smith, "Frustrated director Marshall plans a return to acting," *Los Angeles Daily News*, February 26, 1999.

**She envisioned her friend Mark Wahlberg:** *My Mother Was Nuts*, 272.

**"It was one of the few times":** Ibid.

**As the 1990s waned:** Beck and Smith, "Frustrated director Marshall plans a return to acting," *Los Angeles Daily News*, February 26, 1999.

**some promising news:** Michael Fleming, "Marshall, Col Rev 'Cars,'" *Variety*, May 4, 1999.

**She wasn't gaga over the script:** *My Mother Was Nuts*, 291.

**Penny read:** Ibid.

**"I was furious":** Ibid., 292.

**she replaced David Anspaugh:** Dana Harris, "Marshall Ready to Coach Col's Globetrotters," *Hollywood Reporter*, December 15, 1999.

**Cameras rolled in August 2000:** https://www.tcm.com/tcmdb/title/452811/riding-in-cars-with-boys#notes.

**She didn't like how Penny's cinematographer:** *My Mother Was Nuts*, 292.

**"made me fire Chris":** Ibid.

**"This was the first of all the pictures":** Ibid., 293.

**"she had a problem":** Frank Price to the author.

**"She stayed up all night smoking cigarettes":** Andrew Goldman, "In Conversation: Anjelica Huston," *New York* magazine, May 1, 2019.

**Penny's sports collection was tremendous:** https://www.espn.com/video/clip/_/id/25567192.

**one of the last Bulls jerseys:** Rich Mueller, "Jordan Jersey From Penny Marshall Collection Topps [*sic*] REA Sale," sportscollectorsdaily.com, August 17, 2020.

**She planned to donate some of her keepsakes:** https://www.espn.com/video/clip/_/id/25567192.

**sensed the director and her actress:** Edward Guthmann, "'Riding in Cars' makes a bumpy, irritating trip/Barrymore not right for role, humor too broad," *San Francisco Chronicle*, October 19, 2001.

**"comes off as abrasive":** Rita Kempley, "'Riding in Cars': Gimme a Brake," *Washington Post*, October 19, 2001.

**Ebert hated Bev too:** https://www.rogerebert.com/reviews/riding-in-cars-with-boys-2001.

**Penny had wanted to have a premiere:** *My Mother Was Nuts*, 294.

**Lori Petty was fired three days:** Unbylined, "Petty Differences," *Entertainment Weekly*, April 23, 1993.

**"It was the most uncool day in Hollywood for me":** Marlow Stern, "Lori Petty on 'Orange Is the New Black,' the Halcyon '90s, and Discovering Jennifer Lawrence," *Daily Beast*, June 8, 2014.

**The studio promptly installed Sandra Bullock:** Suzan Ayscough, "Bullock in for Petty on 'Man,'" *Variety*, March 18, 1993.

**In his memoir:** Simon Brew, "Demolition Man: how Nigel Hawthorne hated making the film," filmstories.co.uk, November 24, 2020.
**"liked to parade around":** Ibid.
**"Sly and I were like oil and water":** "Petty Differences," *Entertainment Weekly*, April 23, 1993.
**$4 million:** https://www.boxofficemojo.com/release/rl3061155329/weekend/.
**Lloyd apparently refused to shave her head:** Clark Collis, "'It was a war!': The crazy behind-the-scenes story of *Tank Girl*," ew.com, March 30, 2020.
**"Lori just knew that she was Tank Girl":** Ibid.
**Lori thought an arbitrary R-rating:** Jerilyn Jordan, "Lori Petty reflects on *Tank Girl*, Jennifer Lawrence, and that *Game of Thrones* coffee cup," *Detroit Metro Times*, May 15, 2019.
**"You're gonna have to move your car":** Rosen, "Lori Petty's Hard Look," *New York Times*, June 19, 2008.
**Explaining her roller-coaster trajectory:** Stern, "Lori Petty on 'Orange Is the New Black,' the Halcyon '90s, and Discovering Jennifer Lawrence," *Daily Beast*, June 8, 2014.
**"I guess it's something I had to do to get rid of it":** Rosen, "Lori Petty's Hard Look," *New York Times*, June 19, 2008.
**With a $1 million budget:** Ibid.
**In her first crew meeting:** Hannah Levin, "Lori Petty On Performing With Power," masterchatmag.com, July 20, 2016.
**When people yell at her from their cars:** Baker, "'A League of Their Own' Is an All-Time Great Sports Film," theringer.com, June 30, 2017.
**"I fell off the cliff":** Hadley Freeman, "Geena Davis: 'As soon as I hit 40, I fell off the cliff. I really did,'" *The Guardian*, August 9, 2020.
**She had once been optimistic:** Ibid.
**The screenplay was written with Madonna in mind:** Claudia Eller, "Madonna faxes Roth her wrath," *Variety*, December 13, 1992.
**"I can understand why":** Ibid.
**Angie sputtered:** https://www.boxofficemojo.com/release/rl3292759553/weekend/.
**"In my entire 40s":** Stacey Wilson Hunt, "Geena Davis on Fighting for Female Representation in Hollywood and the Golden Age of Roles for Women," vulture.com, May 4, 2016.
**A League of Their Own taught Geena:** *Dying of Politeness*, 184.
**She took up archery:** Scott Huver, "Geena Davis Explains Why She Took Up Archery—And How She Almost Made the 2000 Olympic Team," *People*, March 23, 2020.
**third most successful soccer:** https://www.boxofficemojo.com/genre/sg1675620609/.
**inspired her to play soccer as a kid:** Abby Wambach to the author.
**schoolgirls' participation in fast-pitch softball surged:** Julien Assouline, "Gender Division in High School Baseball Participation Rates," *Hardball Times*, April 22, 2016.
**There were 353 girls playing high school baseball:** Ibid.
**The girls' numbers:** Ibid.
**Alyssa Nakken of the San Francisco Giants:** Jill Martin, "Alyssa Nakken made MLB history as the first woman to coach on the field during a major league game," CNN.com, July 21, 2020.

**the New York Yankees installed Rachel Balkovec:** https://www.milb.com/tampa/news/new-york-yankees-name-rachel-balkovec-manager.

**since 1994:** Zach Schonbrun, "Always an Outlier, Kelsie Whitmore Just Wants to Play Baseball," *New York Times*, June 12, 2022.

**since the AAGPBL ended:** "Colorado Silver Bullets," encyclopedia.com.

**The Silver Bullets barnstormed:** Scott Allen, "Remembering the Colorado Silver Bullets," mentalfloss.com, November 18, 2008.

**During A League of Their Own's press tour:** Freeman, "Geena Davis: 'As soon as I hit 40, I fell off the cliff. I really did,'" *The Guardian*, August 9, 2020.

**"Can we write that?":** Mark Olsen, "Still in a 'League' of her own," *Los Angeles Times*, July 4, 2017.

**Yes, you can:** Ibid.

**League wasn't a conscious feminist undertaking:** Orenstein, "Making it in the Majors," *New York Times Magazine*, May 24, 1992.

**Ever since *Thelma & Louise*:** *Dying of Politeness*, 167.

**she became a trustee:** Olsen, "Still in a 'League' of her own," *Los Angeles Times*, July 4, 2017.

**"What the heck was this?":** Wilson Hunt, "Geena Davis on Fighting for Female Representation in Hollywood and the Golden Age of Roles for Women," vulture.com, May 4, 2016.

**68 percent of the entertainment companies:** Michelle Penelope King, "Geena Davis Is Creating Opportunities For Women In Hollywood By Tackling Gender Bias," forbes.com, April 3, 2017.

**still wants to make a sequel:** *Dying of Politeness*, 184.

**In 2005, Byron Motley received a handwritten note:** Byron Motley to the author.

**"I read your script":** Ibid.

**"She sometimes was lucid":** Ibid.

**Penny was diagnosed:** *My Mother Was Nuts*, 307–309.

**Tracy cared for her:** Ibid., 310.

**She gained sixty pounds:** Ibid., 314.

**"I can't have just one of anything":** Ibid., 316.

**and still unfinished:** Benjamin Svetkey, "Inside Penny Marshall's Unfinished Film on Dennis Rodman," *Hollywood Reporter*, January 3, 2019.

**"I came to realize":** *My Mother Was Nuts*, 320.

**"enduring importance to American culture":** "2012 National Film Registry Picks in A League of Their Own," loc.gov, December 19, 2012.

**"They're good kids":** Ibid., 319.

**Penny announced:** Jen Yamato, "Penny Marshall Back to Baseball With Biopic of First Female Hall of Famer," deadline.com, December 11, 2014.

**did not have a powerful agent:** Motley to the author.

**But the group struggled:** Ibid.

**She had Motley contact Spielberg:** Ibid.

**"I love the script":** Ibid.

**wrote a curt note back:** Ibid.

**"How can they dismiss":** Ibid.

**called Penny one afternoon:** Paula Herold to the author.

**Herold saw Penny in a wheelchair:** Ibid.

**a thousand attendees streamed into:** Chris Erskine, "With wit and warmth, Hollywood bids goodbye to Garry Marshall, 'an irreplaceable man,'" *Los Angeles Times*, November 14, 2016.

**Carrie went into cardiac arrest:** Joseph Serna and Richard Winton, "Carrie Fisher's autopsy reveals cocktail of drugs, including cocaine, opiates and ecstasy," *Los Angeles Times*, June 19, 2017.

**"My mom battled":** Ibid.

**Penny attended a starry memorial service:** Ella Alexander, "Meryl Streep performed a touching song at Carrie Fisher's memorial," *Harper's Bazaar*, January 6, 2017.

**"I think she just gave up":** Herold to the author.

**Abbi Jacobson and Will Graham declared plans:** Lesley Goldberg, "'A League of Their Own' TV Series in the Works at Amazon," *Hollywood Reporter*, March 30, 2018.

**The reboot's creators received Penny's blessing:** Lesley Goldberg, "Abbi Jacobson on Reimagining 'A League of Their Own' With Late Director Penny Marshall's Blessing," *Hollywood Reporter*, August 5, 2022.

**"We got into the scene with the foul ball":** Ibid.

**Penny died at home:** Anita Gates, "Penny Marshall, 'Laverne & Shirley' Star and Movie Director, Dies at 75," *New York Times*, December 18, 2018.

**Tom memorialized her on Twitter:** Nate Nikolai, "Hollywood Pays Tribute to 'Trailblazer,' 'Pioneer' Penny Marshall," *Variety*, December 18, 2018.

**He said later that A League of Their Own:** https://www.youtube.com/watch?v=Ix6dw8GHPhE.

**"The players are truly grateful":** https://twitter.com/aagpbl/status/1075155803206750208?lang=id.

**The following September:** "A League of Their Own actresses stop in Rockford to celebrate director Penny Marshall," mystateline.com, September 13, 2019.

**At a golf event in the mid-2000s:** Jessica Mendoza to the author.

**"You changed me, like, totally":** Ibid.

**to outlast athletes who were better:** "A League of Their Own—Jessica Mendoza," *This Movie Changed Me* on Apple Podcasts.

**Geena signed her ball:** Mendoza to the author.

**Mendoza cried:** Ibid.

**When Mendoza's five-year-old son:** *This Movie Changed Me.*

**"Mom, I have ticklies in my belly":** Ibid.

**"Ticklies are a good thing, bud":** Ibid.

**"That's what we live for":** Ibid.

# INDEX


Aaron, Hank, 95, 160, 234
Abbott, Elliot, 81, 104, 127, 198
*About Last Night*, 34
Abramowitz, Rachel, 42
*Accidental Tourist, The*, 73
*According to Jim*, 232
Ackmann, Martha, 160
Adams, Chanté, 233
*Addams Family, The*, 217
*Addams Family Values*, 217
Adlard, Shelly, 134, 181
*Advocate, The*, 103
Affleck, Ben, 220
Aikman, Becky, 110
*Aliens*, 40
All-American Girls Professional Baseball League (AAGPBL), 60, 65, 66
  alums, 214
  Black players excluded by, 134, 160
  board, 85, 108
  coaches, 96
  elders, 114
  expansion of, 50
  material collected on, 67
  players, 200
  Players Association, 65, 66
  presentation of, 133
  queer history of, 188
  song's oblique reference to, 198
  vets invited to appear in movie's epilogue, 191
Allen, Woody, 40, 200
*All in the Family*, 15, 18, 21
*Amadeus*, 184
*American Graffiti*, 16
Anderson, Wes, 149
*Angels in the Outfield*, 227
*Angie*, 226
*Annie Hall*, 128, 184
*Another Woman*, 40
Anspaugh, David, 67, 80, 85, 112, 221
*Apocalypse Now*, 195
*Apollo 13*, 214
Arlington, Lizzie, 133
*Arsenio Hall Show, The*, 208
Arvold, Erica, 184
Assante, Armand, 93
*Atlantic*, 131
August, Lissa, 61
*Awakenings*, 71, 72, 76, 123, 138, 184, 194
Aykroyd, Dan, 22

*Babes, The*, 202
Bacall, Lauren, 72
*Bachelor Party*, 39
*Back to the Future*, 217
Bailey, Mary, 151
Ball, Lucille, 15

Bancroft, Anne, 63
Barker, Len, 38
Barrymore, Drew, 221
*Barry Sonnenfeld, Call Your Mother*, 41
Baseball Hall of Fame, 64, 191, 222
Baskin, Josh, 73
Bates, Kathy, 89
*Batman*, 87, 199
*Batman Returns*, 84, 201, 209
Battle Creek Belles, 56, 115, 191
Beatty, Warren, 35, 100, 194, 208
Beck, Marilyn, 220
*Beetlejuice*, 73
Begley, Ed, Jr., 24
*Being There*, 35
Belson, Jerry, 14, 72
Belushi, Jim, 7, 22, 83
Belushi, John, 7, 22, 23, 223
Benatar, Dennis, 158
Bendel, Henri, 110
Bergin, Patrick, 93
Bernhard, Sandra, 102
Bernstein, Carl, 62
Bertolucci, Bernardo, 103
*Beverly Hills, 90210*, 195
*Bewitched*, 110
*Big*, 2, 31, 32, 213, 217
  filming begun on, 40
  gross income for, 62
  idea to flip genders in, 34
  success of, 48
Billington, James, 231
Birnbaum, Roger, 86
*Bishop's Wife, The*, 219
*Black Patch*, 192
*Blood Simple*, 41
*Bloomer Girls: Women Baseball Pioneers*, 132
*Blues Brothers, The*, 22
Blue Sox, 55
*Bonfire of the Vanities, The*, 92, 93, 199
*Booker*, 79
*Bosom Buddies*, 19, 20, 26, 39
Bosse Field, 144, 147, 159, 175, 209
Boston Bloomer Girls, 133
*Boston Globe Magazine*, 66
Bourne, Tim, 47, 194, 216
Bowers, George, 188
*Boys of Neptune, The*, 218
*Boyz n the Hood*, 200
Braddock, James, 220
Brailsford, Pauline, 214
*Brazil*, 217
Breihan, Tom, 198
*Brighton Beach Memoirs*, 34
*Broadcast News*, 34, 195
Brooks, Albert, 15
Brooks, Jim, 15, 32, 46, 195, 221
Brooks, Mel, 214
Brown, Helen Gurley, 165
Browne, Lois, 55
*Bugsy*, 201
*Bull Durham*, 82, 83
Bullock, Sandra, 224
Bunbury, Kylie, 230
*'Burbs, The*, 92
Burns, Ken, 195
Burnstein, Jim, 216
Burton, Tim, 87, 201
*Butch Cassidy and the Sundance Kid*, 37
Butler, Kathleen, 194
*By the Book*, 218
Byrne, Gabriel, 94

*Cadillac Man*, 79
Cahn, Susan K., 53
*Calendar Girl*, 195, 215
Callaghan, Albert, 51
Callaghan, Hazel, 51
Callaghan, Helen, 51–52, 91, 184
Callaghan, Marge, 51–52
Campayno, Joe, 152, 170
Canby, Vincent, 33
Candaele, Bob, 53, 55
Candaele, Helen, 49
Candaele, Kelly, 49, 58–59, 62
Canseco, Jose, 208
Canton, Mark, 199
Capp, Christopher, 198
Capra, Frank, 25, 82
Carden, D'Arcy, 233
Carey, Mariah, 231
Caron, Glenn Gordon, 155
Carson, Johnny, 10
Carter, Graydon, 231
Cartsonis, Susan, 42
Cartwright, Lynn, 192
*Castaway*, 217

*Casualties of War*, 72
*Catcher in the Rye, The*, 37
Cavanagh, Megan ("Marla Hooch"), 105, 172, 188, 213
  alter ego of, 79, 98
  audition of, 78, 148
  post-*League* roles notched by, 214
  pregnancy of, 188
  reaudition of, 98
*Challenge of a Lifetime*, 26
Chase, Chevy, 84
Chattanooga Lookouts, 133
Cher, 218
Chicago Stars, 133
*Chicago Tribune*, 124
*Children of a Lesser God*, 89
Chinn-Tyler, DeLisa, 134, 160, 159, 209
*Chorus Line, A*, 158
Cicotte, Eddie, 123
Cincinnati Reds, 129
*Cinderella Man*, 220
Cinergi Pictures, 218
Clark, Will, 50
Clemmer, Ronnie, 66
Cleveland Indians, 57
Clooney, George, 81
Cobb, Ty, 81
Coen, Erhan, 41
Coen, Joel, 41
Cohen, Andy, 35
Coleman, Renée ("Alice Gaspers"), 99, 111, 114, 188, 206, 211
  comparison of *League* to war movie, 150
  explanation of film by, 188
  reaction to *League* by, 206
Colleton, Sara, 81, 86, 216
Collins, Dottie, 65
Collins, Harold, 149
Colorado Silver Bullets, 229
*Color Purple, The*, 28, 30
Columbia Pictures, 67, 68, 72, 86, 89, 92, 94, 102, 103, 120, 132, 147, 149, 195, 199, 201, 208, 218, 221
Comfort, Alex, 7
*Commander in Chief*, 230
Conte, Lou, 127
Coppola, Francis Ford, 16, 25, 195
Cortino, Anthony, 152
*Cosmopolitan*, 39, 165
Costner, Kevin, 2, 3, 34, 81, 82, 90
Cox, Courteney, 76
Crawford, Cindy, 76
Creative Artists Agency (CAA), 23, 30, 89, 97, 103, 200, 220
Crichton, Charles, 73
Cronin, Brian, 133
Croteau, Julie, 130–132, 170, 229
Crow, Melissa, 117, 147
Crowe, Russell, 220
Cruise, Tom, 3, 92
Crystal, Billy, 90
Cue, Annie, 191
Cusack, Ann ("Shirley Baker"), 99, 112, 118, 142, 149, 206, 216
Cusack, John, 118
*Cut*, 227
*Cutthroat Island*, 226

*Daily Beast*, 225
*Daily News*, 27
Dancer, Faye, 64, 66
*Dances with Wolves*, 90
D'Angelo, Josephine "JoJo," 53
Dangerfield, Rodney, 227
Dash, Stacey, 216
Davis, Geena ("Dottie Hinson")
  acting roles of, 109
  aged (vision of), 192
  as Best Supporting Actress, 73
  body double of, 108
  as bridesmaid, 121
  controlled acting of, 177
  criticism of, 116
  description of *League* as feminist film, 229
  early takes at bat, 1–2
  favorite scene of, 134
  growing confidence of, 157
  height of, 204
  impact of her efforts seen by, 230
  impish side of, 126
  lessons learned from *League*, 227
  Lori Petty's introduction to, 107
  Lori Petty's out-pranking of, 126
  Lori Petty's running faster than, 140
  as member of Mensa, 152
  memoir of, 188, 218–219

Davis, Geena (*cont.*)
 mid-2000s appearance at golf event by, 234
 modeling experience, 110
 praise for "regal" performance by, 203
 reaction to first viewing of *League*, 206
 as role model, 170
 salary of, 111
 stuntwoman for, 181
 test-screening of kiss between Tom Hanks and, 200
 in *Thelma & Louise*, 104
 turning forty, 226
 vocal dubbing by, 196
 as would-be, could-be Kit, 92
Davis, Lavonne "Pepper" Paire, 60, 64, 65, 96, 114, 168, 194, 205
Davis, Willie, 205
Dawson, Andre, 129
Day-Lewis, Daniel, 134
de Becker, Gavin, 146, 205
Dedeaux, Rod, 76, 79
Dedeaux Field, 112
*Deep Impact*, 158
*Demolition Man*, 224
Denby, David, 203
De Niro, Robert, 33, 62, 89, 218
De Palma, Brian, 92
Dern, Laura, 76, 84
*Desperately Seeking Susan*, 100
*Devil's Candy, The*, 93
DeVito, Danny, 215, 218
DiBona, Craig, 129, 153
*Dick Tracy*, 100
*Dick Van Dyke Show, The*, 13, 15
Diller, Barry, 35, 72
Dillingham, Susan, 38
Dillon, Matt, 84
DiMaggio, Joe, 50, 64
Dolly Vardens, 132–133
Doubleday Field, 191
Douglas, Michael, 93
*Dracula: Dead and Loving It*, 214
*Dragnet*, 36
Dreyfuss, Richard, 15, 22, 213
Dries, Dolores, 114
*Driving Miss Daisy*, 198
Drummond, Dennis, 196
Duckworth, Mike, 147
Dukes, David, 22
Dumais, David, 95

*Earth Girls Are Easy*, 73
Ebert, Roger, 33, 82, 204, 220, 223
*Effa*, 232
*Eight Men Out*, 123
Elise, Christine, 214
Elizabeth I, 132
*Elle*, 111
*Enquirer*, 169
*Entertainment Tonight*, 169
*Entertainment Weekly*, 220, 224
*Entourage*, 231
Ephron, Nora, 208
*Erotica*, 198
*Evansville Courier*, 146
Evansville Otters, 145
*Every Time We Say Goodbye*, 39
*Evita*, 155, 226

*Family Feud*, 231
*Family Matters*, 76
*Family Ties*, 26
*Fatal Attraction*, 72, 229
*Father of the Bride*, 195
*Fathers & Sons*, 99
Fawcett, Farrah, 14, 91
Feigen, Brenda, 67, 68
Ferrari, Irene, 153
*Ferris Bueller's Day Off*, 117
FerryHawks, 228
Field, Sally, 226
*Field of Dreams*, 81, 82
Fink, Stuart, 169, 179
Finke, Nikki, 205
*Firm, The*, 93
*Fish Called Wanda, A*, 73
Fisher, Carrie, 6, 22, 26, 213, 215
*Fisher King, The*, 217
*Flamingo Kid, The*, 25, 158
*Flashdance*, 72
*Flintstones, The*, 217
*Flirting with Disaster*, 158
Flores, Abe, 108
*Fly, The*, 73, 111
Flynt, Cynthia, 219
Fonda, Jane, 26

Ford, Harrison, 31, 32, 73
*Forrest Gump*, 215, 217, 218, 219
Fort Wayne Daisies, 50, 96
Fox, Michael J., 26
Foxx, Jimmie, 64, 69, 95, 96
Frattaroli, Frank, 93
Frontier League, 145
Frost, Lindsay, 99
Fuhs, Shannon, 205
F-word, 229

Galvin, Tim, 151
Ganis, Sid, 157, 202
Ganz, Lowell, 17, 62, 69, 71, 93, 124, 175, 203
Garfunkel, Art, 22, 24
Garner, James, 14
Gebbia, Paul, 145, 152, 164
Geffen, David, 86
Gehrig, Lou, 133
Gershon, Gina, 83
*Get Shorty*, 218
*Getting Away with Murder*, 220
*Ghost*, 33, 76
Gilbert, Melissa, 99
Gilliam, Terry, 217
Ginsburg, Ruth Bader, 67
Girardi, Tom, 68
*Girls of Summer*, 55
Gleason, Jackie, 39, 40
*Godfather Part II, The*, 195
Goldberg, Whoopi, 27, 28, 33
Goldblum, Jeff, 99, 108
*Goodfellas*, 90
Goodman, John, 203
Gordon, Larry, 24, 28
Gordon, Leo, 192
gossip hounds, 169
*GQ*, 38
Grand Rapids Chicks, 56
Grant, Cary, 219
Grant, Chet, 57
Greenhut, Bob, 40, 89, 94
Gretzky, Wayne, 130, 158
Grey, Jennifer, 76
Grieco, Richard, 79
Groom, Bill, 138, 149, 219
Guber, Peter, 86, 92, 93, 103
Guest, Christopher, 26
Gumbel, Bryant, 61
Guthmann, Edward, 223

Hackman, Gene, 80
Haines, Randa, 89
hairstyles, 151
Haley, Mike, 140
Hallin, Penny Lee, 142
Hallin, Wendy, 76, 142
Hanks, Colin, 168
Hanks, Tom ("Jimmy Dugan"), 34, 40
  announcement of casting of, 94
  Best Actor Oscar for, 219
  childhood of, 37
  effect of stress on, 97
  funneling of anger by, 172
  genuflection by, 121
  as leading man, 26
  marriage of Rita Wilson and, 47
  memorialization of Penny Marshall by, 234
  nomination of Best Actor for, 73
  test-screening of kiss between Geena Davis and, 200
  wanting the role of Jimmy Dugan, 92
  as wild card, 2–3
Hannah, Daryl, 27, 76, 84
*Happy Days*, 16, 17, 19, 24
  charity baseball game, 22
  *Laverne & Shirley* besting, 18
*Harlem Nights*, 142
Harlin, Renny, 226
Harvey, Walter, 123
Harvey Field, 141, 192
Hathaway, Anne, 221
Hawaii Winter Baseball league, 229
Hawn, Goldie, 26, 218
Hawthorn, Tom, 54
Hawthorne, Nigel, 224
Headly, Glenne, 75
Heard, John, 43
Hemingway, Mariel, 76, 84
Henderson Productions, 17
Henry, Mickey, 11
Henry, Tracy Lee, 11
Hepburn, Katherine, 52
*Hero*, 226
Higgins, Bill, 205
Hill, George Roy, 37

*Hill Street Blues*, 81
Hlinomaz, Bonnie, 137
Hoffman, Dustin, 73, 110, 226
Hoffman, Sam, 135, 139, 164, 188
*Hogan Family, The*, 76
*Hollywood Reporter*, 233
homophobia, 53
*Honey, I Shrunk the Kids*, 201
Hooch, Dave, 148
*Hook*, 201
*Hoosiers*, 67, 80, 81, 83, 197
Hopkins, Gordon, 160
Hopper, Dennis, 80
*Hot Flashes*, 218
Houston, Whitney, 164, 219, 220
Houston Astros, 57
Howard, Ron, 25, 220
*Howard the Duck*, 40
*How Sweet It Is!*, 14
Hubbard Street Dance Company, 117
Hudson, Kate, 221
Hughes, Bo, 76, 108, 114, 118
Hughes, John, 24, 33
*Hunger Games, The*, 227
Hunt, Helen, 78, 84, 130
*Hunter, Holly*, 34
Hurt, William, 93
Huston, Anjelica, 216, 222
Hutton, Timothy, 34

*I Dream of Jeannie*, 110
*I Love Lucy*, 18
*I Love Trouble*, 214
Indiana Film Commission, 149
International Creative Management, 220, 232
*Interview* magazine, 170
*Is That a Gun in Your Pocket?: Women's Experience of Power in Hollywood*, 42

Jackson, Brian, 207
Jackson, Shoeless Joe, 81
Jarrahy, Reza, 230
Jenkins, Marilyn, 56
Jenkinson, Bill, 95
*Jerk, The*, 15
*Jerry Maguire*, 93
*Jesus Christ Superstar*, 170
Jett, Joan, 83
Jim Crow South, 54, 160
*Joe Versus the Volcano*, 92, 121
John Casablancas, 78
Johnson, Mamie "Peanut," 54, 160
Jolie, Angelina, 221
Jones, Eddie, 124
Jones, James Earl, 82
Jones, Janet, 130, 158
Jones, Karen Frankel, 117
Jordan, Michael, 222
Joyner, Florence Griffith (FloJo), 26–27
*Joy of Sex, The*, 7, 24, 25
Judd, Ashley, 132
*Jumpin' Jack Flash*, 27, 28, 30, 32, 33, 40, 142
*Jurassic Park III*, 158

Kane, Carol, 24
Katz, Dan, 179
Keaton, Michael, 7, 201, 226
Keitel, Harvey, 93
Kelly, Moira, 218
Kempley, Rita, 223
Kenosha Comets, 55, 130
Kerwick, Billy, 219
Kestenbaum, Ronnie, 7
Ketcham, Lee Anne, 229
King, Billie Jean, 67
King, Carole, 198
King, Larry, 216
King, Rodney, 195
*Kiss Before Dying, A*, 84
Kleverweis, Jim, 169, 195
Klugman, Jack, 14
Knight, Robin ("Beans Babbitt"), 121, 129, 170, 188, 206
*K-9*, 83
*Kramer vs. Kramer*, 184
Ku Klux Klan, 162
Kunk, Deborah J., 204
Kunkel, Karen, 65, 66, 108

*Ladybugs*, 227
Lamarr, Hedy, 151
Lander, David, 17
Landis, Kenesaw Mountain, 133
Lang, John, 132
Lange, Jessica, 26, 226
Laski, Wendi, 232

*Last Temptation of Christ, The*, 73
*LA Times*, 50, 54, 58, 133, 196, 200, 205, 220
*Laverne & Shirley*, 7, 16, 62
- Carmine "The Big Ragoo" Ragusa on, 116
- debut of, 17
- as favorite show of DeLisa Chinn-Tyler, 161
- Garry Marshall's attempt at big-screen resurrection of, 220
- *Happy Days* bested by, 18
- taping of last episode of, 5
- working conditions during, 17, 19
- the year Penny buried, 24

*LA Weekly*, 25, 53
*League of Their Own, A*
- art director for, 151
- availability in video stores, 211
- as "awakening experience," 169
- awards won on festival circuit, 61
- boy jocks appearing in movies following, 227
- comparison to war movie, 150
- director of. *See* Marshall, Penny
- extras needed for, 178
- as feminist film, 229
- Geena Davis's lesson learned from, 227
- hairstyles of the Peaches in, 151
- as listing in National Film Registry, 231
- marketing of, 202
- merch hawked on QVC, 202
- outtake left in, 141
- pessimistic predictions about, 201
- players of color to try out for, 134
- press tour, 229
- publicity campaign of, 178, 179
- as record-breaking baseball movie, 2
- secret sauce adding zing to, 217
- security expert who advised, 146
- as small-screen sitcom, 214
- standing ovation for, 211
- success of, 2, 3
- union camera operator on, 129
- unofficial DP for, 184
- verbal catfight between Dottie and Kit in, 139
- wardrobe supervisor for, 153

League of Their Own Effect, 228
*Leave It to Beaver*, 154
*Legal Eagles*, 27, 103
Lemisch, Amy, 216
Leo, Melissa, 91
Leonetti, Matt, 28, 29, 40
Leoni, Téa, 83, 130, 158
*Lethal Weapon*, 199
Letts, Tracy, 127
Levinson, Barry, 73
Lewis, Ellen, 93, 127, 191
*Lieutenant, The*, 116
*Like Father, Like Son*, 33
*Lion King, The*, 218
Liotta, Ray, 209
*Little Big League*, 227
Loder, Kurt, 207
Loggia, Robert, 43
Lombard, Carole, 9
London, Roy, 78
Longbow Productions, 66
*Long Kiss Goodnight, The*, 226–227
*Los Angeles* magazine, 205
*Love, American Style*, 7
*Love Thy Neighbor*, 26
Lovitz, Jon ("Ernie Capadino"), 11, 22, 83, 230
- bovine background extra during closeup of, 140
- comic relief provided by, 82

Lowell, Carey, 214
*Lucy Show, The*, 14
Lyons, Jeff, 145

MacLaine, Shirley, 24, 63
*Mad Dog and Glory*, 123
Madonna ("'All the Way' Mae"), 3, 146
- arrival of, 112
- bit-stealing by, 122
- as bridesmaid, 121
- double for, 134
- jitterbug number by, 113
- part wanted by, 100
- Penny Marshall's approach to, 99
- private jet of, 188
- as Queen Bee, 113
- song co-written for the movie's end credits, 198

*Magnum, P.I.*, 20
Mailer, Norman, 127

Mailer, Stephen, 127
*Major League*, 83
Major League Baseball season, 129
Malamud, Bernard, 82
Mallah, Gloria, 137, 164, 213
Mallinger, Mollie, 164, 171, 195
Mamet, David, 28
Mandel, Babaloo, 62, 69, 71, 95, 124, 175, 203, 206
Manley, Effa, 230
Manning, Rick, 38
*Man with One Red Shoe, The*, 39
Mantle, Mickey, 8
Maples, Marla, 75, 79
Maris, Roger, 8
Marjorie Ward Marshall Dance Center, 24
Marks, Mimi, 118
Marks, Richard, 195
Marshall, Garry, 39, 89, 205
  attempt to resurrect *Laverne & Shirley* on the big screen, 220
  call received from distant sister, 13
  casting of Penny as Myrna Turner, 14
  childhood of, 9
  *Happy Days* as top-rated ABC comedy of, 16
Marshall, Kathleen, 142, 182
Marshall, Marjorie, 8, 13
  death of, 24
  diminishing of, 71
  match for Penny dreamed by, 15
  maternal influence of, 10
  plans for youngest child, 9
Marshall, Penny
  accusations of nepotism throughout career of, 15
  as Ado Annie, 13
  complaint revealed by *Newsweek*, 214
  cycle of silence perpetuated by, 187–188
  death of, 234
  ironic statement by, 197
  loneliest time for, 22
  medical emergency of, 216
  as Myrna Turner, 14
  split from Rob Reiner, 21
  trademark whine of, 2
Marshall, Ronny, 9
Marshall, Tony, 5, 9, 17
Marshall Method, 39
Martin, Steve, 218
Maslin, Janet, 204
Matheson, Tim, 22
Maui Stingrays, 229
Mazur, Bernadette, 138, 170
McDonald, Frank, 144
McEnroe, John, 231
McGovern, Elizabeth, 91
McKean, Michael, 17, 26
McMurray, Sam, 214
Meisel, Steven, 116
Mekka, Eddie, 116
Mellencamp, John, 144
*Men in Black*, 217
Mendoza, Jessica, 211, 234, 235
Mensa, Geena Davis as member of, 152
menstrual cycles, syncing up of, 151
Meyer, Ron, 30
Meyerhoff, Arthur, 123
Meyers, Nancy, 28, 195
*Miami Herald*, 220
Michaels, Lorne, 24, 231
Miller, Jeff, 230
Miller, Nicole, 205
*Miller's Crossing*, 41
*Milwaukee Independent*, 162
Minneapolis Millers, 96
*Misery*, 89, 229
*Mississippi Burning*, 73
Mitchell, Jackie, 133
*Money Pit, The*, 39
Monroe, Marilyn, 196
Montana, Joe, 72
Montreal Expos, 57
Moore, Demi, 62, 76, 84
Moore, Mary Tyler, 16
Morales, Tom, 152, 169
Morgan, Connie, 160
Morland, Catherine, 132
Moscow, David, 34, 42
Motley, Byron, 230
*Mr. Destiny*, 38
*Ms.* magazine, 67
*Mulaney*, 231
Muller, Gary, 142, 195
Murphy, Elizabeth, 133
*My Cousin Vinny*, 91
*My Mother Was Nuts*, 35

Naismith Memorial Basketball Hall of Fame, 222
Nakken, Alyssa, 228
*Nash Bridges*, 220
Nass, Connie, 149
Nathanson, Michael, 86, 87, 129, 201
*National Enquirer*, 168
National Federation of State High School Associations, 228
*National Pastime: From Swampoodle to South Philly, The*, 95
National Pro Fastpitch, 234
*Natural, The*, 88
NCAA baseball, 131, 229
Negro Leagues, 54, 160, 230
Negro Leagues Baseball Museum, 222
Nelson, Maud, 133
*Network*, 184
Neuffer, Linda, 168
Newark Eagles, 230
Newman, Paul, 93
*Newsweek*, 214, 229
*New Year's Eve*, 231
*New Yorker*, 204
New York Mets, 129
*New York Times*, 33, 196, 201, 204, 220
Nichols, Mike, 73, 89, 200
Nicholson, Jack, 24, 216
Nicita, Rick, 103
Niemeyer, Shelly, 148
*Nightmare Café*, 99
*1941*, 22
Niven, David, 219
*Northanger Abbey*, 132
*Nothing in Common*, 39, 40
*Nothing but Trouble*, 84
*Not One of the Boys*, 67
*Nutty Professor, The*, 35
N-word, 162, 163

*Odd Couple, The*, 14, 15
O'Donnell, Rosie ("Doris Murphy"), 217
  anger at Lori Petty during scene, 176
  attention in local media, 164
  audition of, 98
  "brief hetero period" of, 165
  as court jester, 113
  daytime talk show of, 98, 220
  difference of opinion with Penny Marshall, 187
  double for, 133
  growing-up years of, 77
  as Madonna's wing-woman, 117–118
  popularity of, 158
  as "Queen of Nice," 220
  skill set of, 108
Office of War Information, 50
*Oh, God!*, 15
*Oklahoma!*, 12
Oliver, John, 62
Ondricek, Miroslav, 129, 184, 219
O'Neal, Tatum, 76
Orenstein, Peggy, 196
*Original Amateur Hour, The*, 11
Otis, Carré, 76
Ovitz, Mike, 200

Pace, Bill, 66, 85
Paige, Satchel, 160
Pakula, Alan J., 97
Paramount, 5, 14, 16, 17, 19, 23, 72
*Parenthood*, 62, 63
Parillaud, Anne, 101
Paris, Francesca, 151
Parker, Alan, 73
Parker, Sarah Jessica, 76
Parkway Productions, 66, 86, 195, 215
Pascal, Amy, 67, 87, 143, 198, 221
Payne, Dale, 147
Peaches. *See* Rockford Peaches
Peck, Gregory, 72
*Peggy Sue Got Married*, 25, 78, 91
Pelton, Patti ("Marbleann Wilkinson"), 130, 170–171, 188, 206, 214
Penn, Sean, 25, 100
Penny Marshall Celebration Weekend, 234
*Penthouse* magazine, 131
*People* magazine, 89
Peoria Redwings, 55
Perelman, Ron, 72, 216
Perkins, Elizabeth, 34, 76, 217
*Personal Best*, 84
Pesci, Joe, 22, 89, 91
Peters, Jon, 86
Pettibone, Shep, 117, 198

Petty, Lori ("Kit Keller")
  acknowledgment of AAGPBL's racist history by, 134
  criticism of, 204
  double for, 181
  firing of (for *Demoliton Man*), 224
  first meeting with Geena Davis, 107
  Geena Davis's introduction to, 107
  Geena Davis's running slower than, 140
  most famous movie for, 226
  out-pranking of Geena Davis by, 126
  scoring the role, 92
Phillips, Nalda "Bird," 65
*Pioneer Press*, 204
*Pitch*, 230
Pitt, Brad, 78
*Playboy*, 32, 36
*Point Break*, 92, 111, 123
*Poker House, The*, 226
Polanski, Roman, 101
*Polar Express, The*, 217
*Police Academy 5*, 158
Pollack, Sydney, 110
*Poltergeist*, 29
*Portlandia*, 231
Posey, Parker, 99
*Postcards from the Edge*, 223
Pounds-Taylor, Connie, 130
Pratt, Mary, 64
*Preacher's Wife, The*, 142, 219, 220
*Press-Telegram*, 204
Preston, Kelly, 76
*Pretty Woman*, 76
Price, Frank, 27, 86, 94, 102
*Pride and Prejudice*, 124
Priestley, Jason, 195–196, 215
Priestley, Tom, 184, 216
*Princess Diaries*, 214
*Prince of Tides, The*, 90
*Project X*, 78
Pullman, Bill, 94, 184
*Punchline*, 36, 37

Quaid, Dennis, 34
*Quarterback Princess*, 78
*Queen of Outer Space*, 192

Racine Belles, 122, 130, 167, 209
*Rain Man*, 73, 87
*Raising Arizona*, 41
Ramsay, Anne ("Helen Haley"), 99, 150, 154, 191
  broken nose of, 114
  as day player on TV, 112
  double for, 130
  opinions given by, 202
  performance in *Jesus Christ Superstar*, 170
Randall, Tony, 14
Raskin, Barbara, 218
*Rear Window*, 46
Redford, Robert, 27, 38, 82, 103
Redmond, J. Patrick, 162
Reeves, Keanu, 92
Reiner, Carl, 15
Reiner, Rob, 15, 21, 26, 89, 213
Reiner, Tracy ("Betty Horn"), 76, 83, 172
Reitman, Ivan, 27, 33
*Renaissance Man*, 215, 216, 217, 218
Reubens, Paul, 179
Reynolds, Debbie, 14
Richardson, Heather Cox, 162
Rickey, Branch, 50
*Riding in Cars with Boys*, 138, 214, 221, 232
*Rifleman, The*, 110
Riley, Pat, 93
Ring, Jennifer, 133
Ritter, John, 26
Roberts, Eric, 93
Roberts, Julia, 76, 214
Robertson, Hugh, 142
*Robin Hood: Men in Tights*, 214
Robinson, Doug, 224
Robinson, Jackie, 50–51, 160
Robinson, Phil Alden, 81
Rockford Peaches
  assembly of, 83
  bus driver for, 171, 186
  casting of, 69
  categories of, 76
  at charm school, 121–122
  in clean and dirty tunics, 153
  competitive spirit of, 158
  custom-made home base for, 149
  during Suds Bucket dance sequence, 118
  fight scene among, 176
  in focus-group screenings, 202

loss as biggest upset in the sports film genre, 181
MVP of, 91
reporting for hair and makeup, 151
schoolgirls' participation in fast-pitch softball after watching, 228
sisterhood of, 70
virtuoso of, 108
young girls' adoration of, 2
Rockwell, Norman, 220
*Rookie of the Year*, 227
Roseanne, 218
Ross, Gary, 31, 73
Roth, Joe, 85, 226
Rubinstein, Helena, 52, 121
Rusk, John, 116, 164, 195
Russo, Joe, 100
Ruth, Babe, 64, 95, 133
Ryan, Meg, 92, 99
Rye Playland, 40–41

Sacks, Oliver, 71
Salamon, Julie, 93
*Sandlot, The*, 227
*San Francisco Chronicle*, 223
*Santa Barbara*, 158
*Sara*, 110
Sarandon, Susan, 109
Sargent, Jim, 52
*Saturday Night Live*, 7, 22, 23, 128, 214
Savino, Tony, 116, 117
Sayles, John, 123
Scheller, Justin, 179, 180, 185, 208
Schmitt, Lita, 133, 158
Schram, Bitty ("Evelyn Garner"), 99, 142, 151, 182
ambushing of, 156
Indiana bubble of, 157
self-consciousness of, 208
silly photograph of, 169
Schwarzenegger, Arnold, 3
Scolari, Peter, 19
Scorsese, Martin, 90
Scott, Ridley, 109
Seahawks, 131
Sedgwick, Kyra, 91
Seidelman, Susan, 100
Selleck, Tom, 20
Sellers, Peter, 35
*September*, 40
Shakur, Tupac, 216
*Shanghai Surprise*, 100
Shannon, Molly, 214
Shattuck, Debra, 132
*She-Devil*, 184
Sheen, Charlie, 83
*Sheltering Sky, The*, 103
Shields, Brooke, 76
*Shoot to Kill*, 142
Shyer, Charles, 33, 195
*Significant Other*, 97
*Silkwood*, 184
Silver, Joel, 28
Simon, Neil, 14
Simon, Paul, 24
Simpkins, Kelli ("Beverly Dixon"), 130, 144, 169, 170
Simpson, Freddie ("Ellen Sue Gotlander"), 112, 185, 206
friendship with Madonna, 123
growing up years of, 78
night before tryout, 77–78
role given to, 99
Skoal-dipping by, 173
Singer, Michele, 89
Singleton, John, 200
*Sister Act*, 33
*Sleeping with the Enemy*, 142
*Sleepless in Seattle*, 208
Slotnick, Joey, 126
Smith, Liz, 208
Smith, Stacy Jenel, 220
Smith, Todd, 23, 89, 218
Snipes, Wesley, 224
Sondheim, Stephen, 218
Sonnenfeld, Barry, 40–41, 89
Sony Pictures Entertainment, 86, 87
*Sophie's Choice*, 184
Sorkin, Arleen, 6
South Bend Blue Sox, 130
*South Pacific*, 12
*Speechless*, 226
*Speed*, 218
Spencer, Ted, 64
Spielberg, Anne, 31, 73
Spielberg, Steven, 22, 23, 31
*Splash*, 26, 39
Sragow, Michael, 204

Stallone, Sylvester, 224
*Stand by Your Man*, 99
*Star Wars*, 22
St. Aubin, Ronald, 57
Steel, Dawn, 68, 72
Steinem, Gloria, 67
*St. Elsewhere*, 81
Stephenson, David Curtis, 162
*Stereogum*, 198
*Stolen Bases: Why American Girls Don't Play Baseball*, 133
Stone, Sharon, 78
Stone, Toni, 160
Strathairn, David, 173
Streep, Meryl, 184, 226
Streisand, Barbra, 90
*Stuart Little*, 227
Swank, Hilary, 221
Sweeney, Julia, 6
*Switch*, 158
Szmidt, Sharon, 130

Tacon, Gary, 124
*Taking Care of Business*, 83
*Taming of the Shrew, The*, 38
Tampa Tarpons, 228
*Tank Girl*, 224–225
Tarleton, Neezer, 78, 130, 206
Taylor, Janis, 60
*Ted Lasso*, 230
*Telegraph, The*, 103
*Terms of Endearment*, 24, 195
*That Thing You Do!*, 214
*Thelma & Louise*, 104, 108, 109
*Then Came Bronson*, 14, 37
*This Boy's Life*, 196
*This Is Spinal Tap*, 26
Thompson, Crystal, 64
Title IX, 62, 67, 77, 131
*Today* show, 61
Tomei, Marisa, 91, 221
*Tootsie*, 110
*Top Gun*, 40, 72
Toppman, Lawrence, 204
Toronto Blue Jays, 38
Touchstone Pictures, 219
*Toy Story*, 219
Trump, Donald, 75
*Truth or Dare*, 102
Turner, Kathleen, 25
*Turning Point, The*, 63
*TV Guide*, 207
*Two Gentlemen of Verona, The*, 38
*2001: A Space Odyssey*, 37

*United States of Tara*, 232
*Unlawful Entry*, 209

Vance, Courtney B., 219
*Variety*, 218
*Vice Versa*, 33
*Village Voice*, 202
*Volunteers*, 39, 47

Wahlberg, Mark, 216, 220
Walken, Christopher, 123
Walt Disney Studios, 97, 201, 215, 219
Wambach, Abby, 228
Ward, Tony, 118
Warner Brothers, 26, 84, 103, 199, 201, 224
Washington, Denzel, 219, 220
*Washington Post*, 131, 223
*Wasp Woman, The*, 192
*Watch What Happens Live*, 35
Watson, Brenda, 134
*Wayne's World*, 201
Webber, Andrew Lloyd, 155
Weingardt, Ellie, 121
Weinstein, Harvey, 220
*Weird Science*, 29
Weiss, Alta, 133
Wells, Linda, 131
Wessler, Charlie, 5, 6, 7, 28, 30, 44, 61
*When Diamonds Were a Girl's Best Friend*, 60
*When Harry Met Sally*, 128
Whitmore, Kelsie, 228
Whitt, Ernie, 38
Wilder, Alan, 120, 127, 168
Willett, Patty, 168
William Morris, 93, 97
Williams, Cindy, 5, 16, 17–18
Williams, Robin, 54, 216, 218
Williams, Ted, 49, 50, 64
Willis, Bruce, 62, 218
Willis, Kaitlyn Marie, 179
Wilson, Hack, 69
Wilson, Kim, 58–59, 62

Wilson, Rita, 47
Winfrey, Oprah, 219
Winger, Debra, 24, 97
Winters, Jack, 23
Witherspoon, Reese, 221
*With Friends Like These*, 220
*Wizard of Oz, The*, 173
Wolfe, Tom, 92
Women's Baseball World Cup, 229
Wong, Frances, 37
*Working Girl*, 73
*Working Stiffs*, 6
Wright, Robin, 91
Wrigley, Philip K., 50
Wrigley Field, 115, 129
Wyeth, Andrew, 80

Young, Loretta, 219
Young, Sean, 84, 85
Young Liberals, 51

Zaillian, Steven, 71
Zemeckis, Robert, 217
Zieff, Howard, 28
Zimmer, Hans, 198
Zoltar machine, 31, 213
Zwecker, Bill, 145